American Technology

BLACKWELL READERS IN AMERICAN SOCIAL AND CULTURAL HISTORY

Series Editor: Jacqueline Jones, Brandeis University

The *Blackwell Readers in American Social and Cultural History* series introduces students to well-defined topics in American history from a socio-cultural perspective. Using primary and secondary sources, the volumes present the most important works available on a particular topic in a succinct and accessible format designed to fit easily into courses offered in American history or American studies.

American Technology

Edited by

Carroll Pursell

First published 2001

2 4 6 8 10 9 7 5 3 1

Blackwell Publishers Inc.
350 Main Street
Malden, Massachusetts 02148
USA

Blackwell Publishers Ltd
108 Cowley Road
Oxford OX4 1JF
UK

Library of Congress Cataloging-in-Publication Data

American technology / edited by Carroll Pursell.
p. cm. — (Blackwell readers in American social and cultural history; 7)
Includes bibliographical references and index.
ISBN 0–631–21996–X (alk. paper); ISBN 0–631–21997–8 (pb.: alk. paper)
1. Technology—United States—History.   I. Pursell, Carroll W.   II. Series.

T21 .A5875 2001
609.73—dc21

00–057933

British Library Cataloguing in Publication Data
A CIP catalogue record for this book is available from the British Library.

Typeset in 10 on 12 Pt Plantin
by Kolam Information Services Pvt. Ltd., Pondicherry, India
Printed in Great Britain by TJ International, Padstow, Cornwall

This book is printed on acid-free paper.

Contents

Series Editor's Preface

The purpose of the Blackwell Readers in American Social and Cultural History is to introduce students to cutting-edge historical scholarship that draws upon a variety of disciplines, and to encourage students to "do" history themselves by examining some of the primary texts upon which that scholarship is based.

Each of us lives life with a wholeness that is at odds with the way scholars often dissect the human experience. Anthropologists, psychologists, literary critics, and political scientists (to name just a few) study only discrete parts of our existence. The result is a rather arbitrary collection of disciplinary boundaries enshrined not only in specialized publications but also in university academic departments and in professional organizations.

As a scholarly enterprise, the study of history necessarily crosses these boundaries of knowledge in order to provide a comprehensive view of the past. Over the last few years, social and cultural historians have reached across the disciplines to understand the history of the British North American colonies and the United States in all its fullness. Unfortunately, much of that scholarship, published in specialized monographs and journals, remains inaccessible to undergraduates. Consequently, instructors often face choices that are not very appealing – to ignore the recent scholarship altogether, assign bulky readers that are too detailed for an undergraduate audience, or cobble together packages of recent articles that lack an overall contextual framework. The individual volumes of this series each focus on a significant topic in American history, and bring new, exciting scholarship to students in a compact, accessible format.

The series is designed to complement textbooks and other general readings assigned in undergraduate courses. Each editor has culled particularly innovative and provocative scholarly essays from widely scattered books and journals, and provided an introduction sumamrizing the major themes of the essays and documents that follow. The essays reproduced here were chosen because of the authors' innovative (and often interdisciplinary) methodology and their ability to reconceptualize historical issues in fresh and insightful ways. Thus students can appreciate the rich complexity of an historical topic and the way that scholars have explored the topic from different perspectives, and in the process transcend the highly artificial disciplinary boundaries that have served to compartmentalize knowledge about the past in the United States.

Also included in each volume are primary texts, at least some of which have been drawn from the essays themselves. By linking primary and secondary material, the editors are able to introduce students to the historian's craft, allowing them to explore this material in depth, and draw additional insights – or interpretations contrary to those of the scholars under discussion – from it. Suggestions for further reading offer depth to the analysis.

Introduction

There is something about the subject of technology that turns people's minds toward the future rather than the past: the *history* of technology, as they say, does not compute. Yet this is both wrong and wrong-headed. Wrong, because technology, like every other aspect of our lives, has come from somewhere – that is, has a history. Wrong-headed, because the future is being shaped right now out of what we have to work with and think about – that is, what we have inherited from the past. Our history does not determine our future, but it provides us with both the material and the understanding with which we built that future.

All too often we fall into the easy understanding called "technological determinism" – that is, the assumption that technology determines what happens in society.[1] This assumption is cunningly used by advertisers to convince us that the new technology they want us to buy – the car, say, or that new dishwasher – will change our lives. If we buy the car we get the partner of our dreams, but if we don't we don't. Sometimes of course it's true – get a gun *and use it*, and we are likely to be in deep trouble. And if we get it, we are probably more likely to use it.

But it's also true that society determines technology. We have a nuclear technology because the United States wanted an atomic bomb. Research on computer technology was pushed by the Pentagon because it decided that it needed the power to crunch big numbers. The result, for many years, was that computers were huge, expensive mainframes, suitable for calculating missile trajectories but not designed to provide personal word processing for students.

Finally, to complicate matters even more, new technologies do not always have the effects they were designed to produce. The historian Joseph Corn has pointed out that when predicting the future of new technologies (that is, the futures which the technologies will determine), we usually make three key mistakes.[2] First, we assume that the new technology will completely replace the technology we used to use for that purpose (the fallacy of total revolution). Second, we assume that this replacement of one technology with a newer and better one is the only change that will take place (the fallacy of social continuity). And, third, we assume that the new technology will only solve problems (the fallacy of the technological fix). In fact, all three of these assumptions are false. Most commonly new technologies are used for some purposes, but join rather than replace the older ones. We now have jet airplanes but we also still use railroads. When we get our music from a CD rather than a piano, more than just the technology changes. And new technologies not only solve problems, they create them as well.

And often both at the same time! "Smart" cars that never crash into each other would solve a huge problem for drivers, but create an equally large problem for that army of auto repair shops, insurance companies, and others who now make a livelihood out of collisions. Results are not simply good or bad, but can often be *both* good and bad depending on where one stands in the situation.

Understanding the role of technology in our lives, in the past as in the present and future, it is important to remember that, like other aspects of our humanity, technology is the result of both choices and accidents. It does not grow out of its own logic nor is it always and inevitably progressive. It is, in fact, largely what we choose to make of it.

There are many questions that the historian of technology can ask of the technology of the past:

- Where did it come from (that is, who designed, invented, engineered it)?
- How did it work?
- Who owned it and who used it (and for what purposes)?
- What effects did it have?
- What did it mean?

When the field of the history of technology first professionalized – that is, when the Society for the History of Technology was organized (1958) and its scholarly journal *Technology and Culture* began publication – some of these questions about the past were more often asked than others. In part because the Cold War had spawned both a Nuclear Age and a Space Age as well as an Arms Race, the origins of technological innovation seemed to have political urgency as well as intellectual appeal. In part because many of those who studied the history of technology at that time had been trained as engineers, the subject of design held an importance and a fascination that cast other questions into the shadow.

The great changes that have taken place in the past generation in the field of history as a whole, however, have left their mark also in the history of technology. For one thing, this sub-field is not alone. During these years other fields, like environmental history and most notably women's history, have also developed into flourishing enterprises with large and sophisticated literatures of their own. Women's history, especially, has been the origin of a host of new and important theories and methodologies that have excited and reshaped the entire historical profession.

More generally, the rise of social history over these same years has led many, perhaps a majority of, historians of technology to switch their focus from questions of where technologies come from to who owns and uses them, and for what purposes. The social context of technologies, as it is phrased, is particularly prone to illusions of determinism, as we see workers thrown off the job, the economy soaring, families weakened (or strengthened), the countryside denuded, and Native Americans driven off the land. At the same time we know that sometimes these are not unforeseen consequences, but the very purposes for which the technology was adopted. It is a thin line, for example, between a "labor-saving" machine, and one that throws people out of work. The anonymously but brilliantly designed American axe of pioneer days devastated the nation's forests, but that is what it was designed to do. Deforestation is a critical part of the social history of the axe, but that implement is only a part of the explanation of why this all took place.

One result of bringing social history into the history of technology is that it allows us to see all those many Americans who were not engineers and inventors, but who lived lives surrounded by technologies. Workers, for example, could now be seen operating machines, breaking them, and sometimes repairing them, maintaining them, and once in a while modifying them in useful ways – a kind of design not taken note of by studies concentrating on engineers. Women working in homes were revealed to be managing sometimes complicated technological systems. Cooking involved not only the design of meals, but the use of energy in specialized stoves to cook food (properly prepared) in a variety of containers, all of which had to be cleaned, repaired and replaced, sometimes with better ones, using a variety of instruments (knives, spoons, beaters, etc.) which also had to be cleaned, repaired and replaced.

Enslaved Africans were discovered to have artisanal skills, some brought over from Africa, like inoculating for smallpox, and others learned in this country, like cooperage or shoemaking. At the turn of the last century African-Americans became electricians and steam engineers, inventors and manufacturers. All of these people had failed to make it onto the pages of histories of technology for a generation, and only now in the twenty-first century are people of color (any color other than white, that is) being recognized as technological players in American history.

Interestingly, Native Americans are still largely invisible in the study of technology in America. Just as Indians are found in *natural* history museums, and not in most history museums, so it has been more often anthropologists than historians who have interested themselves in the technologies of indigenous peoples. What little we do know, however, suggests that it made a difference whether or not Indians had muskets and revolvers, and whether they could repair them and make the ammunition necessary for their use. We also know that, as with other "races," Indians were judged to be savage or civilized in part by their technologies, so "color" was a matter not merely of skin but also of tools.

And so with other groups. Through the lens of social history we can see that children were once thought not to be technologically capable and were therefore subjected to long periods of apprenticeship before being trusted with the tools and machines of grown men and women. (To be manly meant not only to not be womanly, but not to be boyish either.) By the end of the twentieth century, interestingly enough, it was thought that only children and young adults were capable of truly mastering the electronic gadgets that increasingly filled our homes. Through all this time, however, toys scaled down from adult technologies, whether ironing boards or Erector sets, have been thought to prepare the young for the real world of grown-up technology.[3]

In recent years, social history has been joined (though certainly not replaced) by what can be called cultural history. Broadly speaking, cultural history in this field focuses on what technologies mean – or, to use the language of its practitioners, what technologies represent. As the historian Lynn Hunt has written, "the accent in cultural history is on close examination – of texts, of pictures, and of actions – and on an open-mindedness to what those examinations will reveal."[4] I take this to mean that while an internalist might want to investigate who invented the automobile and how it has been changed mechanically over the years, and a social historian might want to know how quickly African-Americans were able to purchase and use automobiles, a cultural historian would want to know what such purchase and use meant to Black Americans – what car ownership and use represented to them (and probably to others as well).

Most of the chapters in this collection could probably be categorized as examples of social history, often with a sensitivity to cultural dimensions in the stories they tell. Theodore Steinberg, for example, looks carefully at how the building of dams in New England during the early years of the Industrial Revolution affected the farmers and fishery workers who had used the waters in radically different ways. Arthur McEvoy, while tracing the way in which industrial workers were endangered in their workplaces, also deals with the meanings attributed to risk and responsibility within the law; a kind of blending of social and cultural history. Bruce Sinclair describes the ways in which the members of one local engineering society represented their professional aspirations and fears in an elaborate pageant. My own contribution acknowledges the social and economic forces which blocked the development of "appropriate" technologies, but insists that the gendered nature of attacks on such technologies as solar power greatly weakened the credibility of their advocates. And Rachel Maines convincingly demonstrates that sexuality can be medicalized in such a way as to socially mask the erotic. Taken together, the ten chapters in this volume, and the primary documents that support them, provide a snapshot of American technologies, and the ways in which we can think about and understand them.

Beginning in the seventeenth century, peoples from different parts of Europe brought their essentially medieval technologies to the Americas, at first blending with and eventually displacing most of the tools and techniques used by the indigenous peoples already living here. Axes and saws were used to convert vast forests into both lumber and farm lands, while water mills and windmills were erected to process the natural and agricultural bounty of the land. In a period when nearly all Americans, enslaved as well as free, worked on the land, the tools of field and farmstead were of critical importance. Neither conservative nor self-sufficient, as Judith McGaw points out in her chapter, colonial Americans applied old technologies to novel materials and situations. Wood was arguably the most important, and certainly the most ubiquitous, material with which people worked, and hand-tools were far more numerous than any machines. People learned to use those tools through experience, either structured as in an apprenticeship or haphazardly through necessity. Despite the growing importance of industries such as iron smelting and fabrication, British economic policy continued to insist that the colonies should avoid manufactures, sending raw materials to the home country to be converted into finished goods.

The year 1763 saw the end of the French and Indian Wars and marked the end also of long years of "salutary neglect" by the British government and the beginnings of heightened tensions between England and

America, as the former searched for ways of better integrating the colonies with imperial policy. The next year, in 1764, James Watt was given a model steam engine at Edinburgh University, and began those improvements which as much as any one cause marked the beginning of the Industrial Revolution. The next quarter century witnessed, in fact, the birth of two great revolutions: the Industrial in the old country and the American in the new.

During this period Watt's improved steam engine was set to work in a number of different industries, not only grinding grain and pumping water, but, as importantly, creating a tremendous demand for both coal and iron. Machines powered by water were invented and set to work to spin and weave cotton and wool. Canals were built to speed commerce and the profession of civil engineer was born. In other words, new industrial technologies were transforming Britain into what would come to be known as the Workshop of the World. This transformation, which ushered in the Modern world, brought with it a vast amount of suffering among what was being formed as a British industrial proletariat.

Having won their political independence from Great Britain during these same years, Americans faced both the opportunity and the necessity of shaping their own political economy. An entirely agricultural society was not possible (indeed, the colonies had never been such), but the twin necessities of importing the industrial technology of the Industrial Revolution without bringing with it the resulting degradation of labor were seen as highly problematic. The enrichment of a few at the expense of the many, as Steinberg's chapter makes clear, was not to be accomplished without resistance. Workshops in the wilderness, as they were sometimes called, were bought at a price. On the other hand, the need to create a balanced economy, with agriculture, manufactures and commerce nicely supporting each other, seemed to require the exploitation of the country's vast natural resources and this, in turn, appeared most easily done by importing the new technologies of England.

The resulting rush to build mills, dig canals, construct turnpikes and eventually railroads, open mines, and raise up great cities (with their own engineering infrastructures of waterworks, sewers, streets, and lighting) created a modern America in which the farmers and artisans of an earlier time became machine-tenders and shop clerks. Slowly, the public and private institutions changed as well, sometimes to accommodate and sometimes to encourage modernization. Corporations replaced partnerships, factories replaced mills, and chattel slavery was eventually replaced with a "free" market of labor, even in the South. In his chapter, Arthur McEvoy traces some of the ways in which these forces created and attempted to control new environments for work.

We easily see factory workers as "labor," and we are not surprised that "labor-saving" machines readily found their way into industrial production during the nineteenth century in America. It is important to also realize, however, that this drive for efficiency and mechanization was broadly felt across the nation and applied to a wide variety of sites and tasks. On farms, such machines as the McCormick reaper were rapidly adopted for harvesting grain crops and by the end of the century electricity was being shown to have a large potential for stationary farm work. In the West, both lumber and mining interests adopted aids such as dynamite and crosscut saws to speed exploitation of the nation's natural resources.

As Rachel Maines shows in her chapter, even physicians eagerly sought mechanical devices which would help them in the diagnosis and treatment of human maladies, including the "hysteria" which many claimed to find in their female patients. In a report on the extent and effects of mechanization in a large number of industries in 1898, the US Commissioner of Labor stated flatly that "hand methods are going out of use."[5] For those who hired labor, increasing productivity and profits proved powerful inducements to mechanize work. For those, like doctors, who did most of their own work, the avoidance of tiring and time-consuming tasks was equally attractive.

If we tend not to think of doctors' offices as sites of production, neither do we automatically think of homes in these terms; the home is more often thought of as a retreat from the modern world of industry and mechanization. But it is, in fact, the traditional workplace of women, where production and reproduction take place. Meals, cleanliness, comfort, and even babies are the results of specific activities and as factories, and later farms, began to adopt machinery so too did the domestic workplace. Christine Kleinegger's chapter argues that the mechanization of both sites of rural production, the farmhouse and the barn, was contentious, contingent, and heavily gendered.

The mechanization of farm and factory, home and white collar office, was accompanied by a dramatic rise in the number of engineers in the country. Beginning early in the nineteenth century, engineering grew to become, by the twentieth, the largest of the new professions spawned by the Industrial Revolution. One by one civil engineers, then mining, then mechanical, then electrical, then chemical, and finally dozens of more specialized engineers organized to meet the needs of both the economy and their own employment prospects. In his chapter, Bruce Sinclair discovers a culture among engineers in St Louis during the early years of the Great Depression which cast an honest, perhaps even a bit cynical, eye on the professional paths they followed, and the social conditions under which they labored. "Progress," both technological and professional, was not the straight, clear, inevitable, and innocent path which they might have wished, and in which many people believed.

The fact that the path of technological development had to be deliberately constructed, rather than simply followed, was obvious also to the post-Second World War generation of engineers, scientists, military leaders, and politicians who wanted very much to enjoy and celebrate a bright, new, "Atomic Age." As the historian Thomas P. Hughes points out, "the long history of projects extends back at least as far as the building of the great Egyptian pyramids and the Middle Eastern irrigation systems." In contrast to those builders, however, he also notes that "those presiding over technological projects today expect the systems they build to evolve continuously and to require new projects to sustain the evolution."[6] Michael Smith's contribution to this volume traces the efforts of nuclear enthusiasts to "sell the atom" to the American public. The cultural link between Hiroshima and Walt Disney's "Our Friend the Atom" was not obvious, nor was it easily drawn.

The fact that nuclear technology could do great harm but also, or so it was alleged, great good should not surprise us; few things are all good or all bad. Indeed, it is not uncommon for the same events to be "good" for some people and "bad" for others at the same time. One example of this is investigated by Venus Green, in her chapter on racial factors in the employment policies of the telephone system. The pursuit of mechanization, to the point, and beyond, of automation, can be undertaken for a number of reasons and often several at the same time. Just as the labor market is segmented – by sex, by race, by skill, and so forth – so can labor-*saving* devices impact different segments of that market differently.

Just as technological "progress" can be instigated and nurtured in different ways and for different purposes, so can it be hindered, even blocked. The so-called oil crisis of the 1970s gave immediacy to growing environmental concerns over the effects of what might be called "over development" in the United States. The large technological systems that appeared to dominate American life, from interstate highways to interlocking electrical grids, began to seem dangerous and undesirable to some, who proposed technologies more "appropriate" to a healthy and sustainable society as well as natural environment. In my own chapter in this collection I point out the ways in which the political economy of technology can work in tandem (or at odds) with cultural constructions such as gender norms.

Notes

1   Merritt Roe Smith and Leo Marx, eds, *Does Technology Drive History? The Dilemma of Technological Determinism* (Cambridge, MA: MIT Press, 1994).

2   Joseph J. Corn, ed., *Imagining Tomorrow: History, Technology, and the American Future* (Cambridge, MA: MIT Press, 1986), pp. 219–21.
3   Carroll W. Pursell, Jr, "Toys, Technology and Sex Roles in America, 1920–1940," in *Dynamos and Virgins Revisited: Women and Technological Change in History*, ed. Martha Moore Trescott (Metuchen, NJ: Scarecrow Press, 1979), pp. 252–67.
4   "Introduction," in *The New Cultural History*, ed. Lynn Hunt (Berkeley: University of California Press, 1989), p. 22.
5   *Hand and Machine Labor. Volume I, Introduction and Analysis. Thirteenth Annual Report of the Commissioner of Labor, 1898* (Washington, DC: GPO, 1899), p. 6.
6   Thomas P. Hughes, *Rescuing Prometheus* (New York: Pantheon Books, 1998), pp. 6, 7.

Further Reading

Corn, Joseph J. *The Winged Gospel: America's Romance with Aviation, 1900–1950.* Oxford: Oxford University Press, 1983.

Douglas, Susan J. *Inventing American Broadcasting, 1899–1922.* Baltimore: Johns Hopkins University Press, 1987.

Friedel, Robert. *Zipper: an Exploration in Novelty.* New York: W. W. Norton, 1994.

Hindle, Brooke, and Steven Lubar. *Engines of Change: the American Industrial Revolution, 1790–1860.* Washington, DC: Smithsonian Institution Press, 1986.

Hughes, Thomas P. *American Genesis: a Century of Invention and Technological Enthusiasm.* New York: Viking, 1989.

Kasson, John F. *Civilizing the Machine: Technology and Republican Values in America, 1776–1900.* New York: Grossman Publishers, 1976.

Lubar, Steven. *InfoCulture: the Smithsonian Book of Information Age Inventions.* Boston: Houghton Mifflin Co., 1993.

Marvin, Carolyn. *When Old Technologies Were New: Thinking About Electric Communication in the Late Nineteenth Century.* New York: Oxford University Press, 1988.

Morison, Elting E. *From Know-how to Nowhere: the Development of American Technology.* New York: Basic Books, 1974.

Nye, David E. *American Technological Sublime.* Cambridge, MA: MIT Press, 1994.

Nye, David E. *Consuming Power: a Social History of American Energies.* Cambridge, MA: MIT Press, 1998.

Pursell, Carroll W. *Technology in America: a History of Individuals and Ideas*, 2nd edn. Cambridge, MA: MIT Press, 1990.

Pursell, Carroll W. *The Machine in America: a Social History of Technology.* Baltimore: Johns Hopkins University Press, 1995.

Pursell, Carroll W. *White Heat: People and Technology.* Berkeley: University of California Press, 1994.

Scharff, Virginia. *Taking the Wheel: Women and the Coming of the Motor Age.* New York: Free Press, 1991.

Smith, Merritt Roe, and Leo Marx, eds. *Does Technology Drive History? The Dilemma of Technological Determinism.* Cambridge, MA: MIT Press, 1994.

Williams, Rosalind. *Notes on the Underground: an Essay on Technology, Society, and the Imagination.* Cambridge, MA: MIT Press, 1990.

1
Early American Technological Possessions

1664	English establish first settlements in New Jersey.
1674	Quakers purchase western half of New Jersey.
1681	William Penn granted land in what is now Pennsylvania.
1700	250,000 settlers in the English colonies.
1710	German immigration begins.
1728	Scottish-Irish immigration begins.
1750	Ninety percent of Americans farm at least part of the year.

Introduction

The historian of technology Tom Misa has wisely suggested that technological determinism is much more persuasive at the macro level than at the micro. As every historian knows, a careful and respectful observance of the particulars of time and space tends to dissolve the easy and comfortable generalizations which can so easily become conventional wisdom on any subject. Looking carefully, through the window of probate inventories, at what early Americans actually owned in the way of technology, Judith McGaw at once undermines the stories of self-sufficient technological conservatism, and suggests some new and surprising sources of the Industrial Revolution in this country.

"So Much Depends upon a Red Wheelbarrow": Agricultural Tool Ownership in the Eighteenth-century Mid-Atlantic

Judith A. McGaw

My title derives from one of the best-known Imagist poems, by William Carlos Williams. The poem goes:

> so much depends
> upon
>
> a red wheel
> barrow
>
> glazed with rain
> water
>
> beside the white
> chickens.[1]

I begin by invoking the Imagist spirit because their mission – replacing the generalizations and abstractions of Victorian poetry with what they called "direct treatment of the 'thing'" – is an approach historians studying early American agricultural technology might profitably emulate.[2] Unfortunately, a salient characteristic of scholarship treating early American farming is nicely captured by a *Peanuts* cartoon a graduate student gave me some years ago. The strip features Sally standing in front of her class and holding a piece of paper. "This is my report on Mr. John Deere," she says. "In 1837, Mr. Deere invented the self-polishing steel plow which was a great help to farmers..." In the next panel she has been interrupted and replies: "Plow? No, Ma'am I've never seen a plow..." After a pause she adds, "I've never even seen a farmer!"[3] Paraphrasing Williams, this essay argues that, for understand-

Taken from Judith A. McGaw, "'So Much Depends upon a Red Wheelbarrow': Agricultural Tool Ownership in the Eighteenth-century Mid-Atlantic," in Judith A. McGaw, ed., *Early American Technology: Making and Doing Things from the Colonial Era to 1850* (Chapel Hill: University of North Carolina Press, for the Institute of Early American History and Culture, 1994), pp. 328–57. Copyright © 1994 by the University of North Carolina Press. Used by permission of the publisher.

ing technological change in America, much depends upon our seeing farmers and plows, red wheelbarrows and white chickens.

The Imagists also set a standard worth emulating by insisting that writers "use the language of common speech, but . . . employ always the *exact* word, not the nearly-exact, nor the merely decorative word," to quote Ezra Pound. Alas, when we read the history of technology, we hear few echoes of common speech, literally or metaphorically speaking. We have mostly studied technology as an expression of leaders – inventors, experimenters, large corporations, or governments; we have mostly ignored common people's technological expression – what tools they chose to own or generally employed, for example.[4]

Nowhere is our ignorance of the mundane more evident than in scholarship on early American agricultural technology. With a few noteworthy exceptions, secondary literature tells us little about which tools, practices, and knowledge early farmers and farm wives customarily employed. Instead, the scholarship features famous firsts – inventors' contrivances and agricultural reformers' proposals, with little sense of how these tools and ideas fared after their debut. We have more often looked at the machine on the drawing board than at the wheelbarrow in the garden.

Despite our inattention to common practice, historians have not been reluctant to characterize early American tool ownership, albeit in highly generalized terms. Indeed, one noteworthy feature of our literature is the virtual absence of clear and specific images of preindustrial technology. Rather than deriving from records that feature farmers, farm wives, and their tools, most scholarship rests on several sorts of unsubstantiated generalizations. One approach has relied heavily on what agricultural reformers and European travelers wrote. It reiterates their claims that common farmers resisted innovation and their assessments of early farm technology as hopelessly primitive, especially on the frontier.

By contrast, the other principal approach portrays the early yeoman as a technological virtuoso. It assumes, albeit implicitly, that tool ownership and tool-wielding skill were common in the preindustrial era. That assumption underlies, for example, the Marxist contention that industrialization degraded work when it shifted tool ownership from tool users to the employers of tool users. It also undergirds revisionist scholarship that depicts industrialization as the demise of an earlier, subsistent, communitarian economy in favor of an increasingly impersonal market-oriented one. Likewise, accounts of women and industrialization contrast restrictive nineteenth-century mill or domestic work with a colonial role presumed to entail an enormous array of agricultural processing tasks, such as spinning, weaving, candlemaking, churning, cheese production, and pickling.

Scholars who assess industrialization more favorably also assume widespread preindustrial tool ownership. For example, one explanation of America's relatively swift industrialization has been that frontier living nurtured technological creativity. Frontiersmen, it argues, had to be jacks-of-all-trades – to know how to use all of the tools that specialists wielded in more settled communities. The unspoken corollary is, of course, that frontiersmen owned all those tools. Nor is this mythic jack-of-all-trades confined to scholarly claims about the frontier. Often, eighteenth- and nineteenth-century northern rural communities are presumed to have nurtured a youthful variant of the type – the Yankee whittling boy. This handy youth figures prominently in the literature celebrating inventors, much of it popular, but some of it scholarly.

My data on tool ownership in the eighteenth-century mid-Atlantic paint a very different picture. I find, for example, that only a little more than half of farmers or yeomen probably owned plows and that, among farm women, about 20 percent made do without either a pot or a kettle, those huge iron or brass caldrons that colonial restorations invariably hang over the fire. The artifact we most often envision in early American hands – the gun – actually existed in only about half of households. And frontiersmen were only slightly more likely to own firearms: about 60 percent versus about 50 percent for inhabitants of longer-settled regions. Nonetheless, early Americans were far more likely to own guns than to possess that other icon of early American life – the Bible – although, surprisingly, frontier households came closest to owning Bibles as often as guns.

These data are arresting. If many, even most, colonial Americans lacked items we have believed common, even essential, our image of America's traditional technology must be quite distorted: a composite of colonial revival stereotypes and an uncritical acceptance of surviving artifacts as representative. We must do better if we would understand what technological experiences and fingertip knowledge the offspring of American farmers brought to the early factories or assess how the shift to industrial production altered people's relationships to their tools.

This essay offers one strategy for doing better. It begins by enunciating why American historians and historians of technology need real knowledge of how early Americans farmed. After articulating the large questions that motivated my data collection and shaped my data selection and analysis, I outline a feasible and promising alternative to the uncritical, anecdotal approach that has predominated in the field. By summarizing my research strategy – describing the sources I exploit and the methods I employ – I hope to evoke emulation: to persuade additional scholars to cultivate the abundant household-level evidence that awaits those willing to venture into new terrain and to challenge yet more colleagues to seek out other promising scholarly resources. The methodological discussion also provides a context for assessing and appreciating the preliminary report of findings on colonial tool ownership to which the essay turns next. As a first step away from the unsubstantiated generalizations to which we have grown accustomed, I present concrete evidence drawn from my research in progress and propose some large conclusions that may be drawn from the presence or absence of winnowing fans, dung hoes, candle molds, and dough troughs in eighteenth-century households. Finally, I conclude with a few brief observations provoked by this look at small things – "red wheel barrows" and "white chickens"; I invite my various colleagues to question our accustomed academic approach to early American technology.

My study of early American agricultural tool ownership derives ultimately from one big question: What accounts for America's sudden, rapid, and comparatively successful early nineteenth-century industrialization? It has seemed to me that most accounts of the American Industrial Revolution, because they begin in 1790, miss a good part of the answer to that question. Likewise, by focusing on manufactures and treating agriculture merely as a belated beneficiary or victim of industry's mechanical creativity, scholarship on technological change in the American Industrial Revolution has begged some critical questions, such as: How did a declining proportion of farm households become able to feed a growing nonfarm population, supply a burgeoning international market, and provide the raw materials most early industry processed? or, What sorts of technical expertise did the sons and daughters of farmers bring to industrial work? or, How did changes in the goods farm households purchased help to create a market for early industrial commodities? or, What toolmaking skills had become common before industrialization?

In contrast to the narrow focus and abbreviated chronology of American scholarship, studies of British industrialization have historically paid at least some attention to prior and simultaneous agricultural innovation. More recently, a number of scholars have given husbandmen a leading role in the British Industrial Revolution. They have shown that most agricultural innovation, both technical and organizational, occurred in the seventeenth and early eighteenth centuries, much earlier than previously believed. Although historians of industry have simultaneously pushed the origins of the manufacturing revolution well back into the eighteenth century, the new "chronology of improvement now makes a strong case for the close interdependence of agriculture and manufacturing, with the springs of much manufacturing improvement to be found in the early dynamism of the agricultural sector."[5]

At the very least, then, understanding the American Industrial Revolution requires that we examine American industry's colonial agricultural roots. But we also need to look at how farm practice changed during the era of the American Revolution and into the nineteenth century if we are to link agricultural innovation to industrial development. Nor can we limit our attention to the farm activities of the late-colonial era. The new scholarship on Britain certainly raises the possibility that the initial British settlers of any given region engaged in agricultural innovation from the outset. Many of their activities paralleled, even when they did not precisely reenact, those of progressive agriculturalists who remained at home. But the innovativeness of colonists who undertook such activities as clearing forests and planting maize has generally escaped notice because farmers undertook these novel tasks from the start of colonial agricultural history, making the new practices appear either "natural" or "necessary." They were neither. The relative ease with which colonists adopted new practices simply reflects that these novel tasks entailed relatively straightforward translations of new British agricultural strategies to the colonial situation.

In the absence of significant scholarly attention to common agricultural practice, I concluded that, before I could begin to document change in early American agricultural technology, analyze its origins, or link it to manufacturing, I needed to find out what American farmers and farm wives had done and how they had done it from the beginnings of settlement to the mid-nineteenth century. In other words, I had somehow to catch a glimpse of all those red wheelbarrows and white chickens. Understanding anything else about early American technology ultimately depended upon seeing those.

After reaching such a disconcerting conclusion, I made several strategic decisions that converted an impossible task into a manageable one. First, I acknowledged that there is no such thing as a representative colonial farm, farm community, or farm region. Indeed, I will argue later that attempting to find a typical farm family and a standard array of farm tools misstates the problem in a way that inevitably misleads us.

I focused on the mid-Atlantic region because it was the only major region where industry and agriculture flourished side by side and because the mid-Atlantic's emphasis on mixed livestock and grain farming set the pattern for much later American agriculture. The Middle Colonies qualify as the quintessential American region in other respects as well. As Frederick Jackson Turner noted nearly a century ago, the region "mediated between New England and the South, and the East and West," and "it had a wide mixture of nationalities, a varied society, the mixed town and county system of local government, a varied economic life, many religious sects."[6] Insofar as these factors influenced agricultural technique, the mid-Atlantic region represents the best microcosm of early American farm practice. Yet, the mid-Atlantic has received far less scholarly attention than has either New England or the South.

Given the rich diversity of the region, five counties warranted close examination. Each county both shares features with and differs from the others. Thus, comparing data from the various counties should indicate which of several relevant factors – length of settlement, ethnic composition, access to markets, relative affluence, and natural endowment, for example – offer the best explanation of particular agricultural patterns. Examining several counties simultaneously should also provide a built-in reminder that there were many "right" answers to the question of how best to farm, a useful corrective to the biases of both secondary literature and the writings of early American agricultural reformers. Limiting my choice of counties to New Jersey and Pennsylvania also kept manageable the number of different currencies and the various legal parameters to be considered. At the same time, my choices were likely to disclose technological differences associated with the westward course of settlement, an aspect of colonial agriculture that has received far less attention than have North–South differences.

Burlington County, New Jersey, offers a case of very early settlement, beginning roughly in the last quarter of the seventeenth century. Close to Philadelphia and to good water transportation, it represents nearly ideal access to a rapidly growing urban market. It also exemplifies a heavily British population with strong Quaker influence. By the nineteenth century, Burlington should illustrate farming practice in a region that rusticated, for its growth slowed early. By contrast, Hunterdon County, New Jersey, the county just north of Burlington in West Jersey, shows a rapid transition from frontier to settled farming region. Initial settlement lagged about two generations behind that of Burlington, but during the second quarter of the eighteenth century Hunterdon's population came to equal and then to surpass that of its neighbor to the south. Hunterdon also differed from Burlington in its significant Dutch and substantial German population, although British and New England influences were also prominent. Like Burlington, the county sent crops by water to Philadelphia, but its northern reaches also traded with New York.

Moving west, York and Adams counties in south central Pennsylvania exemplify a mid-eighteenth-century frontier, a rich natural endowment, and a highly mobile population that went on to shape the southern back-country as well as the near Midwest. Adams, where Gettysburg is situated, was formed out of York in 1800. Settlement of the combined eighteenth-century county began about a generation after that of Hunterdon. Like Hunterdon, it attracted a large German population.

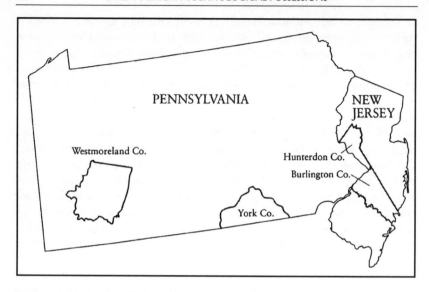

Burlington, Hunterdon, York, and Westmoreland Counties

Unlike Hunterdon, it drew an almost equally large Scotch-Irish contingent, concentrated especially in the newer, western portions of York – those that became Adams County. York and Adams counties also differed from counties to the east in their relatively poor market connections. Navigation on the lower Susquehanna was so poor as to render the river an obstacle rather than a thoroughfare. Instead, as the Baltimore market developed in the late eighteenth century, York citizens petitioned for more roads to nearby Maryland. Overland travel to Philadelphia took far longer, although Harrisburg and Lancaster merchants served as convenient middlemen and attracted substantial York commerce into Philadelphia's commercial orbit before the Revolution.

Located beyond the Appalachian Mountain barrier, Westmoreland County, Pennsylvania, was created on the eve of the Revolution and offers a chance to examine a late-eighteenth-century frontier. After the Revolution, Westmoreland farmers clearly perceived their situation as different from that of farmers to the east, at least judging from their participation in the Whiskey Rebellion. In contrast to York and Adams, Scotch-Irish settlers were a predominant early presence in Westmoreland, making study of the county an opportunity to examine closely generalizations contrasting their slovenly farming methods with those of their German-American contemporaries. Westmoreland also offers a case of dependence on western markets and on Ohio River-borne commerce.

Having selected five sample counties, my first task was to see whether their residents owned "red wheel barrows" and "white chickens." Without a clear image of what tools people commonly owned, I could not deduce what skills farm family members customarily possessed or determine whether agricultural practices were changing. Indeed, with roughly 80–90 percent of the colonial population engaged in agriculture, understanding the cultural and economic significance of any early American technology will entail viewing it within the context of agricultural technology.[7] Since so much depends upon seeing those red wheelbarrows, I wanted to see as many of them as I could – to find a record that exists for enough individuals to capture the mundane technology of ordinary folk.

The record that forms the backbone of this study is the probate inventory, a document created, as the name suggests, when someone died. Probate inventories were not, as the name might suggest, limited to those with wills to probate. They exist for intestate as well as testate decedents. Briefly, inventories were, and are, intended to protect an estate's assets by providing a legal record of personal property ownership. (Real property was not usually listed in Pennsylvania and West Jersey probate inventories.) In some colonies and circumstances they were required whether or not the decedent had much personal property. For example, sometimes the law required an inventory whenever the decedent left minor children. Courts also ordered inventories when a potential heir or other interested party called for one. Those with no assets to protect clearly needed no inventories, so these documents miss the very poor. They do, however, report the assets of many men and women of modest means, and they are clearly more inclusive than other social history sources such as wills, travelers' accounts, account books, or diaries.

They are also far richer in technological detail. Indeed, the level of specificity often astonishes. Inventories distinguish weeding hoes from grubbing hoes, itemize goods of negligible value such as wooden trenchers, and list parts – plowshares, harrow teeth, and wagon covers – as well as plows, harrows, and wagons. All told, then, inventories offer an unparalleled and essentially unutilized resource for historians of technology, both in the attentiveness to tools and in the coverage of the tool-owning population. They also exist continuously from early settlement through the mid-nineteenth century, unlike many social history records that either end or commence with the political transformations of late-eighteenth-century America.

Despite their many assets, like other historical documents, inventories will lead us astray unless we keep in mind why they were created. Otherwise, as one reads through probate inventories, the sense they convey of walking through the house and around the barnyard with the inventory takers can lull one into unwarranted confidence in a document's completeness. Inventories, as noted, were designed to protect an estate's personal property. But inventory takers certainly knew that not all assets needed equal protection. Obviously, listing assets such as cash or silverware afforded insurance against such valuables' disappearance into someone's pocket before settlement.

What is less obvious, until one begins reading wills, inventories, and administrators' accounts, is the need to protect much of the estate's personal property from disappearing into someone's stomach or into the woods. Joseph Wills, administrator of the estate of Daniel Wills of Burlington County, communicated this situation graphically when his 1729 accounts claimed credit for "two hogs appraised in the Inventory at 10/[shillings] Each[,] which either Strayd away with strange hogs or were Destroyd by Wolves or Dogs so that they never came to this Accomptants use"![8]

By contrast, other items were evidently deemed so secure that their absence from inventories does not necessarily spell rarity. Furniture attached to the walls of the house – built-in bedsteads or benches, for example – understandably seemed safe from depredations. In consequence, where featherbeds and other bedding are enumerated but bedsteads not listed, we cannot safely conclude that people were reduced to sleeping on the floor. Nor, of course, can we conclude that they were not.

More important, like all historical documents, inventories were shaped by prevailing gender assumptions. Legally, widows were entitled to a certain share of the property. Sometimes an inventory designates items as "belonging to the wito," to borrow a phrase from one York County inventory. Comparing such inventories with others is important in assessing whether local inventory takers tended to omit goods they assumed to be the widow's. Likewise, certain items were enumerated so rarely as to suggest that some property was commonly perceived as belonging to women, despite the formal legal assumption that a married woman's property belonged to her husband. For example, women's clothing appears almost exclusively in women's inventories; it is rarely listed in the estates of a woman's husband or father. Alternatively, some items associated with women may have been considered by male enumerators to be natural extensions of the woman or deemed so trivial because associated with women that they were not found worthy of enumeration in women's or men's estates. For example, I have found only eight needles and three thimbles in the more than 350 inventories I have examined closely thus far. Other items generally associated with women's work – poultry, for example – were also uncommon, if judged by inventories. Yet we know from other evidence, notably faunal remains in archaeological excavations, that, even in frontier Westmoreland, domestic fowl contributed substantially to the diet.[9]

To generalize, then, our common practice of treating some documents as literary evidence, in which case they receive close reading and attention to nuance and to social construction, and of treating other documents as quantitative evidence, in which case we code them up and crunch out the numbers, entails a false dichotomy between literary and social scientific sources. Certainly inventories are both. They can, for example, be used to tell us that before the American Revolution a significant proportion of Burlington and Hunterdon County households – about 20–25 percent – owned slaves. But they can also be used to reveal something of slavery's meaning in the Quaker mid-Atlantic, if we note that Burlington inventory takers rather consistently listed slaves between the farm tools and the livestock.

Although part of my intention in quoting Williams's poem was to underscore the literary character of the historical enterprise, I do not minimize the importance of the quantitative. For example, I needed to devise a sampling strategy that would avoid aberrant years: times when events such as wars disrupted record keeping or times when epidemics or warfare made the population of decedents unusually young, for example. I found that I could best assure comparability among years if I used a fifteen-year interval in sampling. Starting with 1774, the last good pre-Revolutionary year, I moved forward in fifteen-year increments to 1849, a date chosen so as to conclude my study with results from the first full federal agricultural census, that of 1850. I got as close as possible to initial settlement by moving backward from 1774 in fifteen-year increments, collecting inventories as far back as records permitted.

This strategy has already generated a daunting array of information. My earliest sample comes from Burlington in 1714. Hunterdon supplies inventories beginning in 1729. York, founded in 1749, offers its earliest sample in 1759, and Westmoreland, organized in 1773, provides a small sample the following year. In order to ensure ample representation of inventories compiled in each season of the year and of assets left by various sorts of persons, I chose not to sample within years but to collect all inventories filed in each sample year. I have also chosen to retain virtually all of the original data.

The discussion that follows rests on a data base containing all of the eighteenth-century inventories for Burlington and Hunterdon, New Jersey, and for Westmoreland, Pennsylvania, and all of the York/Adams County inventories prior to 1789, about 350 inventories. That translates into an inventory data base of roughly twenty-six thousand records – individual inventory items, that is. The data I present here are drawn from a subset of 250 inventories chosen to include only individuals who were farmers and who owned at least some household goods.

Before exploring what these data suggest about early American agricultural technology, one final general question remains to be answered: What was early American agricultural technology? To date, restrictive definitions of technology have impeded the study of early farming technology. Accounts of colonial farming in particular regularly dismiss its technology as "primitive" and technological change as "absent." Either characterization reflects an unfortunate tendency "to limit the definition of technology to those things which characterize the technology of our own time, such as machinery and prime movers," a definition that makes the nineteenth-century reaper seem to herald the dawn of American agricultural technology.[10]

Fundamentally, historians' definitions of technology reflect the fact that we have written mostly about nineteenth- and twentieth-century technology and have given little thought to early modern technology or to farm technology generally. It suffices to say here that agricultural technology includes far more than machines, implements, and the knowledge of how to use them. At minimum it must also include the plants and animals that humans have developed, together with knowledge of plant and animal behavior; the methods of identifying land suited to particular purposes and of modifying and organizing that land; the construction methods, structures, and procedures devised for storing crops and housing livestock; and the knowledge of how to modify crops, land use patterns, and storage techniques to adapt to various climates. Under the household organization of labor that characterized early modern agriculture, the tools, skills, and knowledge employed in processing food, fiber, and other farm products – most of them wielded by women – must also qualify as agricultural technology. Assuredly, the agricultural enterprise could not have functioned successfully without them. For purposes of this discussion, then, agricultural tools will include items such as pots, churns, stills, spinning wheels, maize, turnips, cattle, and sheep as well as implements such as plows, wagons, hoes, and axes.

What do probate records of such items allow us to conclude about tool ownership on early American farms? As suggested already, one very clear message is that there was no standard array of household and farm utensils that virtually all colonists owned or needed to own. That many individuals made do without plows, kettles, firearms, or Bibles reminds us, as we need always be reminded when we leave the era of modern technology, that the belief in "one best way" to perform a given task is an artifact of industrialized production. Indeed, the ability of modern households to own a standard array of tools reflects the existence of systems of transportation, communication, and manufacturing inconceivable in early modern societies. I stress the point because the history of technology has focused so narrowly on the recent period that aberrant features of industrial technology easily get read back into discussions of earlier eras.

Another conclusion warranted by these data is that eighteenth-century Americans were not technologically self-sufficient. Patterns of tool ownership imply extensive participation in the market. For example, only five inventories listed candle molds, and only about 5 percent enumerated tallow. A far larger proportion – 24–40 percent – included candles or candleholders, implying the acquisition of candles elsewhere. Likewise, although yard goods appear in most inventories, weaving equipment shows up in fewer than 5 percent of Burlington farm households. Even in more recently settled Hunterdon and York, where poorer transportation limited access to imported textiles and urban weavers, only about 15 percent of farm inventories generally listed looms. Where the prospect of acquiring textiles from Britain or from local population centers was extremely limited, as in the very remote settlements of late-eighteenth-century Westmoreland County or of York in 1759, the proportion of farm households prepared to weave still reached only 25 percent – hardly an impressive tally.

Eighteenth-century farmers not only purchased essential commodities such as cloth but also depended on mills or specialists to process much of what they grew. There is, for example, no evidence that any farmer owned tools to grind his own grain; and, except in frontier York with its exceptionally poor transportation facilities, most people who grew flax lacked both flax brakes to prepare the fiber, and many lacked hackles to comb it. More households owned spinning wheels, although only in York and in early Hunterdon did substantially more than half do so, a pattern probably indicative of the frontier population's relative youthfulness rather than of its relationship to the market. If eighteenth-century agricultural regions had been technologically self-sufficient, we might expect, at the very least, to find a region's ownership of spinning wheels to parallel its fiber production, but, except in York, the proportion of households owning sheep rather consistently outran the proportion prepared to spin wool. Indeed, in many years more Burlington decedents owned herds of sheep (twenty or more) than owned spinning wheels of any sort. Woolen wheel ownership exceeded the number of substantial sheep herds only in York and Westmoreland, where, given the persistence of wolves, large herds of sheep remained uncommon.

Similarly, tool ownership patterns clearly imply extensive wood-processing specialization. Remarkably, even common tasks such as firewood preparation entailed exchanges with outsiders. Throughout

the eighteenth century three-quarters or more of Hunterdon and Burlington households lacked mauls and wedges for splitting wood. Saws of
various sorts and froes, for cleaving shingles, were even less common. As
do the turning lathes listed in craftsmen's inventories, these data remind
us that specialized production and employment long antedated American settlement. It is hardly surprising, then, that colonists presumed
self-sufficiency to be unnecessary and, probably, undesirable. Certainly
they quickly made it uncommon. The most dramatic case in point is that
of frontier farmers, who generally distilled their grain into whiskey, a
commodity whose high value relative to its bulk enabled it profitably
to be transported long distances to market. Despite the relative cheapness of stills, most farmers relied on others to process their grain.
Similarly, in eastern counties, where apple trees had had a chance to
mature, most farmers depended on a small minority who owned cider
mills.

Two additional aspects of tool ownership signal the market's mounting importance over the eighteenth century. First, early in the century
Burlington farmers rarely (less than 15 percent of the time) owned
wagons. Instead, between three-fifths and one-half of households had
carts – relatively small, cheap, two-wheeled vehicles better designed for
hauling small loads around the farm than for carrying crops to market.
After midcentury, this pattern was reversed. About three-fifths to one-
half of Burlington farmers came to own wagons, while cart ownership
declined dramatically. At the same time, roughly two-thirds of Hunterdon farmers owned wagons, the greater proportion reflecting longer
average overland distances to market. Even in York, where wagon trips
to market were less frequent, nearly two-fifths of households owned
them. Only in remote Westmoreland did many farmers have to make
do with pack saddles. During the same years, substantial proportions
(from one-quarter to one-half) of farm households in each county came
to own steelyards, signifying more frequent occasions to weigh goods for
exchange.

Diverse patterns of tool ownership also reveal eighteenth-century
mid-Atlantic farmers to have been a distinctly innovative lot. And, far
from deriving from the romanticized jack-of-all-trades conjured up as
part of the frontier subsistence myth, early American readiness to try
new technology had several more mundane sources. First, it built on the
common experience of the many colonists who came from a place –
Britain – in the throes of an agricultural revolution. If we take differences
in British and colonial circumstances into account, we find that land
reorganization and reclamation, experimentation with and adoption of
new crops, and increased attention to livestock husbandry engaged
colonial yeomen as well as their British counterparts. Whereas the Brit-

ish brought new land into cultivation by adopting crop rotations suited to light, upland soil or by draining swamps or by irrigating meadows, early British Americans achieved the same outcome by acquiring the utterly alien skills needed to clear the continent's dense woodlands. And, like Englishmen at home who acquired their land reclamation technologies from their Dutch neighbors, mid-Atlantic English colonists developed forest destruction to a fine art by borrowing the technology of their Native American and Scandinavian predecessors and of their German contemporaries.

Among their tools, farmers' frequent ownership of axes best documents their openness to new land-making technology. Until relatively late in the eighteenth century, for example, Burlington and Hunterdon County farmers were at least as likely to own axes as plows, and in York and Westmoreland they were far more likely to. Furthermore, despite the near certainty that most arrived from England without axes or tree-felling experience, a substantial proportion (one-quarter to one-third) of Burlington and Hunterdon decedents owned more than one axe.

Mid-Atlantic farmers also paralleled British agricultural revolutionaries in readily adopting new crops, such as Indian corn, listed rather consistently in 50–60 percent of inventories. The extent to which this formerly novel grain had achieved acceptance is best suggested by the evidence that almost all inventories after midcentury employ the words "wheat" or "rye" or "oats" to enumerate European grains; they reserve the word "corn" for maize. Indeed, so early and so thoroughly was Indian corn integrated into the mixed-farming regime brought by English colonists that one of the supreme ironies of eighteenth- and nineteenth-century agricultural history is apparent. The same reformers who praised English husbandmen for their willingness to experiment with new crops ignored the far more general adoption of maize by American farmers and, instead, derided them for their reluctance to grow turnips.[11]

Also like their British contemporaries, mid-Atlantic farmers accorded particular attention to livestock husbandry. In every sample county, horses and cattle were far more common than plows or even axes for most of the century, and hay crops grew in frequency and value. Churn ownership suggests that farm women's work also shifted toward livestock husbandry. Burlington churn ownership increased to nearly one-fifth of estates by the late eighteenth century while in Hunterdon and York more than one-half and about two-thirds, respectively, of all inventories listed churns.

Repeated evidence that York County decedents more often employed progressive technology reflects the prominence of Germans in its population. But the case of German farmers' apparent progressiveness well illustrates that technological progress is always in the eye of the beholder. In fact, for German settlers the techniques that British farmers had recently adopted with so much fanfare represented established practice. So, for example, York farmers often owned tools for manuring: dung forks, dung hooks, and dung shovels appear in two-thirds of their inventories by 1774. By contrast, almost no Burlington farmers' inventories record any such implements. York farmers were also far more likely to wield cradles at harvesttime (20 percent of York farmer decendents versus, at most, 5–10 percent of Burlington farmers). And they generally owned hoes, indicative of more intensive cultivation (about 70–80 percent of York farmers' inventories versus about 30 percent of Burlington farmers' inventories during the same years). York's settlers often used those tools to cultivate potatoes and turnips (about 40 percent and 25 percent, respectively) – "the new root crops" from an English perspective. Farmers in York also employed far more winnowing fans (nearly one-third of York inventories listed them, versus only one Burlington inventory).

However commonplace German farmers may have found these technologies, viewed through British eyes they were innovative. It is all the more noteworthy, then, that by 1774 only about half of York farmers owning dung tools were German and even fewer potato growers were (about one-third). By contrast, fifteen years earlier, Germans had owned most dung tools (about three-fourths of them). In other words, tool ownership patterns show German agricultural technology diffusing earlier and more readily than most secondary scholarship has surmised.

Hunterdon County also had a substantial German population, and one derived from essentially the same sources as supplied York. But whereas York Germans arrived early in that county's history and generally predominated numerically, Hunterdon Germans arrived after their county's other principal ethnic groups and made up only a quarter of the population.[12] As a result, techniques associated with German farming diffused far more selectively in Hunterdon. Where a technology proved well suited to established practice and could be introduced as a solitary innovation, German techniques fared well there. So, for example, winnowing fans became even more common there than in York (they appeared in about 35 percent of Hunterdon farm inventories). This adoption is hardly surprising, for they were clearly well suited to Hunterdon's late-eighteenth-century emphasis on wheat, a crop listed in 65–72 percent of farm inventories. Similarly, although at midcentury Hunterdon farmers, like their Burlington neighbors, rarely harvested with cradles, their increasing reliance on hay reinforced the increased presence of German exemplars to make cradle use more common in Hunterdon than in York. By 1789 two-fifths of Hunterdon farm inventories listed cradles, and only half of these are identifiable as German or Dutch. On the other hand, dung implements appear almost exclusively in German and Dutch inventories in Hunterdon, reflecting both the absence of evident soil depletion and the greater array of new behaviors dunging entailed.

Comparison of York and Hunterdon can also help establish how much of York's apparent innovativeness derived from German influence and how much from the influence of the frontier. Again, data on tool ownership serve as a useful corrective to the belief, pervasive in American popular culture, that frontier living meant being reduced to older, more primitive ways of doing things – a belief we readily incorporate into historical scholarship where evidence is absent. Tool ownership patterns indicate that, far from reverting to obsolete technology, frontiersmen generally brought the latest technology with them. For example, large, heavy, iron-reinforced, covered market wagons (from which the famed Conestoga was derived) showed up far more often in late-eighteenth-century York than in Hunterdon inventories of the same era. And most kettle-owning farm women in Westmoreland and York employed modern iron kettles, whereas traditional brass kettles continued longer in Hunterdon and, especially, Burlington.

Similarly, comparison of Burlington, Hunterdon, York, and Westmoreland inventories indicates that the technological commitments made by a region's pioneers could be hard to break. For example, over the eighteenth century, mid-Atlantic farmers followed a general European trend away from the use of oxen and toward the use of horses as draft animals. Thus, oxen were relatively common in early Burlington, showing up in more than one-quarter of inventories before 1730. By contrast, oxen appear in virtually no inventories in York, where most settlement occurred after midcentury. They are entirely absent from Westmoreland, settled even later. In Burlington, however, oxen represented established practice, and they remained relatively common even late in the century. Hunterdon, settled only a generation earlier than York, also relied heavily on horses from the outset, but a persistent minority used oxen late in the century – apparently Hunterdon immigrants from New England, an early and persistent ox-using region.[13]

Frontier conditions also encouraged technological innovation more directly. Not surprisingly, all of the various rough woodworking tools appeared far more often in York than in Burlington or Hunterdon inventories. Likewise, specialized hoes were a feature of frontier agriculture. Most commonly, inventories distinguished between grubbing hoes and weeding hoes. Such distinctions were especially common in York, ten times more common than in Burlington inventories. Widespread ownership of both weeding and grubbing hoes certainly made sense under frontier conditions. Corn, an ideal crop on new land, generally received hoe cultivation – hence the weeding hoe – and new land also required farmers to use hoes to grub out roots, stones, and other debris.[14]

Frontier and German influence intersected somewhat differently to shape food-processing technology. One of the more striking technological differences between German and British settlers was that Germans were accustomed to cook and heat with stoves, whereas the British relied on open hearth cookery and heating. Like many German technologies, stoves eventually became the British American's modern technology, but there is less evidence of their colonial diffusion. In English Burlington, for example, despite ready access to stoves in nearby Philadelphia, only one stove was enumerated in any eighteenth-century inventory. Rather, food preparation methods appear to have been highly resistant to change, a pattern anthropologists have often ascribed to the deep-seated cultural conditioning of dietary preferences. A look at the technology involved suggests instead that the domestic craftswomen who prepared most meals understandably resisted adopting new tools that threatened their hard-won proficiencies, altered the quality of the work experience, and would have required them to learn a new repertoire of skills.[15]

Domestic tool ownership patterns in York support this interpretation. As a frontier community with a very poor transportation system, York was a difficult place to obtain a stove. Nonetheless, nearly half of York's German decedents had managed to acquire stoves by the 1770s (about 20 percent of all inventories). Even more striking is the suggestion implicit in York's domestic tool ownership pattern that German farm wives who lacked stoves merely tolerated fireplace cooking as a temporary expedient. Trammels, elaborate contrivances for hanging and adjusting pots over the fire, are absent from York inventories although they appear often in Burlington ones. Instead, York mistresses relied on simple pothooks. For varying the heat they applied, they placed their pots on pot racks designed to elevate pots and frying pans over coals on the hearth. Not only did this cooking method come closer to replicating stove cooking, but also pot racks served as complements to legless cooking vessels – vessels one would prefer to retain or purchase if one expected ultimately to acquire a stove.

By contrast, Hunterdon County domestic tool ownership patterns suggest how farm women came to adopt new technology. Although more favorably situated to acquire stoves, few Hunterdon decedents owned them (about 10 percent of inventories). Nor did Hunterdon Germans show a preference for pot racks (fewer than 10 percent of inventories enumerated pot racks, even fewer than in Burlington); county farm wives of all ethnic groups employed trammels. Essentially, this very different behavior reflects differences in the timing of German settlement. As relative latecomers, Hunterdon Germans generally moved into existing houses – houses that embodied a preference for fireplace cooking. Moreover, Hunterdon Germans tended to be poorer than those who could afford the longer trek and greater farm-making investment required in York. Most probably arrived without pots and pans and acquired kitchen utensils from craftsmen accustomed to supplying Hunterdon's established British settlers.

Ethnic differences in food processing are also manifest in the distribution of specialized tubs between York and Burlington. With one exception all of the powdering tubs – tubs used to preserve meat by salting – appear in Burlington inventories. By contrast, all of the pickling tubs show up in York inventories, evidence of a divergent meat preservation tradition. Cabbages and implements for processing cabbage are, likewise, limited almost exclusively to York and Hunterdon German inventories. In sum, the distribution of food processing implements in eighteenth-century inventories hints at a larger, historically invisible array of technologies: the skills and knowledge essential to transforming crops into food.

Although we can glimpse only obliquely the skills and knowledge that constituted most of colonial agricultural technology, inventories offer a rather direct look at the material component of that technology: the tools, livestock, and plants that early Americans commonly employed. This preliminary account of several hundred such documents demonstrates how productive of new and revised understandings of early agricultural practice the actual evidence of tool ownership can be. Looking at farmers' possessions reveals that there existed no standard array of implements farmers and farm wives owned or needed to own; it shows the belief in "one best way" to perform a task to be a historical artifact, an intellectual by-product of industrial society that we inadvertently project onto the preindustrial past.

Certainly, colonial farm household tools show a diversity that we deem uncommon in the world we inhabit. In part this diversity reflected the considerable and growing involvement of farmers and farm wives in networks of exchange – with one another and with the local representatives of distant producers. In part the diversity reveals selective adoption from the varied menu of innovations that American farmers employed virtually from the start of settlement: land-clearing and woodworking tools, new field and garden crops, and the various creatures, structures, and implements that embodied a growing commitment to livestock husbandry. And, whereas the ethnic diversity of the colonial population may have introduced much of this technological diversity, close examination of late-eighteenth-century tool ownership discloses extensive cross-cultural borrowing, especially in regions where ethnic diversity began early. Inventories also reveal diversity emerging from the diverse times at which counties were settled. Technological patterns established early evidently continued to influence local farmers' and farm wives' technological options. Given the continous westward course of settlement, then, temporal diversity gradually assumed a geographic manifestation.

These preliminary observations about early American tool ownership carry obvious implications for the large question with which I began: What accounts for America's sudden, rapid, and comparatively successful early nineteenth-century industrialization? They suggest that the well-springs of American willingness and ability to innovate were mundane rather than mythic, endemic rather than heroic. Judging from these data, the sources of early American technological innovation – and, by extension, America's early industrialization – should sound familiar to American historians: the rise of a market economy, the selective transfer of European culture, the social consequences of ethnic diversity, and the significance of the frontier. These are themes to which students of the American past perennially recur.

If these themes also best elucidate our early technological history, then "so much depends" on closely scrutinizing the small technologies found on early American farms – much more than a new portrait of early tool use. If, as these preliminary findings suggest, traditional historical themes will play a predominant role in explaining America's technological history, historians of technology will have to question the wisdom of their increasing specialization and separation from the larger historical profession. More than most historians, we should recognize and avoid the high cost of unnecessarily reinventing the wheel. Likewise, once early American historians recognize their perennial concerns as having great relevance to understanding the problem of technological innovation, they may wonder at their former willingness to delegate study of this crucial issue to historians of technology. Like all contemporary Americans, early American historians should recognize and avoid the high potential costs of leaving technology solely to the technology experts. Finally, if early American technological diversity helped precipitate America's remarkable nineteenth-century technological innovativeness, the findings discussed above hold a moral for us all, early American historians and historians of technology alike. Studies of early American technology need all of our various approaches; scholarly innovation thrives best when a field's cultivators know there is no "one best way" to farm.

Notes

1 William Carlos Williams, *Collected Poems 1909–1939 – Vol. 1.* Copyright 1938 by New Directions Pub. Corp.

2 F. S. Flint, quoted in William Pratt, ed., *The Imagist Poem: Modern Poetry in Miniature* (New York, 1963), 18.

3 Charles Schultz, *Peanuts* (United Feature Syndicate, Inc., 1981).

4 Pratt, ed., *Imagist Poem*, 22.

5 E. L. Jones, *Agriculture and the Industrial Revolution* (New York, 1974), esp. 86; Maxine Berg, *The Age of Manufactures: Industry, Innovation, and Work in Britain, 1700–1820* (New York, 1986), 93–94.

6 Turner quoted in Sheridan, "The Domestic Economy," in Jack P. Greene and J. R. Pole, eds, *Colonial British America: Essays in the New History of the Early Modern Era* (Baltimore, 1984), 59.

7 Sheridan, "Domestic Economy," in Greene and Pole, eds., *Colonial British America*, 43.

8 Administrator's Accounts, Daniel Wills Estate, Dec. 12, 1729, file no. 1931–37, New Jersey State Archives, Trenton.

9 James B. Richardson III and Kirke C. Wilson, "Hannas Town and Charles Foreman: The Historical and Archaeological Record, 1770–1806," *Western Pennsylvania Historical Magazine*, LIX (1976), 180–181. Without exception, those who signed inventories as enumerators were male, so we know that women's items, if present, were viewed – or ignored – through male eyes.

10 Melvin Kranzberg and Carroll W. Pursell, Jr., eds., *Technology in Western Civilization*, I, *The Emergence of Modern Industrial Society: Earliest Times to 1900* (New York, 1967), 4–6.

11 James T. Lemon, *The Best Poor Man's Country: A Geographical Study of Early Southeastern Pennsylvania* (New York, 1976), 183. Given that Indian corn was unlikely to appear in estate inventories during the months when livestock could be turned out to forage, 50%–60% is an extremely high proportion.

12 Lemon, *Best Poor Man's Country*, 43–50; Hubert G. Schmidt, *Rural Hunterdon: An Agricultural History* (New Brunswick, NJ, 1946), 33–35, 42.

13 Percy Wells Bidwell and John I. Falconer, *History of Agriculture in the Northern United States, 1620–1860* (Washington, DC, 1925), 111–113.

14 Nicholas P. Hardeman, *Shucks, Shocks, and Hominy Blocks: Corn as a Way of Life in Pioneer America* (Baton Rouge, LA, 1981), 55–58, 83–86.

15 Schmidt, *Rural Hunterdon*, 268–269; Stevenson Whitcomb Fletcher, *Pennsylvania Agriculture and Country Life, 1640–1840* (Harrisburg, PA, 1950), 387–388, 399. I am indebted to Stephanie Wolf for suggesting the interpretation of the resistance of craftswomen.

Documents

American Colonial Wealth: Documents and Methods

Alice Hanson Jones

11004
MARGARETA FREDERICK　　*Smithfield Twp*　　*Widow*　　*Acl 4*　　*Pr*　619

A true Appriment of the Estate of Margareta Fredrick Desed. Taken Done by us of the goods & Chattles

	£	s	d
Sundre waring Apperil to the amount of	7	4	–
165 1/2 yds. Lininn £23–7–11 & 4 yds woling Cloth @ 7 yd.	24	15	11
1 1/2 yd. flaxen 4/6d. & 24 lb. Contten yarn @ 4/6	5	12	6
24 lb. flax yarn @ 4/ & 5 lb. Ceverled yarn @ 1/6	5	3	6
12 lb. yarn @ 1/ & 8 lb. @ 9d. & 7 baggs @ 1/3d.	1	7	9
1 Bed & 1 bolster & 2 pillers & 2 Sheets	3	8	–
1 Bed & 1 Rugg & 2 pillers & 1 Bolster	5	–	–
1 Bed & 1 Blanket 40/ & 2 Chists @ 16/ a peace	3	12	–
Shoe Leather 24/ & 12¾ lb. wool @ 1/6d. & 2 Bul. Salt	2	13	1
1 wattering pott 6/ & 3 iron potts 70/ & 3 Tramils 3/	2	9	–
1 Big Bible & Sundre Small Books	3	–	–
4 pales & 1 Cag 6/ & 2 puter Basons & 12 plates & 7 spoons	1	6	–
1 Coffe mill 4/6d. & 1 Tub & 1 Baril & 1 Churn & small Lumber	1	6	6
2 Shovel & 2 axes & 2 forks & 1 grubinghoe	–	16	–
2 Lamps & 1 Candle stick & 2 wedges & 1 pair mall Rings	–	6	–
1 waggon & 1 harrow & 1 flaxbrake 1 iron hopel	4	15	6
1 Cows £8 & 2 steers £5 & 1 heffer 50/ & 1 Calf 20/	16	10	–
1 Rone mare & 1 Brownhorse @ £11 & 8 Sheep @ 9/ 2	25	10	–
4 old Sickels & 2 old sadles 28/ & 1½ Bul. flax seed 7/6d.	1	15	6
8 Reeds & 7 pan of wevers gears & 2 bells & 6 Bul. Corn	2	2	6

Excerpts from Alice Hanson Jones, *American Colonial Wealth: Documents and Methods* (New York: Arno Press, 1977).

16 Bushil Buckwheat 24/ & 1 Stack Wheat £5 & 1 Rye £3:15/	9	19	–
1¾ acers of wheat in the ground & 4½ acors Rye dito	4	–	–
1 Table & 1 small Box & 2 Juggs & 6 hives of Bees	2	6	–
2 iron stoves & 1 small Box old Iron & nales & 3 Chears	3	5	–
2 dozn. knifes & forks & 1 wheal & 8 milk pott & 1 Teapot	–	13	6
1 pair Cards 1/ & 1 hatchel 3/ & 1 smothing iron 4/	–	7	–
6 notes £18:1/ & Cash £50:16:5	68	17	5
120 acres of Land £250:0:0	250	–	–
the 14th Janury. 1774 Appraised by Us	£ 458	4	8

Samuel Drake
Jacob Snell

ACCOUNT OF EXECUTORS:

Dr. The accompt of Jacob Stroud and Abraham Miller Executors the Last Will and Testament of Ann Margaret Frederick Deceased as well of all and Singular the Goods Chattels Rights & Credits which were of the said deced. at the time of her death and which came into the hands & possession of the said Accomptants as of their several payments & disbursements made out of the same Vizt.

Imprs. The said Accomptants charges themselves with all and Singular the Goods Chattels Rights & Credits which came into the hands & possession of the said Executors Specified & contained in an Inventory & Appraisement thereof Exhibited into the Register's Office at Easton amounting to

...Office at Easton amounting to	184	4	4
Item With what the Goods & Chattels sold for at Vendue above the Appraised Value	25	3	7
Item With Cash recd. of Peter Frederick	12	–	–
Item With Cash recd. of Sundry persons	7	1	7

11011
WILLIAM McHENAY   *Mount Bethel Twp*   *Farmer*   *Acl 3*   *Pr 628*

An Inventry of The Goods and Cattel belonging William McHenay Leat of Mount Bethel Desesed Takening This 31st Day of May 1774 and appraised by William McFerrin and Thomas Ross

	£	s	d
To purse and Apparell	17	10	4
To one Wagen	12	–	–
To 2 Horses and 2 Mears	31	–	–
To a Cow and Calfe	4	10	–
To 2 Two year olds and one year old	5	10	–
To Two plows and one slead	1	16	6

	£	s	d
To 2 Grubing Hows and 2 Molding hows and Seaith	–	10	6
To one Herrow and Sheare in The Leane [*Seane?*]	4	–	–
To 21 1/4 Acores of Wheat at 25 shilling per Acors	26	11	3
To one Sow and and [*sic*] 4 Shots	2	5	–
To one ox yoak and Tow Cheans and one Crow Barr	1	4	–
To old Iron and one pich fork	–	7	–
To a Cuting Box and Neck fork	–	11	–
To 2 old Seadels	1	2	6
To 3 Littel wheels and one Clock Reel	1	–	–
To 10 Bags at 5/ per Bag	2	10	–
To 2 old Hogsheds 2 Tubs and one Erthen	–	15	–
To 2 ogers 2 gimblets and Mall Rings	–	3	6
To Inden Corn in the Lump	3	10	–
To 2 Iron poots	–	16	–
To old Books	–	17	–
To 3 peals a half Bushels and Churn	–	6	6
To Sole Lether and a Calf Skin	–	13	6
To 3 Earthen poots 2 Earthen gugs and Crockery Wear	–	8	6
To putter and one Conk-shell	–	13	–
To Forks and knifs and Tea Tackling	–	8	6
To a Beack Iron Candel Sticks and Sundry Articks	–	11	4
To one Firkel of Fish a Gun and Tallow	1	13	–
To one Table Dough Trough and 2 pear of Cards	–	11	–
To one Bead Stead and powdering Tub	–	8	–
To Wheat Rey & Buck wheat in the lump	1	15	–
To Dray Meat and Sealt In the lump	1	2	–
To a poot Reack and Box Iron	–	6	–
To 2 Beads and Beading	2	10	–
To 7 Drinking Glasses	–	3	6
To one Flax Brack	–	5	–

Appraised by us the day & year aforsed.

William McFarnen

Thomas Ross

[*Document presented and sworn to by the signers listed above on June 27, 1774.*]

ACCOUNT OF ADMINISTRATOR:

The account of James McHenny Admr. of the Estate of William McHenny Deced. as of all and singular the Goods Chattels Rights and Credits which were of the Said Deceased at the time of his Death and which Came into the hands and possession of the Said accomptant as of his Several payments & Disbursements made out of the Same as Follows Vizt.

The Said accompt. Charges himself with the following Credits received not Specified in Said Inventory Vizt.

[*Cash received by the estate from six named persons range from £0-3-6 to £18-17-0.*]

The Said accomptant Craves allowance for his Several payments and Disbursements made out of the Same Vizt.

[*Payments from the estate to twelve named creditors range from £0-3-6 to £6-0-0. Eight itemized costs of administration total £20-10-5. Document presented and sworn to January 23, 1778.*]

11012
HENRY NELICH   *Whitehall Twp*   *Farmer*   *Acl 2*   *Pr 61*

Whitehall the 4th June 1774 Inventory of the Goods and Chattles Lands and Credits Belonging to the Estate of Henry Nelich Late of Whitehall Township in the County of Northampton Deceased as Followeth Viz.

	£	s	d
Six Shurds	1	5	–
Two Coads	2	–	–
one Chacket with Sliefs & one Do. without	1	–	–
Britches Stockins & a Had	–	12	–
A Great Coad	–	3	–
Three Bety Coads	1	10	–
one Ebern & other wemon Cloth	–	7	–
Severel other wemen Cloth	–	6	–
Two Shord Gounds	–	6	–
a Clock for wemen	–	12	–
Shifts Seven	–	10	–
handkerchief Caps Stockins & other things	1	–	–
Six Napkins Taple Cloths Six	–	12	–
A Lookin Glass	–	2	6
a Bible	2	–	–
Two Psalm & a prayer boock one Do.	–	12	–
a Daesk	3	–	–
one Dito Shmall	–	14	–
a Clock	11	–	–
a Table	–	15	–
Three Bodles one Gill Glass Reaser Sondiel	–	3	–
Coffe bod Tea Cobs & blads Six Pair a Jack	–	3	–
2 Pair of woll Cards	–	2	–
a Cun	–	2	–
beds One fether bed poulster Sted & Straw bag & Planket	2	10	–
one Dito with 2 poulsters	3	–	–
one Dito	2	–	–
one Do.	1	5	–

	£	s	d
Four bed Stads	1	–	–
a bed Civer	–	2	6
Two Lamps & Lander & oyl bodle	–	3	–
Two hachels	1	–	–
a Chist	–	5	–
a pice of homeSpun Cloth	–	12	–
Sheeps woll	–	6	–
Two Spinning wheals	–	4	–
Eleven bags	1	–	–
Three plans	–	1	6
Twelve bred baskets 2 Straw & one hicry Do.	–	5	–
Three half Bushels	–	3	–
Four Sickels	–	2	–
Two Cheers	–	3	–
Two Pewter Dishes 2 Blades four Drenchers	1	–	–
Sixteen Spoons	–	3	–
Twelve woden Trenchers	–	2	6
Four Erthen plads thre Cups 3 Drenchers	–	–	9
Twelve Erthen Crocks two wot Dishes	–	2	–
one fraying Pan 2 other pans	–	4	–
a Buckwheat plad & a roast	–	6	–
four Ladles & one forcke	–	3	–
2 Pot Civer	–	5	–
a Peper mill & peper box	–	5	–
2 Iron Bots & one Cidtle	1	10	–
one Copper Cidtle	2	10	–
Three Cacks	–	4	–
Six buckets & one wood Can	–	7	6
one Tine quart & one Dramel	–	–	4
one Garter Loom 2 Solt boxes	–	1	6
Three barrel Casks	–	1	3
Two hackfed & two berrel Casks	–	15	–
a Tob for washing & one for cabidge	–	16	–
a Cabidge plain	–	4	–
a Jurn & three buder buckets	–	5	–
a groinding stone	–	8	–
a Saw & Drowing knife	–	5	–
four Oger	–	4	–
five hamer	–	5	–
four Chessels	–	3	–
five bells	–	8	–
Two Hoppels a Chain for waggon tonge	–	6	–
five Siths & one Cutting knife	–	5	–
Three Axes & one hached	–	8	–
five Hows	–	7	6

Three whet Stones & one Camblet	–	1	3
a iren Goos & Shear for Taylor	–	2	6
old Iron ware	–	3	–
2 Ridge 2 Tonge forgs Tonge How & Shovel	–	6	–
three Hamp Brags & a reel	–	3	–
a mall & weches	–	4	–
a Tramel & a Chain	–	4	–
Two Grupping hows	–	7	–
Two Sadles	1	10	–
Two Collers & geers Blind holders & Line	–	10	–
Cutting box & knife	–	8	–
Three Creedles	–	1	6
Two Plows & a Tree	–	15	–
a frow	–	8	–
a new Waggen	3	10	–
a old Waggen The 1/2 of and old waggen	1	10	–
a Sorrel hors	15	–	–
a mere with a Cold	18	–	–
a Cow with a Spot before her face	3	–	–
a Black Dito	2	10	–
a Black Dito with white Spots	2	10	–
a rid Dito	2	10	–
& a haffer	1	10	–
a Calfe	1	–	–
four Cow Cheans	–	7	6
[*illeg.*] hogs	1	12	–
Three Sheep & one young one	1	–	–
Eighteen Bords & Som bees Caps	–	2	–
Boock Debt due to him	3	8	1
Bonds & Notes Due or become Due	42	3	1
a Debt due from Jacob Kendel	13	10	10
The Improvement with all the Grain & Building thereupon	205	–	–

[*sic*] £ 379 8 7

ACCOUNT OF EXECUTOR:

Dr. The Accompt of John Hunsacker Executor of the Last Will & Testament of Henry Nelich deceased as well of all & singular the Goods Chattels Rights & Credits which late were of the said decedt. and which came into the hands & possession of the said Executor as of his several payments & disbursements made out of the same as follows Vizt.

[*The following sum was added to the total physical wealth of the inventory*: "With what the Goods Chattels & Real Estate sold for at Vendue above the Appraisement, £156-11-4." *The real estate sold at vendue for £ 100-0-0 above the appraised value and the goods and chattels sold at £ 56-11-4 above the appraised value.*]

Further Reading

Deetz, James. *In Small Things Forgotten: the Archeology of Early American Life.* New York: Doubleday, 1977.

Green, Jack P., and J. R. Pole, eds. *Colonial British America: Essays in the New History of the Early Modern Era.* Baltimore: Johns Hopkins University Press, 1984.

Hindle, Brooke, ed. *America's Wooden Age: Aspects of Its Early Technology.* Tarrytown, NY: Sleepy Hollow Restorations, 1975.

2

Fighting Technological Change

1769	First water mill in England to utilize Richard Arkwright's spinning machine.
1790	Samuel Slater builds first Arkwright cotton-spinning mill in America.
1811–12	Luddites destroy textile machines in Lincolnshire, England.
1821	Boston Associates discover water powers of Merrimack River at Pawtucket Falls.
1845	Lowell, Massachusetts, has 31 textile mills in operation.
1851	New, larger dam built at Folsom's Falls.
1853	Available mill powers in Lowell increased to just over 139.
1859	Lake Village dam at Folsom's Falls attacked.
1880	US Census shows that 151,923 h.p. were developed by water power at just 55 major sites.

Introduction

The myth has arisen that technological change has always been seen as "Progress" in the American context, and that machine-breakers, like the Luddites of Regency England, had no American counterparts. Theodore Steinberg's story of the New Englanders who attempted to tear down a mill dam gives the lie to this tale of happy accommodation to technological change. Like most changes, those in technologies produce losers as well as winners. Not surprisingly, the winners are often those with the best access to money and political influence, and the losers are left with relatively few resources with which to resist their subordination. Such struggles are rarely between those who are "for" and those who are "against" technology: more often they are about who gets the profit and who pays the price. The fundamental shift from what had been an essentially medieval technological regime to one that relied on the new structures, machines, and productive organizations of the Industrial Revolution introduced many new weapons in the constant contest over and negotiation of advantage.

Dam-breaking in the 19th-century Merrimack Valley: Water, Social Conflict, and the Waltham-Lowell Mills

Theodore L. Steinberg

Historians have studied the large factory towns of the Merrimack River valley for some time, especially the legendary textile city of Lowell, Massachusetts. Within the last decade, Thomas Dublin, Tamara Hareven and others, have enriched our understanding of industrial transformation, exploring the experiences of nineteenth-century workingwomen and men and their families.[1] Central to this work, and to many of the recent studies in social and labor history, is the struggle over the workplace. The conflict over wages and hours, over the enforced discipline of factory life, has dominated much of the historical literature.[2] Industrial capitalism is understood by many to be a vast and thoroughgoing transformation in the social relations of production.

Missing from this view is a discussion of the environment and its role in this process. If industrial capitalism changed the relationship of people to each other (pitting owners of capital against laborers), it also altered human relations with the natural world. Indeed, efforts to control and master nature, in particular water, were a fundamental aspect of industrial change in New England, especially in the Merrimack River valley where water is such an abundant resource. Exploring social conflict over this resource, a facet not fully addressed by historians, promises a richer, fuller understanding of industrial transformation.

Here the focus will be on the Merrimack valley textile cities of Lowell and Lawrence and their relationship to a number of communities in the distant reaches of New Hampshire. As plans were made in 1845 to build the city of Lawrence, the Boston Associates – the group of ingenious New England businessmen who financed the Waltham-Lowell style mills – launched a determined effort to place the water of a number of lakes upstream in the Merrimack valley under their control. The move north into New Hampshire sparked conflict and dissension as those who lived nearby these lakes witnessed this valuable resource controlled for

Excerpted from Theodore L. Steinberg, "Dam-breaking in the 19th-century Merrimack Valley: Water, Social Conflict, and the Waltham-Lowell Mills," *Journal of Social History*, 24 (Fall 1990), pp. 25–45.

the benefit of factories located in another state. Here is an ideal case study in environmental history, one that reveals both the larger dimensions of the industrial revolution and a fascinating mixture of motivation and claims on a natural resource.

The trouble began in the summer of 1859, the same year, as it turns out, that workers at Lowell went out on strike to demand increased pay. This conflict, however, involved water, not wages. The parties concerned included the mills at Lowell and Lawrence, more specifically the waterpower companies – the Proprietors of Locks and Canals on Merrimack River (PLC) at Lowell, and the Essex Company at Lawrence – that controlled water and tended to the energy needs of the factories along the lower Merrimack. These two companies each owned half the shares of stock in a third company, the Winnipiseogee Lake Cotton and Woolen Manufacturing Company (the Lake Company) of New Hampshire. That company, acting as a proxy for the waterpower companies at Lowell and Lawrence, had control over a huge expanse of New Hampshire's water resources in the Merrimack valley, over water that ultimately made its way downstream to the mills along the lower part of the river. The Lake Company managed the water in a way that helped the factories downstream in Massachusetts meet the need for power, particularly during the dry summer months.

During the summer of 1859, Josiah French, the Lake Company's agent, found that he needed to balance the demands for waterpower at Lowell and Lawrence with the available supply in Lake Winnipesaukee. It was to prove no easy task. Controlling the water in the interests of the mills downstream brought French into conflict with those living in the Winnipesaukee region who resented the Lake Company's presence and methods. The company's dam at Folsom's Falls in Lake Village altered the level of the water above in both Paugus [Long] Bay and Lake Winnipesaukee. Catering to the needs of the mills downstream in Massachusetts, the Lake Company flooded land around the bay and lake, and at times injured the interests of navigators who found the water in the lake drawn too low. In early August, French reported that two individuals with land in the area, James Worster and George W. Young, complained that the Lake Village dam had overflowed their property. They apparently bandied threats, and when French anticipated being away during the second week in the month, he wrote James Francis, chief engineer of the PLC, about finding "two or three men that would be sure and reliable in case of trouble ... men that have the right grit."[3]

On 16 August 1859, the Lake Company, in response to a demand for water at Lowell, began drawing water from Lake Winnipesaukee and from other New Hampshire lakes it controlled. French sought to maneuver delicately, insuring the interests of the Massachusetts mills without unduly provoking conflict upstream at the lakes. A drought that descended over the Lakes region in late August complicated matters. Despite the dry conditions, George Young, brandishing an iron bar, tried to damage the company's dam at Lake Village on 3 September.

Several weeks later, on the morning of 28 September, a group of men prepared to attack the Lake Company's dam at Folsom's Falls. The sheriff appeared in time to ward off the clash, but by afternoon several pieces of plank were pulled away from the dam before French could stop George Young and the other intruders. In the course of the struggle, Augustus Owen, French's assistant, struck Young in the left hand with the iron bar he had been using to defend the company's property. About dark the siege began again as the attackers returned – perhaps as many as fifty – this time with an officer who at Young's insistence arrested French and Owen on complaint of assault and battery. "This of course gave the mob the field for a time," French wrote James Francis, "and they used axes and bars to some purpose, although they did no serious mischief." According to a newspaper account, this last attack proved more successful than the earlier one, "but by the assistance of the 'big boys' of this village, the crowd was summarily dispersed, without much regard to ceremony – some of whom were not handled very lightly."[4]

This confrontation was symptomatic, though not exactly typical, of the resistance generated by the Boston Associates' attempt to place New Hampshire's waters under their control. It reflects the tension and conflict that arose over industrial change, a struggle over who would control the natural world and to what ends. Fuller analysis of this episode will offer a sense of the sweeping ambitions of the Boston Associates in their dealings with the natural world. In addition, a clearer understanding will emerge of the enduring and deep-seated current of opposition to their plans for water.

The Boston Associates first discovered the waterpower of the Merrimack River at Pawtucket Falls in 1821. In the next twenty-five years, they transformed this rural precinct of the town of Chelmsford, Massachusetts into the industrial city of Lowell. By 1845, there were thirty-one mills here, and water set in motion 225,000 spindles and more than 6,300 looms for producing textiles.[5] Water from the Merrimack River, distributed through a complicated system of power canals, provided energy to the factories. In 1840, the PLC leased sixty-five mill powers (equal to twenty-five cubic feet per second of streamflow at a fall of thirty feet) to the mills in this city. Three years later that number had grown significantly to ninety-one, a gain of 40 percent.

By the decade of the 1840s, concern surfaced at Lowell over the lack of water. Several of the mills were operating considerably more machinery than before, outstripping the available water supply, and causing the machinery inside the mills to show down. Although the expansion in productive capacity due to the construction of more mills played a part in the perceived shortage, other more obscure forces also may have operated to increase the need for waterpower. In the opinion of James Francis, the experience at Lowell had been that over time, factories, without having added any new machinery, called for more waterpower. This he attributed to the enormous weight of the machinery in the mills which caused the wooden floors to sag. The uneven surface in turn increased the chances for the bearings in the machines to bind, a development creating the need for more power.[6]

The anticipated plans for a major new textile city to be built downstream from Lowell heightened concern over the need for waterpower. With the incorporation in 1845 of the Essex Company, plans went forth for a dam that would average thirty-two feet in height and span a distance of sixteen hundred feet across the river – a massive water control project that furnished power for the factories at Lawrence, Massachusetts. During the summer of 1845, Samuel Lawrence, the brother of the person for whom the textile city was named, turned his attention to the major New Hampshire lakes feeding the Merrimack River: Lake Winnipesaukee and the bays and river leading out of it, the Squam lakes, and Newfound Lake. "After the work on the dam at Lawrence had been commenced," wrote Samuel Lawrence thirty years later, "I became alarmed lest the control of those grand reservoirs should be in the hands of parties not in harmony with the mill-owners on the main stream."[7]

For water to best serve the needs of production it must have a uniform year-round flow, a goal achieved by water storage. In general there were two methods for storing water: Either it could be held directly behind the dam, or in lakes or reservoirs upstream from the factory. In the fall of 1845, Abbott Lawrence, a Boston Associate who played a leading role in the founding of the new city on the Merrimack, attempted to implement the latter approach by gaining control of the waters of New Hampshire. His first move involved the purchase of the Lake Company. That company had been incorporated in 1831, with a capital stock of $100,000 to run two textile mills at Folsom's Falls in Lake Village. Lawrence bought the Lake Company in 1845 for $60,000, a step which gave him control of 250 acres of land, factory buildings and water rights at Folsom's Falls. This marked the start of the Boston Associates' elaborate scheme to take command of New Hampshire's four largest freshwater lakes. Together, Lake Winnipesaukee and the bays and river leading out of it, the Squam lakes, and Newfound Lake comprise well over sixty thousand acres of water, an immense reserve that the Boston Associates resolved to own.

Two other people, Nathan Crosby and John Nesmith, were instrumental in bringing this water into line with the needs of the mills along the lower Merrimack. Both men were born in New Hampshire and had ties to the Boston Associates. Crosby, a neighbor and friend of Samuel Lawrence, was apparently well informed of New Hampshire's water resources. Nesmith was a promoter of the city of Lawrence. During 1846, Crosby and Nesmith both bought land, water rights, and dams in New Hampshire to help secure control of the water that flowed to the Merrimack River. A series of strategic purchases along the bays leading out of Lake Winnipesaukee – later transferred to the Lake Company – gave the company the capability of governing the water level of the lake, of controlling the water as it proceeded downstream to the Merrimack.

Meanwhile, Abbott Lawrence assembled the necessary organizational structure for the new Lake Company. In 1846, he petitioned the Massachusetts legislature to allow the newly formed Essex Company to acquire and hold property in the state of New Hampshire. As he explained it, the Essex Company was interested "in such improvements as shall cause a steady & continuous flow of water throughout the year" in the Merrimack River. Lawrence was not entirely candid in his request. He stated that the intention of the company was to improve *both* the navigation and the waterpower (written in that order) of the Merrimack. This could only be done, he continued, by expenditures in the state of New Hampshire.[8] In March 1846, the governor signed his request, giving the company the privilege of holding stock in the New Hampshire corporation. In addition, the New Hampshire legislature needed to amend the Lake Company's original charter (granted in 1831) so more capital stock could be issued. At the urging of James Bell, a New Hampshire lawyer who preceded Josiah French as the Lake Company's first agent, the New Hampshire legislature approved a bill increasing the company's stock to $1 million.

Its organizational structure and resources in place, the Lake Company began constructing the necessary infrastructure for water control. In the fall of 1846, James Bell had workmen deepening and widening the channel at the outlet of Lake Winnipesaukee. The channel here was lowered several times between 1846 and 1849, resulting in an added depth of from four to six feet. This change allowed the Lake Company to draw down the waters of Lake Winnipesaukee more easily. In 1851, the company completed a new dam about 250 feet in length at Folsom's Falls to replace the old boulder and rubble dam originally built in 1829. Constructed of stone and built to almost exactly the same height as the old dam (approximately ten feet), the Lake Company's new dam was significantly tighter, causing the water to be held back more effectively in Paugus Bay and Lake Winnipesaukee. When completed, the dam served as the primary structure for controlling the water above.

By using a system of gates and sluices at this dam, the Lake Company regulated the flow of water from Lake Winnipesaukee into the bays below. From Paugus Bay, the water passed successively to Opechee [Round] Bay, Winnisquam Lake [Great Bay] and Sanbornton Bay. When factories at Lowell or Lawrence called for water, the company raised the gates at the Pearson Dam at Union Bridge (at the outlet of Sanbornton Bay), allowing the water to pass downstream to the Merrimack River. Simultaneously, it opened the gates at the Folsom's Falls dam to allow an equal amount of water in to replace what had been released. This procedure of filling the intermediate bays shortened the wait for water downstream at Lowell and Lawrence.

For their plan to work, the Lake Company needed authority over the system of dams below the dam at Lake Village (Folsom's Falls). There were three main areas where dams had been erected across the Winnipesaukee River. By the early 1850s, the company had made either purchases or agreements with local milldam owners allowing them the right to control the flow along the roughly thirteen-mile stretch from the outlet of Lake Winnipesaukee to the Merrimack River.

The Lake Company's Winnipesaukee water storage system seemed complete by 1851. But an important addition to it was made in the next few years. By the middle of the 1850s, the Lake Company had purchased mills, land, and water rights at the outlet of Lake Wentworth [Smiths Pond] which flowed into the southeastern corner of Lake Winnipesaukee, thus increasing their control over water in the region. In addition, the company diversified its holdings. It reached out over the waterscape and secured title to property at the Squam lakes, building the necessary water control structures there. The water from these lakes flows into the Pemigewasset River, traveling twenty-three miles from this point to Franklin, New Hampshire, where the Merrimack has its start. A final system of water control operated at Newfound Lake, the waters of which also course downstream into the Pemigewasset and on to the Merrimack.

By 1859 the Lake Company had its three systems of water storage at Winnipesaukee, Squam, and Newfound lakes in operation. But the storage systems they created were a good deal less efficient than the old mill pond directly behind the dam at Pawtucket Falls in Lowell. Because the New Hampshire lakes were far from Lowell and Lawrence (the lakes ranged from eighty-two to ninety-six river miles from Lowell), it took a good deal of time – several days – for the water to make its way downstream. Water directly in back of the Pawtucket or Lawrence dams, in contrast, was available immediately. So in addition to designing a system for controlling the water at the lakes, the Lake Company and its sponsors, the PLC and the Essex Company, needed to develop a faster system of communication. That system took some time to perfect.

Before 1858 James Francis simply sent letters to James Bell conveying his impressions about how high or low the river appeared and what the prospects for waterpower seemed like in the near future. But in the summer of 1858, Francis arranged a more rationalized system with the Lake Company's agent, Josiah French. Instead of giving a general impression of the need for water at Lowell, Francis devised a numeric system that gave a more exact estimation of the water they would need. He let each digit from one to twenty-five represent one hundred cubic feet per second (cfs). In Francis' view, twenty-five hundred cfs was needed night and day to run the mills. Thus if French received the number twenty, he could assume that three days after the letter was written, the Lowell mills would be short five hundred cfs and make the necessary changes to the water at the lakes.[9]

This system would never be perfectly effective, not with the lakes at such a distance from the lower Merrimack River. But control of the New Hampshire lakes unquestionably supplied the mills at Lowell and Lawrence with more water than the river naturally would have conferred. In 1853, after experiments with the volume of flow at Lowell, 47 more mill powers were divided among the corporations there, bringing the total number to just over 139. This was over a 50 percent increase in the number of mill powers leased in 1845 before the acquisition of the lakes. The newly built Northern Canal – completed in 1848 – delivered some of this new found water wealth. James Francis believed the increase in waterpower resulted from the improvements in the canal system at Lowell, but mainly from the New Hampshire purchases. In his opinion, control of the lakes increased the dry season flow (between July and October) by two or three times what it had been. The gain was impressive, and so were the Lake Company's substantial holdings of land and water in New Hampshire. In 1859 Francis calculated the total surface area of water controlled by the Lake Company. The tally came to over 103 square miles.

Several months before the 1859 attack at the Lake Village dam, Josiah French made a remarkably candid, not to say prescient, statement. In submitting a report about the progress of the Lake Company's system of water control to the treasurer of the company he reflected:

> The construction of dams, the widening and deepening of the streams and other improvements of these several Reservoirs, without any other ostensible purpose than the control and use of the water at some distant point, apparently foreign to the interest of of [sic] the people on the Lakes or streams is, and will be more and more, looked upon as an infringement upon the interests of their neighborhood, town, and state, if not upon their individual rights, and the feverish state of public feeling upon the subject of

water rights, and the fact that a great portion of the large bodies of water in the state are owned by the Lake Company, make it important to guard as much as possible against increasing a feeling that is ready to enlist in any crusade against any and all corporations where there is the least ground.[10]

The events of the following autumn would prove French correct. He properly sensed the rising tide of opposition toward the Lake Company. But then again, it was a tide that had been rising for some years.

Broadly speaking, there were four kinds of complaints leveled at the Lake Company. These included claims by farmers that the company flooded land illegally, by mill owners who saw water diverted for factories in another state, by owners of steamboats who found the water level of Lake Winnipesaukee drawn down too low to navigate safely, and by many local citizens who expressed a general dissatisfaction with how the company damaged the overall economy of the area.

Farmers perennially accused the Lake Company of flooding lands, particularly meadows. One source of conflict involved owners of meadow lands in Northfield, downstream from the Union Bridge dam on the Winnipesaukee River. During the period from late July into early August, farmers routinely cut the hay from their meadows on the Winnipesaukee. The trouble arose when the company released water from Sanbornton Bay to supply the mills in Massachusetts with water, flooding the meadows and preventing local farmers from harvesting the hay. But at least in two instances, during the summers of 1853 and 1854, James Bell – the Lake Company agent at this time – agreed to accommodate the nearby farmers. In 1853, for example, Bell closed the gates at both the Lake Village and Union Bridge dams to give farmers a chance to cut their hay. To satisfy the mills at Lowell and Lawrence he simply allowed more water to pass out of Newfound Lake to make up for the deficiency.[11]

At times disputes with landowners proved more intractable, with conflict spilling over into a court of law. John Coe, a wealthy landholder with property on Squam Lake, brought suit against the company before the Supreme Judicial Court of New Hampshire, the state's highest court. Coe sought an injunction preventing the Lake Company from carrying out any further excavations in the channel between Great Squam and Little Squam lakes, and in Squam River below the lakes. If the company proceeded with its plan, he argued, it would result in the destruction of his land, particularly his trees and grass. The company filed a demurrer in response, seeking to have the suit dismissed on the grounds that the plaintiff could not win even if the facts alleged were true. In this case, the company argued that Coe had no right to ask for an injunction because it is an extraordinary remedy, an action of last resort. The following year the court dismissed Coe's bill, denying the equity court's jurisdiction in the case. If the Lake Company did indeed cause damage to Coe's land, the court ruled, he could be compensated by a monetary award; an injunction was not necessary.

A less frequent source of conflict for the Lake Company involved local mill owners. During the 1870s, owners of a woolen mill on the Newfound River sued the company. According to the mill owners, the company's management of the water there made it impossible for them to conduct their business properly. The mill owners specifically alleged that the company did not provide them with adequate water during the dry summer months. Generally, the company tried to satisfy the water needs of local mills, although its primary responsibility of course was to the mills along the lower Merrimack at Lowell and Lawrence. Tensions arose when the Lake Company's decisions to provide water for the Massachusetts factories conflicted with the production schedules and needs of local mills.

Those who owned and operated steamboats also quarreled with the Lake Company. Here the disputes resulted from the company's control of the water level of Lake Winnipesaukee. As noted, the company lowered the level of the water in the lake to supply water to the factories along the lower Merrimack. Such action often made it dangerous, if not impossible, for steamboat pilots to ply the lake as they wished. For example, in 1859, several months prior to the attack on the dam, Josiah French informed the Lake Company's treasurer, F.B. Crowninshield, that such claims were being made against them by the Dover Steamboat Company.[12] And in 1865, B.R. Pipes wrote the company complaining that "you have recently drawn [the water] so low as to interfere seriously with the navigation of" Lake Winnipesaukee.[13]

Finally, a more general form of discontent surfaced in attempts to have the New Hampshire legislature intervene against the Lake Company. In June 1857, the government received a petition bearing an impressive list of 929 names – people living in Laconia, Meredith, Sanbornton, Gilford, and other towns bordering Lake Winnipesaukee, the Pemigewasset River and its tributaries. The petition made three main points. First it accused the Lake Company of misrepresenting its intentions. The company had been established under its original charter (passed in 1831, but amended in 1846 to allow the company to issue more capital stock) to manufacture textiles. The petitioners maintained that the company abandoned this objective in 1846, and "ever since without any legal right or authority so to do continued to devote their capital and resources to the acquisition and maintenance of control over the waters of the Winnipissiogee Lake and River, and the tributaries of the Pemigewasset."[14]

Further, they claimed the Lake Company had managed the water "to the great detriment and loss to the owners of lands and mills" in the region. They had, in short, been economically wronged by the company.

The company's actions, in their opinion, had deprived the region of "a large share of the capital now invested in Lawrence and Lowell." In other words, but for the actions of the Lake Company, large textile towns would have been built along the Winnipesaukee River. The Lake Company's management of the region's water resources evidently had robbed the area of its economic potential.[15] Their own local economy had been sacrificed to the interests of large corporations in another state; one of their most valuable resources had been literally drained away. They asked the legislature to remedy this situation, but their complaints apparently withered. There appears to have been no direct action taken.

It is difficult to say exactly why the issue died in the legislature, but it may have had something to do with the validity of the petitioners' claims. No evidence suggests the Boston Associates ever intended, as the petition charged, to invest capital in mill towns in the area around the New Hampshire lakes. New Hampshire, with its legislature controlled by radical Democrats hostile to business in the early 1840s, was hardly a congenial climate for manufacturing interests. When the Boston Associates were considering plans for the new textile city of Lawrence, it seems unlikely that they would have chosen to build a city anywhere in this state given the legislature's recent hostility toward industry.

Moreover, it was not completely true that the Lake Company had conspired against the local economy. Indeed, the technical infrastructure built by the company seems to have improved the waterpower prospects of some areas in New Hampshire. Before the company's improvements at Newfound Lake, for example, the Newfound River tended to run low during the dry summer months. But by making excavations and managing the water with their dam, the Lake Company improved the natural flow by making it more continuous and reliable. Of course, as mentioned above, the company's plans for water were not always consistent with the production schedules of local mills. Still, the company may have improved the overall reliability of the waterpower in the Winnipesaukee region.

Not everyone who lived nearby the New Hampshire lakes was in a position to benefit from the improved waterpower. To be helped by the company's plans for water, one needed to own property, specifically a mill that could take advantage of better water control. But the group of men who attacked the company's dam owned no mills; indeed most of them owned little if any property at all. The distaste they harbored toward the company then had little to do with whether the company had or had not improved the waterpower of the region. Rather, it seems that their attack on the dam may in part have been the product of economic frustration, of lives caught up in the larger capitalist transformation happening in the region – an economic shift that left them behind.

By the mid-nineteenth century, the regional economy of the towns of Meredith, Gilford, and Laconia – where most of the opposition to the company surfaced – was in flux. (Lake Village itself, the site of the 1859 attack on the dam, was not an official municipality. Originally, half the village belonged to Meredith and half to Gilford. When the town of Laconia was formed in 1855, it assumed Meredith's half of Lake Village.) As Tables 1 and 2 indicate, the local economy of this area diversified in the ten years from 1850 to 1860. A smaller percentage of the workforce farmed the land, although it was still far and away the predominant occupation. Yet there occurred a rise of close to 7 percent in the proportion of the manufacturing workforce, with much of the increase due to the

Table 1   Occupational structure: Meredith and Gilford, New Hampshire, 1850

	Number	Number as % of Total Workforce	Number as % of Total Wealth
Farming	766	46.17	70.37
Building	130	7.83	4.19
Manufacturing	277	16.69	10.62
Metal	57	3.43	2.10
Mechanic	38	2.29	1.07
Clothing	73	4.40	3.02
Homefurnishing	20	1.20	0.83
Food	3	*	*
Jewelry	3	*	*
Print & Art	13	0.78	0.08
Transport Trades	22	1.33	1.91
Building Material	12	0.72	0.40
Other Trades	36	2.17	1.15
Transport	42	2.53	1.40
Commerce	42	2.53	4.69
Professions	56	3.37	4.89
Non-Prof. Services	29	1.75	0.64
Unskilled and Semi-Skilled Labor	310	18.67	2.07
Public Service	7	0.42	1.13

Source: Manuscript Schedules, U.S. Census of Population, 1850. The data are for all adult males 18 and over. Wealth is measured by the reported value of real estate owned. The form of this table and Table 2 is a variation of that used in Michael B. Katz, "Occupational Classification in History", *Journal of Interdisciplinary History* 3 (1972): 83.

Table 2 Occupational structure: Meredith, Gilford, and Laconia, New Hampshire, 1860

	Number	Number as % of Total Workforce	Number as % of Total Wealth
Farming	667	42.67	57.81
Building	113	7.23	5.33
Manufacturing	364	23.29	16.29
Metal	71	4.54	2.62
Mechanic	65	4.16	2.85
Clothing	142	9.09	5.37
Homefurnishing	4	*	*
Food	14	0.90	0.54
Jewelry	1	*	*
Print & Art	10	0.64	0.29
Transport Trades	29	1.86	1.81
Building Material	11	0.70	0.35
Other Trades	17	1.09	1.14
Transport	68	4.35	2.31
Commerce	72	4.61	5.91
Professions	62	3.97	7.98
Non-Prof. Services	26	1.66	0.63
Unskilled and Semi-Skilled Labor	181	11.58	2.16
Public Service	10	0.64	1.58

Source: Manuscript Schedules, US Census of Population, 1860. The data are for all adult males 18 and over. Wealth is measured by the reported value of real estate owned.

growing clothing industry. Smaller gains were made in the still fledgling areas of transportation and commerce (although the percentage gains were substantial). While there was no revolution in the mode of production, the economy was shifting in a somewhat different direction toward a greater emphasis on manufacturing.

The distribution of wealth in these towns can be established by comparing the percentage of property owned with the percentage of the workforce for each occupation. Farmers possessed the bulk of the property wealth in both 1850 and 1860, but their share of such wealth declined relative to their representation in the workforce. Note also that people in manufacturing, although they made up a little over 16 and 23 percent of the workforce in 1850 and 1860 respectively, possessed barely more than 10 and 16 percent of the wealth in these years.

Professionals appear to have secured a sizable share of the total property wealth by 1860 relative to their numbers. But over the ten year period, laborers, who comprised a significantly smaller share of the overall working population, held a mere 2 percent of the wealth. The data offer evidence of an economy that did not reward its participants equally.

Census information for 1860 is available for nine of the men who attacked the dam in 1859. Seven of the nine were living in either Gilford or Laconia, one lived in Northfield and the other in Concord, New Hampshire. Between them they claimed to own $9,000 worth of property. Much of the land belonged to the wealthiest among them, a farmer named Thomas Plumer ($3,500). James Worster valued his real property at $2,500, but most of this land was probably leased or heavily mortgaged. Of the others, one owned land valued at $1,200, four owned $500 or less, and two owned no property at all. Thus most of them owned little or no land.[16]

In addition, an examination of their occupations shows many of the rioters appearing toward the bottom of the region's economic structure. There were two farmers among them, an occupation that in 1860 still accounted for over 50 percent of the total wealth in the area (although the percentage had declined since 1850, see Table 2). The others had jobs in sectors where their relative percentage of the total workforce outstripped the share of total wealth they owned. They worked in manufacturing, transport, and general labor – all occupations possessed of less property than their numbers suggest they should have held.

But the 1859 riot was not simply a case of this society's economically dispossessed rising up in arms. A more complicated interpretation is suggested by examining in detail the motives of the two men who led the attack on the dam, James Worster and George W. Young.

When they hatched their plan to damage the dam, Worster and Young were both in their fifties. Both had also been blacksmiths by trade at an earlier time in their lives. Neither of them seems to have experienced much sustained economic success, their fortunes appearing somewhat checkered. Young, for instance, gives his occupation as laborer in the 1850 census (he is not listed in 1860). When he died in 1870, he owned no real estate.[17] Yet at one point, as we shall see, he managed to rent a factory from the Lake Company for several hundred dollars a year. Worster owned no real estate according to the 1850 census. Although he valued his property holdings in 1860 at $2,500, as mentioned, much of this property was probably either heavily mortgaged or leased. Still, over the course of his life, he had managed to get his hands on some land – more than can be said for many of the other people involved in the attack on the dam.

Worster had a history with the Lake Company that went back ten years before the riot at the dam. In 1849, his daughter, Adeline E. Worster, took the Lake Company to court for flooding her land in Tuftonborough, on the northeast side of Lake Winnipesaukee. She owned the land – amounting to about fifty-two acres – jointly with her father and claimed the Lake Company's dam at Lake Village had so raised the water in the lake as to damage her property. The Lake Company demurred, a move that eventually led to the dismissal of the case in 1852.

Meanwhile, in the period from 1849 to 1853, James Worster made several land transactions: he leased a parcel of meadow land in Sanbornton, a farm bordering Paugus Bay in Gilford, and had a mortgage for a third share of Rattlesnake Island – a cigar-shaped piece of land in Lake Winnipesaukee. It is hard to say precisely why he chose these particular tracts of land. Yet one thing is certain: the land seemed destined to bring him into conflict with the Lake Company. On 14 April 1853, Worster threatened to destroy the company's dam at Lake Village, claiming it injured land he owned and leased in neighboring towns.

As it turns out, Worster had experience with breaking down dams. In December 1847, while still living in Dover, New Hampshire, he tore off an abutment, chopped down planking, and removed stone from a dam across the Salmon Falls River in Somersworth, New Hampshire. The dam and factories belonged to the Great Falls Manufacturing Company, a Boston Associates' venture since the 1830s. Claiming damage to land he leased, Worster sought to abate the nuisance himself – an action which was legal at the time. The Great Falls Company appealed to the Supreme Court of Judicature (SCJ) to issue an injunction barring Worster from doing any further damage. In July 1853, a few months after Worster's threat at the Lake Village dam, the court acceded to the request.

When Worster threatened the Lake Company's dam in 1853, the company must have recognized that this was no idle taunt. Worster's reputation, it seems certain, was well known by then. To protect its property, the Lake Company too attempted to get an injunction and took their case before the SCJ in 1854. Representing himself before the court, Worster submitted a motion to have the company's bill dismissed. He argued, much as the Lake Company had done in a number of its cases (including the one brought by Worster's daughter), that the court should not have jurisdiction over the case. The court disagreed and found for the company. An injunction preventing Worster from interfering with the Lake Company's dam at Lake Village was issued in July 1855. Violation of an injunction, it should be noted, means a contempt charge and possible imprisonment for the offender.

Prevented by the legal authorities from interfering with the dams at Lake Village and Somersworth, Worster in the interim moved to

Concord, New Hampshire. He was probably angry and no doubt frustrated, but for the moment he kept out of the way of the Lake Company. Yet Worster had by no means given up his fight. The following year, he leased a piece of property in Hooksett, New Hampshire – land bordering the Merrimack River – from John Harvey. Two years later, Worster purchased a parcel of land from this same man. Harvey's land was upstream from the Amoskeag Manufacturing Company's dam in Manchester, another waterpower corporation founded by the Boston Associates. It appears that Harvey and other upstream landowners had their property flooded by the Amoskeag Company's regulation of the water. Once again, Worster had placed himself in a position inviting conflict with a company owned by the Boston Associates.

At half past six on the morning of 7 March 1859, Worster and another individual appeared at the Amoskeag Company's dam. The watchman on duty spotted them and ordered them off the premises. They refused to go, and after having words, the watchman pitched a piece of ice at them. A fight broke out and Worster was knocked down three times before he left the dam, sending for a doctor to dress his wounded nose.

The following month, Ezekiel Straw, the Amoskeag Company's agent, retaliated against Worster. Straw obtained an unpaid note in Worster's name, and managed to have the sheriff attach his property in Hooksett for non-payment. Soon after, John Harvey lost a case with the Amoskeag Company for the flooding of his land. By the end of July, tempers once again boiled over. Harvey, Worster, Worster's son, George, and four others made their way to the Amoskeag Company's dam. This time Straw had learned before hand of the attempt to remove the flashboards. He arrived at eleven o'clock in the morning with the sheriff and a posse and had them all arrested for conspiracy as they attempted to tear away at the dam. They were arraigned the following morning.

The summer before the attack on the Lake Village dam, James Worster was on trial, with a number of others, for conspiring to destroy the Amoskeag Company's dam. In a little more than ten years he had made threats or actually destroyed parts of three major water control projects owned by the Boston Associates in the state of New Hampshire.

George Young's confrontations with the Lake Company were somewhat less dramatic. In April 1851, Young leased the Lake Company's cotton factory on the northwest side of the Winnipesaukee River in Lake Village. For four hundred dollars per year, Young got the factory, a machine shop, blacksmith's shop, counting room, machinery, and waterpower to produce textiles. He did not get the right to control the water in the river and mill pond upstream from the factory. The Lake Company reserved that privilege for themselves.

Young does not seem to have done particularly well financially during the following year. In April and July, he mortgaged two pieces of property in Meredith and obtained $750 in the process. The next year, the sheriff attached his property in Gilford and Meredith including his interest in the cotton factory at Lake Village. He had apparently fallen behind by $500 in the payment of his rent to the Lake Company by December 1853; the company brought suit in the Court of Common Pleas and the sheriff was called on to seize his property.

The Lake Company pursued Young in court for seven years, settling finally in the year following the attack on the Lake Village dam. In February 1860, the jury returned a verdict for the company awarding them $373 in damages plus court costs. There is no official record of what was said at the trial. But Josiah French was present and his thoughts are worth noting for the clue they offer to Young's hostility, a fragment which may suggest why Young attacked the dam the year before. Young apparently charged the company with not allowing him enough water to properly operate the machinery in his mill. Moses Sargent, who in 1850 leased the woolen mill from the Lake Company on the same flume below Young, testified at the trial and contradicted Young's contention. But a rather surprising witness came forth to support Young. Thomas Ham, James Bell's assistant during his tenure as agent and briefly in charge before the Lake Company hired French, took the stand to speak on Young's behalf. After the trial, French – still angry but pleased with the outcome – wrote James Francis of his satisfaction with the award, especially "after the evidence given by Mr. Bell's *confidential* assistant and agent as he styled himself *Thomas Ham* Esq. who swore on the stand that Mr. Young could not run his mill at speed with less than ten feet head and fall."[18] It is not possible for us to determine with complete assurance whether Young's charges were true. Ham of course could have been a disgruntled former employee. On the other hand, the jury awarded the company less than what it asked, accounting, almost certainly, for their denial of adequate water.[19] Thus, there is evidence that Young may have been a victim of the company's water control policies.

It may also be true, however, that Young himself tried to take advantage of the company. Several months after he rented the factory from the Lake Company in 1851, Young leased a parcel of land on the shore of Paugus Bay above the dam. This was the same year the company rebuilt the dam at Lake Village, a move which flooded the property Young now leased. It is difficult to say why Young wanted the land, but his action was probably meant to interfere with the company's plans, perhaps to extract some money from the company for the flooding it did. Support for this comes as well from Young's agreement in October 1851 to rent the property to Worster who at the time was already in conflict with the company.

The month before the attack on the Lake Village dam, James Plumer, owner of the property now leased by Young and Worster, sold the land to the Lake Company. When French wrote James Francis to give him the news, a great burden evidently had been lifted. As he put it: "I 'breathe much freer and easier.' "[20] Worster and Young reacted with the expected frustration. On the day the Lake Company took control of the property they leased, they notified French that their lands had been flooded to a depth of four feet by the dam.[21]

Worster and Young were clearly seeking revenge as the fall of 1859 approached. Young may have been victimized by the company, denied enough water to properly run the mill he leased. Worster had spent over a decade attempting to interfere with the company's plans for reasons that are not completely clear. Both may well have been trying to profit from the company's presence in the area. Indeed their failure to obtain damage payments from the company may have frustrated them enough to go forth to wreck the dam.

As for the other rioters, two, Thomas Plumer and Augustus Merrill, had dealings with the Lake Company prior to the attack. Plumer had previously sold the company (in July 1845) the right to maintain its dam at Lake Village at a height that would flood his land in Gilford. But he appears to have sold this right before the Boston Associates took control of the Lake Company. He was paid a mere thirty dollars for granting the right.[22] In the five years after the agreement, the Lake Company embarked on its grand plan for controlling water, and many were able to extract much more money in exchange for the privilege of flooding their land. Perhaps Plumer felt taken in by the company, though he left no record of such feelings.

Augustus Merrill also crossed paths with the Lake Company. The year before the riot he took out a mortgage with them on a small piece of land in Lake Village. This is all that is known: that the company had a legal right to take possession of his land unless he made good on the note. As for the others, nothing can be said about their relationship with the company.

In sum: two people, Worster and Young, out for revenge, urged on a small group of men, most of whom were economically marginal, a few of more substantial means. Frustrated in their dealings with the company, Worster and Young were able to tap into a prevailing current of discontent. In part, we might speculate, that discontent stemmed from the broader economic transformation of the region which did not benefit everyone equally. Whatever bitter feelings there were in this regard were most certainly aggravated by the company's presence in the region, as it tried to profit from the use of New Hampshire's vast water resources. The Lake Company's monopoly over the area's water wealth probably seemed especially galling because it was formed to benefit the financial interests of corporations in another state. To those of little means the company's scheme may well have seemed outrageous, reason enough to make them willing participants in a violent attack on the company's dam.

The 1859 attack on the dam was the start of twenty years of conflict over water involving the Lake Company and those who lived nearby the waters it controlled. The sheer bulk of the litigation was extraordinary. At one point in 1872, the company had become entangled in an astonishing twenty-six cases over water. Litigation continued to be brought against the company for the flooding of land and diversion of water; the company brought action against those who forced their way onto company property to hoist the gates on its dams. In 1877, local residents ventured to the Lake Village dam and, against company wishes, raised the gates to allow logs through. That same year, over eleven hundred people signed a petition sent to the New Hampshire legislature demanding the repeal of the Lake Company's charter. A government investigation ensued that ultimately, in 1879, exonerated the company of any wrongdoing.

The Lake Company, despite all the opposition, was largely successful in exploiting the waters of New Hampshire to the advantage of the factories at Lowell and Lawrence. But the opposition to its plans is a reminder of the importance of the struggle over nature to industrial capitalism. Class conflict over wages and hours has long been at the center of much historical research. But as workers and owners struggled over the workplace, a rather different form of social conflict was taking place as well: one over who would control and profit from the natural world. This too was a struggle central to the emergence of the industrial age.

Notes

1 Thomas Dublin, *Women at Work: The Transformation of Work and Community in Lowell, Massachusetts, 1826–1860* (New York, 1979); Tamara K. Hareven, *Family Time & Industrial Time: The Relationship Between the Family and Work in a New England Industrial Community* (New York, 1982).

2 Paul G. Faler, *Mechanics and Manufacturers in the Early Industrial Revolution: Lynn Massachusetts 1780–1860* (Albany, NY, 1981); Alan Dawley, *Class and Community: The Industrial Revolution in Lynn* (Cambridge, Mass., 1976); Sean Wilentz, *Chants Democratic: New York City & the Rise of the American Working Class, 1788–1850* (New York, 1984).

3 Josiah French to James Francis, 11 August 1859, vol. A-38, file 205, Papers of the Proprietors of Locks and Canals on Merrimack River (PLC).

4   This construction of events comes from two sources: Josiah French to James Francis, 28, 29 September 1859, vol. A-38, file 205, Papers of the PLC; "Trouble at Lake Village," *Winnipisaukee Gazette*, 1 October 1859.

5   Patrick M. Malone, *Canals and Industry: Engineering in Lowell, 1821–1880* (Lowell, Mass., 1983), 9.

6   James Francis to Henry Hall, 21 February 1853, vol. A-18, file 89, Papers of the PLC; James Francis to Isaac Hinckley, 21 February 1859, vol. DA-5, ibid.

7   "Three Letters of Samuel Lawrence, Esq.," *Contributions of the Old Residents' Historical Association, Lowell, Mass.*, 1 (1879), 289.

8   "Petition to the General Court," 4 February 1846, item 2 [3, file 4], Papers of the Essex Company (EC).

9   James Francis to Josiah French, 30 August 1858, vol. A-17, file 82, Papers of the PLC.

10   Josiah French to F. B. Crowninshield, 28 February 1859, item 204 [362], Papers of the EC.

11   James Bell to James Francis, 25 July 1853, 10 August 1854, vol. A-37, file 204, Papers of the PLC.

12   French to Crowninshield, 3 March 1859.

13   B. R. Pipes to Lake Company, 5 October 1865, vol. A-39, file 215, Papers of the PLC.

14   Petition to the New Hampshire Legislature is attached to French's letter to Crowninshield, 28 February 1859.

15   Ibid.

16   Manuscript Schedules, US Census of Population, 1860.

17   George W. Young died intestate. See case #7820, Merrimack County Probate Registry, Concord, NH.

18   Josiah French to James Francis, 10 February 1860, vol. A-38, file 205, Papers of the PLC.

19   Ibid. Young filed a set-off in the case for $1,100. In a case where a plaintiff sues a defendant for damages, a defendant can file a set-off which is simply a sum of money that the defendant holds is due him from the plaintiff. In this case, however, Young was actually using the set-off as his defense. Since the company was not awarded the full amount of the damages it was seeking, the jury must have believed Young's claim that the company had indeed shortchanged him waterpower.

20   Josiah French to James Francis, 15 August 1859, vol. A-38, file 205, Papers of the PLC.

21   French to Francis, 25 August 1859.

22   Thomas J. Plumer to Lake Company, 31 July 1845, book 7:338, Belknap County Registry of Deeds.

Documents

Winnipisiogee Lake Company v. Worster

If a defect in regard to the parties to a bill in equity is apparent upon the bill, and vital to its character, the objection may be taken at any stage of the proceedings.

A defect in a bill in giving the description of the parties, or in properly setting forth their residences or places of doing business, must be taken advantage of by demurrer, or by plea in the nature of a plea in abatement.

Where the complainants were set forth as the Winnipissiogee Lake Cotton and Woolen Manufacturing Company, without stating where they were located, or whether they were a corporation or a partnership; and the defendant was set up as of Meredith, in the county of Belknap, without naming the State – *held*, that whatever defect there might be in the description of the parties could not be taken advantage of upon a motion to dismiss the bill for want of jurisdiction, after the bill had been taken *pro confesso*.

This court, as a court of equity, may grant an injunction to restrain a nuisance or a trespass, where it is made to appear that irreparable mischief will be done if an injunction is withheld.

Where the remedy at law is complete and adequate, an injunction will not be granted.

Where it appeared by the confession of the defendant that the complainants were the owners of a water fall and dam, and had claimed and exercised the right of keeping up the water for more than twenty years, without complaint; and the complainants and others had valuable mills, factories and machinery driven by the water kept up by the dam, which, with other property, would be liable to be destroyed or greatly damaged if the dam was removed; and it also appeared by the defendant's confessions that he threatened and intended to destroy or remove the dam, and that he was insolvent – *held*, that this court, as a court of equity, had jurisdiction of the case, and that an injunction

Taken from *Winnipisiogee Lake Company* v. *Worster*, 29 N.H. 433, December Term 1854, in William L. Foster's *Superior Court of Judicature of New Hampshire*, vol. (2) 9 (Concord, NH: G. Parker Lyon, 1856).

might be issued to restrain the defendant from committing the acts threatened.

IN EQUITY. The bill was filed in the clerk's office on the 18th of April, 1853, and the cause entered in this court at the July term following. At that term the defendant appeared in person, and an order was made that he should answer in ninety days. That order was not complied with; and at the December term, 1853, a further order was made that the defendant should answer in ninety days, or the bill should be taken *pro confesso*. No answer was filed according to the order, and at the last July term the bill was taken as confessed. After the bill was taken as confessed, the defendant moved to dismiss it for want of jurisdiction; and that question was argued by the defendant and the plaintiffs' counsel, and submitted to the court.

The bill states, in substance, that the complainants are, and have long been, seized and possessed of a water fall and mill privilege, called Folsom's Falls and Privilege, upon the Winnipissiogee river in Meredith and Gilford, in the county of Belknap, and of the lands at, near and around the same, and of the mills at the fall; that they hold their land and mills and privilege at the fall, which are situated in Meredith, on the northwesterly side of the river, by a title derived from one Nathan Batchelder, who, on the 20th of October, 1829, and for some years before and after, was lawfully seized and possessed thereof; that they hold their land and mills and privilege on the southeasterly side of said river, in Gilford, by a title derived from the town of Gilford, who were lawfully seized and possessed thereof on and prior to October 10th, 1818, and who on that day conveyed the same to one Jonathan Nelson, from and under whom the complainants, through several mesne conveyances, hold the same.

That they also hold and possess the right to flow and retain the water in the Winnipissiogee lake, to the extent to which they have flowed and retained the same, not only by the titles aforesaid, and by the uninterrupted use and enjoyment of that right for more than twenty years, but that they have derived the right from the owners of mills, dams, and the river at the outlet of the lake, who have maintained said dams and flowed the lake thereby to a greater extent than the same has been flowed by the complainants.

That many mills and a large quantity of machinery have for a long period been kept in operation at these falls by the power created by the dam across the river, and that the complainants have now at the falls a cotton factory, two woolen factories, a grist mill, two double saw mills, a machine shop, and other mills and machinery, driven by said power; and that the Boston, Concord and Montreal Railroad have a repair shop, and Cole, Davis and Company have an iron foundery and a plough manufacturing establishment driven by water leased to them by the complainants, from said dam, from all which they receive a large amount of rents and income.

That in the months of August, September and October, 1829, the then owners of the mills and privilege, built a new dam at the falls, so as to stop the water of the river on the 20th of October of that year, and that the dam soon after became filled with water. And that the dam has ever since its erection been used, occupied and enjoyed in the same manner in which it is now; and occupied for the purpose of creating a water power for the use of said mills, and that the complainants, and those under whom they claim, have, ever since the spring of 1830, claimed, and *have*, except when prevented by the low state of the water in the river, or other accidental causes, *exercised* the right of keeping up the water of the river, by the dam, to as high a level as that to which the same is now usually held and kept, and to which the same was kept at the time of the filing of the bill, at a corresponding season of the year. That from the time of the erection of the dam, no owner of land, in which the defendant has or claims to have any interest, so far as the complainants are informed, has instituted any suit or other proceeding against the owners of the dam, or complained in regard to it, until the proceedings were had by the defendant, as hereinafter stated.

The bill further sets forth, that above the dam are two bodies of water, one called Long bay, lying directly above the dam, and the other is Winnipissiogee lake, which is separated from Long bay by a channel or part of the river, about one hundred rods in length, in which there is a descent of the water of the lake flowing into the bay; that the dam built in 1829 retains the water in Long bay; and that after the erection of the dam, the owners thereof purchased, at great cost, of the many owners of land around the bay, the right to maintain the dam, and to raise the waters of the bay thereby upon said lands, and took conveyances thereof from the owners of land around the bay. That the dam does not, as the same has been and now is used, raise the waters of the lake higher than they had before stood, and been kept in the lake; nor does the dam flow lands owned, if any are owned, by the defendant, upon the shores of the lake, more than the same had been usually flowed; and that the water, both in the bay and lake, does not now, at the time of the filing of the bill, or usually, flow any lands lying upon or adjacent to the lake, more than they have been usually flowed for more than twenty years next before the filing of the complainants' bill.

That since the building of the dam the channel between the lake and the bay has been repeatedly deepened, at the expense of the owners of the mills, by the complainants and others, giving it an increased depth of from four to six feet, and that in consequence thereof the water of the lake now stands at a lower level than if the excavations had not been made, and generally at as low a level as it would stand if there were no dam at the falls, and the excavations had not been made.

That the complainants are ready, and, as they believe, able to establish, at any trial at law, their right, as against the defendant, to maintain and use the dam, as they do use and have used the same, and to prove that he is not injured thereby, nor any of his lands flowed or injured by the water set back or raised by the dam, to any greater extent than the complainants have a right to do.

That the defendant, pretending that he has lands lying upon or near the lake, river or bay, which are injured in consequence of the dam, continually threatens that he will destroy or remove the dam, or some part thereof, and on the 14th day of April, 1853, gave notice to the agent of the complainants of his determination immediately so to do. And that the complainants have reason to believe, and do believe, that the defendant intends to carry his threats into execution.

And the complainants aver that the consequences of carrying the defendant's threats into execution would be to stop and prevent the operation of said mills, or seriously to retard the same, to injure the property of the complainants, and to carry away logs and lumber lying in their mill pond, and to subject the complainants to a heavy expense in repairing or rebuilding the dam, and, also, that there is danger, if the defendant should succeed in his purpose, that great loss and destruction of property might be occasioned thereby, both to the complainants and to others owning property in the river below the dam.

The complainants further aver that if the defendant has any interest in any lands which are in any way affected by the water retained or kept up by the dam, that he acquired such interest with the full knowledge of the existence and effect of the dam, and of the rights claimed by the company, and for the express purpose of making some claim or commencing some proceedings against the complainants on account of some pretended injury to such lands; and that any supposed title he may have therein is contaminated by maintenance or barratry.

The complainants also aver that they, and those from whom they derive title, have for the whole period since the spring of the year 1830, asserted and exercised the right as aforesaid, of keeping up and detaining the water by said dam.

The bill then sets forth the pretences of the defendant; that he has leases of certain lands in Tuftonborough and Wolfborough, and a certain interest in lands in Gilford and Alton. But the complainants aver that these lands are not flowed or affected by the dam more than they have been affected by the water of the lake and bay for more than twenty years last past.

That the defendant also pretends that he has a lease of some interest in land lying in the bed of the river below the dam, in Sanbornton or Northfield, and that he is about to destroy the dam, or a part of it, in order to permit the water of the river to flow naturally over the land; but the complainants aver that they have not been informed by the defendant what lands he owns or has an interest in, in said towns; that the same must be remote from the dam, with other intervening bays, ponds and dams between; and that the value of the land in the bed of the river is in no way impaired or affected by any use which the complainants make of the dam; and that they do not, at the time of filing the bill, detain or use the water of the river thereby, otherwise than as they have a lawful right to do; and as they have used the same for more than twenty years last past; and that an ample and abundant quantity of water now flows from the dam for the supply of all the mills below the dam upon the river, and for all other purposes to which the water is or has been applied.

The complainants further charge that the defendant is wholly unable to respond for the damages which would be occasioned by the execution of his threats, and that he is, as the complainants are informed and believe, wholly insolvent.

The bill states the inadequacy of the common law to render relief in the premises, and prays for an injunction to restrain the defendant from destroying or removing the complainants' dam, until he shall have established his right by a trial at law.

The bill is addressed "To the honorable justices of the superior court of judicature, holding pleas in equity, in and for the fourth judicial district." The complainants are not set up as of any place other than what may be inferred from their holding property and doing business as set forth in the bill. The defendant is set up as of Meredith, in the county of Belknap.

The bill was signed as follows: "The Winnipissiogee Lake Cotton and Woolen Manufacturing Company, by their agent, James Bell." And the following verification was made: "Personally appearing, James Bell, made oath that the charges and allegations contained in the foregoing bill are, according to the best of his knowledge, information and belief, true."

A temporary injunction was granted, *ex parte*, by one of the justices of this court soon after the filing of the bill, upon the condition that the complainants should give bonds, in the sum of $5,000, for the security of the defendant. These bonds were given. At the request of the defendant, a hearing was soon after had upon his motion for a dissolution of the injuction; and upon an investigation of the facts stated in the bill, which were then contested, and evidence submitted upon both sides, the motion to dissolve was denied.

Great Falls v. James Worster

TO THE HONORABLE THE JUSTICES OF THE SUPERIOR COURT OF JUDICATURE, FOR THE STATE OF NEW HAMPSHIRE, NOW IN SESSION, ON THIS TWENTY-FIFTH DAY OF DECEMBER, A.D. 1847, AT DOVER, WITHIN AND FOR THE FIRST JUDICIAL DISTRICT, HOLDING PLEAS IN EQUITY.

HUMBLY represent your petitioners, the Great Falls Manufacturing Company, a Corporation duly by law established, at the Great Falls on Salmon Fall River, in Somersworth, in the County of Strafford, that your petitioners own five cotton mills, and the necessary and proper machinery in the same, for the manufacture of cotton into cloth, at said Great Falls, in said Somersworth, and that your petitioners, for a long time past, have, and they now do, use, occupy, and improve said mills and machinery in manufacturing cotton into cloth, and that, to enable them profitably and successfully, to use said mills and machinery for said purpose, it is necessary for your petitioners to use the water that runs in said Salmon Fall River, to drive said machinery in said mills.

And your petitioners further show unto your Honors, that, to enable them, your said petitioners, advantageously, properly, and profitably, to use said water, in said river, to drive said machinery, for the purposes aforesaid, they have erected, built, and kept up for more than ten years last past, a dam over and across said Salmon Fall River, at the outlet of the three ponds so called, partly in Milton, in said County of Strafford, and partly in Lebanon, in the County of York, and State of Maine, and that said dam has been, during the time aforesaid, and it still is used by your petitioners, to raise and keep back, in said three ponds and river, the water that may accumulate therein in seasons of rain, and abundance of water to be drawn off, and used by your petitioners in driving said machinery, in seasons of drought, and failure of water from other sources, to be used for the purposes aforesaid, and that said dam, so built by your petitioners as aforesaid, cost them about five thousand dollars.

And your petitioners further show unto your Honors, that, for more than fifty years last past, there has been erected and kept up, *partly in said Milton, and partly in said Lebanon, and* on the same place where said dam of your petitioners is situated, a dam, over and across said Salmon Fall

---

Taken from New Hamphire Supreme Court Notes, vol. 17, indexed to *Great Falls* v. *James Worster*, Strafford, June 1854.

River, which has, during all that time, raised, stopped, and kept back the water in said river and three ponds, and that, for more than twenty-three years now last past, said dam over and across said river has kept raised and caused to flow back the water in said river and ponds, to the height to which said dam of your said petitioners, as it now is, will cause said water to rise and flow back, in said river and ponds, unless by reason of the facts hereinafter stated and set forth, said water should, in a freshet, be raised a very little higher, for a very short time.

And your petitioners further show unto your Honors, that your petitioners, and those under whom they claim title, have owned said dams, so erected, and kept up as aforesaid, during all the time they have been so erected and kept up, and the land on which the same have been so erected and kept up, and that your petitioners own all, or nearly all, of the land overflowed by the water raised by said dams, so kept up as aforesaid, and that your petitioners, and those under whom they claim title, have, by conveyance or long continued and uninterrupted use, for more than twenty years, acquired the right to overflow the land, overflowed by the water raised by said dam of your petitioners, and that said land, owned by your petitioners, and overflowed by the water so raised by said dam, is situated partly in said Milton, and partly in said Lebanon.

Your petitioners further show unto your Honors, that sometime between the years A.D. 1819 and 1823, said dam was rebuilt with wood to a given height, and had an overfall of about *seventy-six* feet in length, and was called and known by the name of the Wentworth dam, and that as your petitioners have been informed and believe that said Wentworth dam was not so high as the first dam built over and across said river, at said place, called and known by the name of the Palmer dam, *which was built prior to the year* 1790, and which was carried away by a freshet about 1814, and that a temporary dam was built in the same place soon after, and was continued till said Wentworth dam was built.

And your petitioners further show unto your Honors, that they have been informed, and believe it to be true, that the overfall of said Palmer dam, and temporary dam, was not so long as the overfall of said Wentworth dam by quite a number of feet, but how many feet your petitioners do not know, and cannot set forth, and that there were two saw mills on the Palmer dam and temporary dam, and but one saw mill on the Wentworth dam, which mills reduced, by about their width, the length of the overfall.

And your petitioners further show unto your Honors, that your petitioners, in 1843 or 1844, built a stone dam across said river, immediately below and under the slope of said Wentworth dam, and adjoining the main Wentworth dam, but not the wing, and as high as the bottom of the cap on said Wentworth dam, and placed on said stone dam, timbers and plank, to the height of the top of the cap, on said Wentworth dam, and no higher.

And your petitioners further show unto your Honors, that there was a wing dam, commencing *in said Milton*, on the bank on the westerly side of said river, and extended southerly to a saw mill standing in said Milton, on said Wentworth main dam, *which said wing dam was two feet and more higher than said Wentworth main dam*, and that said overfall, over said Wentworth dam, was easterly of said mill, and that the water did not, except in a high freshet, run over said wing dam, as your petitioners have been informed, and believe to be true.

And your petitioners further show unto your Honors, that, in 1843 or 1844, your petitioners built a stone and gravel abutment on the westerly bank of said river in Milton, extending easterly toward said river, and toward said main Wentworth dam, about sixty feet long, and that said abutment does not extend so far easterly, and toward the thread of said river, as did said wing dam, by at least forty feet, and that the easterly end of said abutment does not extend to the natural westerly shore of said river by more than fifty feet, and your petitioners built a stone dam, *in said Milton, extending* from the easterly end of said abutment sixty-two feet long, to *and uniting with* the stone dam first named, adjoining said Wentworth dam, which said dam, extending from said abutment with the cap and plank thereon, is two feet higher than said Wentworth dam, and that the distance from the easterly end of said sixty-two feet of dam *across* of said Wentworth main dam to the saw mill on the easterly bank of said river is seventy-eight feet, and that, in the Spring of 1836, your petitioners put a superstructure on said Wentworth main dam four feet high, consisting of posts and plank, on the top of the same, forming a platform, and *cut down the top of the cap of the old Wentworth dam, about three inches in all parts of the same, which had not settled that distance, and put a platform of plank across the same, of the thickness of about three inches, forming an overfall for the water of the same height, as your petitioners believe, of the said cap, as it existed prior to that time, and also put* plank, let into grooves, on the upper side of said posts, to stop the water, which last named plank could be removed or drawn up to reduce the water, and that, in the fall of 1836, said posts and plank were raised two feet higher, and constructed in the manner aforesaid, and that when said abutment was built as aforesaid, said superstructure, constructed in the manner aforesaid, was extended westerly to the easterly end of said abutment, and that the tops of said posts were connected by ties of plank, running crosswise of said dam, and caps or stringers running lengthwise of the same, and on the top of said caps or stringers, plank were placed, forming a platform used as a pass-way between the westerly bank of said river and said saw mill on the easterly shore of the same, and that the whole length of the overfall of said Wentworth main dam, after deducting the amount of the breadth of the posts standing in a line thereon is sixty feet, as appears by actual admeasurement, and that the length of the overfall of said sixty-two feet of dam, extending easterly from said abutment, after deducting the amount of the width of the posts standing in a line thereon is fifty-four feet, and that the whole length of said overfall, after deducting the width of said posts as aforesaid, is one hundred and *fourteen* feet.

And your petitioners further show unto your Honors, that your petitioners have, by deed, the right to raise the water in said river and ponds at all times, to the height it might be raised by said Wentworth dam, or any other at the same place of the same height.

And your petitioners further show unto your Honors, that all the plank, the whole length of said overfall, placed in said grooves, have been and are now removed and taken out, except two on the easterly end next to said saw mill, one of which is seven feet and two inches long, and the other eight feet long, and each about one foot wide.

And your petitioners further show unto your Honors, that James Worster, of Dover, in said County of Strafford, blacksmith, pretends to have some interest in certain tracts of land, situated on said river and ponds, and above said dam, and that said tracts of land are overflowed, injured, and rendered spongy and rotten, by water raised and caused to flow back on said tracts of land, by said dam of your petitioners, and that he is deprived of the use of the same land, by means of said water, *and that part of said tracts are situated in said Milton, and a part in said Lebanon, and that your petitioners do not believe said Worster has any legal or equitable right or title to said tracts of land, or either of them, obtained for a valuable or adequate consideration, or bona fide purpose, or with intention to hold or own the same.*

And your petitioners further show unto your Honors, that the said Wentworth dam did not raise the water in said river and ponds, so as to cause the same to overflow, or in any wise injure any of said tracts of land, in which said Worster pretends to have said interest, or in any way to impair his full enjoyment of the same, except one tract called the Fernald lot, which your petitioners have a right to flow, as aforesaid, to the depth the water may be raised by the Wentworth dam as aforesaid.

And your petitioners further show unto your Honors, that your petitioners' said dam, in its present situation, will not and it does not cause the water to rise higher in said river and ponds, than it was raised by said Wentworth dam.

And your petitioners further show unto your Honors, that said James Worster, for a year last past, has not pretended, to your petitioners, that he had any other claim to any of said land, than leases from persons who *pretend to* have some interest therein, *which your petitioners do not admit, but wholly deny that they have any interest therein as against said Wentworth dam, and your petitioners' right to flow all lands that may be flowed thereby,* for the term of thirty to ninety days, some of which were defeasable on notice at any time given to the lessee by the lessor, and the payment of five or six dollars by the lessor, and that some of said leases have been obtained by the said Worster, as your petitioners have been informed, and believe to be true, for the express purpose to give him the color of right to demolish and destroy your petitioners' said dam, or compel your petitioners, *in order* to prevent their said dam from being demolished and destroyed, to pay him, said Worster, such sum of money as he might demand for his said pretended rights, in said tracts of land, *which said leases were taken by said Worster, for the periods aforesaid, and defeasible as aforesaid, for the express purpose of preventing your petitioners from attaching said Worster's right and interest in the lands so leased as aforesaid,* and that said Worster has testified *in* effect under oath, that such was his object, purpose, and design.

And your petitioners further show unto your Honors, that said Worster has, at various times, within fifteen days last past, tore up a part of said abutment, and tore up a part of said platform, westerly of said main Wentworth dam, cut off two of said caps or stringers, and cut off eight of said posts, and torn off the planking from said posts, and thrown out a large amount of the stone of said dam, between said abutment and main Wentworth dam, all which has been wilfully and maliciously done by said Worster, and that the same was not necessary to draw the water from said tracts of land, had the same been overflowed.

And your petitioners further show unto your Honors, that said Worster publicly threatens and declares, that he intends to, and will immediately, tear down and remove said abutment, and all said dam and superstructure, to a level with the top of the old Wentworth dam, and that your petitioners have reason to fear, and they do fear, that said James Worster will immediately tear down, and remove said abutment, and all said dam and superstructure, to a level with the top of said old Wentworth dam, to the irreparable injury of your petitioners.

Your petitioners further show unto your Honors, that said James Worster is poor, destitute of property, and wholly irresponsible.

Now, inasmuch as your petitioners are without remedy in this behalf, by the rules of the common law, and are relievable only in a Court of Equity, where matters of this nature are properly cognizable.

To the end, therefore, that said James Worster, may, upon his corporal oath, to the best and utmost of his knowledge, remembrance, and belief, full, true, direct, and perfect answer, make to all and singular the matters aforesaid, and that as fully and particularly as if the same were here repeated, and he distinctly interrogated thereto, and more especially, that he may, in manner aforesaid, answer and set forth, whether your petitioners own, occupy, and improve the factories, as is in said petition alleged, and for the purpose therein alleged?

Whether your petitioners, and those under whom they claim title, have erected, kept up, and owned the dams and the land on which the same have stood, as is in said petition alleged?

What dams they and each of them have erected, kept up, and owned, at the outlet of said three ponds, and when, and how long?

Whether the water is necessary for said petitioners, for the purposes in said petition alleged, and for what purposes?

When each of said dams, named in said petition, was erected, how long each stood, and by whom each was erected, and the height of each?

Whether said petitioners have the right to raise the water to the height it was raised by the old Wentworth dam, and how high they have a right to raise it?

Whether the land owned by the petitioners, situated above said dam, and flowed by the water raised by the same, is not situated partly in said Milton, and partly in said Lebanon?

What mills have been erected on said dams, when, by whom, where, and how long each stood, and by whom removed?

Whether said Worster has any title to any of the land overflowed by the water, raised by said dam, and what title, from whom, and when, and for what consideration, and for what purpose, and of what land?

Whether said Worster has, in effect, testified that he took leases for the purposes in said petition alleged, and when he so testified, and what he testified in relation to taking leases of said land, or any part thereof, and before what Court or Magistrate he testified?

Whether said Worster will annex to his answer, copies of the lease or leases, or other instrument or instruments, under which he claims any right in or to said tracts of land, and each of them, which he pretends are overflowed by the water raised by said dam, and if yea, he is required to make the same a part of his answer?

Whether said Worster tore up a part of said abutment and platform, cut off said caps or stringers, cut off eight of said posts, tore off the planking from said posts, and threw out a large amount of the stone of said dam, as is in said petition alleged, and what he did, and when, and in what part of said dam?

Whether said Worster has threatened to tear down and remove said abutment, and all said dam and superstructure, to a level with the top of the old Wentworth dam, what threats he has made on that subject, when, and to whom?

Whether said Worster intends to tear down or remove any more of said abutment, dam, or superstructure, and if yea, what part of each?

Your petitioners pray your Honors, that said James Worster, his associates, servants, and agents, and each and every of them may be enjoined and restrained by a decree of this Honorable Court, from tearing down, and removing said abutment, or any part thereof, and said dam and superstructure, or any part thereof, or in any wise intermeddling with the same, and that your Honors will make such further order, and grant such further relief in the premises, as to your Honors shall seem meet. And may it please your Honors to grant unto your petitioners your writ of injunction, under the seal of said Court, directed to said James Worster, his associates, agents, and servants, and each and every of them, enjoining and restraining them from tearing down said abutment, or any part thereof, and said dam and superstructure, or any part thereof, or in any wise intermeddling with the same, *and also enjoining and restraining said Worster from obtaining or acquiring, for the purposes aforesaid, any claim or right in any lands in said Milton, flowed or pretended to be flowed by said dam,* and as in duty bound, &c.

GREAT FALLS MANFTG CO.
By J. A. BURLEIGH, Agent.

I, John A. Burleigh, Agent of Great Falls Manufacturing Company, depose and say, that the facts stated in the foregoing petition, are, in my belief, true.

J. A. BURLEIGH.

New Hampshire, ss., December 25, 1847.
Then personally appearing the above named John A. Burleigh, made oath that the above affidavit by him signed, is true.   Before me,

JOSIAH H. HOBBS,
Justice Peace throughout the State.

I, John A. Burleigh, Agent of Great Falls Manufacturing Company, depose and say, that the facts stated and set forth in the several amendments to the foregoing petition, are, in my belief, true, and existed, and were true at the time the foregoing petition was filed in Court.

J. A. BURLEIGH.

Strafford, ss., August 14th, 1849.

Then personally appeared the above named John A. Burleigh, and made oath that the above affidavit by him signed, is, in his belief, true.

Before me,   NATH. WELLS,
Justice of the Peace.

Further Reading

Marx, Leo. *The Machine in the Garden: Technology and the Pastoral Ideal in America.* New York: Oxford University Press, 1964.

McPhee, John. *The Control of Nature.* New York: Farrar Straus Giroux, 1989.

Steinberg, Theodore. *Nature Incorporated: Industrialization and the Waters of New England.* Amherst: University of Massachusetts Press, 1991.

Wallace, Anthony F. C. *Rockdale: the Growth of an American Village in the Early Industrial Revolution.* New York: Alfred A. Knopf, 1978.

3

The Workplace as an Ecological System

1842	*Farwell* v. *Boston and Worcester Railroad case.*
1844	Friedrich Engels investigates conditions of the working class in Manchester.
1911	Triangle Shirtwaste fire kills 146 workers.
1970	Occupational Safety and Health Administration (OSHA) established.
1982	*Beshada* v. *Johns-Manville Products Corp.*

Introduction

The environmental historian Arthur F. McEvoy is the leader in an effort to see, as he puts it here, "the workplace as an ecological system, of which the worker's body is the biological core." Furthermore, he continues, "Law, business, technology, and the worker's body thus come together in the issue of occupational safety and health. Every work injury," he concludes, "is a text laden with meaning about technology, society, and the law." In this article, McEvoy attempts to bring work accidents out of the background of normal and (regrettably) inevitable events and recontextualize them as events which flow directly from the distribution and legitimization of power relationships occurring in the technological workplace. He makes passing reference to injuries that take place in the home, and none at all to those many thousands that take place on the nation's roads and highways; yet his ecological construction of injury might apply to these other sites as well.

Working Environments: an Ecological Approach to Industrial Health and Safety

Arthur F. McEvoy

One of the many changes that environmentalism has brought to modern historiography is an emphasis on context and contingency. For historians, ecology offers both an object and a method of study. As a subject, it encompasses not only natural objects – plants, animals, the planet itself – but the many different ways in which human and natural systems interact with each other. As a mode of analysis, or what William Cronon called a "habit of thought," environmental history describes change in terms of that interaction, paying attention to the simultaneous and reciprocal influences that work between the natural and the social orders.[1] In both of its guises, ecology highlights the dynamic interrelatedness of things and undermines our efforts to order them neatly. It focuses our attention on the complex interactions between subjects and contexts, on the systemic effects of obscure relationships and unforeseen events.

A penchant for interdisciplinarity is one manifestation of this tendency, as environmental historians harvest other disciplines for ideas and methods to help them highlight interactions between the natural and the cultural. "More than most of the other 'new' histories," Cronon recently observed, "environmental history erodes the boundaries among traditional historical subfields...and suggests new ways of building bridges among them."[2] Ecologically inclined historians in other areas, meanwhile, have lately infused their work with the same kind of attention to context and interdependence that has distinguished environmental historiography for some years now. Inevitably, new methods and new points of view bring into focus new objects of study that earlier works passed by.

In technological history, as in a number of other subfields, environmentalism has reinforced the tendency of recent scholarship to unsettle the systematicity and teleology that characterized earlier work....

A particularly significant locus of contingency in the history of technology is industrial health and safety. Like pollution, occupational injury

Excerpted from Arthur F. McEvoy, "Working Environments: an Ecological Approach to Industrial Health and Safety," *Technology and Culture*, 36 (1995), pp. S145–S172. © 1995 by the Society for the History of Technology. All rights reserved.

and disease are unwanted, unintended consequences of industrial development. They are part of development's social cost, typically falling at random to a diffuse body of victims and figuring only marginally, if at all, in the management decisions that prepare the ground for them. For this reason, perhaps, injuries to workers figure not at all in the field's classic works. Some works that treat technology from the perspective of cultural or intellectual history have dealt at length with the perceived dangers of mechanization, but the danger about which their subjects worry is usually a metaphorical one, not the far more tangible danger of injury and death that machines posed to the historically inarticulate people whose lives they most thoroughly transformed. . . .

Industrial health and safety issues mark out a promising, though as yet largely undeveloped, site at which complementary developments in a great many historical fields come into focus. Environmentally inclined historians of technology have moved into the field by way of a substantial body of work on pollution, both as a product of and as a stimulus to technological change. For their part, environmental historians have lately paid increasing attention to cities and other so-called built environments, although, as Martin Melosi recently observed, urban environmental studies still lack the broad, synthetic focus and theoretical depth of the field's mainstream.[3]

Making occupational safety into an environmental subject would mean attending to relationships between technology and the bodies of people who work with it. Workers' bodies are, after all, biological entities no less than trees or fish and wildlife. Recent work in cultural history that discusses changing attitudes toward the human body is suggestive in this regard, although thinking about the body in ecological rather than cultural terms would underscore not the plasticity of our attitudes but rather the constancy of the body's vulnerability to injury even as technology changes. As a method, ecology points to an analysis of industrial health and safety in terms of the interactions between a number of systems: the worker's body and its maintenance, the productive processes that draw on the worker's energy, and the law and ideology that guide them. The relationship between people who work and the technologies they operate is a complex, dynamic, ecological one that entails elements of sociology and ideology as well as the more direct impacts of technology on worker health. The same political and conceptual barriers that obstruct our understanding of well-recognized environmental problems like pollution and deforestation, however, tend also to obscure the systematic relationships between industrial technology and industrial accidents and make them difficult to describe. The key to the approach is to treat the workplace as an ecological system, of which the worker's body is the biological core.

An Ecological Approach to Technology

Environmental history is a relatively new field, though one of its lines of descent reaches into a distinguished history-of-science literature. Thomas Kuhn's germinal essay, *The Structure of Scientific Revolutions*, was an important catalyst to a contextual study of ecology because it uncovered the contingency of scientific thought, albeit from the internalist perspective that traditionally characterizes the first efforts at historicizing a subject, from law to environment to labor to science and technology.[4] Environmental history portrays nonhuman nature as an active player in human history. Its fundamental insight is that nothing that people do is without causes and consequences in nonhuman nature. The interaction between the two works ecologically, through the medium of biology and adaptation, whether the human protagonists are aware of it or not. Technology is what distinguishes human activity in nature from that of other animals; because technology is a means of interacting with nature, however, it should be amenable to ecological analysis.

Environmental historians for a long time avoided what they call "built" environments such as cities, much less factories. Early studies focused on "natural" subjects such as parks or frontier areas inhabited by hunting-gathering people with low-tech, low-intensity economies. Later work began to analyze the ways in which commercial development has disrupted and degraded natural systems. Several works in this group treat the ecological history of extractive industries, typically in nonurban environments where the ecological impacts of development are relatively easy to trace. Fully developed, industrial-urban environments are dauntingly complex ecologically and received much less attention at first, although the logic of the field's methods and the energy of its practitioners inevitably brought cities into view. Cronon's *Nature's Metropolis*, for example, analyzed the ways in which interactions between Chicago and its hinterland changed each of them over time.[5] Taking their cue from Cronon, environmental historians chose as the theme for their 1993 conference "City and Country: Contrasting and Interacting Environments."

Environmentalists have traditionally preferred "natural" subjects, partly because they are easier to work with but also, doubtless, because of their political interest in nature protection. Beneath the preference, however, lies a distinction between nature and humankind that is fundamental to our culture and whose pervasive influence on our thinking is difficult to escape.[6] According to this view, the terms "nature" and "ecology" refer to that which is not human: the more "artificial" a thing is, the less it is part of nature and the less fit an object of ecological study. Artifacts like cities and factories, conversely, are somehow removed from nature, creatures solely of human planning and artifice. . . .

Environmental history has a characteristic method as well as characteristic subjects. As a method, again, environmental history looks to the ways in which ecology, political economy, and human consciousness interact with each other over time, each continually adapting to a dynamic environment made up of the other two. Nature is an active party to this interaction. Resource endowments influence the development of production and thus of productive technology in particular environments. Local ecologies respond in characteristic ways to human impact and, in turn, present new challenges to production and social organization. People's consciousness of themselves and their place in the world, finally, both guides their activity in the world and alters itself as it confronts environmental changes that activity inevitably calls forth from a responsive nature.[7] Technology is the tangible instrument of the process: it is the point of interaction between the human and the natural.

Modern environmentalism has made it clear that complex social and ecological relations pervade the use of any technology. The biological reproduction of the workforce on a daily and intergenerational basis is as central to human ecology as is the productivity of "natural" resources. Certainly, our experience with toxic chemicals and radiation since 1950 has made it clear that a workplace is a biological environment no less than is a national park. That some hazards work physically on the body rather than biochemically on its processes does not alter the fact.

Technology does not develop autonomously, according to its own logic; it has roots in and impacts on its environment. Every technology entails a politics. Rachel Carson showed how chemical-intensive farming both fed on and, in turn, nurtured a political system dominated by research universities, agribusiness, and chemical companies.[8] Amory Lovins demonstrated the links between nuclear power and corporate giantism, the arms race, and the security state.[9] Every technology entails a particular ecology, moreover, as *Silent Spring* showed most powerfully. Alfred Crosby and other environmental historians have shown that European agriculture brought with it to frontier areas not only plows, pigs, and honeybees, but coherent assemblages of tools, techniques, plants, animals, diseases, and property relations. It was the aggregate working as a system, more than any single part of it, that utterly transformed the ecology of colonized areas and just as utterly displaced the economies of the prior inhabitants.[10]

The relationship between technology and its natural and social environments is not only reciprocal but dynamic as well. Ester Boserup made the point that producing communities always have a large repertoire of techniques available to them; which ones they choose depends on demography, local resource endowments, and other contingencies.[11] Technological innovation, moreover, inevitably changes a community's ecology and social structure. My own work on the California fisheries showed that fishing technology evolved in a dynamic, recursive relationship with the progressive, anthropogenic transformation of entire ecosystems, as well as by strictly "human" market forces and strictly "environmental" changes in climate, currents, and so on. Technology, then, is anything but an autonomous force in history; it develops in continual, reciprocal adaptation with the natural and social environments in which people use it.

A healthy respect for the capricious and the chaotic is a final "habit of thought" that students of biological systems can bring to the historical study of technology. Modern evolutionary theorists, notably Stephen Jay Gould and Niles Eldredge, emphasize the accidental, discontinuous, and, above all, the historical nature of evolution in contrast to the orderly, progressive picture drawn by Darwin and his immediate successors. Life may exfoliate according to pattern, in this view, but it is the occasional, unpredictable catastrophe that winnows out some lines of development and spurs others, essentially at random. Evolution is thus path-dependent, that is to say, historical: it may have an internal logic, but the form it actually takes depends on particular sequences of discrete events.[12] Similar interest in nonlinear, nonprogressive explanation has taken hold in physics and chemistry as well as biology; the new orientation has focused scientists' attention on the kinds of accidents, anomalies, and discontinuities that only fifteen or twenty years ago they would have ignored as errors in perception or experimentation. Economists and other social scientists have applied the new insights to their own work. Mokyr worked with Gould's discontinuous model of evolution in his essay on technological history, though he cautioned his readers not to press the analogy too far.[13]

In many fields, it seems, accidental events and unforeseen consequences of planned activities have taken on new importance in our understanding of the world. The factories and other workplaces that industrial engineers portray as models of order and rationality may, instead, be precisely the kinds of high-energy environments in which the chaotic and the unpredictable are the norm rather than the exception. Tomlins noted that historians have too often taken the word of 19th-century writers that the industrial workplace was orderly and rational and suggested, instead, that "industrial 'order' was, to an important extent a mask for arbitrariness and confusion, a facade behind which employees daily confronted an unpredictable terrain."[14] Tomlins showed that work injuries were a critical problem in industrializing

America and that allocating liability for them was a crucial step in the development of the modern legal system.

Technological accidents, of course, take place in people's homes as well. Domestic injuries are no less crucial to the social experience of industrial technology than are those that take place at work, although the common perception is that they are less systematic, less preventable, and thus rest even more firmly in the natural order of things. The modern law of product liability, for example, owes as much to suits brought by plaintiffs injured at home as by those hurt at the workplace. The workplace, however, is where exposure to technological risk is most immediate, concentrated, and sustained and thus where it comes into focus most sharply as a political issue and as a catalyst for social change, as both Tomlins and Sellers have shown.[15]

Technology and Industrial Accidents

What, then, can we learn about the social history of technology from an ecologically minded study of occupational safety and health? Given that the issue has received little sustained attention from labor historians or historians of technology, occupational safety may be a useful perspective from which to view the development of industrial technology. Cherniak's study of the Hawk's Nest incident, in which miners working on a West Virginia hydroelectric project suffered cruelly from silicosis and were abandoned to their fates by employers and government alike, took this approach in making a statement about government regulation of public health. It may be counterintuitive to discuss the broad sweep of technological development in terms of work accidents; we call them "accidents," after all, because we perceive them as isolated events, unconnected to larger systems or long-term trends. Particular accidents, however, may offer useful texts from which to interpret the role of mayhem in industrial development.

An ecological approach to the problem suggests, further, that we look at the interaction between injuries to workers' bodies – the biological core of the workplace environment – and the technology, organization, and ideology of production. The Industrial Revolution, as Karl Polanyi showed, is a revolution in social organization as much or more than a revolution in production technology.[16] Accidents and disease are an ecological consequence of that organization no less than soil erosion is a consequence of the economics of agriculture or fishery depletion has its roots in the regulatory structure of fishing. Technology, in addition, plays an important role in shaping people's consciousness of occupational hazard, just as it does in the awareness of other social problems, by laying out the boundaries between injuries that society perceives as preventable, as inevitable costs of economic life, or, indeed, as no injury at all. Technology, then structures the ecology of the workplace in three ways: by posing hazards directly, by shaping the social organization that exposes workers to risk, and by influencing society's awareness of danger to its working population.

Sometimes an individual injury assumes historical significance all by itself, by way of its legal or political repercussions. Tomlins's study of employer-liability law in Massachusetts uses the case of *Farwell v. Boston and Worcester Railroad*, which came down from the Massachusetts Court of Appeals in 1842.[17] The railroad was an entirely new phenomenon in the early-19th-century United States; never before had so many workers been brought together in close company with heavy machinery. Economic depression and increased competition in the late 1830s led the roads to intensify operations and generated what Tomlins called a "quickening flood" of derailments, collisions, and injuries.[18]

One of those injured was Nicholas Farwell, who lost his arm when a negligent coworker caused a locomotive to derail. Dismissing the suit in favor of the defendant railroad, the Boston & Worcester, Massachusetts Chief Justice Lemuel Shaw ruled that engineer Farwell had assumed the risk of injury – even at the hands of negligent fellow workers – when he agreed to work on the railroad at a bargained-for wage. *Farwell* thus stood for two of the three great common-law defenses available to defendant employers in work-injury cases: "assumption of risk," the "fellow-servant" rule, and the rule that any contributory negligence on the part of the injured plaintiff was an absolute bar to recovery. Together, the three defenses shielded employers from nearly all liability for worker injuries, thus granting them near-plenary authority to control the pace and conditions of work. As Tomlins put it, Shaw's ruling "endorsed the structure of disciplinary power that permeated the employment relationship and yoked the public interest in industrial safety to its perpetuation."[19]

The decision controlled the law of employer's liability until the advent of workers' compensation in the early 20th century: Tomlins called it "*the* case in the common law of employer liability, treated not only in Massachusetts but throughout the Anglo-American jurisprudential world as the requisite authoritative statement of the limits to an employer's responsibilities, the point of departure in all subsequent litigation in any industrial situation."[20] Another historian, Eric Tucker, wrote that *Farwell* "effectively banished from legal consideration the most important transformation that was taking place in the labor process under industrial capitalism: the shift of control over the labor process from workers to capitalists."[21] One of the earliest injuries involving industrial machinery was thus pivotal for subsequent development. *Farwell* not only encouraged rapid technological development by allocating the costs of accidents to workers rather than to entrepreneurs but did much to structure relations between labor, business, and the state under industrial capitalism.

Another work accident, the Triangle Shirtwaist fire of 1911, was as critical to the evolution of American political economy in the 20th century as engineer Farwell's had been in the 19th. The Triangle fire took place in a New York City garment factory and claimed the lives of 146 workers, many of whom leapt nine stories to their deaths before crowds of horrified onlookers. Neither criminal prosecutors nor civil plaintiffs, however, were able to secure judgments against the factory's owners because at the time the law did not allow them to argue that the employers had been so careless of fire hazard as to make such a tragedy inevitable. Anything more than a misdemeanor conviction under local fire ordinances would have required proof of some act by which the employers directly caused the deaths of their workers. Because prosecutors and plaintiffs were unable to demonstrate such an act, the Triangle employers collected their insurance and were soon back in business.

The fire did expose, however, the deadly consequences of employers' license to maintain unsafe working environments. So great was public outrage over the fire and the employers' escape from liability that within three years of the disaster New York enacted comprehensive changes in factory safety and accident compensation law, changes for which reformers had been struggling with little success for decades. Frances Perkins later wrote that "the extent to which this legislation in New York marked a change in American political attitudes and policies toward social responsibility can scarcely be overrated. It was, I am convinced, a turning point."[22] The fire made clear the ecology of the turn-of-the-century workplace and the law's active role in sustaining it. In so doing, it catalyzed the formation of a modern regulatory state in a key jurisdiction.

Other examples might be found of particular industrial accidents that either contributed directly to changes in the political economy of the workplace or that provide opportunity for "thick description" of ways in which machines transformed the ecology of the workplace.[23] Erickson's study of the Buffalo Creek disaster is a model for this kind of inquiry, though the focus of his interest was the community surrounding the mine rather than the organization of production per se. One spectacular railway accident in Ontario in 1854 both focused public attention on railroad safety at the time and left a detailed record for historians to interpret. Workers frequently come first and most intensively into contact with new technological hazards; their stories tell of technology's social significance not only to later historians but to contemporaries who learn about them as they happen.

In relatively few cases, however – sensational incidents like the Triangle fire or the odd injuries whose victims give their names to legal precedents – do industrial accidents have much direct impact on historical struggles over the social control of industrial technology. This may be one reason they seldom figure in technological historiography. So closely did safety issues cut to the employer's prerogative in the workplace, as Tomlins showed, that legal authorities decided very early that workers would have to fend for themselves for the time being.[24] Tucker concluded that what safety regulation did emerge in 19th-century Ontario did so mainly where public concern over accidents reinforced paternalistic attitudes about the special vulnerability of women and children. It is not clear that late-19th-century factory legislation improved the workers' situation at all. By now it is well-known that Upton Sinclair wrote his exposé of the meatpacking industry out of a concern for industrial safety rather than for the quality of the product, but the latter seized public attention: "I aimed for the public's heart," he wrote later, "and by accident I hit it in the stomach." Economically, the damage that industrial accidents and disease do to workers' bodies is very much like the damage that industry does to the natural environment: both pollution and work injuries are social costs, so broadly diffused over large numbers of politically inarticulate victims that employers are rarely called to account for them. Ecologically, the two are close cousins working on opposite sides of the factory gate: one destroys the productivity of air, water, and other natural systems, while the other destroys a human body's biological capacity to work.

Work accidents are less typically the result of new technologies than they are of more mundane hazards that befall people by way of the political and sociological organization of their workplaces. One might describe the history of machines, for that matter, as a political process as much as a narrowly technical one: machinery, in this view, is the means by which owners and representatives of capital take control over the workplace away from those who do the work. Work accidents, by the same token, are at once the manifestation and the method of that domination. Workers themselves know this: health and safety issues have historically been an important cause of labor unrest, although they are so crucial to employers' authority that workers are seldom able to bring them into serious question. Modern surveys show that union members tend to give higher priority to health and safety issues than to wages and benefits, while the reverse obtains among management and union leadership.

Tomlins and Tucker both noted that 19th-century industry not only exposed people to new hazards but also subjected them to new ways of organizing and controlling production. It was the combination of the two, especially, that put worker health and safety at risk.[25] Workers given the choice of producing faster or facing the wrath of their superiors have always circumvented safety devices and procedures and thus, in the eyes of employers, the law, and the general public, brought their injuries on themselves. Work accidents, then, are often the result of employer decisions to intensify production and reduce investment in safety, thus increasing the danger to workers. Complicit in these decisions, of course, is the legal system that entitles employers to make such decisions. Law, business, technology, and the worker's body thus come together in the issue of occupational safety and health. Every work injury is a text laden with meaning about technology, society, and the law.

Technological change affects the ecology of the workplace in yet a third way, which has to do with people's awareness of the chains of cause-and-effect that link technology with its impacts on worker health and safety. As a cognitive activity, causal attribution is as much a social process as it is an objective, "scientific" one: it takes different patterns in different social/cultural environments according to prevailing standards of judgment and what Michel Foucault called "the architecture of knowledge" in a culture.[26] The process is thus necessarily a historical one, though it has been little studied. Spectacular accidents teach people about the meaning of technology in their lives. Technology itself, however, is an important engine of change in people's understanding of the world because it influences their ability to manipulate reality and thus to grasp cause-and-effect relationships in the world around them: "The notion of causation," one philosopher wrote, "is essentially connected with our manipulative techniques for producing results."[27] Social experience, and work experience in particular, is a key source of heuristics and paradigms for attributing causality not only in social life but in the natural world as well. . . .

Like poverty in the preindustrial era, industrial injuries frequently offer themselves to view as an inevitable part of life in a technologically advanced society, a necessary cost of innovation. Observers attribute accidents to poor equipment or, more typically, the carelessness of the injured worker, but seldom to the technologies themselves and the social relations that surround their use. Even late-20th-century observers often attribute accidents to "operator error" when they are, in fact, necessary complements to working with highly complex, dangerous technologies under legal arrangements that guarantee employer prerogative to determine the conditions under which they are to be used. Legal doctrines that shield employers from liability for accidents play a major role in narrowing the available scope of causal attribution. Work accidents are powerful indicators of maladjustment in the ecology of production, although it takes more than the mere knowledge that suffering exists to motivate social action. People must first recognize the suffering as systematic rather than random, as "caused" by something and thus preventable. It is people's social experience, of which both law and technology are a part, that enables that recognition.

Laissez-faire in industrial safety came to an end at the turn of the 20th century as people recognized the systemic causes of accidents and conceived political remedies for them. In the words of J. Willard Hurst, "sharper perception of cause–effect relations, developed out of increasing science-and-technology-based manipulation of affairs, generated political pressures for more rational and humane arrangements, given form, however inadequately, in factory safety laws and workmen's compensation."[28] What Hurst did not mention was the fact that public outrage over the enormous toll that work accidents took at the turn of the century, as well as the litigation crisis they spawned, was a significant impetus to industrial reform in the Progressive Era. The relationship between technology and injury was recursive: life in an advanced, interdependent industrial society taught people to look for the systemic causes of industrial mayhem, while the mounting toll of accidents generated political pressure for controlling industrial hazards. Economic life also provided a repertoire of remedies for social ills: experience with the executory contract suggested the boycott, casualty insurance suggested workers' compensation, work on the assembly line suggested the sit-down strike.

Technology, then, structures the ecology of the workplace in a number of ways. Particular machines and processes may pose direct hazards to worker health and safety. A more subtle, pervasive threat to workers may stem from the social organization of the workplace, which is a product not only of the labor requirements of particular technologies but of the legal arrangements under which employers hire and control their workers. Finally, by conditioning social awareness of the causes of industrial health and safety problems, technology plays a role in motivating public action to control those hazards that appear controllable. Like all environments in which humans are active, the workplace is the product of ongoing, reciprocal interaction between biology, political economy, and consciousness. What distinguishes a workplace from a forest or a fishery is that its biological heart is the worker's body itself.

Denaturalizing Industrial Accidents

Occupational injury, then, is a key aspect of life for industrial workers; the historiography of technology is seriously incomplete without it. Every technology nests in a dynamic system that includes the worker's body, the social conditions under which production takes place, and the ideology that both springs from and mediates the interaction between biology and production. As the means of production, technology structures the workplace environment by posing direct threats to the worker's body, by influencing the social relations of work, and by molding social perception of the industrial order. For too long, as Tomlins put it, "the maiming or death of employees at work could be treated as part of the social landscape – a routine, if regrettable occurrence" that is just part of the price we pay for progress.[29] Ironically, perhaps, highlighting the role of the human body in workplace ecology may help to "denaturalize" industrial accidents, that is, remove them from the background against which technology develops and expose them as contingent phenomena, systematically related to their social and historical contexts.

Scholars concerned with explaining the historical degradation of the natural environment have faced a similar task in developing their field. Nineteenth-century Americans typically thought environmental destruction a necessary companion to social progress, if only because it seemed impossible to do anything about it. To many, indeed, the extermination of Indians and wildlife, the clearing of the forests, and the fouling of city air by smoking factories signified progress and were thus to be welcomed: efforts to interfere with the process were not only pointless but positively vicious. Critical to the success of modern environmentalism were the efforts of Carson and others to portray nature as an active partner in human life as opposed to a passive victim; that insight, which George Perkins Marsh had articulated in 1864 but which went unnoticed for many years, has lately enabled historians to explain the nation's progress in a different and more sophisticated way.

The task of denaturalizing industrial mayhem is a difficult one, however, politically as well as historiographically. This is because, like our historical abuse of nature, industrial accidents nest in a set of social relations that we perceive as "natural" and hence ineluctable. If work accidents appear "inevitable" to us, it may be because our habits of thought and action render their systemic causes invisible. Writing the history of industrial accidents, like the task of controlling them politically, requires bringing them into relief against that background. The problems involved in doing so are nearly identical with those of highlighting the causes of environmental destruction. They involve the voluntarism, the mechanism, and the teleology that color our view of history and politics. These problems are, of course, interrelated.

The problem of *voluntarism* refers to our tendency to see human will as the prime mover of social change and to focus our attention narrowly on the intended consequences of human behavior. When 19th-century Americans thought about their use of natural resources, they looked first at the wealth they intended to create and only as an afterthought, if at all, at the devastation they left in their wake. A related tendency was to look for the causes of environmental and other social problems in the intentional acts of individuals; because pollution, species extinction, soil erosion, and so on, are social problems with systemic causes, courts and legislatures were thus ill-equipped to deal with such problems when they took note of them at all. This reflex is still common and confounds modern efforts to fix liability for many environmental problems, particularly those involving toxic substances. Historians are not immune, either: this is why environmental studies focused first on what historically articulate people have thought about nature, then on political controversies over how to use nature, and only then on how nature and society create each other.

Voluntarism suffuses our thinking about industrial accidents, as well. The persistent, reflexive tendency to blame accidents on "operator error" is the clearest manifestation of this. Inventors may make technological innovations so as to exploit the labor power of workers more efficiently, but they seldom mean to push that exploitation to the point of killing and maiming. The killing and maiming that do result are unintended and thus (we think) incidental consequences. Industrial safety regulation in Ontario, Tucker found, ran up against the background assumption of many factory inspectors that the interests of workers and employers were fundamentally compatible: their attitude, then, was that accidents reported to them were for the most part inevitable, given the fact of employer control over plant safety and work discipline.[30] Employers avoided having to account for accidents for as long as they did partly because liability depended on finding some individual directly at fault for mishaps, many of which stemmed from causes over which no individual had real control.

More subtle was the law's ability to obfuscate the systemic causes of accidents by portraying working conditions as the product of the individual worker's voluntary choice. The judge in the *Farwell* case reasoned that the injured plaintiff had taken his job at a bargained-for wage and thus assumed the "normal" risks of his job, including the negligence of coworkers. The court would not hold the defendant railroad liable for the chance consequences of Farwell's voluntary act. Factory laws and workers' compensation came about around the turn of the century once a militant workforce and an outraged public became unwilling any longer to think of existing rates of injury as "normal" and realized that choice had little to do with workers' exposure to them. Once the horrible toll of industrial accidents had systemic, articulable causes and thus imaginable cures, the laissez-faire regime in industrial relations began to collapse. Legal scholars have sometimes portrayed the workers'-compensation regimes that supplanted it as a product of rational public choice, although it is not clear that "rationalizing" the liability system in this way either compensated workers adequately or improved workplace safety to any great degree. Here again, the rhetoric of voluntarism rendered invisible the power of the employer to expose defenseless workers to the risk of injury and disease.

The problem of *mechanism* refers to the tendency to describe both nature and society in mechanical terms: composed of interchangeable parts, rationally ordered, and manipulable through technology and experimentation. This view came into being in the 17th century as the Scientific Revolution, the emergence of new theories of political sovereignty, and the diffusion of capitalist economic relations fundamentally altered the architecture of knowledge in Western culture, teaching people to understand themselves and the world around them in new ways. As Carolyn Merchant has shown, the change in view entailed "the death of nature": the earth, no longer perceived as an organism but as a mechanical system of inert matter in motion, could be taken apart and rearranged with impunity to serve exclusively human needs.[31] Ecological disruption on a scale hitherto unknown ensued as people assumed voluntaristic control over the planet, unable or unwilling to account for the real complexity of the natural systems they overwhelmed. Americans, to whom voluntarism was an article of faith, believed that science and technology could make a more orderly, more productive nature and that any problems they might encounter would have technological solutions.

A product of the 17th century, mechanism most thoroughly transformed the ecology of the workplace with the spread of industrialism and the division of labor in the 19th century. The worker's personality disappeared from social view as labor became an abstract factor of production, to be bought at a price determined by impersonal market forces and combined with capital and resources at the will of the entrepreneur. The worker's body became a mere appendage of the machine, subject to the impersonal discipline of employers who attended to health and safety concerns only to the extent that they entailed out-of-pocket costs. Nineteenth-century writers analyzed the worker's body itself as a species of machine. Visiting Manchester in 1844, Friedrich Engels was stunned by the manifestations of this transformation – in poverty, in illness, and especially in workplace injuries.[32] The law's representation of the employment relation as a voluntary, contractual agreement between equal bargainers further obscured what Foucault called the "new mechanism of power" that allowed "time and labor, rather than wealth and commodities, to be extracted from bodies."[33]

One important manifestation of mechanism in modern industrial safety law is the economic approach to safety and liability issues in current vogue among judges and legal scholars. Neoclassical economics is a supremely mechanistic discipline, postulating as it does an economy made up of atomized, rational utility-maximizers moved this way and that by Newtonian market forces. A substantial law-and-economics literature, then, has emerged around problems of accident liability and safety regulation, much of it taking the view that market incentives generally deter accidents by leading employers to maintain appropriate levels of safety in their plants. Some scholars, echoing the argument in *Farwell* v. *Boston and Worcester Railroad*, claim that industrial wages include a premium for the risks entailed in particular jobs. Just as they do in environmental areas, however, market forces overdiscount the costs of industrial injuries (thus subsidizing employers at the expense of injured workers), particularly when the harms involved are long-term, hard to identify, or difficult to value in money terms. Injuries to workers from asbestos and other toxic substances are the clearest example of this kind of market failure in the safety area. Just as the industrial economy extracts resources from nature, it extracts labor from the bodies of workers with insufficient regard for the complexity of their ecology and thus their ability to sustain the yield.

The problem of *teleology*, finally, refers to the notion, embedded deep in our culture, that technological development is progressive, self-motivating, and benign. The idea of autonomous technological progress, of course, is a cornerstone of modern Western culture: Polanyi called it "a mystical readiness to accept the social consequences of economic improvement, whatever they might be."[34] Nowhere is this more prevalent than in the United States, where, at least until the late 20th century, private initiative in science and technology was a powerful engine of economic growth and social progress. That the course of development was left to market forces made it look autonomous and inevitable. The size and natural wealth of the country, meanwhile, combined with chronic shortages of labor and capital to place a premium on the rapid development of resources; for a long while the environmental costs that came with headlong development were simply not noticed. As Hurst put it, "We would realize the greatest present production we could from the land, though in the contemporary state of the economy this meant throwing away much that a broader future development could use."[35]

Only after the turn of the century did the law reflect any effort to slow the pace of destruction, of the country's workforce as well as its natural wealth. Only late in the 20th century did it attempt, haltingly, to direct the course of innovation and to assess rationally the social costs and benefits of developing particular technologies. The Office of Technology Assessment is one institutional manifestation of this new concern; environmental impact statements are probably the best procedural example.

One of the environmental costs of progress, of course, was the toll in industrial accidents. Because people did not recognize their systemic causes, however, accidents became a necessary evil, to be tolerated on the way to the brighter future that technology would bring. This spirit suffuses the opinion in the *Farwell* case of 1842, which makes vague but repeated references to "considerations of policy": Shaw and his contemporaries would not let sporadic damage to individuals stand in the way of technological innovation and economic growth, in which the future of the country lay. Technological change was one of the impersonal, Newtonian forces that drove social change. Its progress, moreover, was benign. Given the presumed teleology of technological development, the law's unwillingness to control it, and the instinct to blame individuals for what accidents did occur, the tendency to perceive the cost as "inevitable" – like taxes, paid in blood and bone – seems only natural.

Conclusion

It seems remarkable that industrial health and safety has so seldom figured in analyses of technological change, given the pervasive influence of injury on the lives of the people who work most closely with industrial technology and the significance of accident liability in allocating the social costs of industrial production. Treating the workplace as an ecological system, however, taking into account the dynamic, reciprocal interaction between the worker's body, the political economy of technological development, and changing perceptions of the role of machines in social life, may offer a broader perspective on the problem of industrial safety and thus highlight its importance in a way that other approaches to technology and labor historiography cannot. Work accidents contribute to the social meaning of technology in three ways: they constitute the most dramatic and immediate social cost of mechanization, they catalyze the construction of power relations in the workplace, and they contribute to public consciousness of the industrial order. Highlighting that role is as difficult an intellectual process as it has been historically because the habits of mind that condition our thinking about technology and industrial accidents – voluntarism, mechanism, and teleology – obscure the systemic relationships between them. That we call workplace injuries "accidents" rather than, say, "production costs" illustrates the tendency to think of them as somehow peripheral and not central to the role of technology in our lives.

That we can now talk about industrial safety in this new way is itself a product of a significant shift in the architecture of our knowledge of the world, a shift that has gathered momentum since the middle of this century. Late-20th-century environmentalism, itself catalyzed by qualitatively new hazards posed by developments in chemical and nuclear technology, as well as by developments in information sciences that have made those hazards comprehensible, is both symptom and cause of the current, ongoing change in our understanding. Industrial health and safety have come into sharper relief with the gathering scholarly emphasis on the role of accident, of unforeseen consequences, and of complex interaction in history and social life as well as in the natural world. Reemphasizing the significance of industrial accidents in the ecology of the workplace may highlight the hidden truth that labor is more than just an economic activity controlled by impersonal market forces: it is the manifestation of the worker's life force, the expression of which makes human life distinctively human.

Notes

1 William Cronon, "The Uses of Environmental History," *Environmental History Review*, 17 (1993): 1–22, esp. 12–16.
2 Ibid., p. 5.
3 Martin V. Melosi, "The Place of the City in Environmental History," *Environmental History Review*, 17 (1993): 1–24, esp. 2.
4 Thomas Kuhn, *The Structure of Scientific Revolutions* (Chicago, 1962). See also Carolyn Merchant, *Ecological Revolutions: Nature, Gender, and Science in New England* (Chapel Hill, NC, 1989), p. 3.
5 William Cronon, *Nature's Metropolis: Chicago and the Great West* (New York, 1991).
6 Cronon, "The Uses of Environmental History" (n. 1 above), pp. 10–11.
7 Cronon, "The Uses of Environmental History" (n. 1 above), pp. 12–14.
8 Rachel Carson, *Silent Spring* (Boston, 1962).
9 Amory B. Lovins, "Energy Strategy: The Road Not Taken?" *Foreign Affairs*, 55 (1976): 65–96; Amory B. Lovins, L. Hunter Lovins, and Leonard Ross, "Nuclear Power and Nuclear Bombs," *Foreign Affairs*, 58 (1980): 1137–77.
10 Alfred W. Crosby, *Ecological Imperialism: The Biological Expansion of Europe, 900–1900* (Cambridge, 1985), pp. 188–190; William Cronon, *Changes in the Land: Indians, Colonists, and the Ecology of New England* (New York, 1983), pp. 135–40; Arthur F. McEvoy, *The Fisherman's Problem: Ecology and Law in the California Fisheries, 1850–1980* (Cambridge, 1986), pp. 41–51.

11 Ester Boserup, *The Conditions of Agricultural Growth: The Economics of Agrarian Change under Population Pressure* (Chicago, 1965), pp. 117–18; see Joel Mokyr, *The Lever of Riches: Technological Creativity and Economic Progress* (Oxford, 1990), pp. 190–92.

12 Stephen Jay Gould, *Wonderful Life: The Burgess Shale and the Nature of History* (New York, 1989), pp. 50–52, 283–85; Gould, *Ontology and Phylogeny* (Cambridge, Mass., 1977), and "Evolution and the Triumph of Homology, or Why History Matters," *American Scientist*, 74 (1986): 60–69.

13 Mokyr (n. 11 above), p. 279.

14 Christopher L. Tomlins, "A Mysterious Power: Industrial Accidents and the Legal Construction of Employment Relations in Massachusetts, 1800–1850," *Law and History Review*, 6 (1988): 375–438, esp. 385.

15 Tomlins, "A Mysterious Power" (n. 14 above), p. 421; Christopher Sellers, "Factory as Environment: Industrial Hygiene, Professional Collaboration and the Modern Sciences of Pollution," *Environmental History Review*, 18 (1991): 55–83, esp. 57.

16 Karl Polanyi, *The Great Transformation: The Political and Economic Origins of Our Time* (New York, 1944), pp. 40–41.

17 *Farwell* v. *Boston and Worcester Rail Road*, 45 Mass (4 Met) 49 (1842); Christopher L. Tomlins, *Law, Labor, and Ideology in the Early American Republic* (Cambridge, 1993), pp. 347, 352–63.

18 Tomlins, "A Mysterious Power" (n. 14 above), pp. 391–92.

19 Ibid., p. 415.

20 Tomlins, *Law, Labor, and Ideology* (n. 17 above), p. 303.

21 Eric Tucker, *Administering Danger in the Workplace: The Law and Politics of Occupational Health and Safety in Ontario, 1850–1914* (Toronto, 1990), p. 44.

22 Frances Perkins, *The Roosevelt I Knew* (New York, 1946), p. 23.

23 The phrase is Geertz's: see Clifford Geertz, "Thick Description: Toward an Interpretive Theory of Culture," in Geertz, *The Interpretation of Cultures: Selected Essays* (New York, 1973), pp. 3–30.

24 Tomlins, "A Mysterious Power" (n. 14 above), p. 421; Michel Foucault, *Discipline and Punish: The Birth of the Prison* (New York, 1979), pp. 137–38; Robert W. Gordon, "Critical Legal Histories," *Stanford Law Review*, 36 (1984): 57–126, esp. 122.

25 Tucker, *Administering Danger in the Workplace* (n. 21 above), p. 15.

26 Michel Foucault, *The Order of Things: An Archaeology of the Human Sciences* (New York, 1970), p. xx.

27 Douglas Gasking, "Causation and Recipes," *Mind*, 64 (1955): 479–87, esp. 483.

28 J. Willard Hurst, *Law and Social Order in the United States* (Ithaca, NY, 1977), p. 198.

29 Tomlins, "A Mysterious Power" (n. 14 above), p. 421. See also Karl Figlio, "What Is an Accident?" in Paul Weindling, ed., *The Social History of Occupational Health* (London, 1985), pp. 197–201.

30 Tucker, *Administering Danger in the Workplace* (n. 21 above), pp. 161, 173.

31 Carolyn Merchant, *The Death of Nature: Women, Ecology, and the Scientific Revolution* (New York, 1980), pp. 216, 227–35, 290–93.

32 Friedrich Engels, *The Condition of the Working Class in England* (Stanford, Calif., 1968), pp. 185–88.

33 Michel Foucault, *Power/Knowledge: Selected Interviews and Other Writings, 1972–1977* (New York, 1980), pp. 104–7.

34 Polanyi (n. 16 above), p. 33.

35 J. Willard Hurst, *Law and the Conditions of Freedom in the Nineteenth-century United States* (Madison, Wisc., 1956), p. 70.

Documents

Nicholas Farwell v. The Boston and Worcester Rail Road Corporation

Where a master uses due diligence in the selection of competent and trusty servants, and furnishes them with suitable means to perform the service in which he employs them, he is not answerable to one of them, for an injury received by him in consequence of the carelessness of another while both are engaged in the same service.

A rail road company employed A., who was careful and trusty in his general character, to tend the switches on their road; and after he had been long in their service, they employed B., to run the passenger train of cars on the road; B. knowing the employment and character of A. *Held,* that the company were not answerable to B. for an injury received by him, while running the cars, in consequence of the carelessness of A. in the management of the switches.

March, 1842, Decided

In an action of trespass upon the case, the plaintiff alleged in his declaration, that he agreed with the defendants to serve them in the employment of an engineer in the management and care of their engines and

Excerpted from *Nicholas Farwell* v. *The Boston and Worcester Rail Road Corporation,* Supreme Court of Massachusetts, Suffolk and Nantucket. 45 Mass. 49; 1842 Mass.; 4 Met. 49.

cars running on their rail road between Boston and Worcester, and entered on said employment, and continued to perform his duties as engineer till October 30th 1837, when the defendants, at Newton, by their servants, so carelessly, negligently and unskillfully managed and used, and put and placed the iron match rail, called the short switch, across the rail or track of their said rail road, that the engine and cars, upon which the plaintiff was engaged and employed in the discharge of his said duties of engineer, were thrown from the track of said rail road, and the plaintiff, by means thereof, was thrown with great violence upon the ground; by means of which one of the wheels of one of said cars passed over the right hand of the plaintiff, crushing and destroying the same.

The case was submitted to the court on the following facts agreed by the parties: "The plaintiff was employed by the defendants, in 1835, as an engineer, and went at first with the merchandize cars, and afterwards with the passenger cars, and so continued till October 30th 1837, at the wages of two dollars per day; that being the usual wages paid to engine-men, which are higher than the wages paid to a machinist, in which capacity the plaintiff formerly was employed.

"On the 30th of October 1837, the plaintiff, then being in the employment of the defendants, as such engine-man, and running the passenger train, ran his engine off at a switch on the road, which had been left in a wrong condition, (as alleged by the plaintiff, and, for the purposes of this trial, admitted by the defendants,) by one Whitcomb, another servant of the defendants, who had been long in their employment, as a switch-man or tender, and had the care of switches on the road, and was a careful and trustworthy servant, in his general character, and as such servant was well known to the plaintiff. By which running off, the plaintiff sustained the injury complained of in his declaration.

"The said Farwell (the plaintiff) and Whitcomb were both appointed by the superintendent of the road, who was in the habit of passing over the same very frequently in the cars, and often rode on the engine.

"If the court shall be of opinion that, as matter of law, the defendants are not liable to the plaintiff, he being a servant of the corporation, and in their employment, for the injury he may have received from the negligence of said Whitcomb, another servant of the corporation, and in their employment, then the plaintiff shall become nonsuit; but if the court shall be of opinion, as matter of law, that the defendants may be liable in this case, then the case shall be submitted to a jury upon the facts which may be proved in the case; the defendants alleging negligence on the part of the plaintiff."

C. G. Loring, for the plaintiff. The defendants, having employed the plaintiff to do a specified duty on the road, were bound to keep the road in such a condition that he might do that duty with safety. If the plaintiff had been a stranger, the defendants would have been liable; and he contends that the case is not varied by the fact that both the plaintiff and Whitcomb were the servants of the defendants; because the plaintiff was not the servant of the defendants in the duty or service, the neglect of which occasioned the injury sustained by him. He was employed for a distinct and separate service, and had no joint agency or power with the other servants whose duty it was to keep the road in order; and could not be made responsible to the defendants for its not being kept in order. He could not, by any vigilance or any power that he could exercise, have prevented the accident. His duties and those of Whitcomb were as distinct and independent of each other, as if they had been servants of different masters.

The plaintiff does not put his case on the ground of the defendants' liability to passengers, nor upon the general principle which renders principals liable for the acts of their agents; but on the ground, that a master, by the nature of his contract with a servant, stipulates for the safety of the servant's employment, so far as the master can regulate the matter.

The defence rests upon an alleged general rule, that a master is not liable to his servant for damage caused by the negligence of a fellow servant. But if that be sound, as a general rule, it does not apply here; for Whitcomb and the plaintiff, as has already been stated, were not fellow servants – that is, were not jointly employed for a common purpose.

The case of *Priestley* v. *Fowler,* 3 Mees. & Welsb. 1, on which the defendants will rely, was rightly decided. The case was clearly one of equal knowledge on the part of the two servants, and of voluntary exposure by the plaintiff to a known hazard not required by his duty; and both servants were jointly engaged in the same business when the accident happened to the plaintiff. But the reasoning and *dicta* of the court went much beyond the case – in undertaking to lay down a general rule, as applying to all cases of damages sustained by a servant in the employment of his master, without discrimination as to the peculiar relations of the servant, and the causes of the injury received by him – and lead to unsound conclusions.

No general rule can be laid down, which will apply to all cases of a master's liability to a servant. But it is submitted that a master is liable to one servant for the negligence of another, when they are engaged in distinct employments, though he is not so liable, where two servants are engaged jointly in the same service; because, in the latter case, each servant has some supervision and control of every other. This principle may be illustrated by the relation which subsists between the owner of a ship and the master and crew. The owner contracts with them to navigate his ship, and of necessity he impliedly contracts that she is capable of navigation – seaworthy for the voyage. And if she prove otherwise, by reason of the carelessness of the builder or the shipwright employed to repair her, and the master and crew lose their wages, the owner must be liable and pay a full indemnity; and he has his remedy against the shipwright. See *Eaken* v. *Thom*, 5 Esp. R. 6. Abbott on Ship. (4th Amer. ed.) 457. In such case, the master and crew have no remedy against the shipwright by whose misconduct they suffer, because there is no privity of contract between him and them. But there is a privity of contract between them and the ship-owner, and this gives a perfect remedy, in the theory of the law. Many similar illustrations of the principle might be given. And unless the servant has a remedy against the master, in such cases, the great fundamental legal rule, that where there is a wrong there is a remedy, is violated or departed from.

In case of servants jointly employed in the same business, it may reasonably be inferred that they take the hazard of injuries from each other's negligence; because such hazard is naturally and necessarily incident to such employment; because they have, to a great extent, the means of guarding against such injuries, by the exercise of mutual caution and prudence, while the master has no such means; and because, between persons employed in a joint service, there is a privity of contract, that renders them liable to each other for their carelessness or neglect in the discharge of such service.

It is a well settled general rule, that a servant is not liable to third persons for his neglect of duty. Story on Agency, @@ 308, 309. If that principle applies to this case, so that the plaintiff has no remedy against Whitcomb, it would seem to be a sufficient reason for holding the defendants liable.

It is also a well established rule, that if an agent, without his own default, has incurred loss or damage in transacting the business of the principal, he is entitled to full compensation. Story on Agency, @ 339.

Fletcher & Morey, for the defendants. The plaintiff must maintain his action, if at all, either on the rule of *respondeat superior*, as for a tort, or on an implied contract of indemnity. The early cases in which masters were held liable to a stranger in an action of tort, for the misconduct of their servants, were mostly those which respected the safety of passengers on highways, and were decided on grounds of policy. The doctrine of such liability was afterwards extended to cases that were deemed analogous. See 1 Bl. Com. 432, *Christian's note*. But no rule of policy requires that masters shall be liable to one servant for injuries received by him from a fellow servant. On the contrary, policy requires an entirely different rule, especially in the present case. The aim of all the statutes concerning rail roads is to protect passengers; and if this action is maintained, it will establish a principle which will tend to diminish the caution of rail road servants, and thus increase the risk of passengers.

The defendants have been in no fault, in this case, either in the construction of their road, the use of defective engines, or the employment of careless or untrusty servants. So that the question is, whether they are liable to the plaintiff, on an implied contract of indemnity. The contract between the parties to this suit excludes the notion that the defendants are liable for the injury received by the plaintiff. He agreed to run an engine on their road, knowing the state of the road, and also knowing Whitcomb, his character, and the specific duty intrusted to him. The plaintiff therefore assumed the risks of the service which he undertook to perform; and one of those risks was his liability to injury from the carelessness of others who were employed by the defendants in the same service. As a consideration for the increased risk of this service, he received higher wages than when he was employed in a less hazardous business.

The defendants are doubtless bound, by an implied contract, to use all the ordinary precautions for the safety of passengers, and are liable for injuries which a passenger may receive in consequence of the negligence of their servants. But the plaintiff was not a passenger, and his counsel does not place his claim on that ground.

The only cases in which a servant has attempted to recover of a master for another servant's misconduct, are *Priestley* v. *Fowler*, 3 Mees. & Welsb. 1, and *Murray* v. *South Carolina Rail Road Company*, 1 McMullan, 385; and in both those cases, it was held that the action could not be maintained. In those cases, it is true that both servants were on the same carriage when the accident happened by which one of them was injured. And the counsel for the present plaintiff has invented a rule of law, in order to escape from the pressure of those decisions. But admitting the distinction, and the rule which he advances, to be sound, the case at bar is not thereby affected. The plaintiff and Whitcomb were not engaged in distinct and separate employments, but in the same service. They both were acting to the same end, although they had different parts to perform.

It will not be necessary for the court to lay down a general rule, in order to decide this case for the defendants. Ordinary care is all that a master is bound to use in behalf of his servants; and the defendants have used such care. They used due diligence in selecting Whitcomb, who was careful and trustworthy. The case is analogous to that of a ship-owner, who is insured, and who has employed a competent master and crew. Though his ship is lost by the negligence of some of the crew, yet he does not thereby suffer the loss of his insurance. *Walker* v. *Maitland*, 5 Barn. & Ald. 174.

Loring, in reply. In the case in 1 McMullan, 385, the plaintiff, as in the case in 3 Mees. & Welsb. 1, was jointly engaged in the same service with the other servant, whose negligence caused the injury. It therefore does not affect the principle on which the present plaintiff rests his cause.

Shaw, C. J. This is an action of new impression in our courts, and involves a principle of great importance. It presents a case, where two persons are in the service and employment of one company, whose business it is to construct and maintain a rail road, and to employ their trains of cars to carry persons and merchandize for hire. They are appointed and employed by the same company to perform separate duties and services, all tending to the accomplishment of one and the same purpose – that of the safe and rapid transmission of the trains; and they are paid for their respective services according to the nature of their respective duties, and the labor and skill required for their proper performance. The question is, whether, for damages sustained by one of the persons so employed, by means of the carelessness and negligence of another, the party injured has a remedy against the common employer. It is an argument against such an action, though certainly not a decisive one, that no such action has before been maintained.

It is laid down by Blackstone, that if a servant, by his negligence, does any damage to a stranger, the master shall be answerable for his neglect. But the damage must be done while he is actually employed in the master's service; otherwise, the servant shall answer for his own misbehavior. 1 Bl. Com. 431. *M'Manus* v. *Crickett*, 1 East, 106. This rule is obviously founded on the great principle of social duty, that every man, in the management of his own affairs, whether by himself or by his agents or servants, shall so conduct them as not to injure another; and if he does not, and another thereby sustains damage, he shall answer for it. If done by a servant, in the course of his employment, and acting within the scope of his authority, it is considered, in contemplation of law, so far the act of the master, that the latter shall be answerable *civiliter*. But this presupposes that the parties stand to each other in the relation of strangers, between whom there is no privity; and the action, in such case, is an action sounding in tort. The form is trespass on the case, for the consequential damage. The maxim *respondeat superior* is adopted in that case, from general considerations of policy and security.

But this does not apply to the case of a servant bringing his action against his own employer to recover damages for an injury arising in the course of that employment, where all such risks and perils as the employer and the servant respectively intend to assume and bear may be regulated by the express or implied contract between them, and which, in contemplation of law, must be presumed to be thus regulated.

The same view seems to have been taken by the learned counsel for the plaintiff in the argument; and it was conceded, that the claim could not be placed on the principle indicated by the maxim *respondeat superior*, which binds the master to indemnify a stranger for the damage caused by the careless, negligent or unskillful act of his servant in the conduct of his affairs. The claim, therefore, is placed, and must be maintained, if maintained at all, on the ground of contract. As there is no express contract between the parties, applicable to this point, it is placed on the footing of an implied contract of indemnity, arising out of the relation of master and servant. It would be an implied promise, arising from the duty of the master to be responsible to each person employed by him, in the conduct of every branch of business, where two or more persons are employed, to pay for all damage occasioned by the negligence of every other person employed in the same service. If such a duty were established by law – like that of a common carrier, to stand to all losses of goods not caused by the act of God or of a public enemy – or that of an innkeeper, to be responsible, in like manner, for the baggage of his guests; it would be a rule of frequent and familiar occurrence, and its existence and application, with all its qualifications and restrictions, would be settled by judicial precedents. But we are of opinion that no such rule has been established, and the authorities, as far as they go, are opposed to the principle. *Priestley* v. *Fowler,* 3 Mees. & Welsb. 1. *Murray* v. *South Carolina Rail Road Company,* 1 McMullan 385.

The general rule, resulting from considerations as well of justice as of policy, is, that he who engages in the employment of another for the performance of specified duties and services, for compensation, takes upon himself the natural and ordinary risks and perils incident to the performance of such services, and in legal presumption, the compensation is adjusted accordingly. And we are not aware of any principle which should except the perils arising from the carelessness and negligence of those who are in the same employment. These are perils which the servant is as likely to know, and against which he can as effectually guard, as the master. They are perils incident to the service, and which can be as distinctly foreseen and provided for in the rate of compensation as any others. To say that the master shall be responsible because the damage is caused by his agents, is assuming the very point which remains to be proved. They are his agents to some extent, and for some purposes; but whether he is responsible, in a particular case, for their negligence, is not decided by the single fact that they are, for some purposes, his agents. It seems to be now well settled, what ever might have been thought formerly, that underwriters cannot excuse themselves from payment of a loss by one of the perils insured against, on the ground that the loss was caused by the negligence or unskillfulness of the officers or crew of the vessel, in the performance of their various duties as navigators, although employed and paid by the owners, and, in the navigation of the vessel, their agents. *Copeland* v. *New England Marine Ins. Co.* 2 Met. 440–443, and cases there cited. I am aware that the maritime law has its own rules and analogies, and that we cannot always safely rely upon them in applying them to other branches of law. But the rule in question seems to be a good authority for the point, that persons are not to be responsible, in all cases, for the negligence of those employed by them.

If we look from considerations of justice to those of policy, they will strongly lead to the same conclusion. In considering the rights and obligations arising out of particular relations, it is competent for courts of justice to regard considerations of policy and general convenience, and to draw from them such rules as will, in their practical application, best promote the safety and security of all parties concerned. This is, in truth, the basis on which implied promises are raised, being duties legally inferred from a consideration of what is best adapted to promote the benefit of all persons concerned, under given circumstances. To take the well known and familiar cases already cited; a common carrier, without regard to actual fault or neglect in himself or his servants, is made liable for all losses of goods confided to him for carriage, except those caused by the act of God or of a public enemy, because he can best guard them against all minor dangers, and because, in case of actual loss, it would be extremely difficult for the owner to adduce proof of embezzlement, or other actual fault or neglect on the part of the carrier, although it may have been the real cause of the loss. The risk is therefore thrown upon the carrier, and he receives, in the form of payment for the carriage, a premium for the risk which he thus assumes. So of an innkeeper; he can best secure the attendance of honest and faithful servants, and guard his house against thieves. Whereas, if he were responsible only upon proof of actual negligence, he might connive at the presence of dishonest inmates and retainers, and even participate in the embezzlement of the property of the guests, during the hours of their necessary sleep, and yet it would be difficult, and often impossible, to prove these facts.

The liability of passenger carriers is founded on similar considerations. They are held to the strictest responsibility for care, vigilance and skill, on the part of themselves and all persons employed by them, and they are paid accordingly. The rule is founded on the expediency of throwing the risk upon those who can best guard against it. Story on Bailments, @ 590, & *seq.*

We are of opinion that these considerations apply strongly to the case in question. Where several persons are employed in the conduct of one common enterprise or undertaking, and the safety of each depends much on the care and skill with which each other shall perform his appropriate duty, each is an observer of the conduct of the others, can give notice of any misconduct, incapacity or neglect of duty, and leave the service, if the common employer will not take such precautions, and employ such agents as the safety of the whole party may require. By these means, the safety of each will be much more effectually secured, than could be done by a resort to the common employer for indemnity in case of loss by the negligence of each other. Regarding it in this light, it is the ordinary case of one sustaining an injury in the course of his own employment, in which he must bear the loss himself, or seek his remedy, if he have any, against the actual wrong-doer.

In applying these principles to the present case, it appears that the plaintiff was employed by the defendants as an engineer, at the rate of wages usually paid in that employment, being a higher rate than the plaintiff had before received as a machinist. It was a voluntary undertaking on his part, with a full knowledge of the risks incident to the employment; and the loss was sustained by means of an ordinary casualty, caused by the negligence of another servant of the company. Under these circumstances, the loss must be deemed to be the result of a pure accident, like those to which all men, in all employments, and at all times, are more or less exposed; and like similar losses from accidental causes, it must rest where it first fell, unless the plaintiff has a remedy against the person actually in default; of which we give no opinion.

It was strongly pressed in the argument, that although this might be so, where two or more servants are employed in the same department of duty, where each can exert some influence over the conduct of the other, and thus to some extent provide for his own security; yet that it could not apply where two or more are employed in different departments of duty, at a distance from each other, and where one can in no degree control or influence the conduct of another. But we think this is founded upon a supposed distinction, on which it would be extremely difficult to estab-lish a practical rule. When the object to be accomplished is one and the same, when the employers are the same, and the several persons employed derive their authority and their compensation from the same source, it would be extremely difficult to distinguish, what constitutes one department and what a distinct department of duty. It would vary with the circumstances of every case. If it were made to depend upon the nearness or distance of the persons from each other, the question would immediately arise, how near or how distant must they be, to be in the same or different departments. In a blacksmith's shop, persons working in the same building, at different fires, may be quite independent of each other, though only a few feet distant. In a ropewalk, several may be at work on the same piece of cordage, at the same time, at many hundred feet distant from each other, and beyond the reach of sight and voice, and yet acting together.

Besides, it appears to us, that the argument rests upon an assumed principle of responsibility which does not exist. The master, in the case supposed, is not exempt from liability, because the servant has better means of providing for his safety, when he is employed in immediate connexion with those from whose negligence he might suffer; but because the *implied contract* of the master does not extend to indemnify the servant against the negligence of any one but himself; and he is not liable in tort, as for the negligence of his servant, because the person suffering does not stand towards him in the relation of a stranger, but is one whose rights are regulated by contract express or implied. The exemption of the master, therefore, from liability for the negligence of a fellow servant, does not depend exclusively upon the consideration, that the servant has better means to provide for his own safety, but upon other grounds. Hence the separation of the employment into different departments cannot create that liability, when it does not arise from express or implied contract, or from a responsibility created by law to third persons, and strangers, for the negligence of a servant.

A case may be put for the purpose of illustrating this distinction. Suppose the road had been owned by one set of proprietors whose duty it was to keep it in repair and have it at all times ready and in fit condition for the running of engines and cars, taking a toll, and that the engines and cars were owned by another set of proprietors, paying toll to the proprietors of the road, and receiving compensation from passengers for their carriage; and suppose the engineer to suffer a loss from the negligence of the switch-tender. We are inclined to the opinion that the engineer might have a remedy against the rail road corporation; and if so, it must be on the ground, that as between the engineer employed by the proprietors of the engines and cars, and the switch-tender employed by the corporation, the engineer would be a stranger, between whom and the corporation there could be no privity of contract; and not because the engineer would have no means of controlling the conduct of the switch-tender. The responsibility which one is under for the negligence of his servant, in the conduct of his business, towards third persons, is founded on another and distinct principle from that of implied contract, and stands on its own reasons of policy. The same reasons of policy, we think, limit this responsibility to the case of strangers, for whose security alone it is established. Like considerations of policy and general expediency forbid the extension of the principle, so far as to warrant a servant in maintaining an action against his employer for an indemnity which we think was not contemplated in the nature and terms of the employment, and which, if established, would not conduce to the general good.

In coming to the conclusion that the plaintiff, in the present case, is not entitled to recover, considering it as in some measure a nice question, we would add a caution against any hasty conclusion as to the application of this rule to a case not fully within the same principle. It may be varied and modified by circumstances not appearing in the present case, in which it appears, that no wilful wrong or actual negligence was imputed to the corporation, and where suitable means were furnished and suitable persons employed to accomplish the object in view. We are far from intending to say that there are no implied warranties and undertakings arising out of the relation of master and servant. Whether, for instance, the employer would be responsible to an engineer for a loss arising from a defective or illconstructed steam engine: Whether this would depend upon an implied warranty of its goodness and sufficiency, or upon the fact of wilful misconduct, or gross negligence on the part of the employer, if a natural person, or of the superintendent or immediate representative and managing agent, in case of an incorporated company – are questions on which we give no opinion. In the present case, the claim of the plaintiff is not put on the ground that the defendants did not furnish a sufficient engine, a proper rail road track, a well constructed switch, and a person of suitable skill and experience to attend it; the gravamen of the complaint is, that that person was chargeable with negligence in not changing the switch, in the particular instance, by means of which the accident occurred, by which the plaintiff sustained a severe loss. It ought, perhaps, to be stated, in justice to the person to whom this negligence is imputed, that the fact is strenuously denied by the defendants, and has not been tried by the jury. By consent of the parties, this fact was assumed without trial, in order to take the opinion of the whole court upon the question of law, whether, if such was the fact, the defendants, under the circumstances, were liable. Upon this question, supposing the accident to have occurred, and the loss to have been caused, by the negligence of the person employed to attend to and change the switch, in his not doing so in the particular case, the court are of opinion that it is a loss for which the defendants are not liable, and that the action cannot be maintained.

Plaintiff nonsuit.

Is It Safe to Work? A Study of Industrial Accidents
Edison L. Bowers

Injuries Are Very Costly

The average fatality cuts off twenty years of productive labor. This means that the country as a whole, on the basis of 20,000 fatalities per year, is deprived of 380,000 man-years of labor because of each year's fatal accidents. The serious permanent disabilities result, on the average, in a reduction in earning capacity of nearly 50 per cent. This is equivalent to the loss of some 350,000 man-years of labor. The less serious injuries account for probably 3,000,000 weeks of lost labor annually. All types of injuries taken together cause an annual loss of time of more than 280,000,000 working days.

The annual wage loss attributable to industrial injuries amounts to more than a billion dollars; the annual total loss, to probably four billion. In this are included the cost of medical and surgical attention, and the overhead cost in connection with the payment of claims, as well as a heavy indirect cost. The indirect loss of production is very significant. Whole processes may have to wait because of a single accident. The injurious effect of accidents on the morale of the workers is almost impossible to estimate, but that it is considerable is evident to any one who has seen a serious accident where large numbers of persons are employed.

There Are Many Causes for Injuries

The customary way of placing fault for injuries is to say that a certain part of the blame is due to the negligence of the employee; another part is due to the failure of the employer to provide proper working conditions, tools and equipment, and so forth; and all injuries not thereby accounted for are thought of as being nobody's fault. Some accidents appear to be due to carelessness, foolishness, or seemingly inexcusable ignorance of employees. The following cases may be cited in point:

Excerpt from Edison L. Bowers's *Is It Safe to Work? A Study of Industrial Accidents* (Boston: Houghton Mifflin Company, 1930), pp. 4–9.

1 A helper on a shears in a rolled steel mill was in the habit of asking the shearman on the opposite side of the shears for tobacco. Becoming tired of getting up and walking around the shears, this man put his hand under the shears just in time to have the big blade sever his right hand at the wrist.

2 An employee for a gasoline distributing company, although he had been cautioned many times, lighted a match and tried to place it inside an automobile gasoline tank to determine if the tank would hold more gasoline. In the explosion that followed, the employee lost the use of an arm and the sight of an eye, and had in addition a badly burned body.

It must not be assumed that the above examples are typical accidents, but undoubtedly the records of every State reveal many such unfortunate experiences. How may these accidents be explained? They may be due to fatigue, lack of sleep, or inability to comprehend and interpret orders. They may be due to mental causes. Mr. Boyd Fisher believes that mental causes are primary in explaining accidents. In his book, *Mental Causes of Accidents*, he divides these causes into five heads: ignorance, predisposition, inattention, preoccupation, and depression.

A study of 75,000 industrial accidents by the Travelers' Insurance Company revealed the fact that only about 10 per cent of accidents are due to physical and mechanical causes, whereas nearly 90 per cent are attributable to the human factor – faulty instructions, poor discipline, unsafe practice, and so forth.

Just as some accidents may be definitely traced to the negligence of the employee, so may others be attributed to the employer. Here are two examples:

1 A planing mill had in operation a large circular saw with no guards around it. An employee had his thumb taken off. Another employee was put in his place. Within a few days this man had his wrist so badly cut that an amputation was necessary. Meanwhile, State officials insisted that the saw be guarded. The guard was not immediately supplied, the blame for the delay being placed upon the foreman in charge. A short while later this same foreman, having some work to do, and nobody available to do it, began operating the unguarded saw. He was fatally wounded after a few minutes of work. Then, and then only, did the company, under the compulsion of the State, guard the machine.

2 A steel company, specializing in the production of iron bars, made a practice of using hand trucks in moving steel about the plant. These trucks, when loaded, weighed as much as 15 tons, and ran from the

stock room to the loading car by gravity. Many times one truck would run into another truck with tremendous force. Occasionally, an employee would have a finger smashed or a glove caught between the protruding bars. Requests were repeatedly made that brakes be put on the trucks, but the company did nothing. One night the foreman of the shipping department did not move quite quickly enough, was caught between two trucks, and pierced as if by a hundred spears.

Conditions such as these testify to poor shop management, or insufficient State inspection, or both. Some employers will not make their plants safe because they fear that the expense involved will reduce profits. Further, many a factory manager lives under the delusion that in his plant a serious accident will never occur.

That State inspection is sorely deficient is apparent to all who are familiar with the situation. It is not uncommon for one inspector to have under his jurisdiction all the factories in several large industrial cities. In a territory so large, it is impossible to give adequate attention to each plant. Often the result is a superficial inspection and a duplicate of the previous inspection report with the date changed. An example of the inadequacy of State inspection is found in this extract from the annual report of the Louisiana Commission of Labor: "In the discharge of routine duties, practically every industry in the State has been visited and inspected by some attaché of this department during the last year, and in many industrial centers, even more inspections have been made."

Aside from those accidents which are caused directly by somebody's negligence, there are many others in which it is difficult to determine fault. The general explanation of the causes of these accidents is to be found in the inherent hazards of industry as it has been conducted since the coming of the machine process, and as it is likely to be conducted in the future, with the ever-increasing intensity of the newer and more powerful machinery. The very nature of modern production seems to demand the hands and legs and arms and eyes and even the lives of men and women. There are punch presses which smash fingers; metal shears which cut off hands; calendering machines which tear off arms; giant rolls which smash bodies; falls which break legs; cave-ins which wrench backs; flying dust which blinds eyes. These are the concomitants of machine production.

Throughout modern industry, the human organism is expected to adapt itself to an ever-changing mechanical environment. Machine production is increasing in its complexity; speed has become synonymous with efficiency; unskilled and less responsible workmen have replaced old-line mechanics. It is a constant race between man's powers of adaptability and industry's changes in its methods of production. There is good reason to believe that workers unaided would be the losers in the race, and that the only thing that prevents them from losing entirely is the constant assistance given them through safety devices of all kinds.

Edward J. Besheda v. Johns-Manville Products Corporation

April 19, 1982, Argued
July 7, 1982, Decided

Prior History:

On appeal from the Supreme Court, Appellate Division . . . .

Opinion: The sole question here is whether defendants in a product liability case based on strict liability for failure to warn may raise a "state of the art" defense. Defendants assert that the danger of which they failed to warn was undiscovered at the time the product was marketed and that it was undiscoverable given the state of scientific knowledge at that time. The case comes to us on appeal from the trial court's denial of plaintiffs' motion to strike the state-of-the-art defense. For the reasons stated below, we reverse the trial court judgment and strike the defense.

I

These six consolidated cases are personal injury and wrongful death actions brought against manufacturers and distributors of asbestos products. Plaintiffs are workers, or survivors of deceased workers, who claim to have been exposed to asbestos for varying periods of time. They allege that as a result of that exposure they contracted asbestosis (a non-malignant scarring of the lungs), mesothelioma (a rare cancer of the

---

Excerpt from *Edward J. Besheda v. Johns-Manville Products Corporation.* A-162/163/175, Supreme Court of New Jersey. 90 N.J. 191; 447 A.2d 539; 1982 N.J. LEXIS 2153; 33 A.L.R. 4th 353; CCH Prod. Liab. Rep. P9344; 13 ELR 20533.

lining of the chest, the pleura, or the lining of the abdomen, the perito-
neum) and other asbestos-related illnesses.

These cases involve asbestos exposure dating back perhaps as far as
the 1930s. The suits are first arising now because of the long latent
period between exposure and the discernible symptoms of asbestosis
and mesothelioma. See *Borel* v. *Fibreboard Paper Products Corporation*,
493 F. 2d 1076, 1083 (5th Cir. 1973). Plaintiffs have raised a variety of
legal theories to support their claims for damages. The important claim,
for purposes of this appeal, is strict liability for failure to warn. Prior to
the 1960s, defendants' products allegedly contained no warning of their
hazardous nature. Defendants respond by asserting the state-of-the-art
defense. They allege that no one knew or could have known that asbestos was dangerous when it was marketed.

There is substantial factual dispute about what defendants knew and
when they knew it. A trial judge in the Eastern District of Texas, the
forum for numerous asbestos-related cases, has concluded that "[k]now-
ledge of the danger can be attributed to the industry as early as the mid-
1930s .... " *Hardy* v. *Johns-Manville Sales Corp.*, 509 F. Supp. 1352,
1355 (E. D. Texas 1981). Defendants respond, however, that it was not
until the 1960s that the medical profession in the United States recognized that a potential health hazard arose from the use of insulation
products containing asbestos. Before that time, according to defendants,
the danger from asbestos was believed limited to workers in asbestos
textile mills, who were exposed to much higher concentrations of asbestos dust than were the workers at other sites, such as shipyards. Defendants claim that it was not discovered until recently that the much smaller
concentrations those workers faced were also hazardous.

We need not resolve the factual issues raised. For purposes of plaintiffs' motion to strike the defense, we assume the defendants' version of
the facts. The issue is whether the medical community's presumed
unawareness of the dangers of asbestos is a defense to plaintiffs' claims.

II

As noted, this case involves six consolidated cases. *Jarusewicz, et al.* v.
Johns-Manville, et al. is a suit by eighteen workers who were employed by
Jersey Central Power and Light Company for various periods between
1930 and 1981, all of whom allege that they used asbestos, asbestos
products or asbestos materials in the course of their work. They allege
that they were given no warning, handling instructions or safety equipment to protect them from the dangers of asbestos. *Beshada, et al.* v.
Johns-Manville, et al. is a suit by twenty-one current or former pipefitters

employed at Hercules, Inc. between 1935 and the present, who allege that they worked with and around insulation products containing asbestos. *Blazewicz, et al.* v. *Johns-Manville, et al.* and *Hann, et al.* v. *Johns-Manville, et al.* involve respectively twelve and six employees of Research Cottrell, Inc., between 1936 and 1979. Plaintiff in *Beckwith, et al.* v. *Johns-Manville, et al.* is the widow of an electrician, Earl Beckwith, who was exposed to finished asbestos products during his work. She alleges that her husband's exposure to asbestos caused various illnesses which resulted in his death. Finally, *Crilley* v. *Cork, et al.* is a wrongful death action by the widow of James Crilley, who died allegedly as a result of occupational exposure to insulation products containing asbestos.

A single trial judge has been specially assigned to hear all asbestos-related litigation in Middlesex County. On September 9, 1981, counsel for plaintiffs in four of the cases filed a Motion for Partial Summary Judgment seeking to strike the state-of-the-art defense. Subsequently, plaintiffs in the other two cases joined the motion.

Plaintiffs based their motion on *Freund* v. *Cellofilm Properties, Inc.*, 87 N.J. 229 (1981), our most recent case concerning product liability. In *Freund*, Justice Handler elaborated the difference between negligence and strict liability in a failure to warn case. He explained that in strict liability cases knowledge of the dangerousness of the product is imputed to defendants. Plaintiff need not prove that defendant knew or should have known of its dangerousness. The only issue is whether the product distributed by defendant was reasonably safe. Plaintiffs urge that *Freund* disposed of the state-of-the-art issue. Since defendant's knowledge of the dangers of the product is presumed, it is irrelevant whether the existence of such dangers was scientifically discoverable. Defendants respond that *Freund* imputes to defendants only "existing knowledge, the technical knowledge available at the time of manufacture."

The trial judge denied the motion to strike. Reading *Freund* in conjunction with prior cases, *Suter* v. *San Angelo Foundry & Machine Company*, 81 N.J. 150 (1979) and *Torsiello* v. *Whitehall Laboratories*, 165 N.J. Super. 311 (App. Div. 1979), the judge concluded that *Freund* merely created a rebuttable presumption that defendants had knowledge of the dangers of their product. That presumption could be overcome by proof that the knowledge at issue was "unknowable" at the time of manufacture.

Plaintiffs sought leave from the Appellate Division to appeal the trial court's interlocutory order and filed a motion with this Court for direct certification. The Appellate Division denied plaintiffs' motion for leave to appeal. In all but the *Crilley* case, plaintiffs moved before this Court for leave to appeal the Appellate Division order. We granted their motion on February 25, 1982, and subsequently granted plaintiff Crilley's late motion for leave to appeal.

III

Our inquiry starts with the principles laid down in *Freund* v. *Cellofilm Properties, Inc., supra, Suter* v. *San Angelo Foundry & Machine Company, supra,* and *Cepeda* v. *Cumberland Engineering Company, Inc.,* 76 N.J. 152 (1978). In *Suter,* we summarized the principle of strict liability as follows:

> If at the time the seller distributes a product, it is not reasonably fit, suitable and safe for its intended or reasonably foreseeable purposes so that users or others who may be expected to come in contact with the product are injured as a result thereof, then the seller shall be responsible for the ensuing damages. [Id. at 169]

The determination of whether a product is "reasonably fit, suitable and safe" depends on a comparison of its risks and its utility (risk–utility equation). Central to this theory is the risk–utility equation for determining liability. The theory is that only safe products should be marketed – a safe product being one whose utility outweighs its inherent risk, provided that risk has been reduced to the greatest extent possible consistent with the product's continued utility. [*Freund,* 87 N.J. at 238, n. 1]

In *Cepeda,* we explained that in the context of design defect liability, strict liability is identical to liability for negligence, with one important caveat: "The only qualification is as to the requisite of foreseeability by the manufacturer of the dangerous propensity of the chattel manifested at the trial – this being imputed to the manufacturer." *Cepeda,* 76 N.J. at 172. See *Freund* v. *Cellofilm Properties, Inc.,* 87 N.J. at 239. In so holding, we adopted the explication of strict liability offered by Dean Wade:

> The time has now come to be forthright in using a tort way of thinking and tort terminology [in cases of strict liability in tort]. There are several ways of doing it, and it is not difficult. The simplest and easiest way, it would seem, is to assume that the defendant knew of the dangerous condition of the product and ask whether he was then negligent in putting it on the market or supplying it to someone else. In other words, the scienter is supplied as a matter of law, and there is no need for the plaintiff to prove its existence as a matter of fact. Once given this notice of the dangerous condition of the chattel, the question then becomes whether the defendant was negligent to people who might be harmed by that condition if they came into contact with it or were in the vicinity of it. Another way of saying this is to ask whether the magnitude of the risk created by the dangerous

condition of the product was outweighted by the social utility attained by putting it out in this fashion. [Wade, "On the Nature of Strict Tort Liability for Products," 44 Miss.L.J. 825, 834–35 (1973), quoted in *Cepeda*, 76 N.J. at 172]

Stated differently, negligence is conduct-oriented, asking whether defendant's actions were reasonable; strict liability is product-oriented, asking whether the product was reasonably safe for its foreseeable purposes. *Freund*, 87 N.J. at 238.

"Warning" cases constitute one category of strict liability cases. Their relation to the strict liability principles set forth above can best be analyzed by focusing on the definition of safe products found in footnote 1 of *Freund*. See *supra* at 200. For purposes of analysis, we can distinguish two tests for determining whether a product is safe: (1) does its utility outweigh its risk? and (2) if so, has that risk been reduced to the greatest extent possible consistent with the product's utility? Id. at 238, n. 1. The first question looks to the product as it was in fact marketed. If that product caused more harm than good, it was not reasonably fit for its intended purposes. We can therefore impose strict liability for the injuries it caused without having to determine whether it could have been rendered safer. The second aspect of strict liability, however, requires that the risk from the product be reduced to the greatest extent possible without hindering its utility. Whether or not the product passes the initial risk–utility test, it is not reasonably safe if the same product could have been made or marketed more safely.

Warning cases are of this second type. When plaintiffs urge that a product is hazardous because it lacks a warning, they typically look to the second test, saying in effect that regardless of the overall cost–benefit calculation the product is unsafe because a warning could make it safer at virtually no added cost and without limiting its utility. *Freund* recognized this, noting that in cases alleging "an inadequate warning as to safe use, the utility of the product, as counter-balanced against the risks of its use, is rarely at issue." Id. at 242.

Freund is our leading case on strict liability for failure to warn. In *Freund*, Justice Handler applied the principles set forth above, initially laid down in *Suter* and *Cepeda*, to warning cases. The issue there was whether there is any difference between negligence and strict liability in warning cases. We stated unequivocally that there is. That difference is the same difference that we noted in *Suter* and *Cepeda* concerning other design defect cases:

when a plaintiff sues under strict liability, there is no need to prove that the manufacturer knew or should have known of any dangerous propensities of its product – such knowledge is imputed to the manufacturer. [*Freund* v. *Cellofilm Properties, Inc.*, 87 N.J. at 239]

Thus, we held in *Freund* that it was reversible error for the trial judge to instruct the jury only with a negligence charge.

With these basic principles of design defect strict liability in New Jersey as our framework for analysis, we turn now to a discussion of the state-of-the-art defense.

IV

As it relates to warning cases, the state-of-the-art defense asserts that distributors of products can be held liable only for injuries resulting from dangers that were scientifically discoverable at the time the product was distributed. Defendants argue that the question of whether the product can be made safer must be limited to consideration of the available technology at the time the product was distributed. Liability would be absolute, defendants argue, if it could be imposed on the basis of a subsequently discovered means to make the product safer since technology will always be developing new ways to make products safer. Such a rule, they assert, would make manufacturers liable whenever their products cause harm, whether or not they are reasonably fit for their foreseeable purposes.

Defendants conceptualize the scientific unknowability of the dangerous propensities of a product as a technological barrier to making the product safer by providing warnings. Thus, a warning was not "possible" within the meaning of the *Freund* requirement that risk be reduced "to the greatest extent possible."

In urging this position, defendants must somehow distinguish the *Freund* holding that knowledge of the dangers of the product is imputed to defendants as a matter of law. A state-of-the-art defense would contravene that by requiring plaintiffs to prove at least that knowledge of the dangers was scientifically available at the time of manufacture.

Defendants argue that *Freund* did not specify precisely what knowledge is imputed to defendants. They construe *Freund* to impute only that degree of knowledge of the product's dangerousness that existed at the time of manufacture or distribution.

While we agree that *Freund* did not explicitly address this question, the principles laid down in *Freund* and our prior cases contradict defendants' position. Essentially, state-of-the-art is a negligence defense. It seeks to explain why defendants are not culpable for failing to provide a warning. They assert, in effect, that because they could not have known the product was dangerous, they acted reasonably in marketing it without a warning. But in strict liability cases, culpability is irrelevant. The product was unsafe. That it was unsafe because of the state of technology does not change the fact that it was unsafe. Strict liability focuses on the product, not the fault of the manufacturer. "If the conduct is unreasonably dangerous, then there should be strict liability without reference to what excuse defendant might give for being unaware of the danger." *Keeton*, 48 Tex.L.Rev. at 408.

When the defendants argue that it is unreasonable to impose a duty on them to warn of the unknowable, they misconstrue both the purpose and effect of strict liability. By imposing strict liability, we are not requiring defendants to have done something that is impossible. In this sense, the phrase "duty to warn" is misleading. It implies negligence concepts with their attendant focus on the reasonableness of defendant's behavior. However, a major concern of strict liability – ignored by defendants – is the conclusion that if a product was in fact defective, the distributor of the product should compensate its victims for the misfortune that it inflicted on them.

If we accepted defendants' argument, we would create a distinction among fact situations that defies common sense. Under the defendants' reading of *Freund*, defendant would be liable for failure to warn if the danger was knowable even if defendants were not negligent in failing to discover it. Defendants would suffer no liability, however, if the danger was undiscoverable. But, as Dean Keeton explains,

> if a defendant is to be held liable for a risk that is discoverable by some genius but beyond the defendant's capacity to do so, why should he not also be liable for a risk that was just as great but was not discoverable by anyone? [*Keeton*, 48 Tex.L.Rev. at 409]

We are buttressed in our conclusion that the state-of-the-art defense is inconsistent with Freund by the recent decision of Judge Ackerman in *Marcucci* v. *Johns-Manville Sales Corp.*, Nos. 76–414, 76–604 and 76–1510 (D.N.J. Feb. 19, 1982), in which he applied New Jersey law to strike defendants' state-of-the-art defense.

The most important inquiry, however, is whether imposition of liability for failure to warn of dangers which were undiscoverable at the time of manufacture will advance the goals and policies sought to be achieved by our strict liability rules. We believe that it will.

Risk Spreading. One of the most important arguments generally advanced for imposing strict liability is that the manufacturers and distributors of defective products can best allocate the costs of the injuries resulting from those products. The premise is that the price of a product should reflect all of its costs, including the cost of injuries caused by the product. This can best be accomplished by imposing liability on the manufacturer and distributors. Those persons can insure against liability and incorporate the cost of the insurance in the price of the product. In this way, the costs of the product will be borne by those who profit from it: the manufacturers and distributors who profit from its sale and the buyers who profit from its use. "It should be a cost of doing business that in the course of doing that business an unreasonable risk was created." *Keeton*, 48 Tex.L.Rev. at 408. See Prosser, *The Law of Torts*, @ 75, p. 495 (4th Ed. 1971).

Defendants argue that this policy is not forwarded by imposition of liability for unknowable hazards. Since such hazards by definition are not predicted, the price of the hazardous product will not be adjusted to reflect the costs of the injuries it will produce. Rather, defendants state, the cost "will be borne by the public at large and reflected in a general, across the board increase in premiums to compensate for unanticipated risks." There is some truth in this assertion, but it is not a bad result.

First, the same argument can be made as to hazards which are deemed scientifically knowable but of which the manufacturers are unaware. Yet it is well established under our tort law that strict liability is imposed even for defects which were unknown to the manufacturer. It is precisely the imputation of knowledge to the defendant that distinguishes strict liability from negligence. *Freund*, 87 N.J. at 240. Defendants advance no argument as to why risk spreading works better for unknown risks than for unknowable risks.

Second, spreading the costs of injuries among all those who produce, distribute and purchase manufactured products is far preferable to imposing it on the innocent victims who suffer illnesses and disability from defective products. This basic normative premise is at the center of our strict liability rules. It is unchanged by the state of scientific knowledge at the time of manufacture.

Finally, contrary to defendants' assertion, this rule will not cause the price and production level of manufactured products to diverge from the so-called economically efficient level. Rather, the rule will force the price of any particular product to reflect the cost of insuring against the possibility that the product will turn out to be defective.

Accident Avoidance. In *Suter*, we stated:

> Strict liability in a sense is but an attempt to minimize the costs of accidents and to consider who should bear those costs. See the discussion in Calabresi & Hirschoff, "Toward a Test for Strict Liability in Torts," 81 Yale L.J. 1055 (1972), in which the authors suggest that the strict liability issue is to decide which party is the "cheapest cost avoider" or who is in

the best position to make the cost–benefit analysis between accident costs and accident avoidance costs and to act on that decision once it is made. Id. at 1060. Using this approach, it is obvious that the manufacturer rather than the factory employee is "in the better position both to judge whether avoidance costs would exceed foreseeable accident costs and to act on that judgment." Id. [*Suter* v. *San Angelo Foundry*, 81 N.J. at 173–74]

Defendants urge that this argument has no force as to hazards which by definition were undiscoverable. Defendants have treated the level of technological knowledge at a given time as an independent variable not affected by defendants' conduct. But this view ignores the important role of industry in product safety research. The "state-of-the-art" at a given time is partly determined by how much industry invests in safety research. By imposing on manufacturers the costs of failure to discover hazards, we create an incentive for them to invest more actively in safety research.

Fact Finding Process. The analysis thus far has assumed that it is possible to define what constitutes "undiscoverable" knowledge and that it will be reasonably possible to determine what knowledge was technologically discoverable at a given time. In fact, both assumptions are highly questionable. The vast confusion that is virtually certain to arise from any attempt to deal in a trial setting with the concept of scientific knowability constitutes a strong reason for avoiding the concept altogether by striking the state-of-the-art defense.

Scientific knowability, as we understand it, refers not to what in fact was known at the time, but to what could have been known at the time. In other words, even if no scientist had actually formed the belief that asbestos was dangerous, the hazards would be deemed "knowable" if a scientist could have formed that belief by applying research or performing tests that were available at the time. Proof of what could have been known will inevitably be complicated, costly, confusing and time-consuming. Each side will have to produce experts in the history of science and technology to speculate as to what knowledge was feasible in a given year. We doubt that juries will be capable of even understanding the concept of scientific knowability, much less be able to resolve such a complex issue. Moreover, we should resist legal rules that will so greatly add to the costs both sides incur in trying a case.

The concept of knowability is complicated further by the fact, noted above, that the level of investment in safety research by manufacturers is one determinant of the state-of-the-art at any given time. Fairness suggests that manufacturers not be excused from liability because their prior inadequate investment in safety rendered the hazards of their product unknowable. Thus, a judgment will have to be made as to whether defendants' investment in safety research in the years preceding distribution of the product was adequate. If not, the experts in the history of technology will have to testify as to what would have been knowable at the time of distribution if manufacturers had spent the proper amount on safety in prior years. To state the issue is to fully understand the great difficulties it would engender in a courtroom.

In addition, discussion of state-of-the-art could easily confuse juries into believing that blameworthiness is at issue. Juries might mistakenly translate the confused concept of state-of-the-art into the simple question of whether it was defendants' fault that they did not know of the hazards of asbestos. But that would be negligence, not strict liability.

For precisely this reason, Professor Keeton has urged that negligence concepts be carefully avoided in strict liability cases.

> My principal thesis is and has been that theories of negligence should be avoided altogether in the products liability area in order to simplify the law, and that if the sale of a product is made under circumstances that would subject someone to an unreasonable risk in fact, liability for harm resulting from those risks should follow. [*Keeton*, 48 Tex.L.Rev. at 409]

This Court has expressed the same concern in *Freund*, reversing the trial court's jury charge because the "terminology employed by the trial judge was riddled with references to negligence, knowledge and reasonable care on the part of a manufacturer." 87 N.J. at 243. "[W]e must be concerned with the effect of the trial judge's articulation upon the jury's deliberative processes." Id. at 244.

V

For the reasons expressed above, we conclude that plaintiffs' position is consistent with our holding in *Freund* and prior cases and will achieve the various policies underlying strict liability. The burden of illness from dangerous products such as asbestos should be placed upon those who profit from its production and, more generally, upon society at large, which reaps the benefits of the various products our economy manufactures. That burden should not be imposed exclusively on the innocent victim. Although victims must in any case suffer the pain involved, they should be spared the burdensome financial consequences of unfit products. At the same time, we believe this position will serve the salutary goals of increasing product safety research and simplifying tort trials.

Defendants have argued that it is unreasonable to impose a duty on them to warn of the unknowable. Failure to warn of a risk which one could not have known existed is not unreasonable conduct. But this argument is based on negligence principles. We are not saying what defendants should have done. That is negligence. We are saying that defendants' products were not reasonably safe because they did not have a warning. Without a warning, users of the product were unaware of its hazards and could not protect themselves from injury. We impose strict liability because it is unfair for the distributors of a defective product not to compensate its victims. As between those innocent victims and the distributors, it is the distributors – and the public which consumes their products – which should bear the unforeseen costs of the product.

The judgment of the trial court is reversed; the plaintiff's motion to strike the state-of-the-art defense is granted.

Further Reading

Aldrich, Mark. *Safety First: Technology, Labor, and Business in the Building of American Work Safety, 1870–1939*. Baltimore: Johns Hopkins University Press, 1997.

Bergstrom, Randolph. *Courting Danger: Injury and Law in New York City, 1870–1910*. New York: Columbia University Press, 1992.

Environmental History Review, 18 (Spring 1994), ed. Joel A. Tarr and Jeffrey K. Stine.

Stine, Jeffrey K., and Joel A. Tarr. "At the intersection of histories: technology and the environment." *Technology and Culture*, 39 (October 1998), 601–40.

4

Sexuality, Women, and the Social Camouflage of Technology

c.150 AD	Aretaeus Cappadox recommends digital massage.
1880s	Electromechanical vibrator introduced for office use.
1876	J. H. Kellogg takes over sanitarium at Battle Creek, Michigan.
1900–3	Electromechanical vibrator introduced for home use.
1952	American Psychological Association abandons "hysteria" as a disease paradigm.

Introduction

In this selection, Rachel Maines brings together three subjects which are too little studied in the history of technology: sexuality, women, and what she calls the "social camouflage" of technology. It is only recently that historians have looked at issues of sexuality, a subject that famously belongs to the "private sphere" of personal lives rather than the "public sphere" thought appropriate for historical inquiry. Although women, especially as producers and consumers, are beginning to be more studied by historians of technology, gender is more often used as a lens through which to view them than is sexuality. And the role of social camouflage has been little noticed and commented upon. The idea that technologies are socially "constructed" – that is, that they are deliberately shaped for social purposes – is now widely accepted, but the phenomenon of camouflage is less familiar. Not surprisingly, when this article first appeared in the journal of an engineering society, it was the subject of sexuality which caused the most alarm and controversy.

Socially Camouflaged Technologies: the Case of the Electromechanical Vibrator

Rachel Maines

Certain commodities are sold in the legal marketplace for which the expected use is either illegal or socially unacceptable. Marketing of these goods, therefore, requires camouflaging of the design purpose in a verbal and visual rhetoric that conveys to the knowledgeable consumer the item's selling points without actually endorsing its socially prohibited uses. I refer not to goods that are actually illegal in character, such as marijuana, but to their grey-market background technologies, such as cigarette rolling papers. Marketing efforts for goods of this type have similar characteristics over time, despite the dissimilarity of the advertised commodities. I shall discuss here an electromechanical technology that addresses formerly prohibited expressions of women's sexuality – the vibrator in its earliest incarnation between 1870 and 1930. Comparisons will be drawn between marketing strategies for this electromechanical technology, introduced between 1880 and 1903, and that of emmenagogues, distilling, burglary tools, and computer software copying, as well as the paradigm example of drug paraphernalia.

I shall argue here that electromechanical massage of the female genitalia achieved acceptance during the period in question by both professionals and consumers not only because it was less cumbersome, labor-intensive and costly than predecessor technologies, but because it maintained the social camouflage of sexual massage treatment through its associations with modern professional instrumentation and with prevailing beliefs about electricity as a healing agent.

The case of the electromechanical vibrator, as a technology associated with women's sexuality, involves issues of acceptability rather than legality. The vibrator and its predecessor technologies, including the dildo, are associated with masturbation, a socially prohibited activity until well into the second half of this century. Devices for mechanically-assisted female masturbation, mainly vibrators and dildoes, were marketed in the popular press from the late nineteenth century through the early thirties in similarly camouflaged advertising. Such advertisements temporarily

Excerpted from Rachel Maines, "Socially Camouflaged Technologies: the Case of the Electromechanical Vibrator," *IEEE Technology and Society Magazine*, 8, 2 (June 1989), pp. 3–11, 23. © 1989 IEEE. Reprinted with permission.

disappeared from popular literature after the vibrator began to appear in stag films, which may have rendered the camouflage inadequate, and did not resurface until social change made it unnecessary to disguise the sexual uses of the device.

For purposes of this discussion, a vibrator is a mechanical or electro-mechanical appliance imparting rapid and rhythmic pressure through a contoured working surface usually mounted at a right angle to the handle. These points of contact generally take the form of a set of interchangeable vibratodes configured to the anatomical areas they are intended to address. Vibrators are rarely employed internally in mastur-bation; they thus differ from dildoes, which are generally straight-shafted and may or may not include a vibratory component. Vibrators are here distinguished also from massagers, the working surfaces of which are flat or dished. It should be noted that this is a historian's distinction imposed on the primary sources; medical authors and appliance manufacturers apply a heterogeneous nomenclature to massage technologies. Vibrators and dildoes rarely appeared in household advertising between 1930 and 1955, massagers continued to be marketed, mainly through household magazines.

The electromechanical vibrator, introduced as a medical instrument in the 1880s and as a home appliance between 1900 and 1903, repres-ented the convergence of several older medical massage technologies, including manual, hydriatic, electrotherapeutic and mechanical methods. Internal and external gynecological massage with lubricated fingers had been a standard medical treatment for hysteria, disorders of menstruation and other female complaints at least since the time of Aretaeus Cappadox (circa 150 A.D.), and the evidence suggests that orgasmic response on the part of the patient may have been the intended therapeutic result. Douche therapy, a method of directing a jet of pumped water at the pelvic area and vulva, was employed for similar purposes after hydrotherapy became popular in the eighteenth and nine-teenth centuries. The camouflage of the apparently sexual character of such therapy was accomplished through its medical respectability and through creative definitions both of the diseases for which massage was indicated and of the effects of treatment. In the case of the electro-mechanical vibrator, the use of electrical power contributed the cachet of modernity and linked the instrument to older technologies of electro-therapeutics, in which patients received low-voltage electricity through electrodes attached directly to the skin or mucous membranes, and to light-bath therapy, in which electric light was applied to the skin in a closed cabinet. The electrotherapeutic association was explicitly invoked in the original term for the vibrator's interchangeable applicators, which were known as "vibratodes." Electrical treatments were employed in hysteria as soon as they were introduced in the eighteenth century, and remained in use as late as the 1920s.

Hysteria as a disease paradigm, from its origins in the Egyptian medical corpus through its conceptual eradication by American Psychological Association fiat in 1952, was so vaguely and subjectively defined that it might encompass almost any set of ambiguous symptoms that troubled a woman or her family. As its name suggests, hysteria as well as its "sister" complaint chlorosis were until the twentieth century thought to have their etiology in the female reproductive tract generally, and more particularly in the organism's response to sexual deprivation. This physiological condition seems to have achieved epidemic proportions among women and girls, at least in the modern period. Sydenham, writing in the seventeenth century, observed that hysteria was the most common of all diseases except fevers.[1]

In the late nineteenth century, physicians noted with alarm that from half to three-quarters of all women showed signs of hysterical affliction. Among the many symptoms listed in medical descriptions of the syndrome are anxiety, sense of heaviness in the pelvis, edema (swelling) in the lower abdomen and genital areas, wandering of attention and associated tendencies to indulge in sexual fantasy, insomnia, irritability, and "excessive" vaginal lubrication.

The therapeutic objective in such cases was to produce a "crisis" of the disease in the Hippocratic sense of this expression, corresponding to the point in infectious diseases at which the fever breaks. Manual massage of the vulva by physicians or midwives, with fragrant oils as lubricants, formed part of the standard treatment repertoire for hysteria, chlorosis and related disorders from ancient times until the post-Freudian era. The crisis induced by this procedure was usually called the "hysterical paroxysm." Treatment for hysteria might comprise up to three-quarters of a physician's practice in the nineteenth century. Doctors who employed vulvular massage treatment in hysteria thus required fast, efficient and effective means of producing the desired crisis. Portability of the technology was also a desideratum, as physicians treated many patients in their homes, and only manual massage under these conditions was possible until the introduction of the portable battery-powered vibrator for medical use in the late 1880s.

Patients reported experiencing symptomatic relief after such treatments, and such conditions as pelvic congestion and insomnia were noticeably ameliorated, especially if therapy continued on a regular basis. A few physicians, including Nathaniel Highmore in the seventeenth century and Auguste Tripier, a nineteenth century electrotherapist, clearly recognized the hysterical paroxysm as sexual orgasm.[2] That many of their colleagues also perceived the sexual character of hysteria treatments is suggested by the fact that, in the case of married women, one of the therapeutic options was intercourse, and in the case of single women, marriage was routinely recommended. "God-fearing physicians," as Zacuto expressed it in the seventeenth century, were expected to induce the paroxysm with their own fingers only when absolutely necessary, as in the case of very young single women, widows and nuns.[3]

Many later physicians, however, such as the nineteenth century hydrotherapist John Harvey Kellogg, seem not to have perceived the sexual character of patient response. Kellogg wrote extensively about hydrotherapy and electrotherapeutics in gynecology. In his "Electrotherapeutics in Chronic Maladies," published in *Modern Medicine* in 1904, he describes "strong contractions of the abdominal muscles" in a female patient undergoing treatment, and similar reactions such that "the office table was made to tremble quite violently with the movement."[4] In their analysis of the situation, these physicians may have been handicapped by their failure to recognize that penetration is a successful means of producing orgasm in only a minority of women; thus treatments that did not involve significant vaginal penetration were not morally suspect. In effect, misperceptions of female sexuality formed part of the camouflage of the original manual technique that preceded the electromechanical vibrator. Insertion of the speculum, however, since it travelled the same path as the supposedly irresistible penis during intercourse, was widely criticized in the medical community for its purportedly immoral effect on patients. That some questioned the ethics of the vulvular massage procedure is clear; Thomas Stretch Dowse quotes Graham as observing that "Massage of the pelvic organs should be intrusted to those alone who have 'clean hands and a pure heart'."[5] One physician, however, in an article significantly titled "Signs of Masturbation in the Female," proposed the application of an electrical charge to the clitoris as a test of salacious propensities in women. Sensitivity of the organ to this type of electrical stimulation, in his view, indicated secret indulgence in what was known in the nineteenth century as "a bad habit."[6] Ironically, such women were often treated electrically for hysteria supposedly caused by masturbation.

However they construed the benefits, physicians regarded the genital massage procedure, which could take as long as an hour of skilled therapeutic activity, as something of a chore, and made early attempts to mechanize it. Hydrotherapy, in the form of what was known as the "pelvic douche" (massage of the lower pelvis with a jet of pumped water), provided similar relief to the patient with reduced demands on the therapist. Doctors of the eighteenth and nineteenth centuries frequently recommended douche therapy for their women patients who could afford spa visits. This market was limited, however, as both treatment and travel were costly. A very small minority of patients and doctors could afford to install hydrotherapeutic facilities in convenient locations; both doctor and patient usually had to travel to the spa. Electrically-powered equipment, when it became available, thus had a decentralizing and cost-reducing effect on massage treatment.

In the 1860s, some spas and clinics introduced a coal-fired steam powered device invented by a Dr. George Taylor, called the "Manipulator," which massaged the lower pelvis while the patient either stood or lay on a table.[7] This too required a considerable expenditure either by the physician who purchased the equipment or by the patient who was required to travel to a spa for treatment. Thus, when the electromechanical vibrator was invented two decades later in England by Mortimer Granville and manufactured by Weiss, a ready market already existed in the medical community. Ironically, Mortimer Granville considered the use of his instrument on women, especially hysterics, a morally indefensible act, and recommended the device only for use on the male skeletal muscles.[8] Although his original battery-powered model was heavy and unreliable, it was more portable than water-powered massage and less fatiguing to the operator than manual massage.

Air-pressure models were introduced, but they required cumbersome tanks of compressed air, which needed frequent refilling. When line electricity became widely available, portable plug-in models made vibratory house calls more expeditious and cost effective for the enterprising physician. The difficulty of maintaining batteries in or out of the office was noted by several medical writers of the period predating the introduction of plug-in vibrators. Batteries and small office generators were liable to fail at crucial moments during patient treatment, and required more engineering expertise for their maintenance than most physicians cared to acquire. Portable models using dc or ac line electricity were available with a wide range of vibratodes, such as the twelve-inch rectal probe supplied with one of the Gorman firm's vibrators.

Despite its inventor's reservations, the Weiss instrument and later devices on the same principle were widely used by physicians for pelvic disorders in women and girls. The social camouflage applied to the older manual technology was carefully maintained in connection with the new, at least until the 1920s. The marketing of medical vibrators to physicians and the discussion of them in such works as Covey's *Profitable Office Specialties* addressed two important professional considerations: the respectability of the devices as medical instruments (including their reassuringly clinical appearance) and their utility in the fast and efficient treatment of those chronic disorders, such as pelvic complaints in women, that provided a significant portion of a physician's income.[9]

The importance of a prestige image for electromechanical instrumentation, and its role in the pricing of medical vibrators is illustrated by a paragraph in the advertising brochure for the "Chattanooga," at $200 in 1904 the most costly of the physicians' office models:

> The Physician can give with the "Chattanooga" Vibrator a thorough massage treatment in three minutes that is extremely pleasant and beneficial, but this instrument is neither designed nor sold as a "Massage Machine." It is sold only to Physicians, and constructed for the express purpose of exciting the various organs of the body into activity through their central nervous supply.[10]

I do not mean to suggest that gynecological treatments were the only uses of such devices, or that all physicians who purchased them used them for the production of orgasm in female patients, but the literature suggests that a substantial number were interested in the new technology's utility in the hysteroneurasthenic complaints. The interposition of an official-looking machine must have done much to restore clinical dignity to the massage procedure. The vibrator was introduced in 1899 as a home medical appliance, and was by 1904 advertised in household magazines in suggestive terms we shall examine later on. It was important for physicians to be able to justify to patients the expense of $2–3 per treatment, as home vibrators were available for about $5.

The acceptance of the electromechanical vibrator by physicians at the turn of this century may also have been influenced by their earlier adoption of electrotherapeutics, with which vibratory treatment could be, and often was, combined. Vibratory therapeutics were introduced from London and Paris, especially from the famous Hôpital Salpêtrière, which added to their respectability in the medical community. It is worth noting as well that in this period electrical and other vibrations were a subject of great interest and considerable confusion, not only among doctors and the general public, but even among scientists like Tesla, who is reported to have fallen under their spell. " . . . [T]he Earth," he wrote, "is responsive to electrical vibrations of definite pitch just as a tuning fork to certain waves of sound. These particular electrical vibrations, capable of powerfully exciting the Globe, lend themselves to innumerable uses of great importance . . . "[11] In the same category of mystical reverence for vibration is Samuel Wallian's contemporaneous essay on "The Undulatory Theory in Therapeutics," in which he describes "modalities or manifestations of vibratory impulse" as the guiding principle of the universe. "Each change and gradation is not a transformation, as mollusk into mammal, or monkey into man, but an evidence of a variation in vibratory velocity. A certain rate begets a *vermis*, another and higher rate produces a *viper*, a *vertebrate*, a *vestryman*."[12]

In 1900, according to Monell, more than a dozen medical vibratory devices for physicians had been available for examination at the Paris Exposition. Of these, few were able to compete in the long term with electromechanical models. Mary L. H. Arnold Snow, writing for a medical readership in 1904, discusses in some depth more than twenty types, of which more than half are electromechanical. These models, some priced to the medical trade as low as $15, delivered vibrations from one to 7,000 pulses a minute. Some were floor-standing machines on rollers; others could be suspended from the ceiling like the modern impact wrench.[13] The more expensive models were adapted to either ac or dc currents. A few, such as those of the British firm Schall and Son, could even be ordered with motors custom-wound to a physician's specifications. Portable and battery-powered electromechanical vibrators were generally less expensive than floor models, which both looked more imposing as instruments and were less likely to transmit fatiguing vibrations to the doctor's hands.

Patients were treated in health spa complexes, in doctors' offices or their own homes with portable equipment. Designs consonant with prevailing notions of what a medical instrument should look like inspired consumer confidence in the physician and his apparatus, justified treatment costs, and, in the case of hysteria treatments, camouflaged the sexual character of the therapy. Hand or foot-powered models, however, were tiring to the operator; water-powered ones became too expensive to operate when municipalities began metering water in the early twentieth century. Gasoline engines and batteries were cumbersome and difficult to maintain, as noted above. No fuel or air-tank handling by the user was required for line electricity, in contrast with compressed air, steam and petroleum as power sources. In the years after 1900, as line electricity became the norm in urban communities, the electromechanical vibrator emerged as the dominant technology for medical massage.

Some physicians contributed to this trend by endorsing the vibrator in works like that of Monell, who had studied vibratory massage in medical practice in the United States and Europe at the turn of this century. He praises its usefulness in female complaints:

> ...pelvic massage (in gynecology) has its brilliant advocates and they report wonderful results, but when practitioners must supply the skilled technic with their own fingers the method has no value to the majority. But special applicators (motor-driven) give practical value and office convenience to what otherwise is impractical.[14]

Other medical writers suggested combining vibratory treatment of the pelvis with hydro- and electrotherapy, a refinement made possible by the ready adaptability of the new electromechanical technology.

At the same period, mechanical and electromechanical vibrators were introduced as home medical appliances. One of the earliest was the Vibratile, a battery-operated massage device advertised in 1899. Like the vibrators sold to doctors, home appliances could be handpowered, water-driven, battery or street-current apparatus in a relatively wide range of prices from $1.50 to $28.75. This last named was the price of a Sears Roebuck model of 1918, which could be purchased as an attachment for a separate electrical motor, drawing current through a lamp socket, which also powered a fan, buffer, grinder, mixer and sewing machine. The complete set was marketed in the catalogue under the headline "Aids That Every Woman Appreciates." Vibrators were mainly marketed to women, although men were sometimes exhorted to purchase the devices as gifts for their wives, or to become door-to-door sales representatives for the manufacturer.[15]

The electromechanical vibrator was preceded in the home market by a variety of electrotherapeutic appliances which continued to be advertised through the twenties, often in the same publications as vibratory massage devices. Montgomery Ward, Sears Roebuck and the Canadian mail order department store T. Eaton and Company all sold medical batteries by direct-mail by the end of the nineteenth century. These were simply batteries with electrodes that administered a mild shock. Some, like Butler's Electro-Massage Machine, produced their own electricity with friction motors. Contemporaneous and later appliances sometimes had special features, such as Dr. H. Sanche's Oxydonor, which produced ozone in addition to the current when one electrode was placed in water. "Electric" massage rollers, combs and brushes with a supposedly permanent charge retailed at this time for prices between one and five dollars. Publications like the *Home Needlework Magazine* and *Men and Women* advertised these devices, as well as related technologies, including correspondence courses in manual massage.

Vibrators with water motors, a popular power source, as noted above, before the introduction of metered water, were advertised in such journals as *Modern Women*, which emphasized the cost savings over treatments by physicians and further emphasized the advantage of privacy offered by home treatment. Such devices were marketed through the teens in *Hearst's* and its successors, and in *Woman's Home Companion*.[16] Electromechanical vibrators were sold in the upper middle class market, in magazines typically retailing for between ten and fifteen cents an issue. As in the case of medical vibrators, models adapted to both ac and dc current were more expensive than those for use with dc only; all were fitted with screw-in plugs through the twenties.

All types of vibrators were advertised as benefiting health and beauty by stimulating the circulation and soothing the nerves. The makers of the electromechanical American vibrator, for example, recommended their product as an "...alleviating, curative and beautifying agent...It will increase deficient circulation – develop the muscles – remove wrinkles and facial blemishes, and beautify the complexion."[17] Advertisements directed to male purchasers similarly emphasized the machine's advantages for improving a woman's appearance and disposition. An ad in a 1921 issue of *Hearst's* urges the considerate husband to "Give 'her' a Star for Christmas" on the grounds that it would be "A Gift That Will *Keep* Her Young and Pretty." The same device was listed in another advertisement with several other electrical appliances, and labelled "Such Delightful Companions!"[18] A husband, these advertisements seem to suggest, who presented his wife with these progressive and apparently respectable medical aids might leave for work in the morning secure in the knowledge that his spouse's day would be pleasantly and productively invested in self-treatment. Like other electrical appliance advertising of the time, electromechanical vibrator ads emphasized the role of the device in making a woman's home a veritable Utopia of modern technology, and its utility in reducing the number of occasions, such as visiting her physician, on which she would be required to leave her domestic paradise.[19]

Advertisements for vibrators often shared magazine pages with books on sexual matters, such as Howard's popular *Sex Problems in Worry and Work* and Walling's *Sexology*, handguns, cures for alcoholism and, occasionally, even personals, from both men and women, in which matrimony was the declared objective. Sexuality is never explicit in vibrator advertising; the tone is vague but provocative, as in the Swedish Vibrator advertisement in *Modern Priscilla* of 1913, offering "a machine that gives 30,000 thrilling, invigorating, penetrating, revitalizing vibrations per minute...Irresistible desire to own it, once you feel the living pulsing touch of its rhythmic vibratory motion." Illustrations in these layouts typically include voluptuously proportioned women in various states of *déshabillé*. The White Cross vibrator, made by a Chicago firm that manufactured a variety of small electrical appliances, was also advertised in *Modern Priscilla*, where the maker assured readers that "It makes you fairly tingle with the joy of living."[20] It is worth noting that the name "White Cross" was drawn from that of an international organization devoted to what was known in the early twentieth century as "social hygiene," the discovery and eradication of masturbation and prostitution wherever they appeared. The Chicago maker of White Cross appliances, in no known way affiliated with the organization, evidently hoped to trade on the name's association with decency and moral purity.[21] A 1916 advertisement from the White Cross manufacturer in *American Magazine* nevertheless makes the closest approach to explicit sexual claims when it promises that "All the keen relish, the pleasures of youth, will throb within you." The utility of the product for female masturbation was thus consistently camouflaged.

Electromechanical vibrator advertising almost never appeared in magazines selling for less than 5 cents an issue (10 to 20 cents is the median range) or more than 25 cents. Readers of the former were unlikely to have access to electrical current; readers of the latter, including, for example, *Vanity Fair*, were more likely to respond to advertising for spas and private manual massage. While at least a dozen and probably more than twenty U.S. firms manufactured electromechanical vibrators before 1930, sales of these appliances were not reported in the electrical trade press. A listing from the February 1927 *NELA Bulletin* is typical; no massage equipment of any kind appears on an otherwise comprehensive list that includes violet-ray appliances.[22] A 1925 article in *Electrical World*, under the title "How Many Appliances Are in Use?", lists only irons, washing machines, cleaners, ranges, water heaters, percolators, toasters, waffle irons, kitchen units and ironers.[23] *Scientific American* listed in 1907 only the corn popper, chafing dish, milk warmer, shaving cup, percolator and iron in a list of domestic electrical appliances.[24] References to vibrators were extremely rare even in popular discussions of electrical appliances. The U.S. Bureau of the Census, which found 66 establishments manufacturing electro-therapeutic apparatus in 1908, does not disaggregate by instrument type either in this category or in "electrical household goods." The 1919 volume, showing the electromedical market at a figure well over $2 million, also omits detailed itemization. Vibrators appear by name in the 1949 *Census of Manufactures*, but it is unclear whether the listing for them, aggregated with statistics for curling irons and hair dryers, includes those sold as medical instruments to physicians.[25] This dearth of data renders sales tracking of the electromechanical vibrator extremely difficult. The omissions from engineering literature are worth noting, as the electromechanical vibrator was one of the first electrical appliances for personal care, partly because it was seen as a safe method of self-treatment.

The marketing strategy for the early electromechanical vibrator was similar to that employed for contemporaneous and even modern technologies for which social camouflage is considered necessary. Technologically, the devices so marketed differ from modern vibrators sold for explicitly sexual purposes only in their greater overall weight, accounted for by the use of metal housings in the former and plastic in the latter. The basic set of vibratodes is identical, as is the mechanical action. The social context of the machine, however, has undergone profound change. Liberalized attitudes toward masturbation in both sexes and increasing understanding of women's sexuality have made social camouflage superfluous.

In the case of the vibrator, the issue is one of acceptability, but there are many examples of similarly marketed technology of which the expected use was actually illegal. One of these, which shares with the vibrator a focus on women's sexuality, was that of "emmenagogues" or abortifacient drugs sold through the mail and sometimes even off the shelf in the first few decades of this century. Emmenagogues, called in pre-FDA advertising copy "cycle restorers," were intended to bring on the menses in women who were "late." Induced abortion by any means was of course illegal, but late menses are not reliable indicators of pregnancy. Thus, women who purchased and took "cycle restorers" might or might not be in violation of antiabortion laws; they themselves might not be certain without a medical examination. The advertising of these commodities makes free use of this ambiguity in texts like the following from *Good Stories* of 1933:

> Late? End Delay – Worry. American Periodic Relief Compound double strength tablets combine Safety with Quick Action. Relieve most Stubborn cases. No Pain. New discovery. Easily taken. Solves women's most perplexing problem. RELIEVES WHEN ALL OTHERS FAIL. Don't be discouraged, end worry at once. Send $1.00 for Standard size package and full directions. Mailed same day, special delivery in plain wrapper. American Periodic Relief Compound Tablets, extra strength for stubborn cases, $2.00. Generous Size Package. New Book free.[26]

The rhetoric here does not mention the possibility of pregnancy, but the product's selling points would clearly suggest this to the informed consumer through the mentions of safety, absence of pain, and stubborn cases. The readers of the pulp tabloid *Good Stories* clearly did not require an explanation of "women's most perplexing problem."

Distilling technology raises similar issues of legality. During the Prohibition period, the classified section of a 1920 *Ainslee's* sold one and four gallon copper stills by mail, advising the customer that the apparatus was "Ideal for distilling water for drinking purposes, automobile batteries and industrial uses."[27] Modern advertisements for distilling equipment contain similar camouflage rhetoric, directing attention away from the likelihood that most consumers intend to employ the device in the production of beverages considerably stronger than water.

Although changes in sexual mores have liberated the vibrator, social camouflage remains necessary for stills and many other modern commodities, including drug paraphernalia. The Deering Prep Kit, for example, is advertised at nearly $50 as a superlative device for grinding and preparing fine powders, "such as vitamin pills or spices."[28] Burglary tools are marketed in some popular (if lowbrow) magazines with the admonition that they are to be used only to break into one's own home or automobile, in the event of having locked oneself out. The camouflage rhetoric seems to suggest that all prudent drivers and homeowners carry such tools on their persons at all times. Most recently, we have seen the appearance of computer software for breaking copy protection, advertised in terms that explicitly prohibit its use for piracy, although surely no software publisher is so naive as to believe that all purchasers intend to break copy protection only to make backup copies of legitimately purchased programs and data.[29] As in vibrator advertising, the product's advantages are revealed to knowledgeable consumers in language that disclaims the manufacturers' responsibility for illegal or immoral uses of the product.

The marketing of socially camouflaged technologies is directed to consumers who already understand the design purpose of the product, but whose legally and/or culturally unacceptable intentions in purchasing it cannot be formally recognized by the seller. The marketing rhetoric must extoll the product's advantages for achieving the purchaser's goals – in the case of the vibrator, the production of orgasm – by indirection and innuendo, particularly with reference to the overall results, i.e., relaxation and relief from tension. The same pattern emerges in the advertisement of emmenagogues: according to the manufacturer, it is "Worry and Delay" that are ended, not pregnancy. In the case of software copyright protection programs, drug paraphernalia and distilling equipment, the expected input and/or output are simply misrepresented, so that an expensive finely-calibrated scale with its own fitted carrying case may be pictured in use in the weighing of jelly beans. As social values and legal restrictions shift, the social camouflaging of technologies may be expected to change in response, or to be dispensed with altogether, as in the case of the vibrator.

Notes

1 Sydenham, Thomas, "Epistolatory Dissertation on Hysteria," in *The Works of Thomas Sydenham*, transl. by R. G. Latham. London: Printed

for the Sydenham Society, 1848, vol. 2, pp. 56 and 85; and Payne, Joseph Frank, *Thomas Sydenham*. New York: Longmans, Green and Co., 1900, p. 143.

2 Gall, Franz Josef, *Anatomie et Physiologie du Systeme Nerveux en Général*. Paris: F. Schoell, 1810–1819, vol. 3, p. 86; Tripier, Auguste Elisabeth Philogene, *Leçons Cliniques sur les Maladies de Femmes*. Paris: Octave Doin, Editeur, 1883, pp. 347–351; Highmore, Nathaniel, *De Passione Hysterica et Affectione Hypochondiaca*. Oxford: Excudebat A. Lichfield impensis R. Davis, 1660, pp. 20–35; and Ellis, *Studies in the Psychology of Sex*, vol. 1, p. 225; see also Briquet, Pierre, *Traite Clinique et Thérapeutique de l'Hystérie*. Paris: J. B. Baillière et Fils, 1859, pp. 137–138, 570 and 613.

3 Zacuto, Abraham. *Praxis Medica Admiranda*. London: Apud Ioannem-Antonium Huguetan, 1637, p. 267.

4 October–November, p. 4. Kellogg's background is described in detail in Schwarz, Richard W., *John Harvey Kellogg, MD*. Nashvill: Southern Publishing Association, *c*.1970.

5 Dowse, Thomas Stretch, *Lectures on Massage and Electricity in the Treatment of Disease*. Bristol: John Wright and Co., 1903, p. 181.

6 Smith, E. H., in *Pacific Medical Journal*, February 1903.

7 Taylor wrote indefatigably on the subject of physical therapies for pelvic disorders, and devoted considerable effort to the invention of mechanisms for this purpose. See Taylor, George Henry, *Diseases of Women*. Philadelphia and New York: G. McClean, 1871; *Health for Women*. New York: John B. Alden, 1883 and eleven subsequent editions; "Improvements in Medical Rubbing Apparatus," US Patent 175,202 dated March 21, 1876; *Mechanical Aids in the Treatment of Chronic Forms of Disease*. New York: Rodgers, 1893; *Pelvic and Hernial Therapeutics*. New York: J. B. Alden, 1885; and "Movement Cure," US Patent 263,625, dated August 29, 1882.

8 Mortimer Granville, Joseph, *Nerve-Vibration and Excitation as Agents in the Treatment of Functional Disorders and Organic Disease*. London: J. & A. Churchill, 1883, p. 57.

9 Covey, Alfred Dale, *Profitable Office Specialities*. Detroit: Physicians Supply Co., 1912, pp. 16, 18, and 79–85.

10 Vibrator Instrument Company, *Chattanooga Vibrator*. Chattanooga, TN: Vibratot Instrument, 1904, pp. 3 and 26.

11 O'Neill, John J., *Prodigal Genius: The Life of Nikola Tesla*. New York: Ives Washburn, Inc., 1944, p. 210.

12 *Medical Brief*, May 1905, p. 417. See also the theory of light vibrations employed in the Master Electric Company's advertising brochure *The Master Violet ray*. Chicago: n.d.

13 Monell, Samuel Howard, *A System of Instruction in X-Ray Methods and Medical Uses of Light, Hot Air, Vibration and High Frequency Currents*. New York: E. R. Pelton, 1902.

14 Monell, *A System of Instruction...*, p. 591.

15   See for example, "Wanted, Agents and Salesman..." Swedish Vibrator
     Company, *Modern Priscilla*, April 1913, p. 60.

16   "Agents! Drop Dead Ones!" Blackstone Water Power Vacuum Massage
     Machine, *Hearst's*, April 1916, p. 327; and "Hydro-Massage"
     Warner Motor Company, *Modern Women*, vol. 11, no. 1, December 1906,
     p. 190.

17   "Massage Is as Old as the Hills...," American Vibrator Company,
     Woman's Home Companion, April 1906, p. 42.

18   "Such Delightful Companions!" Star Electrical Necessities, 1922,
     reproduced in Jones, Edgar R., *Those Were the Good Old Days*. New York:
     Fireside Books, 1959, unpaged; and "A Gift that Will Keep Her Young and
     Pretty," Star Home Electric Massage, *Hearst's International*, December
     1921, p. 82.

19   See for example, the Ediswan advertisement in *Electrical Age for Women*,
     January 1932, vol. 2, no. 7, p. 274, and review on page 275 of the same
     publication.

20   "Vibration Is Life," Lindstrom-Smith Co., *Modern Priscilla*, December
     1910, p. 27.

21   Pivar, David J. *Purity Crusade: Sexual Morality and Social Conscience, 1868–
     1900*. Westport, CT: Greenwood Press, 1973, pp. 110–117.

22   Davidson, J. E., "Electrical Appliance Sales During 1926," *NELA Bulletin*,
     vol. 14, no. 2, pp. 119–120.

23   December 5, 1925, vol. 86, p. 1164. See also Hughes, George A., "How the
     Domestic Electrical Appliances Are Serving the Country," *Electrical Review*,
     June 15, 1918, vol. 72, p. 983; Edkins, E. A., "Prevalent Trends of Domes-
     tic Appliance Market," *Electrical World*, March 30, 1918, pp. 670–671; and
     "Surveys Retail Sale of Electrical Appliances," *Printer's Ink*, vol. 159, May
     19, 1932, p. 35.

24   "Electrical Devices for the Household," *Scientific American*, January 26,
     1907, vol. 96, p. 95.

25   US Bureau of the Census, *Census of Manufactures*, 1908, 1919, and 1947,
     pp. 216–217, 203, and 734 and 748 respectively.

26   *Good Stories*, October 1933, p. 2; see also similar advertisement in the same
     issue for Dr Roger's Relief Compound, p. 12.

27   "Water Stills," *Ainslee's Magazine*, October 1920, p. 164.

28   *Mellow Mail Catalogue*. Cooper Station, New York City: 1984, pp.
     32–39.

29   Levy, Steven, *Hackers: Heroes of the Computer Revolution*. Garden City, NY:
     Anchor Press/Doubleday, 1984, p. 377.

Documents

Improvement in Medical Rubbing Apparatus

George H. Taylor

To all whom it may concern:

Be it known that I, GEORGE H. TAYLOR, of New York, in the county and State of New York, have invented an Improved Medical Rubbing Apparatus; and I do hereby declare that the following is a full, clear, and exact description of the same, reference being had to the accompanying drawing, forming part of this specification.

The object of my invention is to produce effects on different parts of the human body similar to those produced by rubbing with the hands, and to afford facility to the patient for directing and controlling the rubbing operation; and it consists in a novel combination of reciprocating rubbers, an adjustable seat, a treadle or lever, and connecting devices, whereby the pressure of the rubbers may be controlled at the pleasure of the patient.

In the accompanying drawing, Figure 1 is a side view of my improved apparatus. Fig. 2 is a top view of the same.

A represents a base or platform, in which rests the lower end of a standard, B, at the upper end of which is pivoted the inner ends of two arms, C C, which are provided with springs $d\,d$ having a tendency to keep them pressed outward from each other. The outer end of each of the arms C terminates in two lugs, $c\,c$, between which is journaled a friction-roller, f.

On the rear side of the standard B is a vertical shaft, E, the ends of which work in suitable bearings provided for the purpose. At the upper end of this shaft is attached, midway of its length, a horizontal arm, G, to the ends of which are pivoted the rear ends of the rubbers, which consist of strips or bars H, the inner sides of which, near the front ends, are covered with rubber, leather, fibrous fabric, or other suitable material, h, attached in any suitable manner. The rear portions of the bars H pass

Taken from George H. Taylor's "Improvement in Medical Rubbing Apparatus," Specification forming part of Letters Patent No. 175,202, dated March 21, 1876; application filed May 17, 1875. United States Patent Office.

between the lugs *c* and the rollers *f*, the rollers bearing on the outer sides of the bars.

Near the outer ends of the arm C are attached the upper ends of two straps, cords, or bands *i*, which pass over pulleys *l*, journaled in a frame, *k*, attached to the upper end of the standard B, and have their lower ends attached to a treadle or lever, M, the rear end of which is hinged or pivoted to the base or platform A.

The vertical shaft E is provided with a projecting arm or crank, *e*, to which power may be applied in any suitable manner to rock the shaft E and oscillate the arm G, so as to give a reciprocating motion to the rubbers H.

The seat P for the patient is attached by pivots to the front ends of two arms, R R, the rear ends of which are pivoted to the standard. Said seat is also pivoted to the front ends of two levers, S S, which have their fulcra on the standard B, by which means the seat is adjusted to different heights, and always remains in a horizontal position, the arms R and lever S being parallel with each other.

The rear ends of the levers are united, so as to operate as one lever, and may be provided with a seat, V, for the attendant. The seat P is held in place, at different heights, by means of a pawl, *t*, on the lever S, and a ratchet, *r*, on the standard B, engaging with each other, as shown in Fig. 1.

The patient sits on the seat P when at its lowest position, and by means of the feet on the treadle or lever M regulates the pressure of the rubbers H H, which are then set in motion by the attendant by any suitable means. The upper part of the body is rubbed first, and then the seat is gradually raised, either by the feet of the patient pressing against the floor, or by the attendant pressing down the rear end of the lever S, by which means the lower parts of the body are brought in contact with the rubbers.

I do not claim, in this application, the rising and falling seat, or the reciprocating rubbers, either separately or in combination.

What I claim as new herein, and desire to secure by Letters Patent, is –

The combination, with the seat P and rubbers H H, of the treadle or lever M, straps or bands *i i*, and arms C C, substantially as and for the purpose herein described.

GEO. H. TAYLOR.

Witnesses:
BENJAMIN W. HOFFMAN,
F. HAYNES.

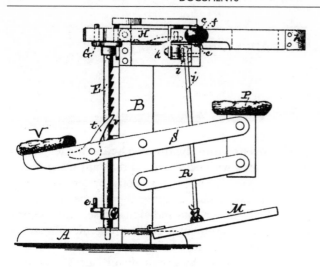

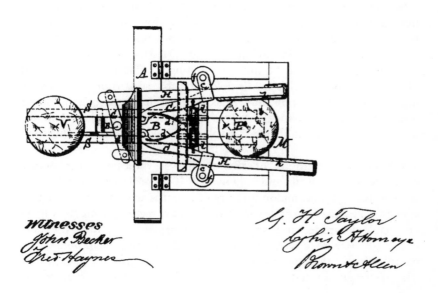

Witnesses
John Becker
Fred Haynes

G. H. Taylor
by his Attorneys
Brown & Allen

Mechanical Vibration and Its Therapeutic Application

M. L. H. Arnold Snow

Pelvic disorders, amenorrhea and dysmenorrhea in the female are probably more often associated with neurasthenia than any other condition. The treatment of pelvic derangements, constipation and other associated conditions will be considered under their respective heads. The length of time necessary to treat an individual case, and the prognosis will depend upon the chronicity, whether organic disease be present, and on how amenable the cause is to treatment.

Neurasthenia may also be caused by gastric disturbances as chronic gastritis, and gastroptosis, or by derangements and displacements of other abdominal viscera.

Sexual neurasthenia, impotency and **prostatitis** may also be treated by vibration either alone or in connection with static electricity. For the treatment of which employ the rectal vibratode for five minutes or so, using the minimum stroke and a fairly rapid speed, taking care that the treatment be not too prolonged. The best vibratode, in the writer's opinion, is a flexible one of soft rubber about six inches long. The application has a soothing effect and is not disagreeable to the patient. As yet little has been published in this line of treatment, but it offers a splendid field for rational investigation. . . .

Vibratory treatment of the vagina is indicated in rectocele, cystocele, relaxed walls and vaginismus. If there be general relaxation or prolapsus lift the abdominal organs, uterus and bowels, and then vibrate the vagina either per vagina or from the rectum, using the vaginal or rectal vibratode, and apply interrupted vibration over the perineum to increase circulatory activity and produce dilatation of the blood vessels, thereby imparting warmth and promoting nutrition. The treatment should not be continued for more than four or five minutes.

The application of spinal treatment over the sacrum will vary with indications and must be left to the discretion of the operator. The perineal treatments may be supplemented by stretching the tissue out-

Excerpted from M. L. H. Arnold Snow, *Mechanical Vibration and Its Therapeutic Application* (New York: The Scientific Authors' Publishing Co., 1904), pp. 192–3, 237, 238–9.

ward "from the median line" with the thumbs, "the fingers resting upon the buttocks. " ...

For the treatment of the *coccyx* introduce the rectal vibratode into the rectum a short distance, the left hand being placed over the coccyx, the patient lying on her right side with knees drawn up. Use compressing interrupted vibration if the coccyx is bent inward, great care being taken to avoid causing pain. If the parts are sensitive very light pressure if any should be used at first and pressure should be gradually increased.

Vibratory treatment of the rectum with the rectal vibratode for five minutes, employing the shortest stroke, will tone up the parts and relax spasm of the sphincters. Spinal stimulation may or may not be necessary. In the treatment of *hemorrhoids* vibration lessens pelvic congestion, and stimulates the venous circulation. Apply a prolonged rectal treatment for inhibition. In the treatment of pelvic conditions vibration can be employed to advantage in connection with electricity, hydrotherapy, or exercise according to indications.

A Brief Guide to Vibratory Technique

Noble M. Eberhart

Vibrators

It is not the purpose of this condensed guide to give any extended description of the many instruments on the market.

It is desirable, however, to consider briefly the various points which go to make up a good vibrator.

It must have sufficient power; be capable of delivering an even stroke, both deep and penetrating, as well as medium or light; be capable of quick adjustment from the light to the heavy stroke and from one kind of stroke to another; be capable of giving a rotating or lateral stroke, as well as an up and down stroke. It should give little or no vibration to the operator's hand, and be easily brought to bear upon various parts of the body, without any cumbersome mechanism.

Excerpted from Noble M. Eberhart, *A Brief Guide to Vibratory Technique* (Chicago: New Medicine Publishing Co., *c.*1910), pp. 41–6, 58, 95–6, 108–10, 122–3, 147–8.

Again, it should be capable of giving a considerable range of speed in the number of vibrations.

There are three principal types now in use: the rigid arm vibrator, the flexible shaft vibrator, and the portable vibrator.

There has been much controversy between the advocates of different makes of vibrators, and frequently it is claimed that certain machines do not have sufficient power for the purposes demanded of them.

This is a matter that depends largely upon what is understood by sufficient power.

It is apparent that for many conditions only a moderate amount of power is demanded or may be tolerated; hence in these cases nearly all machines will answer the purpose.

In the case of deep spinal stimulation, the result is more quickly obtained by a heavy machine, and lighter vibrators require a relatively longer application to accomplish the same result; but when this end is finally reached there can be but little choice.

It is equally obvious that the weight or pressure increases rapidity of action, although the length of stroke remains the same.

The friends of the larger machines claim that the smaller ones have insufficient penetrating power and the advocates of the latter claim that some of the larger machines have too much power and may have harmful by-effects.

I must repeat that it is merely a question of having force enough, beyond which the power is wasted.

Only a certain degree is necessary or can be tolerated by the tissues.

One might illustrate this by comparing the vibrators to various-sized hammers. If one wished to drive a small nail, he could do so with either a sledge hammer, an ordinary hammer or a tack hammer.

The sledge hammer would drive it at one blow, but there would be much superfluous power; the ordinary hammer would drive it in four or five strokes; and the tack hammer would possibly require a dozen blows. However, the final result would be the driving of the nail.

More importance in the selection of a vibrator will naturally be attached to the character of stroke; convenience of adjustment, speed, etc.

Whatever the type of machine used, the general results have been very gratifying, as evidenced by the multitude of clinical reports by operators all over the country. Naturally, the better the instrument and the more it is adapted to the character of work required of it and also the greater the knowledge of the operator, the more successful must be the results. A good operator will obtain results with a comparatively poor machine; he will obtain much better results with a first-class machine.

Applicators

A number of different styles of applicators are on the market. The applicator is the part of the vibrator which transmits the vibration directly to the body and it is commonly known as the vibratode. Some of the principal forms are shown in Plate III. . . .

Rhythm and Pitch

Attention has been called to the necessity of a vibrator giving even strokes with a wide range of speed.

An even, regularly recurring stroke causes each subsequent one to accentuate the former and gradually increases the strength and penetration of the vibratory wave, as well as developing a rhythm that facilitates cellular processes. Eventually it will probably be found that each organ has its proper vibrating pitch and can be reached and influenced by rhythmic vibrations of that pitch, whether mechanical, electrical, thermal or light vibrations.

Dysmenorrhea

In cases where the pain occurs during the commencement of the flow, being of a cramping nature and disappearing when the menses are well established, I have ordinarily found that vibration with rotary or percussion stroke, medium or rapid speed and fairly deep pressure directly over the painful areas; would give relief in five to eight minutes.

The vibrator is held steadily over a painful spot for two or three minutes or even longer.

Inhibitive vibration to the third, fourth and fifth lumbar centers is indicated where the regional vibration is insufficient.

In treating a case where dysmenorrhea regularly occurs, the treatment between menstrual periods should be applied from the tenth dorsal down to the coccyx, giving inhibitory treatment over the sensitive areas which will be found.

For a few days before menstruation is expected, daily treatments should be given, or, if possible, twice a day.

Intra-vaginal treatment with special applicator may be indicated between periods. Common sense will tell the physician not to expect success in dysmenorrhea where mechanical obstruction occurs.

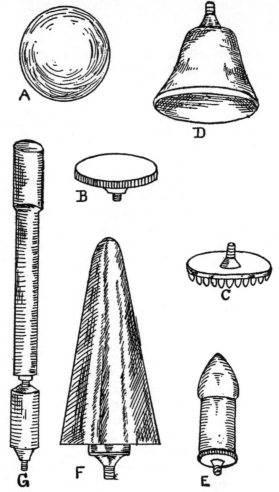

PLATE III. Applicators. A. Ball. B. Flat disk. C. Brush. D. Vacuum cup. E. and F. Rectal applicators. .G. Prostatic vibratode.

Associated troubles, such as constipation, neurasthenia and pelvic disorders, when present, must also receive attention.

Hysteria

In hysteria vibration is simply an adjunct to other measures.

(1) General spinal treatment with ball applicator and deep pressure; regulating the length of treatment as required.

(2) Lateral or gyrating stroke with rubber brush over anesthetic areas.

High frequency and static electricity are useful.

Impotency

There is a mass of clinical evidence to indicate that a reasonable percentage of cases of functional impotency have been cured by vibration.

The technique which I have found most satisfactory is:

(1) Deep vibration to spinal centers from tenth dorsal to the coccyx; with ball vibratode and long stroke; medium speed; six or eight seconds or more as required over each center.

(2) Short gyrating or side-to-side stroke with soft rubber brush to inguinal region; to base and dorsal surface of penis; and to perineum.

Treat daily at first, then every other day.

Vibration is, of course, useless in impotency arising from locomotor ataxia or other constitutional diseases, its sphere being limited to functional cases.

Improvement has occasionally manifested itself in locomotor ataxia where the vibratory stimulation has caused improvement in the tabes itself.

Intra-rectal massage to the prostate, with short gyrating stroke, as described under diseases of the prostate, is often useful; also the sinusoidal or the high frequency current in connection with vibration.

Metrorrhagia and Menorrhagia

To lessen the excessive flow during the menstrual period, give inhibitive treatment, with ball applicator; medium stroke and pressure; over eighth to twelfth dorsal and all of lumbar and sacral centers.

Treatments between periods should be in the nature of a general, but mild spinal stimulation, with attention to any accompanying symptoms.

The judicious use of the author's special uterine vibratode will be found of great value, especially where sub-involution or enlarged cervix exists, or where there is general atony of the parts.

Use rotary or lateral stroke with this applicator. The vaginal vibratode to reach the hypogastric plexus on the anterior aspect of the sacrum and the ganglion impar in front of the coccyx is sometimes indicated.

Deep vibration over the uterus itself, through the abdominal wall, is another efficacious method, when sub-involution is present.

Uterine Diseases

In diseases of the uterus, vagina and ovaries vibration is given to the third, fourth and fifth lumbar centers. "Stimulation of these nerve centers causes vaso-constriction and muscular contractions also." (Schafer.)

Inhibitory treatment would have the opposite effect.

Practically, however, it is usually found desirable in diseases of these organs to vibrate from about the tenth dorsal down to the coccyx.

In addition to spinal vibration, local treatment over the lower part of the abdomen with rotary or percussion stroke and as deep pressure as can be tolerated, ordinarily will be indicated.

Finally, intra-vaginal treatment with the special vaginal applicator, or with author's uterine applicator, and short or medium rotary stroke, lasting one and one-half to three minutes, may be required.

A physician who condemned the vaginal applicator severely at first, reported recently a cure of a case of retro-flexion with adhesions and now considers this one of the most valuable applicators in the list.

Intra-vaginal treatment is also indicated in vaginismus; relaxed walls; cystocele; and rectocele.

Profitable Office Specialties

A. Dale Covey

Office Equipment

Modern inventive genius has made great advancements within the last few years, and today the physician can install scientific appliances, and apparatus at almost any price that will fit his purse.... Physicians can also make as large a display with their apparatus as they desire, or have it condensed in as small a space as they wish. This is exemplified by one of

---

Excerpted from A. Dale Covey, *Profitable Office Specialties* (Detroit: Physicians Supply Co., *c.*1912), pp. 14–17, 79.

the latest creations, which is known as the Siebert–Welch apparatus. This wonderful little piece of condensed mechanism only occupies a space fifteen inches square by forty-five inches high, and weighs not to exceed one hundred pounds; yet within its walls are contained a complete atomizing and nebulizing outfit, hot air douch, vacuum apparatus for conducting Bier's hyperemic treatment, tankless compressed air, complete vibratory massage outfit, superheated air and vacuum combined. Galvanic electricity and a combination of vibration, dilation, contraction and massage are possible of administration at one time, known as the Intro-gymnastic treatment. This equipment may not be as attractive as the different instruments stretched along the walls where they will make a better display, but such an apparatus will be exceedingly convenient for the physician with small office space. . . .

Vibrotherapy

Physicians, as a rule, never take very kindly to the manual methods of massage, which are outlined in the foregoing chapters. One possible reason may be that it involves too much labor, but when some mechanical genius invented the Vibrator about twelve years ago, it was immediately recognized by the medical profession, and received as hearty welcome from the physicians as the sulky plow did from the farmer: "It's the easy way."

One of the most important things to be considered in adopting Vibratory therapeutics in office practice is the selection of a vibrator. There are many types, with varying degrees of efficiency. Therefore, in selecting a vibrator the following points should be considered: The instrument should have sufficient motive power to deliver long, penetrating strokes, as well as medium and light ones, in order to receive the degree of stimulation or inhibition desired; it should also be capable of changing from a heavy to a light stroke, and vice versa, without any delay. It should have a well localized stroke and also a rotary and lateral stroke, for treating cavities.

A well constructed vibrator should never give any vibration to the operator's hand; by observing these points we really have a scientific instrument with which excellent results can be obtained.

Enjoy Life!

Enjoy Life!

Get *all you can* out of it.
Live every minute. **Vibration is life.** It is the very
foundation of all existence.
It will give you the power
to *see clearly—think keenly—act quickly.* It will fill
you full of the **real joy of
living.**

Rests, Strengthens, Renews, Repairs

Every vital organ is *crammed full
of vitality.* The clogging waste is
swept away by the coursing blood
which this marvelous force sets leaping through every vein and artery
with the virile strength of perfect health.
You sleep as restfully **as you used
to.** You awaken, *refreshed* mentally—physically—*strong in mind and
body* and **glad to be alive.**

A 60 Day Special Offer

For a *limited time* we are making
a remarkable Special Offer on the famous
White Cross Electric Vibrator. The
wonders of **Vibration**—the same treatments for which specialists charge huge
fees. It also gives Faradic and Galvanic
Electricity, Swedish Movements, etc.—
**All within your reach if you act at
once.**

FREE Handsomely Illustrated Book
on "Health and
Beauty" tells you
**FREE
BOOK
COUPON** just what you want to know—
tells you fully, clearly, just
what vibration is, how it
acts, and what it will do
for you. Get posted
LINDSTROM, SMITH CO. now—right away. Your
name and address on
Desk 1051 coupon or on a postal
or letter is all—send
218 S. Wabash Ave., Chicago now.

Gentlemen: Please send
me free and without obligation on my part, copy of
your Free Book on "Health
and Beauty" and full explanation of Special Limited
Offer on the WHITE CROSS
ELECTRIC VIBRATOR.

**LINDSTROM,
SMITH CO.**

Desk 1051

218 S.
Name............................. **Wabash Ave.**

Chicago

Advertisement for White Cross Vibrator by Lindstrom,
Smith Co., Chicago, in *The American Magazine*, no. 75,
January 1913, p. 118.

Further Reading

Hynes, H. Patricia, ed. *Reconstructing Babylon: Essays on Women and Technology.* Bloomington: Indiana University Press, 1991.

Maines, Rachel P. *The Technology of Orgasm: "Hysteria," the Vibrator, and Women's Sexual Satisfaction.* Baltimore: Johns Hopkins University Press, 1999.

Reiser, Stanley Joel. *Medicine and the Reign of Technology.* Cambridge: Cambridge University Press, 1978.

Rothman, Barbara Katz. *Recreating Motherhood: Ideology and Technology in a Patriarchal Society.* New York: W. W. Norton & Co., 1989.

5

The Culture of Engineers

1880	Establishment of the American Society of Mechanical Engineers.
1928	Herbert Hoover, a prominent mining engineer, elected President of the USA.
1929	Stock market crashed on October 24 and 29.
1929	Eugene O'Neill writes the play Dynamo.
1930	Engineers Club of St Louis stages "Every Engineer: An Immorality Play."

Introduction

Along with inventors, engineers have claimed special attention from historians of technology. Together both these groups, which became large bodies of self-conscious social actors with the coming of the Industrial Revolution, are assumed to have designed the technological world within which we live. Most of these studies, not surprisingly, focus on the way elite engineers are educated, how they organize professionally, and how they go about their work of design and management. We know relatively little about them, however, as cultural figures – that is, about what meanings they drew from their lives. The decades between the wars are a particularly rewarding time to look for these meanings because engineers, like others, organized plays and pageants in which they were able, though a cast of allegorical figures, to give expression to some of their hopes and fears about themselves and their futures. Sinclair examines one such entertainment put on by the engineers of St Louis in 1930.

Local History and National Culture: Notions on Engineering Professionalism in America

Bruce Sinclair

On the face of it, we know more about the engineering profession than practically any other large topic in the history of American technology. There are eight historical monographs explicitly concerned with the subject, half a dozen relevant biographies, and at least as many books that deal with the profession indirectly. So it might seem fanciful to argue that we lack important details or that major questions remain to be addressed.

Yet those are just the claims I want to make. After a quarter-century of historical attention, we still know very little of the vast majority of American engineers. The actual case is that this extensive literature tells us mostly about the profession's central characters and the organizations those kinds of men established and perpetuated. The rank and file of any large group are always harder to apprehend than its leading figures, but in this well-studied profession the discrepancy is especially glaring. Nor do we know much of anything about what other Americans thought of these engineers. We claim that they symbolize technology, or reflect America's commitment to it, or in some other way provide insight into big issues like that. But, in fact, none of us has more than a slight grasp on the way the work and lives of engineers might illuminate the study of American culture.

Think about the paradoxes. More American men follow engineering than any other profession. Yet the vast majority – 75–80 percent – of those identified with the principal branches of the field do not belong to their national societies and do not participate in the activities of those organizations. That was true in the past, and it is still so. Furthermore, those organizations – which ostensibly exist to serve their members – not only have no historical records of their memberships, they know surprisingly little about those who currently belong and nothing at all about the great numbers of engineers who might logically join.

If this state of affairs conjures up a mental picture of one of those buildings of the Old West, where there is more in front than there is

---

Taken from Bruce Sinclair, "Local History and National Culture: Notions on Engineering Professionalism in America," *Technology and Culture*, 27 (1986), pp. 683–93. © 1986 The Society for the History of Technology. All rights reserved.

behind, the difference between the claims engineers make for themselves and the way they appear to others is equally anomalous. Ever since John Alexander Law Waddell started telling engineering students to clean their fingernails and comb their hair, it has been easy to caricature the profession. Herbert Hoover's biographer said of the Great Engineer, for example, that he had all the emotions of "a slide rule."[1] Or, as the editor of *Toronto Life* recently described the grammar and punctuation programs of his word processor, "they seem to have been designed by engineers, not writers; they force your prose into a stuffy and predictable style."[2] Instead of the portrait of a profession, what we have is a grab bag of stereotypical images and they picture a group that seems politically inflexible, socially awkward, culturally limited, and ethically inert.

In the late 1890s, the civil engineer George R. Morison argued that the coming potential for generating unlimited amounts of electrical energy would inaugurate a revolutionary stage in human development, unlike anything that had gone before, and that engineers would be the "priests of the new epoch."[3] Why, then, didn't Theodore Dreiser or Frank Norris or Sinclair Lewis write a novel about these powerful characters in the American drama? How is it that Eugene O'Neill's 1929 play, *Dynamo*, which so caught the spirit of that great transformation Morison had in mind, mentions engineers only to dismiss them as irrelevant? If technology really stands at the center of the American experience, if its history tells us something both novel and essential about the country's past, as Brooke Hindle has said, why are engineers so invisible in American culture?[4] Is it because, after all, they are not synonymous with technology? Or is it that, in any event, elevated literature is the wrong place to look for them? And if existing historical scholarship does not answer these kinds of questions, what sort of an approach would?

Population biologists struggle with the problem that, in groups large enough to be statistically significant, individual complexities are lost, while aggregations small enough to make individuals significant become numerically irrelevant. Our difficulties with the existing literature are analogous. Edwin Layton and David Noble deal with essentially the same group of people, and, by making national engineering societies and corporate industry the principal settings for their stories, each implies a scale of historical action grand enough to describe important truths. However, they characterize this group in two quite different ways. Those engineers who for Layton are riven by ambivalence – pulled in opposite directions by science and business and consequently unable to realize either their professional aspirations or their economic ambitions – are for Noble a powerful and cohesive group, quick to identify their interests and to plot strategies that gain them their objectives. So it is apparently difficult simply to characterize the profession's leadership and the effect of occupational circumstance. But even if we could, we would still be talking about a small fraction of the total population and one in most respects unrepresentative. Nor does either analysis reflect that more individualistic, solitary, creative, and aesthetically satisfying side of engineering that Eugene Ferguson and Brooke Hindle talk about and that is presumably an important element of the engineer's self-image as well as of his work. Thus – and to overstate the case for the sake of argument – the existing literature not only fails the test of statistical validity; it yields an insufficient amount of information about individual variety.

There is another, more promising, avenue of attack open to us. I think the vital core of the profession might best be discovered at the level of local engineering associations. The membership, activities, and orientation of these groups are more representative of the profession than are the national societies. And it also strikes me that a study of them will most probably lead to a synthesis of our knowledge of this subject as well as to its integration into main themes of American culture. It may seem unpromising to seek in parochial associations the national dimensions of engineering professionalism, but there is where we will find most of the country's engineers, and there is where we are also more likely to get an enriched sense of their lives.

It is not, of course, that the concerns of national society leaders are irrelevant to the rank and file or that there is not an overlap in their interests, but rather that, besides the congruences, there are differences. For example, it has been clearly shown that the officers of national organizations are more conservative in their economic and social views than the membership. Conversely, city engineering societies in places like Cleveland, St Louis, and Boston, institutions more likely to enroll those men who were not members of a national organization, were leading elements in the profession's reform movement of the early 20th century. The discourse in these local clubs is less self-conscious, too, and more likely to suggest what people feel as well as what they think.

There is to hand a neat case study to support the proposition. In 1930, when the American Society of Mechanical Engineers wanted to mark its fiftieth anniversary (and also to combat those critics of mechanization who blamed it for causing unemployment and dehumanized working conditions), the New York officers and staff planned an elaborate, week-long celebration carefully designed to publicize the claim that engineering was the basis of modern civilization. The festivities featured a gathering of prominent engineers from all over the world, a special banquet addressed by the president of the United States, and a unique theatrical production entitled *Control* that aimed to dramatize the connection between engineering and human progress.[5] Besides the novel use of light, sound, and motion pictures, that pageant employed a cast of allegorical characters – Curiosity, Intelligence, and Beauty, among others – to illustrate engineering's professional and intellectual development. The proofs of that maturation, according to the pageant, were the readiness of engineers to assume a leading role in the solution of the world's economic and social problems and the ability of engineering to provide consumers with aesthetic satisfaction as well as material abundance.

Now, it happens that in 1930 the Engineer's Club of St Louis also staged a play about the profession. Topical, funny, irreverent, and sardonic, it conveys a very different message than the pageant organized by ASME's elite, and thus we have the ingredients for an unusual comparison. Peter Gay, in his *Education of the Senses*, reminds us of Freud's argument that "institutions, whether of society or of the mind, at once control passions and satisfy human needs."[6] In these two theatrical presentations, then, what can be discovered about the passions and needs of engineers?

The St Louis engineers titled their production *Every Engineer: An Immorality Play*. It was, of course, to be a sort of *Pilgrim's Progress*, and it depicts the career of a naive young engineering graduate as he discovers what a professional life is really like. This play also has its allegorical characters – Youth, Ambition, and Ingenuity – who are Every Engineer's companions on his journey, as well as a cast of villains, called "robbers" on the program, which identifies them as St Louis private utility corporations.

As the play opens, we learn two things about Every Engineer, that he is powerfully educated and enormously, indeed brashly, self-confident. Here is how he describes himself:

> Building a bridge is merely childish play,
> Electric theories are at my finger's ends
> The methods of the laboratory, say:
> I know how every beam of concrete bends!

Ambition echoes the extent of the engineer's learning with the observation, "All the professors passed him in their courses / He knows the laws which govern mass and forces." Nor is this the extent of his knowledge, as Youth advises us, "And he can juggle chemistry to boot / And as for handling men, that's his long suit." These lines may sound like one of Gilbert and Sullivan's patter songs, but it is not difficult to hear in them the language engineers of that era used when seriously describing themselves.

In Every Engineer this sense of commanding knowledge generates a considerable audacity, and he says,

> Before me mighty work is all I see
> Perhaps some trifling task to fill the hour
> Until the ginks with money come to me
> And give me a position of much power.

So, full of himself, Engineer breezily approaches Corporation I, a private utility company of the city, for a job. The dialogue makes it plain, however, that these sorts of firms are put off by his independent cockiness, that they want experienced men, and that they want them cheaply, too. There is also, behind these lines, something of the painful knowledge of personal experience, of having learned the difference between school and the world, between mastery of knowledge and control over one's life.

Chastened by this rebuff, Every Engineer next approaches "Municipality" for a job and in that exchange is taught the realities of local politics. He is hired only because he knows someone and then discovers that, besides having to make a contribution to party funds out of his salary, he will be judged on his ability to win votes rather than on his technical skills.

After a brief piece of dialogue that satirizes the laziness and incompetence of city engineers, all the corporations reappear on stage, swaying gently to the "Flower Maiden" music from *Parsifal*. And now we come to the central confrontation. Attracted by Every Engineer's moral pliability, they introduce themselves one after another in a wonderfully scurrilous fashion:

Corporation II	We are bold Corporation
	The terror of this nation.
	In Jersey we incorporate
	But take our compensation
	From every man in this wide land
	Of high or lowly station.
Corporation III	Our stock on its own water
	Floats, though it shouldn't oughter,
	Our rights they are inviolate
	As Pharo's only daughter....
Corporation IV	Precision such as yours, sir,
	Efficiency so sure, sir,
	We yearn to hire and consecrate
	To uses high and pure, sir;
	Come! find your ends in dividends.

As clearly ironic as their blandishments are, Every Engineer is easily persuaded. His acceptance speech reveals his awareness of the potent consequences in the combination of capital and technical skill, just as the corporations know that too, and they rejoice:

> We are together now and will
> Make the dear people foot the bill.
> And by alchemic methods surer
> Squeeze dividends from Aqua Pura.

Yet even as Every Engineer contemplates the bargain, he feels a sense of responsibility to his new employer, and his words reflect the profession's claim of ethical obligation to the client:

> I hold a job, but bet your cash,
> They'll get their money's worth.
> No more on petty work
> Have I a minute's leisure
> No time to eat, no time to sleep,
> No hour consigned to pleasure.

Youth joins the engineer in this commitment with the pledge, "I willingly will give my finest days / If for their wasting Corporation pays." His loyalty is met with scorn, however, as, *sotto voce*, the corporations mock Youth's poignant declaration with derisive laughter.

Oblivious to these portents, Every Engineer now calls on another allegorical familiar, Ingenuity, who with Youth and Ambition will raise him to success in his new job. Naturally, Ingenuity finds Every Engineer's situation appealing, and in a bit of stage business characteristic of this broad farce, slips an idea under his hat. When he sees it, Every Engineer exclaims:

> Now will fat corporation
> Be pleased with me. He'll pat me on the back,
> And raise my pay: I should worry now!
> Here's the stunt and it's a cracker-jack
> A scheme to bring a joy to Jonny Hunter's heart,
> A plan to use electric currents in plumb tarts!
> T'will flatten out the peak, the hollows fill
> And we'll get profits from every grocery bill!

But the corporation, in this case the United Electric Light and Power Company of St Louis, has been looking over the young man's shoulder and snatches the idea from him. "Here, give me that you mutt," the corporation says, "I own the product of your festering nut." Youth and Ambition are pretty badly jolted by the experience, but Ingenuity slips another idea under the engineer's hat, with the advice, "Next time, my friend, make corporation *buy!*"

The second idea is directed toward one of the city's transit companies:

> A plan to make the seats so darn unpleasant
> That no one, whether Lord or lowly peasant,
> Will stand for them, but *on* them, then you see
> They'll hold not two unfortunates, but three.

This corporation, too, has sneaked up on the engineer and says, "I'll take that stunt, so come across / You are my hireling and I am your boss." When the young man tries to hold it back, the corporation knocks him to the floor and takes the idea anyhow. In the struggle Youth has been struck down. Indeed, that is the end of him and, as the subsequent dialogue makes plain, of innocence besides.

Every Engineer is momentarily saddened by this turn of events, but Ambition cheers him on and Ingenuity gives him yet another idea, which this time, with a craftiness matching that of his adversaries, he hides for safekeeping. Boldly, then, he goes up to the local gas utility and tells the corporation, "This is a stunt, a peacherino true, / for multiplying all gas bills by two." As the others did, this corporation also grabs the engineer and searches him for the idea. When it isn't found, however, the corporations realize they must revise their tactics, and they invite the engineer to lunch where, after some bargaining, they agree to make him their consulting engineer. As one of them puts it, "My man, you've got a nifty little thinker / With all our properties we'll let you tinker."

The post of consulting engineer is the pinnacle of achievement for Every Engineer, and, in unison, the corporations sing with him a brief but deliciously ironic chorus that makes it seem as if he has acquired the position as a result of an arduous though honorable climb to the top. Then Municipality, politically reformed now, appears back on stage and joins in to say, "But talent such as yours I cannot buy," to which Every Engineer adds the refrain, "Can't buy." Municipality promises, however, in another of the play's topical references, that, if the new city charter is adopted, things will change for the better. Here again, the message – so reminiscent of Morris L. Cooke's anti-utility campaign two decades earlier – is obvious.

At that point the play's focus shifts as the last of the allegorical characters, Success, comes on stage, laurel wreath in hand. Every

Engineer turns eagerly toward Success, casually leaving Ambition, his youthful companion, to depart the stage alone. As if it were not already clear, Success then describes the human costs of Every Engineer's achievement:

> Few men attain my friendship without sin,
> My presence is no mark of purity
> No guaranty of firm security,
> The gaunt wolf "Want" may yet be heard
> Outside your door.

In the 1930s these references to the unpredictable nature of economic life were real enough, and Success continues to mix harsh imagery with idealism. Indeed, Success's speech is a curious one. It ends the play and one might expect an upbeat, lighthearted tone. Instead, Success compares engineering with the other professions, to its detriment. The format is a familiar one in the contemporaneous engineering literature and in that context should have produced the old joke about doctors who bury their mistakes. But Success tells the engineers that they cannot hope to enjoy the status or financial rewards of the independent consultant, despite the learning and labor their profession demands. They have in their hands the "instruments that lay the *real* truth bare"; they can make "the poets' dreams" come true, he says. But few will value their achievement, and if they fail – an idea that consistently appears in these kinds of professional comparisons – they alone will bear the burden of it.

The play's authors meant by this astringent, Grail-like characterization of the engineering profession to close on an elevated, though somewhat elegiac, note. One could decide, despite those intentions, that this stark contrast with the funny and pointed material that came earlier was simply due to a failure of imagination. But there are other, more interesting ways to look at the play, the most obvious of which is that to some degree the production mirrors in both its humorous and serious modes the actual circumstances of St Louis engineers during the 1930s. There is, for instance, an inescapably rueful undertone in the way they kidded themselves about their educations, employers, and careers. And in a similar fashion, the discontinuity between those jokes and the play's somber ending also suggests that, beneath the surface, there are attitudes and ideas worth exploring. But most of all, the play indicates how important such ephemeral, local sources can be in getting us closer to our subjects. And that possibility points toward another simple truth, namely, that the specifics of time and place are still the essential ingredients of the historian's work and that even such conventional tools are useful in the understanding of engineering professionalism.

It must be admitted, however, that in selecting this odd and fugitive document as case study, I also want to argue that the history of engineering professionalism is ripe for new adventures in analysis. One example of the different kind of interpretive modes that lie waiting for us is that book of Peter Gay's. The first of a projected multivolume analysis of the bourgeoisie in the 19th century, *Education of the Senses* is full of ideas and approaches that seem valuable. Gay alerts us to the fact that documents like *Every Engineer* carry latent meanings, that people orient themselves by cultural signals, and that out of "varieties of experience," the historian can construct "a recognizable family of desires and anxieties."[7] This approach encourages us to see the full nature of people; it helps correct the tendency to typecast engineers in the flat, one-dimensional terms we so often resort to; and it indicates how we might more successfully deal with the contradictions that currently hamper our efforts to describe the profession and its relation to American life.

Gay's use of Freudian psychoanalytic concepts, particularly aggression, suddenly made me realize how much an engineer's ordinary experience is dominated by adversarial relations of all sorts. And they are an accepted part of life; at one point in his speech, Success tells Every Engineer, "So I the men of all professions seek, / Saving the strong and grinding down the weak." Aggression also encompasses the notion of. mastery – I am reminded of Sally Hacker's study of the function of the calculus in engineering education – and it includes domination over the environment.[8] George Babcock, the founder of Babcock and Wilcox, provided a telling example of that kind of attitude when he claimed that engineering's principal mission was to bring about the day "when every force in nature and every created thing shall be subject to the control of man."[9]

What Gay makes us realize, however, is that in these respects engineers do not stand apart from the rest of American culture. To the contrary, engineering professionalism is a cultural artifact, just as fashion, family life, or the language of the marketplace is, too. And if materialism and a certain difficulty with ideals are hallmarks of bourgeois culture, as Gay claims, then we can begin to recognize characteristics of the engineering population in terms that connect them directly to American history. The sense of impotence that *Every Engineer* expresses is not then a simple function of the terms of employment of engineers but a result besides of the pressures most Americans felt to get ahead and their fear of the consequences if they failed. Or, to put it somewhat differently, it was not simply corporate power or professional status that disturbed engineers but also the rapidly evolving nature of their work, and they felt themselves ground between the millstones of past and present – between an old mechanic arts tradition that spoke to enduring American values and the engineering science of the 20th century that promised insulation both from corporate cupidity and the condescension of aesthetes. So it is out of the processes of bourgeois culture that we get professionalism and specialization, but also, as the St Louis play suggests, conflicting feelings of helplessness and confidence, of loyalty and isolation.

Thus, to insist on the complexity of human experience and on broad definitions of culture as our points of departure means, for the historian, access to a stock of emotional responses as well as political reactions or economic concerns. And that fuller kind of information yields, I think, better insight into the ways engineers and people like them tried to manage their lives during periods of great change.

Notes

1 The remark about Hoover comes from Robert S. McElvaine, "An Uncommon Man: The Triumph of Herbert Hoover," *New York Times, Book Review Section*, September 2, 1984, p. 4.
2 *Toronto Life*, May 1984, p. 5.
3 As quoted in Edwin T. Layton Jr, *The Revolt of the Engineers: Social Responsibility and the American Engineering Profession* (Cleveland, 1971), p. 59.
4 Brooke Hindle, ed., *Technology in Early America: Needs and Opportunities for Study* (Chapel Hill, NC, 1966).
5 That pageant and the other ceremonials of the ASME's fiftieth anniversary celebration are described in my *Centennial History of the American Society of Mechanical Engineers*.
6 Peter Gay, *The Bourgeois Experience – Victoria to Freud*, vol. 1, *Education of the Senses* (New York, 1983), p. 459.
7 Gay, p. 5.
8 Sally Hacker, "Mathematization of Engineering: Limits on Women and the Field," in *Machina ex Dea: Feminist Perspectives on Technology*, ed. Joan Rothschild (Elmsford, NY, 1983), pp. 38–58.
9 American Society of Mechanical Engineers, *Transactions*, 9 (1888): 37.

Documents

Some Notes on Vocational Guidance

J. A. L. Waddell

Introductory Notes

There are few engineering matters of more importance than the subject of this address, which is a signal factor not only for individual engineers and the entire profession itself but also for other callings and professions and for public prosperity and the welfare of society.

Engineering, and after it surgery and medicine, may well be considered the most vital and critical of professions. The achievements of its motives are of immeasurable importance to the welfare and progress of humanity; equally, its mistakes may, and sometimes do, involve heavy losses and even fatalities.

It is, therefore, essential to the safety and increasing prosperity of the community that those entering the engineering profession should certainly possess the principal requisite natural qualifications and, unquestionably, characters of high ability and reliability. Equally the profession needs only recruits that will extend its field and increase its fame, while the disciples themselves should be well assured of their qualifications before undertaking even the novitiate that, together with the ensuing career, demands, to the last stage, the highest, most complete, responsible, and arduous continuous service. Making good is to reach that highest eminence of distinction – service to mankind, as well as the satisfaction of ambition, material compensation, and general appreciation.

If a man is not qualified to undertake this arduous enterprise, he still may possess many valuable qualities: possibly even the deficiencies which militate against engineering may be utilized in another direction, enabling him to achieve great success in some other line and thereby benefit both the world and himself. It has been truly said that many an obscure man might have been a Napoleon, had he known in what direction to exert his energy.

Excerpted from J. A. L. Waddell, *Memoirs and Addresses of Two Decades* (Easton, PA: Mack Printing Company, 1928), pp. 297–302.

It is equally evident that the unreliable, incompetent, or misfit aspirant for engineering laurels is likely to make mistakes and fail in important duties that might well bring great loss and disaster to innocent parties – errors that rarely, if ever, can be redeemed.

The profession of engineering is a glorious one, but it is also very exacting; and only those willing, able, and determined to give it complete allegiance for a life-time should enter it.

No man governed by impulse or prejudice, or deficient in health, strength, mental ability, integrity of the highest order, or unlimited persistence, or who is unable or unwilling to endure hardships, or who lacks patience and determination should consider entering the profession.

The highest rewards of the engineer are the splendid pride of achievement that goes with creation and successful execution, and the exhilaration of directing and watching the growth of great structures, together with the stimulation of invention and the solution of difficult problems. If engineering is considered from the side of the material reward alone or for easy and luxurious conditions, it offers small inducement for a life's work.

It is unquestionably true that far too many aspirants try to embark on the career of engineering – many of them carelessly, and some of them through a very much mistaken idea that the engineering curriculum is an easy one to pass and demands less study than do the others. Many young men are graduated from engineering colleges who should never have entered them – and the sooner their mistakes are rectified the better. It would be much preferable if they had never commenced the study of engineering, and if the requirements of the colleges had been much more severe and the duration of their instruction longer. Even a man passing all the usual specific tests may be totally unfitted by temperament for engineering – and to such the catechism suggested by Dr Waddell would be invaluable.

Some Notes on Vocational Guidance

Were there definitely established in America some effective method of determination concerning the fitness of young men for the engineering field and some means of arriving at a specific decision in regard to the best line of activity in that calling for any individual to follow, much benefit would result to numerous persons and much more to the engineering profession as a whole.

Again, such a measure would be fraught with great economy for our nation, in that it would materially reduce the cost of technical education, would increase the individual efficiency of graduate engineers, and would improve the character of professional output by the elimination of a large percentage of the unfit from engineering practice.

Is such a method of determining the suitability or unsuitability of any young person for any particular calling truly feasible, or is it altogether chimerical, as many claim it to be? In the writer's opinion, it ought to be within the realm of possibility to evolve and establish upon a permanent basis a satisfactory means of analyzing the mental equipment of almost any young man or woman for any walk of life, but not without first expending much time and money on systematic psychological research.

The mental tests that thus far have been tried are good enough in a general way to "separate the sheep from the goats"; but no absolute reliance can be placed on the correctness of their results in any special case. These tests need elaboration after much grey matter has been expended upon their consideration by some of the best intellects of our country.

The selection of desirable candidates for the engineering profession would be immensely facilitated, were the general public properly and authoritatively informed concerning what an engineer's work consists of, the kind of life he leads, his earning capacity (maximum, average, and minimum, *especially average* as compared with the earnings of other men), the amount of study requisite for graduation from a technical school, the satisfactions and the hardships of a technical man's life, etc. If the parents of the aspirants were thoroughly posted on these matters, their offspring would not be so utterly ignorant of them as they are today.

But how are we to instruct these parents? The writer can conceive of no better way than to have a book prepared jointly by a number of engineers of the highest standing, selected by the Council of some national engineering society, so that the treatise may be accepted as authoritative; and have it distributed broadly and in such a way as to be accessible by the masses.

For instance, it could be placed in all the public libraries and in those of the high schools; and gratis copies could be distributed by the secretaries of all the technical schools of the country to those persons making enquiries about technical education for themselves, their children, or their young friends. Write-ups from time to time in the newspapers most generally read by the farmers and the working classes of the cities, and in the popular magazines, telling about the engineering profession in general, and incidentally referring to the suggested book, would be exceedingly helpful.

If the youth of the country were thoroughly posted about the profession of engineering, its scope, its difficulties, and its rewards, there would be fewer applicants for admission to its ranks, and those applicants would be of much greater mental calibre and moral courage than the ones who at present are seeking entrance.

The set subject of this paper, however, is not "The Selection of Applicants for Technical Courses" but "Vocational Guidance" – quite a different matter – nevertheless the preceding general remarks are pertinent as an introduction to the said set subject, which the writer will now proceed to treat.

Owing to the known interest he takes in ambitious men, he is called upon a number of times per annum to give advice to either boys who contemplate entering the engineering profession or to young men who are already practising it. Almost always the petitioner for advice goes away satisfied with the information he has received; because the writer always gives of his best without stint, often supplementing his counsel with the gift of some pertinent literature. Quite often he hears later on from such young men to the effect that they have profited by his suggestions and have adopted his recommendations with resultant advantage. This is one of his greatest "satisfactions of life."

Sometimes the problem set has been difficult of solution – for instance, on several occasions graduates of West Point, serving in the army, have come to the writer to confer about the advisability of dropping their military career and entering civil life. To solve such queries, knowing that one's advice will be followed, involves great responsibility. Sometimes the writer after a long conference can give the questioner a decided answer, but occasionally the problem is so complex that he evades the responsibility by presenting the young man with some literature to read and by telling him, after reading it, to settle the question for himself.

Sometimes a middle-aged engineer asks whether he should remain in the rut where he has let himself enter, or venture to strike out in a new line of endeavor. The correct answer to this query involves a number of considerations, for instance, the man's age and condition of health, the extent of his ambition, the income he must have to support himself and his dependents, the possibility of receiving some day a retiring pension and its amount, the possession of a home that he might have to abandon at pecuniary loss, etc. These matters must be studied carefully before a correct answer can be given.

To settle whether a youth is mentally fitted for engineering is often a simple matter – especially if the answer be in the negative – and, in some unusual cases, also when it is in the affirmative. There are occasions, though, when considerable uncertainty exists; but in these, after prolonged investigation, the decision is generally adverse.

Among other questions to propound to an aspirant are the following:

A.   What are your reasons for thinking that an engineer's life would be to your liking?

B.   What is your school record in mathematics – excellent, fair, or poor? Do you like or dislike mathematics?

C. Have you any marked mechanical taste?

D. Are you fond of using tools?

E. How does research work appeal to you?

F. Is it your ambition to become wealthy or to establish for yourself a high reputation as an engineer?

G. Are you fond of study and reading?

H. What class of literature do you prefer?

I. What appeals to you most in college life – scholarship, athletics, or social functions?

J. As a student, do you desire to make the best record possible, or would you be content to receive merely passing marks?

K. Have you the ambition to attain one or more of the honor-society grades – Phi Beta Kappa, Sigma Xi, or Tau Beta Pi; or like many others do you look down upon the so-called "grinds" and prefer to establish your college record on the basis of popularity?

L. Are you provided with sufficient funds to take the full course of instruction, or must you earn additional money by doing some outside work?

M. Do you think that after graduating you would prefer adhering to strictly professional work at small pay or entering some affiliated line with larger compensation?

N. Do you really love to study and investigate, or does it bore you? Are you glad or otherwise when quitting time comes?

O. Does your sympathy lie with labor or capital – and why?

P. Are you interested in matters pertaining to political economy?

Q. What are your ideas about national defense?

R. Outside of your technical career, what ambitions have you?

S. What is your opinion on the subject of immigration?

T. What importance do you place on engineering economics, and what is your conception of the meaning of that term?

U. Have you studied at all about general ethics, and what are your guiding rules for conduct?

V. What men of history do you desire to emulate, and why?

W. How many hours per day do you think a man should actually work, first at college, and afterwards in practice?

X. Do you believe in extra pay for overtime work by engineers; and, if so, should the hourly compensation be greater therefor?

Y. What are your sentiments concerning the question of "valuable experience *versus* large earnings?" Give the reasons for your views thereon.

Z. Describe in detail your conception of the characteristics and attributes of an ideal member of the engineering profession.

Such a quiz as the preceding, covering an uninterrupted hour or two, ought to give the examiner a very fair impression concerning the general ability of the young man, his ambitions, his fitness or unfitness for a technical life, his courage, and his probable success or failure in any professional career.

There is another suggestion of importance regarding "Vocational Guidance," viz., that every young engineer, as soon as possible after graduation, should select some middle-aged or elderly member of the profession to serve as his "guide, philosopher, and friend," find some way to become acquainted with him, impress upon him favorably the tyro's personality, and ultimately persuade him to act as monitor or general adviser. If the choice made is truly a happy one, the benefit that can thus be received is almost incalculable.

In selecting such a guide, the young man for various reasons should choose a busy engineer, one of which reasons is that a hard-working practitioner is much more likely to spare the time necessary for the consultations than is one who is not fully occupied; because it is undoubtedly true that the more work a man has to do, the more extra or outside work he can undertake, and the better he can do it. This is a strange characteristic of human nature, and is good evidence of the correctness of the old statement that "humans are queer creatures."

It ought not to be an imposition on any professional man to look after the general interests of half a dozen young fellows, to the extent at least of furnishing them with sound advice and guiding their footsteps into the paths they ought to follow in order to attain the worthy objects of their ambitions.

Unemployed Engineers, 1932

J. P. H. Perry

For many engineers the central fact of the Depression was their own unemployment. In some industrial centers the problem was acute; it has been estimated that by 1932 some 112,000 engineers, perhaps half the profession, were without jobs. There was a great deal of talk about increasing job opportunities by stimulating public works and about limiting the number of

Taken from J. P. H. Perry, "New York Engineers' Successful Efforts to Relieve Unemployment," *Civil Engineering*, II (June 1932), pp. 404–7.

engineers through smaller college enrollments and strict licensing. But for the unemployed the immediate problem was solved by direct relief.

In the February issue of *Civil Engineering* there appeared an article outlining the organization, aims, and activities of the Professional Engineers Committee on Unemployment up to the middle of January 1932. It is believed that members of the Society in general, as well as the various committees scattered over the country that have been organized to deal with the relief of unemployed civil engineers, may be interested in this latest report of the work of the Professional Engineers Committee on Unemployment of the four Founder Societies in the New York Metropolitan District, known locally as the "P.E.C.U."

The organization of the P.E.C.U. has been changed but very slightly from that described in my article in the February issue of *Civil Engineering*. The work has gone on steadily and fairly successfully. Up to May 14, 1932, our organization had registered unemployed members of the four Founder Societies and non-members to a total number of 2,689.

Of this total registration, 526 were not regarded as active applicants for relief since 139 had stated on a reclassification that they were definitely interested only in permanent engineering jobs, not in relief, and 249 had not replied to a series of letters asking if they still desired assistance, thereby indicating to the P.E.C.U. that they were no longer interested, while 138 had registered for educational courses.

Distribution of Registered Unemployment

Of the active registrants, totaling 2,163 men, P.E.C.U. has made 1,389 placements divided as follows:

On P.E.C.U. payrolls.....	307
Receiving other relief, such as that given by the Gibson, Bliss, and general public committees in the Metropolitan District of New York	879
In permanent engineering jobs.....	203

The division among society members and non-members, both for registrations and placements, is as [shown in the first half of the table].

The analyses of registration and placements by married and single classifications and also by groupings of salaries received by the registered man in his last employment, are shown in the [second half of the table].

The division among Society members and non-members

Society	Registered	Percentage of total registration	Placed	Percentage of total placed	Percentage of registered placed
American Society of Civil Engineers	239	11.0	184	14.9	77.0
American Institute of Mining and Metallurgical Engineers	35	1.6	31	2.8	88.6
American Society of Mechanical Engineers	345	15.9	248	20.2	71.9
American Institute of Electrical Engineers	210	9.6	157	12.7	74.8
Western Society of Engineers	4	0.2	4	0.3	100.00
Non-Members	1,339	61.7	603	49.1	45.03
	2,172	100.0	1,227	100.0	
Duplicate Memberships	9		7		
	2,163		1,220		
Men placed more than once			169		
Total			1,389		

Marital Status	Registered		Placed
Single	648		228
Married	1,431		964
Widower	33		18
Divorced	29		10
	2,141		1,220
Unaccounted for	22	Replacements	169
Totals	2,163		1,389

Salary	Registered		Placed
$6,000 or better	127		92
$3,600–$6,000	505		352
$2,400–$3,600	1,016		576
$2,400 and below	493		200
	2,141		1,220
Unaccounted for	22	Replacements	169
Totals	2,163		1,389

Types of Relief Provided

The average relief afforded the individual unemployed engineer through the P.E.C.U. has been $19.05 per week. This sum has varied somewhat depending upon where the relief was obtained. The average under different conditions varied as follows:

For those paid direct through P.E.C.U.'s payroll	$18.82
For those who obtained relief through the Gibson, Bliss, and other relief committees	$21.50
For those who got engineering jobs through the P.E.C.U. and other sources	$32.50

There have been 73 loans granted in amounts in excess of $15, totaling $3,355, and averaging $45.18 per man. There have been 60 emergency loans granted in amounts less than $15, totaling $248 and averaging $4.13 per man.

These loans were on demand notes without interest. The expectation is that ultimately a considerable percentage of the borrowers will repay them. The notes are made payable to the United Engineering Trustees, Inc., the official treasurer of the P.E.C.U. Should these loans be repaid, the funds collected will be reserved in a permanent fund to be managed by the presidents of the four local sections of the four Founder Societies for the relief of destitute engineers, or they will be held in reserve to meet another business depression.

The relatively small number of loans made and the meager sums of money required surprised those active in the P.E.C.U. At the inception of our organization the forecast was that the loaning of money would be one of our chief activities. Apparently engineers (especially our members) are extremely loath to apply for loans. They much prefer wages from made work or even direct relief from city bureaus. Also, a loan meets only the momentary emergency, whereas a wage, even at a trifling rate, makes possible the planning of one's life. Loans, to be satisfactory, must be at a continuing rate, and this is impossible, in our experience, to contemplate.

In addition to its other activities, the P.E.C.U. has been very active in using the influence of its personnel to persuade the gas and electric light companies to forebear as far as possible enforcing routine orders to discontinue their services to destitute engineers who were being aided in other ways by the P.E.C.U. In some instances it has been possible to persuade holders of mortgages to be more lenient in the terms on which they extended or renewed them. Occasionally money has been loaned to pay interest on mortgages.

A legal aid department has been established, whose function has been to give free legal advice to registered unemployed whose circumstances were such that they required such advice. Similarly, an agency has been set up to assist registered unemployed who had developed inventions or processes possibly warranting patents. Occasionally the P.E.C.U. has been of help through various hospitals in the city in getting special terms or special admittance for its registered unemployed.

It has been found that many unemployed engineers lack the knack of writing suitable and effective letters applying for jobs. Engineers seem to have difficulty in "selling" themselves. Therefore the P.E.C.U. organized a little department, the function of which has been to help registered men prepare letters outlining their past experience in a way to interest the prospective employer. This has been supplemented with a mimeographing service to produce multiple copies of such letters.

Another way of stating P.E.C.U.'s accomplishments is that through February, March, and April it was responsible for building up a payroll of about $21,000 a week for unemployed engineers. Of this, about $4,000 was met directly by the P.E.C.U. from its own funds; the balance, by public or other agencies.

As regards clothing, in the early winter the McGraw-Hill Company generously donated floor space in its building on West 42d Street. Two unemployed engineers were set to work to operate this clothing bureau. To date 203 men, 61 women, and 58 children have been provided with clothing, which has been contributed largely through the kind efforts of the Engineering Woman's Club of New York. This clothing has been a godsend to many unemployed men, who, if they had not had the clothing from the P.E.C.U., in many cases could not have taken the positions which were found for them.

The Engineering Woman's Club not only did a splendid work in collecting and distributing clothing but also initiated and managed in a fine way a charity bridge party which was held in the rooms of the Engineering Societies Building. Some 700 tickets were sold at $2 apiece, and between 400 and 500 members of the Founder Societies played bridge one evening. The result was that a net contribution of $1,160 was made to the funds of the P.E.C.U. This report would not be complete without including words of warm appreciation and gratitude to the officers and members of the Engineering Woman's Club for their active assistance to the P.E.C.U. throughout the past winter.

Another successful activity of the P.E.C.U. was that of certifying unemployed engineers to Columbia University so that they could attend classes without academic credit and without expense. Early in the campaign it was felt that in addition to affording financial relief to unemployed men, we must do something to sustain the morale of those who were not as yet in dire need of financial relief. Columbia University responded very generously to the suggestion, and to date we have sent there 138 men, who made 564 registrations in 163 different courses for the winter and spring terms. The subjects elected by these men cover a wide range. They may be summarized briefly as embracing architecture, chemistry, civil engineering, electrical engineering, industrial engineering, geology, mechanical engineering, mathematics, languages, metallurgy, mining, physics, accounting, finance, industrial relations, and economics.

Another important committee which was recently established is known as the Committee on Industrial Opportunities. This committee endeavors to place engineers outside the profession. It has prepared a list of some 800 industrial concerns which in its judgment could use engineers for cost studies and in other ways where their technical training and mathematical ability would make them more useful than the ordinary layman. This committee plans to continue its work all summer, and has been reinforced by two other groups who will solicit positions of a permanent nature.

Advertisements in the daily and technical press are being posted on a bulletin board in the Engineering Societies Building, and, as has been mentioned, assistance is being rendered in preparing letters of application. . . .

Another committee, known as the Committee on Construction Legislation, under the able leadership of Malcolm Pirnie, John P. Hogan, and R. C. Marshall, Members Am. Soc. C. E., has been active in Washington and Albany in endeavoring to persuade Congressmen and other legislators that the cutting out of construction enterprises from Federal, state, and municipal budgets is fallacious economy, results in great increase in unemployment, and is particularly distressing to engineers. It is believed that the work done by this committee has been, or will be, fruitful in part.

Reviewing the activities of the past seven months, the greatest accomplishment of the P.E.C.U. has been to convince the semi-public relief agencies in the Metropolitan District of the desirability, from their point of view, of using unemployed engineers in supervising capacities or as key men in directing the 35,000 or 40,000 individuals to whom these agencies have had to give unemployed relief in the form of made work or as direct relief in New York this past winter. Extreme care was taken in certifying P.E.C.U. registrants to these public bodies, notably to the Gibson and Bliss Committees, to make certain that the candidates sent down for employment were qualified for the job in question.

A large part of the work of the Registration Committee, ably led by Ernest S. Holcombe, as a part of the General Relief Committee under the fine management of George L. Lucas, M. Am. Soc. C. E., has been to classify all registrants as to their prior experience and their fitness for different types of work. In other words, it was a "selling proposition" and we had to be sure that the goods we were offering were satisfactory. Our care along these lines in the early stages of our activities has been rewarded many times over. The fact that wages paid by these relief agencies to our unemployed engineers totaled $307,119 is distinctly "proof of the pudding."

Although the raising directly by P.E.C.U. of $107,841.69 may be regarded as satisfactory, it is only proper to call attention to the fact that this has come from only 3,286 men out of over 12,000 members of the four Founder Societies in the Metropolitan District, to say nothing of an estimated non-membership of at least 10,000 more. This estimate is based on the fact that our registrations indicate that the division between members and non-members among unemployed engineers is almost exactly half and half. It is also distressing to report that in spite of four letters of appeal, over 5,000 members of the societies failed to reply in any way. Some 4,000 members who did not contribute did accord the P.E.C.U. the courtesy of acknowledging its appeals and giving reasons why they could not contribute. In most cases the reason for non-contribution was loss of job or extreme outside relief burdens to which the member was committed.

Plans for the Future

As to the immediate future, the Relief Committee after mature study submitted a written report to the Executive Committee, which in turn, after consideration, made a written recommendation to the General Committee to the effect that registration of unemployed engineers should cease April 9. The General Committee unanimously approved the recommendation. The branch offices of the P.E.C.U. in New Jersey and in Westchester and Nassau counties in New York State were closed on the same date. A nucleus of the normal staff of some 60 paid and volunteer P.E.C.U. workers on registration, classification, vital statistics, certification of unemployed to vacant jobs, and other work will be maintained until October 1 to the number of about 16.

Announcements were sent out giving two weeks' notice to unemployed non-members that they were to go off the P.E.C.U. payrolls on April 15; a month's notice was given to married non-members and unmarried members that they would go off the P.E.C.U. payroll on May 1; and a month's notice was given to married members other than those falling within Class A destitution that they would go off the payroll on May 15.

A reserve of money to start up the activities of the P.E.C.U. on October 1 was set aside and the remainder of its funds were held to take care of married members in Class A destitution from May 15 to October 1. The general feeling of those active in the P.E.C.U. is that the problem of relief for unemployed engineers will be more serious in the winter of 1932–1933 than in the past winter and that the number of members of the four Founder Societies falling within Class A destitution will increase throughout the summer months, not only because of the tapering off of direct relief from the P.E.C.U. but also because of the laying off of the engineers placed through the P.E.C.U. with other relief agencies in New York City, notably with the Gibson and Bliss committees, which began to occur in April and will continue throughout the summer, and further because of the continued loss of employment by engineers throughout the summer months.

It was felt that above all the P.E.C.U. must keep itself in such financial condition that it can take care of all married members of the four Founder Societies whose situation now places them, or may place them within the next few months, within our Class A destitution. To be in Class A destitution a man must have three or more dependents, must have exhausted all personal resources and all personal credit. He may be briefly described as one with his back to the wall.

Starting in October 1931, the P.E.C.U., on instructions from the four Founder Societies, rendered assistance to members and non-members without discrimination. About February 8, when we had more knowledge of the problem confronting us, the Executive Committee, with the support of the General Committee, reached the conclusion that inasmuch as substantially 90 per cent of the money contributed to the P.E.C.U. had come from members of the four Founder Societies and yet more than 50 per cent of its registrations and more than 50 per cent of its registrations and more than 50 per cent of its placement of unemployed engineers had been of non-members of the Societies, it was necessary from that date on to use the funds contributed to the P.E.C.U. only for the assistance of members or former members of the four Founder Societies. We continued, however, to place our registered men with public or semi-public agencies without discrimination between members and non-members. In the face of present conditions, the decision has been made that the P.E.C.U. will use its own funds only for the relief of members of the Founder Societies. In deciding for the present to relieve only Class A destitute married members, we interpret the word "married" to include a single man with dependents. We also interpret "members" to include former members of the Founder Societies whose membership ceased because of their loss of position and inability to pay dues.

In concluding this report, on behalf of the General Executive Committees of the Professional Engineers Committee on Unemployment, I
desire to make public our gratitude to the rank and file of our organization, including particularly the committee chairmen, who have done
such spendid work and have given of their time and energy so unselfishly
and with such splendid results. I believe that the thanks of the four
Founder Societies are also due to all these men.

Further Reading

Beers, David. *Blue Sky Dream: a Memoir of America's Fall from Grace*. New York:
Doubleday, 1996.
Cather, Willa. *Alexander's Bridge* [1912]. Lincoln: University of Nebraska Press,
1977.
Oldenziel, Ruth. *Making Technology Masculine: Men, Women and Modern
Machines in America, 1870–1945*. Amsterdam: Amsterdam University
Press, 1999.
Reynolds, Terry S. *The Engineer in America: a Historical Anthology from Techno-
logy and Culture*. Chicago: University of Chicago Press, 1991.
Sinclair, Bruce. *A Centennial History of the American Society of Mechanical
Engineers, 1880–1980*. Toronto: University of Toronto Press, 1980.
Tichi, Cecelia. *Shifting Gears: Technology, Literature, Culture in Modernist America*.
Chapel Hill: University of North Carolina Press, 1987.
Ullman, Ellen. *Close to the Machine: Technophilia and Its Discontents*. San Fran-
cisco: City Lights Books, 1997.

6

Technology on the Farm

1831	First American cheese "factory."
1862	US Department of Agriculture established.
1910	88 percent of US farms raise chickens.
1923	USDA Bureau of Home Economics established.
1928	NBC begins broadcasting "National Farm and Home Hour."
1936	REA (Rural Electrification Administration) established.
1940	Only 17.8 percent of US farms have running water.

Introduction

Until 1920, the United States was a rural and agricultural nation. Not until that year did the federal census show that a bare majority of Americans lived in cities. Despite the political clout and cultural valorization of "the farmer," however, life on the land had never been easy or romantic. As new technologies became available in America, they usually appeared first in the cities, and in general terms, this was true of both those designed for the home and those for other workplaces; in farm terms, the kitchen and the barn. In the barn and field, the Industrial Revolution that swept urban industries in the United States did not take place until after the First World War, with the gasoline tractor, electric power, and chemical fertilizers and pesticides. In the kitchen, lighting, plumbing, and appliances which were widely available, at least in middle-class homes, in the nation's cities were long delayed in the countryside. The decision as to which if any new technologies to invest in was based on economic calculations, but it was also a decision that was deeply gendered.

Out of the Barns and into the Kitchens: Transformations in Farm Women's Work in the First Half of the Twentieth Century

Christine Kleinegger

In 1917 Susan Keating Glaspell published an extraordinary story called "A Jury of Her Peers" about the grim life of a farm woman. The story is both a psychological drama and a murder mystery about a farmer who has been strangled to death. The sheriff and deputy, accompanied by their wives, go to the isolated farm to investigate the murder. While the men search the barn and yard for clues, they leave the ladies to putter among "the insignificance of kitchen things," since the sheriff wonders, "would the women know a clue if they did come upon it?" Ironically, all the clues to who strangled the farmer (his wife) are in the kitchen, in the form of domestic irregularities that only the women detect – half-done chores, erratic sewing on a quilt – and the lack of labor-saving devices, which suggests the wife's motive in killing her husband. Gradually the two women perceive who committed the murder, and their horror turns to sympathy for the murderess. The sheriff's wife observes, "The law is the law – and a bad stove is a bad stove. . . . Think of what it would mean, year after year, to have that stove to wrestle with. The thought of Minnie Foster trying to bake in that oven!" Ultimately these law-abiding ladies destroy the evidence that points to the guilt of the farm wife. They clean up the kitchen and rip out the quilting, while the men continue their fruitless search for clues in all the wrong places. It is a remarkably subversive story in that it suggests that the lack of a good cooking stove justifies homicide. Glaspell powerfully illustrates the drudgery, isolation, and frustration of many farm women's lives.

The story also serves as a cautionary tale for historians, showing that the "insignificance of kitchen things" – so long ignored by historians – holds clues to the meaning of women's work and women's lives. The context of women's work must be examined with a critical eye, in much the same manner that the sheriff's wife scrutinized the farm kitchen –

Taken from Christine Kleinegger, "Out of the Barns and into the Kitchens: Transformations in Farm Women's Work in the First Half of the Twentieth Century," in Barbara Drygulski Wright et al., eds, *Women, Work, and Technology: Transformations* (Ann Arbor: University of Michigan Press, 1987), pp. 162–81. © 1987 University of Michigan Press.

with "that look of seeing into things, of seeing through a thing to something else . . . as if seeing what that kitchen meant through all the years."[1]

What the kitchen, the barn, and the yard have meant for farm women through all the years – or, more accurately, during the first half of the twentieth century – is the main subject of this article. Our focus is the domestic labor of farm women in the first half of the twentieth century, with special attention given to the transition from household production to consumerism, the sexual division of labor on the farm, and the role of labor-saving devices as an oft-proffered panacea for the ills of farm women.

In the late nineteenth century there existed a traditional integration of women's household production in the farm economy. In the twentieth century much of this production was removed from the home and female supervision, as dairying, poultry, and truck farming were ultimately organized as agribusinesses. This can be viewed as a stage in the "masculinization of agriculture," a process that can be traced back to earliest times when primitive women were primarily responsible for agricultural production. In the twentieth century, "masculinization" consists of increased mechanization, specialization, capital outlay, and scientific expertise. To none of these did the average farm woman have direct access.

Before the mid-nineteenth century almost all cheese, in the United States as well as Europe, had been made at home by women. A common saying in Great Britain was, "What does a man know about cheese?" and in France all the principal cheeses were created by women.[2] Madame Harel developed Camembert in 1781 and passed the recipe on to her daughter. While a woman invented the sublime Camembert, it was a man who is responsible for "American" cheese as we know it today. J. L. Kraft "perfected" processed American cheese in the first decades of this century, and through mass production, heavy advertising, and mass selling he built his business up to a $30 million concern by 1925.[3]

Cheese was the first dairy product to leave the purview of women for the factory. The first cheese factory in the United States was founded in 1831; by 1869, two-thirds of all cheese in the United States was manufactured in factories.[4] By 1910, 99 percent of all cheese was made in factories.[5] Although in the late nineteenth century a few women served as head manufacturers in the factories at salaries as high as one hundred dollars per month, more commonly women were employed in subordinate positions at sixteen to twenty dollars a month. A man with only a year or more of experience might earn thirty-five to forty-five dollars.[6]

The extent to which women were no longer involved in dairy production can be discerned from a survey conducted in Wisconsin in 1918. Managers of creameries, condenseries, cheese factories, and milk plants were asked whether hiring women workers would be a feasible solution to war-related labor shortages in the dairy industry. That several establishments had "already demonstrated that women *can learn* to . . . make cheese" suggests that most women no longer possessed this skill.[7] Some of the obstacles in hiring women included: protective legislation setting maximum hours, the inability of women to lift ten- and twenty-gallon cans of cream, and cultural proscriptions such as "a woman is out of place working in a creamery as women were intended by the Creator to make a home for men. . . ."[8] On the other hand, one milk plant manager reported that "it is an advantage to use women in this work because more hands can be employed for the same amount of money."[9] Most women workers in dairy plants did office work, washed bottles and milk cans and performed other janitorial duties, wrapped butter, and ran laboratory tests on the milk and cream.

In 1863 the *Rural New Yorker,* a farm weekly, praised the establishment of cheese factories by noting, "They save labor, relieving the 'women folks' of nearly all the drudgery of cheese making . . . besides they increase the quantity and generally improve the quality."[10] The *Rural New Yorker*'s concern about the dubious quality of home-produced cheese is not an isolated remark. One finds ample evidence in the farm literature that challenges any nostalgic notions about the intrinsic wholesomeness of farm-produced dairy products. One historian of the dairy industry declared in 1926 that in the nineteenth century "sanitary methods were unknown; science, art or skill in connection with the handling of dairy products were unheard of."[11] While this is probably an unjust exaggeration, there is no reason to believe all farm women were equally skilled in the tricky tasks of making butter and cheese. The problem seemed not so much consistently bad cheese and butter but an unevenness of quality that gave farm products a bad reputation. Yet, surely, the farm wife was not entirely to blame, since the system of marketing in the nineteenth century consisted of selling a few pounds of butter at a time to the local storekeeper, who would lump all the butter of varying quality together in a tub. He then waited until he had enough butter to make it worth transporting to a city. No wonder it arrived a rancid mess.

Butter factories, or creameries, it was believed, would produce a more reliable product. The first creamery in the United States was established in 1856 in Orange County, New York.[12] Yet creameries did not monopolize butter making in the early twentieth century to the same degree that cheese factories monopolized the production of cheese. In 1925, when 1.3 billion pounds of butter were produced in factories, there were still 600 million pounds of butter produced on farms.[13] And farm periodicals such as the *Rural New Yorker* and the *Farmer's Wife* continued to publish advice directed to women on butter making for both home use and market sale.

It is possible that because of factory competition, many farm women no longer trained their daughters in the tasks of butter making. A 1925 farm novel, *The Trouble Maker,* by *American Agriculturist* editor E. R. Eastman, alludes to the decline of butter-making skills in the farm households around Binghamton, New York, in 1916. The story recounts the great New York milk strike of 1916 organized by the Dairymen's League. The manufacturers had refused to pay what farmers considered a fair price for raw milk. Dairy farmers struck by withholding all their milk from market, but because milk is very perishable, they hoped to cut their losses by converting the milk into less perishable butter and cheese. For this the women were called into service. One character observes:

> Do you know, I've been surprised to find out that right here in this cow country, there's few people left who really know how to make good butter. Butter-making on the farms is a lost art and it's kind of too bad. Some of the homemade butter I've bought in the store would drive a dog off a garbage wagon...when all this homemade rotten butter is put on the market as a result of this strike, I can see how a lot of people are going to be driven to eat oleomargarine.[14]

The author calculates that milk had been sold in fluid form to factories for "a generation," which was long enough for the skills of butter making to become obsolete.[15] Thus, this farm writer placed butter making as a thriving art prior to 1900. Similarly, a California farm woman reflected somewhat wistfully in a letter to the U.S. Department of Agriculture (USDA) in 1915, "Our modern creamery is fast displacing the golden butter churned by our *grandmothers....*"[16]

Since all cheese and two-thirds of butter was made in the factory, what dairy work did remain for women to do in the early twentieth century? (See table 1, p. 182.) The main function of dairy farms became the production of raw fluid milk, which was delivered to factories to be transformed into cheese, butter, or ice cream, or sold as a beverage. On the farms the cows still had to be milked, and although women still helped out with this, milking machines were increasingly utilized. One job that remained "women's work" was operating the cream separator on farms that supplied cream to "gathered cream" factories. Advertisements for cream separators almost always showed women (and sometimes children) operating the machine, to show how easy it was to operate. Before 1879, women had separated the cream by putting milk in a shallow pan (which was relatively easy to clean) and skimming the cream that floated to the top. Because this gravity method proved inefficient in collecting all the valuable cream, a centrifugal cream separator was developed. It was a more sophisticated piece of machinery and its daily cleaning fell to women. If advertisements are any indication, it was a chore that women did not particularly enjoy. That it had to be done each day made it monotonous, and rising standards of sanitation required that it always be performed thoroughly and not just given "a lick and a promise."

Several factors led to the greater mechanization of dairying. The rapidly increasing population in urban centers created a demand for milk far greater than immediately surrounding farm areas could meet. Developments in transportation and refrigeration in the late nineteenth century allowed outlying farm areas to supply the expanding markets. Increased demand required larger herds, which required either more labor, which was often too costly or in short supply, or more machines. Moreover, the development in 1890 of the Babcock test for measuring butterfat demonstrated the need for dairy farmers to specialize in superior breeds of cattle that produced milk with higher butterfat content, and thus greater profits.[17] Cattle breeding required a scientific expertise and an understanding of genetics that could be acquired at any agricultural college, but generally "book farming" was reserved for farmers' sons, not their daughters. The typical farm woman did not have access to the capital or education to compete with the producers for Borden or the contented cows of the Carnation Company.

On the other hand, poultry raising was not transferred to Frank Purdue-style factories until after World War II. A 1910 farm census revealed that 88 percent of farms raised chickens, with an average of 80.4 chickens per farm.[18] An estimate for 1939 indicated that 70 percent of poultry production was still carried out by women.[19] Even so, big business principles had to be applied in order to meet the increasing demand for poultry and eggs. In 1927 the poultry column of the *Farmer's Wife* reported the case of a farm woman who sent a dozen eggs to a large buyer. The columinist concluded, "Imagine the lady's consternation when she received an order by telegraph for 30 cases each week for a year! Because she was producing them by the dozen instead of by the case, she was unable to take advantage of the order...she may have the quality, but not the quantity."[20] In 1930 in the same farm woman's magazine, a poultry expert advised that flock owners keep a *minimum* of five hundred hens for a profitable business; otherwise a small flock of fifty would suffice to supply the farm table.[21] Thus, while many women did continue to raise poultry, others found that their usual round of housework did not leave them enough time or energy to tend to such large flocks. The 1945 novel *The Egg and I* is a frantic account of one woman who tried. After the Second World War, a minimum of two thousand layers was necessary to support a family,[22] and vast "chicken ranches" dominated the market. In the late 1960s, twelve thousand hens would be considered "a very small flock."[23]

As in the dairy industry, advances in technology ultimately demanded specialization and high volume production. Some of the major innovations that transformed poultry raising from the housewife's sideline to an automated agribusiness include the development of incubators for hatching large numbers of chicks, trap-nests (which allowed the producer to identify the poor layers to be culled since the hens were "trapped" on the nest), advances in genetics to breed better layers, use of artificial light to increase laying, and the development of expensive commercial feeds and conveyor-belt feeders.

For those farm women who forsook the production of poultry and dairy products even for home use, it became easier to buy the food the family consumed. Yet there is evidence of tension between the farm woman's role as consumer and her role as the wife of a producer. This conflict is evident in a letter a New York State farm woman wrote to the USDA in 1915:

> I am convinced that the brain work I have expended [on buying household supplies] has done more than any other agency toward building up our farm business. It is so much more the woman's province to buy than to sell that it seems to me here lies her greatest opportunity. Now here is where I encounter the blank wall. I find in the current number of [a farm journal] when the best time is to sell wheat.... Where, tell me, shall I look for information as to the best time to buy flour?[24]

Obviously, the best time for farmers to sell wheat is when prices are high, and the best time for housewives to buy that wheat-milled-into-flour is when prices are low. The farmer's wife is caught in the middle – wanting low prices for the food she has to buy in the marketplace and high prices for the food her husband is producing for the same marketplace.

During the Depression overproduction, considered to have driven down agricultural prices, was a perennial problem for egg producers. Thus, in a 1930 editorial in the *Farmer's Wife*, farm women were encouraged not to *produce* more eggs but to *consume* more. The writer noted, "If... 6 million farm families ate a dozen or two eggs more per week, it would reduce the number of eggs taken to market by ten or twelve million dozen a week....[That] would help to keep the egg supply down and prices up...."[25]

This conflict between the interests of the producer and those of the consumer was highlighted by a new emphasis on sticking to budgets in a cash economy. Budget (and cholesterol) notwithstanding, one finds numerous editorials in the *Farmer's Wife* urging farm women to cook generously with butter, eggs, and cream. Readers were warned, "The eggless cake is just as big a mistake on the general farm as the butterless table...."[26] A 1938 article admonished frugal housewives:

> The butter-saving woman is not as scientific or wise a planner as it might seem if she looks to a cream check for cash. Multiply butter-saving and butter-substituting country cooks many times and it does things to the national supply of butter. Folks must use butter a bit more freely if the surplus is to be reduced and the price of butter kept stable.[27]

The harshest indictment was reserved for the farm wife who bought margarine, a product seen as a great threat to the dairy industry. The *Farmer's Wife* asked rhetorically, "Why shouldn't farm folks save money by using cheaper butter substitutes instead of higher priced butter?" It answered its own question emphatically by stating that the few cents the farm wife saved per pound on purchased margarine could not possibly equal the loss her husband would sustain when he sold his milk and cream at a lower price.[28]

The producer-versus-consumer conflict over the use of margarine is graphically illustrated by a 1930s controversy that resulted when the Federal Bureau of Home Economics endorsed the use of margarine as economical. The Bureau of Home Economics was a subdivision of the USDA, and the National Cooperative Milk Producers were indignant that a federal agency devoted to farming interests should favor the dread ersatz. Similarly, when the Bureau of Home Economics distributed bulletins on the relative cost and nutritional value of various foods, wheat producers and millers protested that the bureau did not tout the virtues of wheat vigorously enough. The chairman of the House Agriculture Committee proposed an amendment "which would prohibit any employee of the Department from making any statement that gave the impression that it was harmful or undesirable to consume wheat or anything manufactured from wheat." This amendment passed in the House, but not in the Senate.[29]

Tension also existed in the academic disciplines of home economics and agriculture. At Cornell University, where the Department of Home Economics was part of the College of Agriculture, there existed "a fundamental conflict of interest between the constituency of home economics and agriculture ... the former represented the interests of food and fiber consumers [and] the latter represented the interests of food and fiber producers."[30] Dairy farmers tried to obstruct the home economists' efforts to objectively evaluate oleomargarine.

Recipes can be viewed as directives to women regarding what products to use or buy; the *Farmer's Wife* made the claim that its "recipes ... consistently boosted farm products."[31] Ironically, though, advertisements that appeared in this farm magazine did not consistently boost farm products. For instance, during the Depression advertisements for Junket rennet tablets told farmers' wives "How to make smoother ice cream with less cream," and numerous advertisements for Swan's Down cake flour promised that one could use "half as many eggs, half as much butter" for their one-egg cake. Swan's Down included a cartoon of two housewives bemoaning the high price of eggs and butter.[32] The presence of such conflicting messages about household economy within the pages of a farm women's magazine that counted a large dairy audience among its subscribers reflects the contradictions inherent in the farm woman's *new* role as a consumer and her *old* role as the wife of a producer.

"Out of the Barns and into the Kitchens" can be understood not just as a metaphor for changes that occurred in the *nature* of women's work, but also as a literal description of a change – or rather a contraction – in the *site* of that work. In what may be called "the geography of gender," the male workplace had long been the fields and the female sphere the house,[33] with the yard and barn constituting more or less shared, androgynous zones. As the sexual division of labor on the farm became more sharply defined in the twentieth century, the outdoor/indoor dichotomy also became more defined and the barn and yard were seen by many women (and men) as obviously outdoors and outside of the female domain. Some women viewed this with regret or rebellion; others welcomed the diminished productive role. The following letter, written in 1915 to the USDA by a Kansas woman, indicates an astute appreciation of what today would be called the "double burden" and expresses very definite ideas about the geography of gender. She begins with the pronouncement, "I protest against the Hens," and goes on to ask:

> This is my question: When I have cooked, and swept, and washed, and ironed, and made beds for a family of five ... and have done the necessary mending and some sewing, haven't I done enough? In any fair division of labor between the farmer and his wife the man would take the outdoors and the woman the indoors. That would drop the chickens on the man's side, with the probable result that on most farms there would be no chickens; on some there would be big flocks.[34]

The distance between men's and women's separate spheres was not only a matter of *how* the work was divided and *where* the work was conducted;

there is evidence to suggest that distance between their work sites was increasing in terms of *physical* proximity as well. A study done in 1953 showed that on prosperous farms, farmers were choosing to build their barns farther away from the house.[35] Moreover, the trend was toward larger farms. It can be argued that farm families were experiencing to a lesser degree what the urban and suburban household had already experienced – a separation of home and work for men, with the husband leaving the home for his work site, in this case the barn or the field. To what extent did the farm family maintain the preindustrial integration of personal life and work if it was not as convenient for husbands, wives, and children to physically interact? It follows that if wives did not frequent the barns and the fields, they had less practical knowledge of the farm business, which in turn might hinder their participation as truly equal partners in the business. The 1928 *Farmer's Wife*'s claim that "The woman on the farm is in the very *center* of the farm business and knows the details of sowing and planting, of harvesting and marketing the crops *just as intimately as her husband*" is not entirely convincing.[36]

The early twentieth-century literature for, by, and about farm women was divided as to whether farm women were drudges or equal partners on the farm. Many farm women did consider themselves equal partners in the family farm. For instance, a Michigan woman described pitching in to help milk the cows one evening, a chore she indicated was ordinarily her husband's. A female neighbor dropped in and commented, "I wouldn't milk any man's cows." "Well," the farm woman replied, "I'm not milking 'any man's' cows; I'm milking *our* cows."[37]

Yet some women felt the need to protect themselves from being exploited by their husbands as unpaid hired hands. A farm wife from New York State who wrote a letter to the *Farmer's Wife* entitled "Don't Start" and simply signed "Overworked" had this to say about helping with outdoor work in emergencies: "Show me a man who won't take any amount of help if his wife is willing to give it. From my experience and that of friends and neighbors I have found the more you 'help out' the more you will have to."[38] Similar advice came from a woman calling herself "Go Slow" from Iowa, who cautioned women, in a letter entitled "Let Brides Beware," not to let emergencies occur too often since women had enough to do cooking, cleaning, and raising children.[39] That many women were reluctant to take on the double burden is reflected in other letters to the *Farmer's Wife*, such as one from "Out-of-Breath Betty," who asked, "Is it really worth while to try to do the work of two or three women in a day? It is two or three, isn't it, when a woman does all the necessary work in a home and then helps her husband in the field, and raises a hundred chickens?" "Betty" concluded by saying that she tried to do her share by saving, apparently quite satisfied with her consumer role, and added that she "wouldn't milk [a cow] on a bet."[40]

Of course, some farm women were not just resisting the double burden but were enthusiastically embracing a feminine mystique. In a letter dated 1940 an Oregon wife observed, "To me it seems that mamma in a pretty housecoat, putting the children to bed and making coffee to share with Daddy in the living room, is doing her part better than if she drags in from the barn in dirty overalls to a dull and disorderly house and neglected children."[41]

Women today might have more sympathy with the farm woman who in 1938 resented the image of a rural "Superwoman" as portrayed in the prescriptive literature. She wrote, "I have read the Success Stories of money-making women. Some of them, it seemed to me, must have gotten in 48 hours in the 24 to accomplish what they did. Some I just couldn't believe accomplished it all."[42]

There is an important difference in strategy between women today and these earlier twentieth-century women in resisting the double burden: working wives today often attempt to equalize the domestic work load by trying to get men to take on some of the "women's work," whereas earlier farm women tried to equalize it by saying no to "men's work." Apparently it was not common (and arguably not even possible given agricultural conditions) for farmers to share in the housework, except occasionally in the arduous task of doing laundry. In 1914 the *Country Gentleman* columnist Nellie Kedzie Jones noted, "I wish it could be burnt into the consciousness of every man and every woman that washing under average farm conditions is man's work, not a woman's."[43] Such a "redivision" of the sexual division of labor did not come to pass. Instead, farm women in their consumer role turned to a technological solution – the washing machine – rather than challenging the sexual division of labor.

Like their suburban and urban counterparts, most farm women looked to consumerism, in the form of privately owned labor-saving devices, as an individual solution to housework. Thus, while there existed a few examples of cooperative laundries, such as the first one opened in 1912 in Chatfield, Minnesota, where the boiler system of the local creamery provided the power to clean fifty families' clothing at five cents a pound,[44] most farm wives aspired to purchase their own washing machines.

It is important to note that "labor-saving devices" in the context of rural America in the first half of the twentieth century included utilities such as running water and electricity as well as major appliances and small tools. In fact, to understand how primitive the work conditions were in some farm households we must view a sink with a drain (for instance) as a modern "convenience": the agricultural census of 1945 revealed that three out of five farm households did not have this fundamental equipment.[45] Obviously the lack of a drain meant that all the water carried *into* the house for cooking, washing dishes, laundry, bathing, and so on had also to be carried *out* of the house, a function of modern plumbing we probably take for granted. The rural sociologist Carl Taylor asked numerous farm women in the 1930s which modern convenience they would choose first and reported that they were "unanimous in saying they would take running water and a kitchen sink."[46] Only 17.8 percent of farm households had running water in 1940. By 1950 only 42.7 percent of farm households had running water, and as recently as 1960 only 74.8 percent of farm households had acquired running water.[47] By one estimate, a farm household of five persons needed 175 gallons of water a day for household use alone,[48] and much of this water was carried by farm women. In a 1919 survey of farm households conducted by the USDA, 61 percent of women reported that carrying water was one of their chores and that they hauled it an average distance of thirty-nine feet many times a day. (Out West farm women "fetched" water an average of sixty-five feet!)[49] (See table 1, p. 182.) Electricity was also lacking on most farms. In 1930 only 10.6 percent of farm households had electricity; by 1940 only 32.6 percent of farm households were electrified.[50]

In some instances the lack of modern conveniences was a direct result of poverty, and *both* farm men and women made do with obsolete tools and labor-intensive, back-breaking methods of running farms and farm households. Yet over and over again farm women complained that they put up with antiquated equipment while their husbands enjoyed the latest in agricultural machinery.

The hard life of some farm women was summed up in a 1915 rural sociology textbook:

> Perhaps the sorest spot in the rural problem is the lot of the neglected farm wife and mother. Even where agricultural prosperity is indicated by great barns filled with plenty, often a dilapidated farm-house nearly devoid of beauty, comfort, or convenience, measures the utter disregard of the housewife's lot. Money is freely spent, when new machinery is needed on the farm, or another fifty-acre piece is added after a prosperous season, but seldom a thought to the needs of the kitchen. While the men of the farm ride the sulky plough or the riding harrow of the twentieth century, the women have neither a washing-machine nor an indoor pump, to say nothing of running water, sanitary plumbing, or a bath-tub. Sometimes the drudgery of the farm is endured by the mother uncomplainingly, or even contentedly; but the daughter recoils from it with a growing discontent.[51]

The fear of discontented daughters was a real one, as the "woman question" for rural America became "How ya gonna keep 'em down on the farm?" The mass exodus from rural areas in the twentieth century was led by women, and in 1917 in New York State the sex ratio on farms was 120 men to every 100 women.[52] By 1984 the imbalance in the Farm Belt had grown to 134 men to every 100 women.[53]

In 1917 the *Farmer's Wife* informed fathers that they could stem this female out-migration and keep their daughters on the farms by providing them with labor-saving devices.[54] Even an advertisement aimed at men for Ford tractors appealed to farmers' concerns about their daughters, suggesting that a farmer who owned a Ford tractor would be a better dad to his daughter since he would be less tired. Furthermore, his daughter would have a more positive view of the farm and be more inclined to stick with it herself.[55] The implication of the "if not for your wife, then for your daughter" theme suggests that men may have been more responsive to egalitarian appeals on behalf of their daughters than on behalf of their wives, who may not have been as mobile.

A USDA survey of farm households conducted in 1919 found that 42 percent of the farms surveyed had power-driven farm machinery, while only 15 percent of the homes had power-driven appliances for household use.[56] To equalize this uneven distribution of modern equipment, a group of Nebraska farm women put forth this six-point technological agenda in 1923:

1   A power washing machine for the house for every tractor bought for the farm.
2   A bath tub in the house for every binder on the farm.
3   Running water in the kitchen for every riding plow for the fields.
4   A kerosene cook-stove for every auto truck.
5   A fireless cooker for every new mowing machine.
6   [Their] share of the farm income.[57]

This question of a fair share of the farm income is at the heart of the drudge-versus-equal-partner debate. While it is true that in the early twentieth century many women still earned money from marketing poultry and dairy products (generally butter) or selling garden produce, these women often did not get to keep their earnings for their own use. As illustrated in table 1, the 1919 USDA survey discovered that only 11 percent of the farm women surveyed kept their butter money, 22 percent kept their poultry money, and 16 percent kept their egg money.[58] Farm women often commented that their work in running

Table 1 Farm women's work, 1919

	Eastern States	Central States	Western States	United States
Helps to milk cows	24%	45%	37%	36%
Makes butter	43%	66%	74%	60%
Sells butter	31%	33%	33%	33%
Keeps butter money	9%	9%	16%	11%
Cares for poultry	69%	89%	84%	81%
Average size flock	90 hens	102 hens	71 hens	90 hens
Keeps poultry money	13%	25%	21%	22%
Keeps egg money	16%	16%	17%	16%
Carries water	54%	68%	57%	61%
Distance water carried	23 ft.	41 ft.	65 ft.	39 ft.
Helps in fields[a]	27%	22%	23%	24%
Cares for garden	41%	67%	57%	56%

Source: Derived from Florence Ward, "The Farm Woman's Problems," U.S. Department of Agriculture Circular no. 148 (Washington, D.C.: GPO, 1920), a survey of 10,044 farm women conducted in 1919.
[a]An average of 6.7 weeks per year

the household – which included raising much of the food for the table, preserving foods, feeding threshing crews and hired hands, caring for children, cleaning, and sewing – was not rewarded with an equal share of the family income or in decision making.

A common bit of nineteenth-century folk wisdom was that where the farm home was more imposing than the barn, "the woman is the boss."[59] This suggests that some rural people identified a "battle of the sexes" or at least tension between farmers and their wives over financial decisions, family resources, and competing priorities in the adoption of modern technology. The most famous fictional representation of this struggle is, of course, Mary Wilkins Freeman's 1891 short story "The Revolt of Mother." "Mother" moves her family out of the shack that has long been their home into the palatial new barn, a kind of "out of the barns and into the kitchens" in reverse.[60] For some reason Freeman later repudiated her own story. She wrote:

all fiction ought to be true and "The Revolt of Mother" is not true.... There never was in New England a woman like Mother. If there had been she certainly would not have moved into the palatial barn.... She simply would have lacked the nerve.... She would also have lacked the imagination. New England women ... coincided with their husbands that the sources of wealth should be better housed than the consumers.... Mother would never have dreamed of putting herself ahead of Jersey cows which meant good money....[61]

That cows had better accommodations than people was a common assertion. A Kansas farm woman wrote a sarcastic letter to *Farm Journal* in 1948 charging that "It seems that the cows, calves, horses, sheep, hogs, chickens, and turkeys must be made *comfortable* first, then if the machinery and house are paid for, if there's time and money left, the little woman may get her sink and drain." She added that running water had recently been put in for the chickens and turkeys on her farm, although she herself still labored in a kitchen without piped-in water or a drain in her sink.[62] That this letter hit a raw nerve in many other farm women is reflected by the fact that it was voted the best letter to the editor by the (mostly female) readers of *Farm Journal*'s women's section.

And yet there was a logic to providing fowl with running water first, for elsewhere *Farm Journal* advised that running water could increase the chicken's winter egg production by 19.5 percent and thus increase profits.[63] In their quest for modern conveniences farm women had to struggle against a compelling economic imperative requiring that limited resources be reinvested in the farm in the form of more land, more labor, or more machines, because that was where the income was. This hard-headed reality was summed up in the aphorism, "A barn can build a house sooner than a house can build a barn."[64] Unfortunately, many farm women like "Mother" discovered that a barn only built another barn.

It would be too simple to suggest that farmers were acting in an economically "rational" way in their single-minded devotion to profit while farmers' wives were "irrational" in valuing family comfort, leisure, and health over profits. In fact, as capitalist expansion in the twentieth century depended on consumer purchasing, I would suggest that farm women, in their desire to buy major applicances, were every bit as "modern" as their husbands in integrating farm households into the consumer economy.

Farm women were encouraged in their roles as consumers on many fronts: the USDA, agricultural colleges, extension services, and farm journals all offered consumer information to farm women. A New York State farm woman answered a 1915 USDA query as to what were the needs of farm women by saying, "To my mind the Department can do no better for the country woman than to help her buy intelligently."[65]

Naturally, farm women had their allies in the world of finance as well as in their desire to own labor-saving devices. A trade journal devoted to

rural banking called the *Banker-Farmer*, published in the 1910s and
1920s, had a surprising number of articles devoted to women. The
thrust of most of these articles was to urge the purchase of large appliances, preferably bought on credit or on the installment plan. To this
end rural bankers advocated that farm women have their own checking
and savings accounts, accompany their husbands when conferring with
local bankers about loans, and generally be given a greater say in the
financial decisions on the farm – in short, that farm wives be treated as
genuine business partners. The *Banker-Farmer* put this on a sound
financial basis by observing, "It pays to make the women happy. It
pays to emancipate the slaves, and especially when those slaves are our
wives, our mothers, our daughters. It pays in money, indirectly, if not
directly, but whether or not it pays in money it must be done."[66] Bankers
recognized that farm women as equal partners were bigger spenders than
drudges were.

The *Farmer's Wife* is another source rich in information and messages
to farm women about consumerism. With a circulation of 1.25 million
readers by 1939, when it was absorbed by *Farm Journal*, the *Farmer's
Wife* was the most popular women's magazine aimed at a rural audience.
The magazine was established in 1896 and was originally more a primer
for production with many columns on dairying, poultry, gardening, and
the production of other marketable items. By the 1920s and 1930s the
Farmer's Wife gradually put more emphasis on consumerism, including
the establishment of a test kitchen and a *Farmer's Wife* seal of approval to
endorse products and appliances. Articles that promoted brand names
also demystified the new stoves, refrigerators, cleaning products, miracle
fabrics, and convenience foods on the market. So engaging seemed
consumer culture that an article on organizing community get-togethers
went so far as to suggest an entertainment called "Advertise," in which
teams matched up products and slogans.[67]

No surprise, then, that the advertisements in the magazine reinforced
its consumer emphasis. For instance, an advertisement for overalls
depicted a winsome farm wife in a feminine frock announcing, "I
don't wear the pants, but I buy 'em...."[68] Similarly, an advertisement
for a new stove asked readers, "What makes a man brag about his wife?
The answer you hear most often is that she knows how to buy wisely."[69]
This emphasis on buying as opposed to producing (and selling) marked
a departure from the traditional nineteenth-century integration of farm
women's household production into the farm economy.

In 1917 the *Farmer's Wife* printed a virtual prose poem to self-actual-
ization through labor-saving devices, entitled "I Resolve to Grow." The
author conceded, "I am not developing as a woman should develop for
the sake of herself and all whom she is associated." She observed that

"Time is necessary for Growth and Development" and concluded, "I resolve to buy not less than one first-class time-and-strength saving tool every year. . . ." The resulting free time would be spent on leisure pursuits such as music, reading, outings, and establishing closer ties with family and the community.[70]

Compare this to a feature about another farm woman who we are told saved seven hours a week by trading in her old wood stove for an electric range in 1948.[71] She used her newly acquired "free" time to do all the family sewing, which she had previously hired someone else to do. The point of the article, of course, was that free time gained from a labor-saving device can translate into a cash saving, since in this case the wife was able to produce goods and services that she had formerly bought. But her story also illustrates the point that new tasks (or higher standards) rush in to fill the "free" time that labor-saving devices "save."

Not only did the *Farmer's Wife* urge the purchase of labor-saving devices, it addressed the problem of persuading reluctant husbands to agree to these investments. An article called "600 Ways to Get That Running Water" noted that a farm woman who has to lug water may have forgotten how to "manage" her husband. Earlier, the editors had suggested that lack of modern conveniences was not a matter of money but a "human relations problem." They solicited readers' suggestions on the "psychology" they had used on their husbands, which implies that many farm women did not have direct access to the purse strings and were actually less than equal partners.

The six hundred replies from readers ranged from the coy to the militant. Strategies included feigning illness, going on strike, placing the order for the pipes and installing them oneself (even bungling the job to secure male assistance), and calculating the net savings from the investment and presenting the figures to one's husband. Not infrequently farm women reported that all it took was to have their husbands tote the water for even a short while to convince them to pipe in water.[72] An inventive – if somewhat vindictive – strategy was organized by the We Want Water for Christmas Club: this group of Illinois farm wives published the names of their husbands in a public newsletter until one by one the recalcitrant husbands surrendered and installed running water.[73] Strategies such as this suggest that Mary Wilkins Freeman was shortsighted in repudiating "The Revolt of Mother": real-life farm women did exist who had the nerve and the imagination to revolt against a division of labor that assigned decision making and money spending to men. The method the *Farmer's Wife* endorsed over all others was the idea of partnership. It concluded, "If you can make your husband think of you as his partner, the rest is easy. . . ."[74]

The *Farmer's Wife* summed up its philosophy that the quality of life on the farm was as important as the profits in its motto, "A good life as well as a good living." Yet, as we've seen, messages abounded that "a good life" could be purchased – that in fact, it required "a good living" to afford "a good life."

Labor-saving devices failed to liberate women from housework; on the contrary, women spent at least as much time as before meeting higher standards, and the sexual division of labor in the home was reinforced. All of this has been well demonstrated by historians of technology such as Joann Vanek, Ruth Schwartz Cowan, and Charles Thrall. With disturbing prescience the *Rural New Yorker* reflected in 1900:

> So many labor-saving devices have been common that woman's work should now be simpler, but with these improvements, our standard of comfort has been so greatly raised that the present-day housewife seems more overworked.... It is indeed unfortunate if we permit labor-saving devices to increase our work, rather than to lessen it.[75]

The promise of "a good life" in the form of consumerism blended with domesticity was one that many farm women ultimately found to be elusive.

Notes

1   Susan Keating Glaspell, "A Jury of Her Peers," in *American Voices, American Women*, ed. Lee R. Edwards and Arlyn Diamond (New York: Avon Books, 1973), 359–81.

2   T. R. Pirtle, *History of the Dairy Industry* (Chicago: Mojonnier Bros., 1926), 213, 327.

3   Pirtle, *History of the Dairy Industry*, 102.

4   Pirtle, *History of the Dairy Industry*, 110–12.

5   Elmer O. Fippin, *Rural New York* (New York: Macmillan Co., 1921), 279.

6   Eric Brunger, "New York State Dairy Industry, 1850–1900" (Ph.D. diss., Syracuse University, 1954), 72.

7   E. H. Farrington, "Women in Dairy Manufacturing," *American Produce Review*, July, 1918, 366. Emphasis mine.

8   Farrington, "Women in Dairy Manufacturing," 368.

9   Farrington, "Women in Dairy Manufacturing," 368.

10 *Rural New Yorker*, Dec., 1863, 398. Cited in Brunger, "New York State Dairy Industry," 64.

11 Pirtle, *History of the Dairy Industry*, 74.

12 Fippin, *Rural New York*, 278.

13 Pirtle, *History of the Dairy Industry*, 99, 101, 102.

14 E. R. Eastman, *The Trouble Maker* (New York: Macmillan Co., 1927), 125.

15 Eastman, *The Trouble Maker*, 189.
16 US Department of Agriculture, *Domestic Needs of Farm Women*, Report no. 104 (Washington, DC: GPO, 1915), 73. Emphasis mine.
17 Pirtle, *History of the Dairy Industry*, 80.
18 Page Smith and Charles Daniel, *The Chicken Book* (Boston: Little, Brown, 1975), 232.
19 "We Honor the Hen," *Farm Journal*, Feb., 1939, 3.
20 "Poultry and the City Market," *Farmer's Wife*, Oct., 1927, 56.
21 "Fifty Hens or Five Hundred?" *Farmer's Wife*, Feb., 1931, 52.
22 "How Many Chickens?" *Farm Journal*, Apr., 1946, 124.
23 Smith and Daniel, *Chicken Book*, 292.
24 US Department of Agriculture, *Economic Needs of Farm Women*, Report no. 106 (Washington, DC: GPO, 1915), 64.
25 "Have Another Egg, Dear?" *Farmer's Wife*, Oct., 1930, 3.
26 "Better Prices for Better Eggs," *Farmer's Wife*, May, 1930, 60.
27 "Use Butter Generously," *Farm Journal*, Nov., 1938, 11.
28 "Is It True?" *Farmer's Wife*, Mar., 1930, 3.
29 Gladys Baker, "Women in the USDA," *Agricultural History*, Jan., 1976, 197.
30 Gould P. Colman, *Education and Agriculture: A History of the New York State College of Agriculture at Cornell University* (Ithaca: Cornell University, 1963), 284.
31 "Frugal or Economical?" *Farm Journal*, Dec., 1938, 16.
32 See the *Farmer's Wife*, Jan., 1931, 21; Feb., 1936, 21; *Farm Journal*, Feb., 1937, 27; June, 1937, 30.
33 Mary P. Ryan, *Womanhood in America: From Colonial Times to the Present*, 2d ed. (New York: New Viewpoints, 1979), ix. Sex Roles," in *Energy and Transport: Historical Perspectives on Policy Issues*, ed. George H. Daniels and Mark H. Rose (Beverly Hills: Sage Publications, 1982), 235–59.
34 US Department of Agriculture, *Social and Labor Needs of Farm Women*, Report no. 103 (Washington, DC: GPO, 1915), 51.
35 James W. Green, "Distance as a Factor in Farmhouse Location," *Rural Sociology*, Sept., 1953, 261–62.
36 "A Portrait: The Typical Farm Homemaker," *Farmer's Wife*, July, 1928, 9. Emphasis mine.
37 "Are Wives Loyal?" *Farm Journal*, Feb., 1938, 10.
38 *Farmer's Wife*, Jan., 1936, 18.
39 *Farmer's Wife*, Nov., 1935, 13.
40 *Farmer's Wife*, Oct., 1929, 18.
41 *Farm Journal*, Dec., 1940, 52.
42 *Farm Journal*, Aug., 1938.
43 Jeanne Hunnicutt Delgado, "Nellie Kedzie Jones' Advice to Farm Women: Letters from Wisconsin, 1912–1916," *Wisconsin Magazine of History*, Autumn, 1973, 14.
44 E. B. Forney, "How Farmers Formed the World's First Cooperative Laundry," *Banker-Farmer*, Apr., 1916, 12.
45 "Are You Emancipated?" *Farm Journal*, Nov., 1947, 124.

46 Carl C. Taylor, "Address to the Associated Country Women of the World," in *Proceedings of the Third Triennial Conference, May 31–June 11, 1936*, US Department of State Publication no. 1092, Conference Series 34 (Washington, DC: GPO, 1937), 198.

47 Joann Vanek, "Keeping Busy: Time Spent in Housework, United States, 1920–1970" (PhD diss., University of Michigan, 1973), 2.

48 "Running Water Runs Up Profits," *Farm Journal*, Mar., 1946, 125.

49 Florence Ward, *The Farm Woman's Problems*, US Department of Agriculture Circular no. 148 (Washington, DC: GPO, 1920), 8.

50 Vanek, "Keeping Busy," 3.

51 Albert H. Leake, *The Means and Methods of Agricultural Education* (Boston: Houghton Mifflin, 1915), 201–2.

52 Fippin, *Rural New York*, 40.

53 "A Growing Question: How Can You Keep Women on Farms?" *Wall Street Journal*, Aug. 30, 1984, 1.

54 "Daughter Chooses the Farm," *Farmer's Wife*, June, 1917, 8.

55 *Farm Journal*, Sept., 1944, 37.

56 Ward, *Farm Woman's Problems*, 8.

57 Newell Leroy Sims, *Elements of Rural Sociology* (New York: Thomas Y. Corwell, 1928), 274–75.

58 Ward, *Farm Woman's Problems*, 11.

59 Fred A. Shannon, *The Farmer's Last Frontier: Agriculture, 1860–1897* (New York: Holt, Rinehart and Winston, 1945), 368–69.

60 Mary E. Wilkins Freeman, *The Revolt of Mother and Other Stories* (Old Westbury, NY: Feminist Press, 1974).

61 Mary E. Wilkins Freeman, "Who's Who and Why," *Saturday Evening Post*, Dec. 8, 1917, 25, 75.

62 *Farm Journal*, Jan., 1948, 92–93.

63 "Running Water Runs Up Profits," 125.

64 Sims, *Elements of Rural Sociology*, 264.

65 US Department of Agriculture, *Economic Needs of Farm Women*, 64.

66 "Giving the Farm Girl Her Chance," *Banker-Farmer*, Apr., 1914, 7.

67 *Farm Journal*, Jan., 1944, 44.

68 *Farm Journal*, May, 1947, 117.

69 *Farmer's Wife*, May, 1938, 30.

70 "I Resolve to Grow," *Farmer's Wife*, Jan., 1917, 173.

71 "Electric Cooking Saves *Me*!" *Farm Journal*, Oct., 1948, 93.

72 "600 Ways to Get That Running Water," *Farm Journal*, Apr., 1948, 138, 140–41.

73 *Farm Journal*, Feb., 1942, 45.

74 "600 Ways to Get That Running Water," 141.

75 *Rural New Yorker*, Jan. 20, 1900.

Documents

Social and Labor Needs of Farm Women

Extracts from letters received from farm women in response to an inquiry "how the US Department of Agriculture can better meet the needs of farm housewives," with special reference to the provision of instruction and practical demonstrations in home economics under the Act of May 8, 1914, providing for cooperative agricultural extension work, etc.

Woman's Labor

Long Hours and Overwork

The long hours of labor and the overworking of women on the farms form the major part of many letters. Several of the writers stated that it was impossible for them to get any kind of domestic help, even in time of sickness, and commented on the difference between the country home and the city home, where day workers can be obtained in emergencies. Some saw a solution for this difficulty in properly directed immigration. Others suggested inducing the surplus from the overcrowded sections to enter domestic employment on the farm. Coupled closely with this complaint is the fact that conditions of farm life tend to make the younger generation leave the farms and seek employment in city factories and urban occupations, thus making it more difficult for the overworked farm woman to employ the daughter of a neighbor as her assistant.

A large number speak of the extra work put upon women by the employment of large numbers of field laborers who have to be housed and fed; and one or two, while stating that farm help no longer comes from the neighboring farms, object seriously to introducing into their families the rough element now hired. Others seem not to object to the work, but state that under present marketing conditions the returns they

Excerpted from *Social and Labor Needs of Farm Women*, Report no. 103 (compiled in the Office of Information, G. W. Wharton, Chief), United States Department of Agriculture, Office of the Secretary. Issued February 17, 1915, Government Printing Office, Washington, DC, pp. 42–9, 54–5.

receive from the sale of garden truck, poultry and eggs, and milk and butter, do not constitute a legitimate wage.

Many letters from Southern States complain of the heavy work that women have to do in the fields. Cotton hoeing and picking are frequently mentioned as one of the chief hardships. This field work, it is said, leaves the woman no time for anything else.

The following are some of the significant extracts from letters dealing with these phases of the subject:

Northeastern Quarter

Maine

"One great trouble, perhaps the greatest, is the fact that here in New England whatever help is employed on the farm must to some extent be taken into the house. Formerly the 'hired man' was the son of a neighbor or perhaps the cousin or relative of the proprietor, so was not so bad; but now the help that it is possible to obtain is usually a very undesirable member of the household, besides being another for the housewife to provide food for. I see no remedy for this. I know several cases where farms that have been for several generations in one family are being sold because no really efficient help can be obtained either indoors or out."

Massachusetts

"Too little attention has been given to the part and importance of the woman on the farm. Probably this is so because of the ideal which prevails but which now gives some promise of change. This ideal assigns to the farm woman almost constant work that is heavy, and provides for her too few (if any) and insufficient conveniences and improvements for doing her work. She goes at it largely as a matter of brawn, exercising too meagerly her intelligent thought. But often, too, the man is held as tightly to his daily routine and fails to have time for thinking how he may do his work by better methods – or improve the conditions of the farm woman whose part in rural economy is rated too low. This ideal, in the second place, provides too inadequately for the farm woman's leisure and cultivation of interest in other things than her daily routine of household cares. Her sphere of thought and activity is frequently limited and often her work is drudgery."

"It seems to me that the farmers' wives' work is more laborious than the farmers'. The farmer has one day in seven for comparative rest, but

Sunday is often the hardest day in the week, especially during the summer, for the farmer's wife."

New York

"It may be summed up in two words – drudgery and economy. These seem to pursue her from the time she signs her name to the mortgage that is given in the purchase of the farm until that other time when, weary and worn, she gives up the unequal struggle and is laid at rest. This interest (paid on farm mortgages) robs the farm woman of much.

"We bought a 110-acre farm; my husband was a good dairyman and a first-class butter maker, but we could scarcely pay taxes and interest and live, until I took up crochet work. I managed thus to pay $200 on the mortgage every year, but the strain was too great, and overwork ruined my health – but the mortgage was paid. Meantime I have had only one new hat in eight years and one secondhand dress, earned by lace work. We are of the better class and have to keep up appearances, but the struggle is heartbreaking and health destroying. We have worked night and day. Our two sons have had to give up a higher education to work, and both have decided mechanical and constructive ability."

"Suggest some feasible plan for caring for the farm help without making them a part of the family. Many of them are dirty, vulgar, profane, and drunken, yet they eat at table with us; our children listen to and become familiar with their drunken babblings. Our privacy is destroyed, our tastes and sense of decency are outraged. We are forced to wait upon and clean up after men who would not be allowed to enter the houses of men of any other vocation. Do not misunderstand; the farmers' wives care little for social status. It is not because they are hired men that we wish them banished, but because oftentimes they are personally unworthy."

Pennsylvania

"Lack of proper literature and time to read it; almost impossible to employ girls or women to help with housework. How to provide board and lodging for farm laborers without taking them into the home and table with the family (they often being very undesirable foreigners and tramps who only work for a few days to earn money for drink)."

"I have in mind a small, delicate woman, with a family of small children, that does all her own housework, milks four or five cows, cooks for extra help, carries from a spring all the water – no time to read a paper or book. Late to bed and early to rise, yet neither he nor she has any idea they could make her burden easier."

A man: "The average farmer's wife is unable to devote her best energies to the bigger problems of farm housekeeping owing to the fact that she is obliged to be more or less of a drudge. Surely among the vast numbers of immigrant girls to this country there must be some who would welcome an opportunity to identify themselves with a well-kept home; thus to be taught to become economical and progressive farm women. If the Government could establish and maintain a bureau, with agencies at the principal landing stations, to this end it would work a great benefit to the farm women. I think the farm woman is in many instances overburdened with work and the care of a family; so much so that many of the farmers' daughters are looking upon farm life with a shudder."

Ohio

A man: "Under present conditions it is impossible most times to get help even in case of sickness. The farm wife can not reach a laundry or a bakery, nor can the husband and his help get their meals at a hotel or restaurant, as can be done oftentimes in the city. She is depended on to feed her own people, and often to appear hospitable and generous. She feels she must be in readiness to feed wayfarers that are hardly able to reach a hotel and very much wish to dine at a farm-house."

Illinois

"My first complaint is hard work, no profits, and an exceedingly small sum upon which to live and supply her children. If city people could see the farmers' wives and children work and sweat in the fields in June, July, and August, when they are going to the beach or some summer resort or to cool in the mountains, they would not wonder at our complaint. When our work is over we could go, too, if we got any profits."

A man: "It is the wife of the tenant and poor farmer who needs help. She has a hard row to hoe. She has very few labor-saving implements, no electrical or gasoline power, but does nearly all her work by 'main strength and awkwardness.' Thousands rise at 4 a.m. and peg away until 10 p.m. That game finally puts her down and out. The union man and 'industrial worker' does his eight-hour stunt and then agitates for shorter hours and more pay, but the wife of the tenant or poor farmer has no time to 'agitate', strike, or walk out. Her pay is plain board and clothing. Very few ever see a State fair, get a week's vacation, or even an auto ride. She is a slave to long hours of work and her husband is a slave to the landlord, for whom he works two-fifths or one-half his time, and who is determined to have every dime, peck, or pound of his rent."

Michigan

"I am not writing as a practical farm woman but as one who has recently lived three years on a large farm. Those three years gave me an opportunity to observe and understand the hardships and isolation, the waste of time with the tiresome traveling back and forth, constant contact with uncongenial laborers and many other unpleasant features. I do not complain so much of the labor. Work is honorable and health-giving. There were weeks when I accomplished more than many other farmers' wives. The work of the farmer's wife is hard, but unless she takes part in the more laborious operations in the field and stables, I think it is not more so than many other women in town who have their homes to keep up and take boarders or sew or in some way assist in providing for the family."

"The necessity of taking the farm men into the family is the most unfortunate of any condition of the home. Labor is scarce and the farmer must take such labor as he can get, often changing several times during the year, with rough and uncouth fellows who have to sit with the family at table and evenings, and their manner and language make this intimate association undesirable for all members of the family, especially the boys and girls. I think the farmer should have a men's room where they can sit and have a separate table for eating. When it so happened that we had to give the men meals, I gave them a separate table with food neatly prepared and we thought they liked it better than eating with the family."

"The woman in town can always hire some one to help by the day at least, but in the country that is not so – if she hires help she must make a companion of the girl and often take her along when she goes to town. There is no family privacy in the farm home where help is kept. The average farmer, or better than the average, does not care for the privacy of life. I can see no possible way of improving the home life and giving the family life more thought unless the farmer can afford a home for his men."

Wisconsin

A man: "On the large farms where men must be boarded at the farm home, and where it is hard to get servants and where there may be several small children, the wife and mother is to be pitied. It seems the owner should build small cottages for his help as the Southerners did for their slaves and thus keep work from the home. Where the wife has to cook for hands such good packers' goods as possible should be used."

Minnesota

"The farm work which has to be done is nothing but drudgery for the whole family from the age of 12 years and upward and it has least pay for our services. We have on an average from ten to fifteen thousand dollars invested in our farms and personal property and we have to work from 12 to 13 hours a day to make a living."

"I asked the sister of my housekeeper, who has tried both city and country, and she said it was about equal for her in this way: On the farm her husband managed to work 200 acres without a hired man most of the time with her help. In the city he worked as a day laborer for $2.50 per day and she kept 12 boarders and took care of her two children."

"I have always lived on a farm except the first five years of my marriage, and I think I might almost as soon have been in jail, because the work is so hard and is never done. The hardest is the washing."

A man: "From the experience of 30 years in the store business in rural parts of northern Minnesota, I do not hesitate to say that over one-half of the total work done on the farm has been done by the women of the house, besides they have done all their cooking and mending and have raised the families."

Iowa

"The majority of farmers' wives are simply overburdened with summer company from the city, either relatives or friends, who if they were forced to change places with us would soon realize what it meant to be considered the one to make life lovely for them during the long hot days of harvest, haying, and all. We think articles written on this subject might bring them to realize we are not machines of perpetual motion with no chance of a feeling of physical exhaustion."

"There is almost every kind of machinery and utensils made to lighten her work, as well as machinery to lighten man's work. Therefore the fault must lie somewhere else. To my mind a great deal of it is their own choosing. I think the marked clause in an editorial taken from the Chicago Tribune of November 10, 1913, tells quite a story, and I know that it is a true statement of affairs in a great many cases. The marked sentence is: 'The average farmer, says this bulletin (referring to bulletin of Wisconsin country life conference), has until recently been interested in his crops, cattle, and a bank account more than he was in the comfort of his wife and children.' I am glad to say, however, that the more progressive class of farmers are putting in modern homes. In a great many – I could say the majority – of new houses built, gas or electric lights, heating plants, running water, with modern plumbing, etc., are being installed.

"If it were not for the long, hard hours with poor remuneration the majority of farmers' wives would be content. We are told to be more sociable – have picnics and merrymakings so as to be content with our lot. Why, we can hardly find time, as we are, to visit a neighbor, and are too tired on Sunday for church. A good rest would be a more cheerful prospect than any picnic. While city women are having parties and the children doing nothing but attending school, all hands on the farm are at work."

Missouri

"I have been a farmer's wife for 30 years and have never had a vacation."

"The laws are all right for the women. In my mind the worst trouble is with the women themselves. They spy around and talk of each other, making remarks about a speck of dirt or any disorder in a neighbor's house. Awfully nice housekeeping is the tyrant the women bow down to. It is a poor excuse of a woman who can not get help from her husband. I read somewhere of a woman who asked her husband for a wringer and sewing machine the first summer of their marriage. On being refused she hired out in harvest to make the money. After that lesson she had every labor-saving appliance she saw fit to ask for. I serve good, clean, whole-some food to the men folk, hire my washing, and do not scrub my kitchen floor."

"Every one is urging the farmer to raise crops. Now all this means extra help for the woman to cook for, since all these crops have to be attended, harvested, and marketed. From one to four extra men to board during the hottest part of the year is the rule, provided you can get the men. We would not complain if we could see the bank account growing in proportion to the work, or if there were any permanent improvement in our surroundings, but a good many of us are beginning to ask, Who gets the benefits of all the hurry and work necessary to produce the big crops? I heard a very practical farmer say last summer, when the corn was drying up, that he did not care, for he had noticed that he always made more on a bad crop year than on a good one. He was judging entirely by financial results and not taking into account the difference in labor to himself and his family.

"This question was brought up at a women's meeting recently, and all agreed that they were tired of this continual urging the farmer to so-called better farming, since it only meant more work for the whole family with no real gain. These were not dissatisfied women, but just average Middle-West farmers' wives and daughters who can help with the milking or take a team to the field if the hired man leaves suddenly or the exigencies of the case demand it – women physically and mentally alive, who feel the joy of achievement. Better homes and better living generally in the country will do more than all the back-to-the-land jargon. Farmers should be induced to pay more attention to the house, garden, and orchard, for these are badly neglected and will continue to be so long as all the time and attention are given to stock and field crops. With farm homes once made attractive, the high cost of living will settle itself. People will come back and raise their own living partly from choice and partly from necessity."

Southeastern Quarter

Virginia

"I am living in the most prosperous – at least said to be the richest county of Virginia, in the beautiful Shenandoah Valley. Most of the women live the lives of slaves – slaves to their farms and families. Help is hard to obtain and keep. The strong, hearty woman doesn't mind the work, and there are a great many of this class. The delicate, broken-down, and overworked are filling the hospitals."

North Carolina

A man: "The women here carry water one-quarter mile and go one mile to milk."

Georgia

A man: "On the cotton farms the women and children generally hoe out the cotton, putting it to a stand and cleaning the row of grass and weeds. Then in the fall of the year the women and children pick out the bulk of the cotton crop. This is the life of the average tenant of the South. The poor tenant mothers are deserving of the sympathy and encouragement of all. It often happens that our best and most prosperous farmers come from these poor children who have been taught to labor and learn the cost of a dollar, but the mothers toil on with no hope of anything except to raise their children."

Florida

"In almost all of the one-crop cotton-growing sections the labor question is narrowed down to the farmer, his wife, and children. The wife, if able to work, regardless of condition, makes a full hand at whatever the occasion demands – plowing, hoeing, chopping, putting down fertilizer, picking cotton, etc. The same is required of the children almost regardless of age, sex, or condition. In many cases this seems unavoidable. Poverty is the word that covers the condition."

Kentucky

A man: "The woman does 50 per cent of all the work on the farm except at the plow, such as cleaning up the land, hoeing the corn, potatoes, cabbages, and beans, etc. – the woman does the same as the man – in gathering the corn, potatoes, etc. The woman does the work at 50 cents per day and will ask for the work, while the men hands can't be employed on the farm for less than $1 a day. I employ women when I can't get men hands, and at half the cost."

Tennessee

"The two greatest problems that confront women in the rural districts are overmuch work and little strength. We need domestic help. We do not claim all wisdom in doing things, yet our knowledge surpasses our strength to do the many different tasks incumbent upon us in farm life.

Mississippi

"To look at the careworn, tired faces, and bent forms of the 'bride of a few years' in our hill sections, where servants are scarce, we realize at once our personal and National neglect and are astounded at the enormity of it."

"The woman living on farms, in addition to bearing and caring for her children, does her own housework – cooking, and washing the clothes once a week, and then works in the fields during the months of May, June, and July, which is the hoeing season, and in September, October, November, and December, which is the cotton-picking season."

A man: "I wonder if the gentleman has ever seen a woman plowing cotton with oxen, and what he would think if he knew that this woman's husband was working at a sawmill several miles away, and it was her duty to get up and cook his breakfast so he can be at his work at 6 – and yet this is a common sight in the rural districts. What is needed, and what can help this life? Go to that man and show him that the life he is living is wrong. What power can raise them from the neglected position this gentleman sees them in? I would answer: Educate the man who is her husband."

A man: "After consulting some of the women in this part of the woods I find that a majority want a law passed to this effect: Make it read that any man who marries a girl in the rural districts who requests or allows his wife to go to the field and work as a hand in making or gathering a crop be subject to a fine and imprisonment. The claim is that it is injurious to the offspring of such to be in the hot sun and laboring in the same."

Arkansas

A man: "The long hours of labor that the farmer's wife has to contend with and the constant drudgery ought to be mitigated – if there was a system of education taken up by the Government, which has been to some extent already, to explain to the farmers that the extremely long hours and constant drudgery is not economy and does not necessarily work toward prosperity in a financial way; that conservation of strength, energy, and health brings the best results; and that it doesn't pay to work such long hours and have no recreation to break the monotony of hard, constant labor. If farmers generally would not make the day's work longer than 10 hours, or at the least 8 hours, it would give some chance for recreation and rest, and a half holiday on Saturday if it was practiced generally would no doubt generally afford the necessary recreation and rest. When the housewife's labor commences at 5 o'clock in the morning and continues until bedtime, no wonder they get dissatisfied with their lot in life and break down in health and often suffer from nervous prostration on account of this unreasonable method and unhealthful practice of so many long hours."

A man: "They claim they have to work from sunup to sundown, hoeing, picking cotton in the mud and dew. I saw a man and his wife, while I was walking around among them. Their baby was fastened up in the house 400 yards from them. They said it stayed there from morning until dinner and from dinner until night (while the man and his wife were working in the field). I find some of them in bad shape."

"If we had time out of the cotton patch to learn how to can fruit for the market so we could can our fruit as it ripens, even if we only got pay for our labor, we would be no worse off and the world much better."...

Texas

"Her life in a majority of homes is one of constant physical labor and many hardships, and her constant exertions with no remission bring her to a premature grave. A neighbor farmer worth at least $30,000 lives as frugal, as hard as the poorest tenant on his farm. He arises at 4 o'clock each workday. The wife and daughter prepare the breakfast for the family and two hired men. At daylight, or soon after, the wife milks the cows, usually three or four, in an open lot. This duty is followed by house cleaning – in the spring house cleaning is followed by efforts to make a garden. At the approach of daylight the hands are in the field ready for the day's labor and remain there as long as they can see to work. The work teams are usually fed after dark, at which time the wife and daughter milk the cows, followed by the last meal of the day. If the farmer has had an unusually hard day's work, he and his men retire soon after supper, leaving the wife and daughter to wash dishes, prepare the kitchen for morning, undress and put to bed one, two, or more small children, making her bedtime at 10 or 11 o'clock. This farmer has all of the latest improved machinery for good and successful farming, but no equipment beyond a sewing machine to lighten his wife's burden. The wife and her daughter not only do the laundry work for the family but for the help as well. At the time of corn harvesting and gathering of cotton in the fall, the feminine labor is increased, and not only the daughter (the mother's only help) but every child, from 6 years up, is driven to the cotton field and often work in cotton wet with or dampened with rain. A regretful circumstance in connection with the children picking cotton is the further fact that he requires each child to pick a certain quantity of cotton each day. After all the crops are harvested, the children are sent to school during the winter months until time to commence preparations for a new crop, when those large enough to handle a plow are withdrawn from school.

"Let us state a remarkable fact. The wife cooperates with her husband in his strenuous efforts to make money on the farm, by performing her duties with a degree of pleasantness that is surprising, and not only acquiesces in his undertakings, but urges on and drives the children the same as he. Their philosophy is that it doesn't hurt children to work them, and trains them well to know how to work when grown – and to be successful at farming one must go early and late. The farmer now at the age of 55 years is practically a physical wreck, and his wife, stooped and wrinkled, has the appearance of a grandmother at the age of 75, although she has just passed the forty-ninth milepost in life's sojourn. What is said here respecting this family will apply to thousands of others in the South, and paradoxical as it may appear, the wife of the well-to-do farmer has the greatest burdens to bear. There are exceptions, of course."

"Two-thirds of the farm girls are denied an education by being kept in the fields or at routine housework until all their hopes and ambitions are crushed and blighted. The usual result is they reach maturity with little or no education, marry, and bring into the world children to rear like unto themselves; and so on and on, each generation forming a link in the chain that has no end. Compulsory education would break this chain."

California

"There is a question in my mind as to what to 'aid' us farm women means to you. Is it that you wish us to increase farm production, and are contemplating sending us a lot of pamphlets to 'help' us make more butter, raise more vegetables, supply the markets with more eggs than we do now, and be better cooks than we are? If that is what your 'service' to us would imply, I decline it with thanks. Not that I think we have reached perfection in our line of work, but because we already have many ways open to learn if we earnestly wish to do our work better, and also many of us have our hands too full without any increase in our amount of work. Therefore I do not believe it is literature on our work that we really need. But if such a thing is possible, that your department wishes to do something to make our lives a little easier and a little more pleasant, we certainly appreciate even your wishing such things for us. If you could be instrumental in actually helping us to get some of the 'good things' – by 'good things' I mean such conveniences as the average city woman accepts as a matter of course. The luxury of having the water right in the house, sinks, and a really, truly bathtub are some of the principal things we long for. Then, too, we have few books to read."

Power on the Farm
Guy E. Tripp

There is a wide-spread public interest in the reports that the farming in-dustry is less prosperous than most of the other industries of the country.

If this is true, then it certainly becomes a matter of importance to everybody because there are over 6,000,000 farms in the United States and more than 30,000,000 people, or nearly a third of our population, live on them.

The trouble with the farming industry can be stated in a word, and that is it yields unsatisfactory profits. There have been various reasons given for this condition of affairs:

One, that the farmer is caught between the upper millstone of high prices for the things which he must buy due to special conditions produced in the main by our protective tariff system, and the nether millstone of low prices for the bulk of his products which are influenced largely by the world markets where competition is free and unrestricted.

Another is that the high cost of distribution of his products in our home markets consumes too much of the margin between the prices which he receives and the prices which the ultimate consumer pays.

There are other things such as unsatisfactory farm labor conditions, lack of a system under which his products may be warehoused pending favorable market conditions, over-production, etc.

Any one, or all, of which may be factors in the situation.

The plight of relatively small margin of profits to the average farmer is a frequently recurring one, and in at least two outstanding cases the remedy which I am going to talk about has been successful in killing the patient, but I do not believe it will do so this time. I certainly hope not because, as they say down East, there is only one thing that can be cured after you kill it and that is a pig; a saying that I recommend to the earnest consideration of radical statesmen.

Apologizing for leading you back into ancient history, you will remem-ber that one of the principal causes of what is popularly known as "The Fall of the Roman Empire" was the unfortunate condition of the average farmer brought about by the employment of slaves on the large farms of the aristocracy which made it impossible for a free farmer to compete;

Excerpted from Guy E. Tripp, *Electric Development as an Aid to Agriculture* (New York: The Knickerbocker Press, 1926), pp. 1–3, 8–9, 39–40.

and, again, coming down to our own day, perhaps the unfortunate condition of the so-called poor white in the South was brought about by precisely this same cause.

Power an Important Factor in Improving Conditions

Now, since I endorse the introduction of the slave on the farm as an important factor in the improvement of farming conditions in this country, it becomes necessary to point out the difference between the kind I recommend and the kind which has always brought disaster in its train. I approve the use of the power slave; and since electric power is the most convenient and flexible for many purposes, I shall specifically deal with electric power.

Of course, there are other forms of power also adapted for farm use – farm tractors, gasoline engines, and the like – and wherever I speak of the general virtues of power, I include machines of this sort, although we electricians hope to supplant some of them in time. . . .

Electricity Not an Extravagance

If for much more practical reasons the majority of our farmers should adopt the general use of electric power on the farms, would it be an extravagance which they could not afford? I do not think so. I think it would tend to so improve and develop the man himself that out of the additional cost there would arise a profit from his greater alertness and efficiency.

Man is the all important thing in this world. Except for man, Pittsburgh would today be a wilderness filled with bears and woodchucks; and, in proportion as man supplements the pitiful power of his own muscles by an expanded and alert mind, so he surmounts all obstacles toward a higher standard of living.

I know enough about farming to realize that there is room for more efficiency in farm labor and that better tools make better workers. It is human nature for a man to use a tool until it is almost blunt rather than to treadle a grindstone, whereas a switch on a motor-driven grinder invites his soul.

The life of the farmer's wife, through the use of domestic electric appliances and other conveniences, would be emancipated, and her spirit either improves or depresses the family.

Better living conditions on the farm would make it easier to obtain efficient labor during harvest time, and so on.

But these things are all details. The important thing is to place 30,000,000 people alongside the rest of us in use and effect of use of modern industrial tools and most important of all to stimulate them to take a more active interest in the movement of industrial decentralization which I venture to hope has set in in this country. There are indeed many indications of this tendency. . . .

Now, the chief obstacle to the electrification of our farms is the high cost of bringing electric service to them. It usually does not pay to tap a high-tension line and build a low-tension line to take care of the relatively small demand of a few scattered farms, but it frequently does pay to do these things to serve an industry; and, when once a service connection is made and a line is built, neighboring farms can then be supplied with electric power at reasonable cost.

To cite a specific case, a group of southern farmers applied to their electric power company for service, but were told, after investigation, that this could not be supplied unless a nearby cotton-gin could also be included. The farmers called on the owner of the gin, with the result they got what they wanted.

Hence, as small factories multiply in the rural districts, more and more farms will be electrified.

No one questions the great value of electric power to the farmer. Give the farmer electric power at a reasonable cost, and he can immediately relieve himself and his family of a large portion of their burden of labor, reduce his costs, make his profits more certain, and, what is of equal importance, raise his standard of living to a level corresponding to that of the city dweller, which will improve the morale of his family, help to keep his children at home, and make it more easy for him to secure efficient labor when he needs it.

The Farm House

Newell Leroy Sims

Modern Conveniences and Farm Homes

Water piped into the house is one of the requirements of a modern dwelling. However, relatively few farm houses have such arrangements.

Excerpted from Newell Leroy Sims, *Elements of Rural Sociology* (New York: Thomas Y. Crowell Company, 1928), pp. 270–6.

"There is every gradation from the most unmodern and unsanitary open well, from which water is drawn with wheel and bucket and carried to the house, on thru the more convenient arrangement of pump in the kitchen or water piped into the house to the truly modern water system with hot and cold water flowing on one or more floors of the house."

About 10 per cent of the farm houses in 1920 reported "water piped into the house." ... There is the greatest difference in various sections. New England and California show nearly half the houses provided with such arrangements; New York, Pennsylvania, Oregon and Washington, one fourth; the Corn Belt, one eighth; and the Cotton Belt, one in 50. This does not in most cases really mean modern water systems. Nebraska, for instance, reported one in six houses with "water piped in" but only one in sixteen had modern water systems. [A] survey of 1,000 farm homes in North Carolina ... disclosed but 1.66 per cent of land owners whose houses had running water and but .885 per cent of all farm houses. No Negro farm whatever had any convenience of this sort.

The real test of a modern water system is the presence of a bath tub and indoor toilet. The two states for which data are available make a very unequal showing on these points but they illustrate the general difference between North and South. In Nebraska the sample survey indicated that about 16.7 per cent of all operators had bath tubs in their houses. It varied from about 23 per cent of owners to 10 per cent of tenants. In North Carolina the average for the area surveyed was only .885 per cent of farm houses. The range was from 1.84 per cent for land owners to 1.23 per cent for landless farmers among the whites and none at all for Negroes. Indoor toilets were found in 1.24 per cent of owners' houses and in .82 per cent of the houses of the landless among the whites in North Carolina. The blacks were wholly without such facilities. The average for all farm homes was .591 per cent. In Nebraska 10.2 per cent of all farm homes had indoor toilets. For owners it was 14.2 and for tenants 5.9 per cent.

Perhaps no improvement for the farm is so useful as a modern water plant. A Minnesota engineer has calculated that the average housewife who carries water from an outdoor well or rain-barrel will spend 20 eight-hour days a year in doing it. If she carries the waste water out again, it will add 10 more days of work. Thus, the farm woman is sentenced "to 30 days hard labor every year carrying water."

Heating by modern means, i.e., by other than stoves or fireplaces, is less common than water piped into the house. In Nebraska only 6.3 per cent of the houses had modern heating. Among owners it was 8.8 per cent; part owners, 9.4 per cent; and tenants, 2.8 per cent. In North Carolina the sample surveyed showed but 3.1 per cent of all houses with "other than fireplace."

Lighting by modern means is not much more in use. Gas or electric lighting is found in about 7 per cent, or one out of fourteen farm houses, thruout the United States. The following table shows the percentage of such lighting by geographic sections.

Table Per cent of farm houses with modern lighting

New England..................	15.3	South Atlantic................	3.9
Middle Atlantic...............	14.1	East South Central.........	2.0
East North Central...........	10.5	West South Central........	1.9
West North Central..........	8.9	Mountain......................	10.3
	Pacific........................19.6		

It seems that a very small per cent of the houses even in the most progressive states of the Union have all three of the conveniences mentioned. In Nebraska, for instance, only about 2 per cent of all houses are so equipped.

Screening is indispensable for comfortable and sanitary living. The Nebraska data indicate from 95 to 99 per cent of all farm houses as having screened windows and doors. No great difference is seen between owners and tenants in this respect. Screened porches are less prevalent but average from 41 to about 47 per cent for back porches and around 16 per cent for front porches. The contrast with North Carolina conditions is striking. In the latter state only 30.4 per cent of the land owners and 12 per cent of the tenants had houses with doors and windows fully screened. The averages are 27.5 per cent for whites, 3.9 per cent for Negroes, and 20.9 per cent for all the homes surveyed.

Telephones may be listed as another convenience in the home. On this we have the data of the Federal Census for the whole country.

For 1920, 38.7 per cent of all farm houses were reported supplied with telephones. It varied from 69.5 per cent in the West North Central to 14.2 per cent in the South Atlantic states. In the corn belt and Kansas they are most common. In the hay and pasture regions of the Northwest, the spring wheat region of the Northwest, and the Pacific Coast region about half the homes have this convenience. In the South West it is about one-third. In the winter wheat region except Kansas, in the Great Plains and the Rocky Mountain region about one-fourth are supplied. In the cotton belt east of Texas and Oklahoma the percentages are only five to fifteen.

Needs of Farm Homes

The foregoing canvass of home equipment is not exhaustive. No attention, for instance, has been given to the use of motor and electric power for lightening labor. Satisfactory data showing the use of such power are not available. However, there are many indications that it is rapidly coming into vogue. Mechanical devices, such as cream separators, washing machines and vacuum cleaners are being introduced. These greatly lighten the heavy burdens that country women have to bear. Labor-saving power and mechanisms, coupled with modern housing, are unquestionably the great needs of homes on the farms today.

These needs are becoming wants of the present generation of farm women, and the farmer's habitual indifference toward the equipment of his home is being broken down. The following declaration of a group of Nebraskan farm women seems fairly typical of the new attitude. They called for:

1 "A power washing machine for the house for every tractor bought for the farm."
2 "A bath tub in the house for every binder on the farm."
3 "Running water in the kitchen for every riding plow for the fields."
4 "A kerosene cook-stove for every auto truck."
5 "A fireless cooker for every new mowing machine."
6 "Our share of the farm-income."

These modest demands are no doubt quite within the financial reach of a large majority of country homes in a state like Nebraska and indeed in the homes of a few other states where farm incomes range above the average for America. But in the majority of states and for the majority of farms this standard does not come within easy grasp. Hence, the landless farmer, the debt-burdened farmer, and the tenant farmer will long continue to live in a house without modern conveniences.

This will be so because the cost of many of these things is much higher for the farm than for the city home. Modern lighting and water systems are thus reserved chiefly for the most prosperous farms. Still, there are possibilities of cooperation in securing improvements at a cost not beyond the reach of the average farmer in many sections of the country.

The problem, however, is not altogether economic. There are too many cases where farmers can easily afford modern houses equipped with modern conveniences and do not, to lay the deficiency all to inadequate incomes. It is often a matter of educating country people to a proper standard of living. Primitive standards carried over from pioneer days too often prevail. The habit of doing without things too often reigns. But when once the benefits to be derived are clearly demonstrated old standards and habits tend to give way. If one farmer in a neighborhood instals a modern heating, light or water plant others are likely to see the advantages and follow suit.

Country homes have many advantages over those of the city in the matter of location and surroundings. They do not suffer from inadequate light and fresh air. There is no lack of the great out-of-doors. They are not beset by the filthy dust of streets, the noisome smells of urban districts, nor the din of crowded thoroughfares. The peaceful, wholesome, open spaces are theirs. In these things many find deep satisfaction. But these advantages, in the estimation of many others, are more than outweighted by the lack of modern houses and of conveniences that are a matter of course in every city. Good surroundings do not recompense for the dreadful burdens of home-making that the average farm woman is compelled to carry. Much dissatisfaction springs from this source and until these handicaps are pretty generally removed, the ordinary country home will not hold its own against the lure of the city.

The need therefore for modern houses with comfort-giving and labor-saving equipment on the farms is, in the last analysis, a distinctively sociological need. To supply it is to emancipate the country woman from much drudgery, increase her leisure, give a larger measure of contentment, and withal strengthen the ties that bind her to the rural community.

Further Reading

Cowan, Ruth Schwartz. *More Work for Mother: the Ironies of Household Technology from the Open Hearth to the Microwave.* New York: Basic Books, 1983.

Horowitz, Roger, and Arwen Mohun, eds. *His and Hers: Gender, Consumption, and Technology.* Charlottesville: University of Virginia Press, 1998.

Jellison, Katherine. *Entitled to Power: Farm Women and Technology, 1913–1963.* Chapel Hill: University of North Carolina Press, 1993.

Kleinberg, S. J. *The Shadow of the Mills: Working-class Families in Pittsburgh, 1870–1907.* Pittsburgh: University of Pittsburgh Press, 1989.

Power and the Land. Film by the US Department of Agriculture, 1940.

7

"Selling" Nuclear Energy

1945	First atomic bomb dropped on Hiroshima, with at least 160,000 casualties.
1946	Atomic Energy Commission established.
1949	North Atlantic Treaty Organization (NATO) formed.
1953	President Eisenhower announced "Atoms for Peace" program.
1956	Walt Disney produces "Our Friend the Atom."
1956–71	Government pursues "Project Plowshare."
1957	Nation's first nuclear power plant opens at Shippingport, PA.
1957	Price–Anderson Act protects nuclear power industry from lawsuits.
1974	Nuclear Regulatory Agency carved off from AEC.
1979	Accident at Three Mile Island.
1986	Accident at Chernobyl power plant in the USSR.

Introduction

The government (especially the federal government) and corporations (especially large corporations) were the only likely sources of new technologies within the United States in the late twentieth century, and, not surprisingly, these two centers of innovation often cooperated to bring technologies into common use. Nuclear technologies, which had begun with the Manhattan Project's effort to create an atomic bomb, immediately became a key element of the Cold War competition between the United States and the Soviet Union and, as such, was considered to be a natural monopoly of the government itself. As that technology was shaped to produce power as well as weapons, the balance between public and private interests was accompanied by a need to "sell" it to a public traumatized by the fear of nuclear war. Like private corporations, and often in conjunction with them, the government undertook a public relations campaign to create and shape consumer acceptance of this new product.

Advertising the Atom

Michael Smith

Compared with the other subjects in this volume, nuclear power is a relative newcomer to environmental policy. Officially, no civilian nuclear program existed before the Atomic Energy Act of 1954. In its short lifetime, however, nuclear power has become one of the most controversial issues in the history of American environmental politics. For roughly the first fifteen years after the 1954 act, the peaceful atom enjoyed widespread popular support, enthusiastic press coverage, and optimistic government predictions of imminent growth. In the late 1960s, questions began to surface, and over the next decade, virtually every aspect of nuclear-generated electricity attracted environmental concern. The mining and processing of uranium; the location, construction, and operational safety of nuclear power plants; thermal pollution from those plants; disposing of radioactive waste; and emergency evacuation plans for communities near nuclear plants all became contested terrain among policymakers, regulators, and their critics. The national news media, once uncritically enthusiastic toward nuclear power, had become openly antagonistic by the time of the accident at Three Mile Island in March 1979. An unofficial moratorium on new nuclear plant orders has remained in place ever since.

What caused the peaceful atom's fall from grace? Is it permanently discredited, or only temporarily deflected? Is nuclear power an environmental blessing, a nightmare, or something in between? Although opposing sides in the nuclear debate tend to give equally brief replies to these questions, the answers are embedded in an intricate history of policy objectives, controversies, and crises that led to the current impasse. Since no brief essay could treat this history in adequate detail, I have chosen instead to address the social context of nuclear power in the United States: to trace the broader political and social pressures that shaped its early development, and to suggest how that pattern of development contributed to the environmental crisis that followed. Examined in this context, nuclear power is above all a product of federal

Excerpted from Michael Smith, "Advertising the Atom," in Michael J. Lacey, ed., *Government and Environmental Politics: Essays on Historical Developments since World War Two* (Baltimore: The Woodrow Wilson Center Press and The Johns Hopkins University Press, 1991), pp. 233–62. Reprinted by permission of the Woodrow Wilson Center Press.

promotional objectives in the 1950s and 1960s. To understand the clash between the atom and the environment in the 1970s, we must begin with the assumptions and goals that shaped early nuclear power policy.

Origins of Federal Nuclear Policy

On July 18, 1945, Major General Leslie Groves, officer-in-charge of the Manhattan Project, wrote a top secret memorandum to Secretary of War Henry Stimson, who was with President Truman at the Potsdam conference. Groves's memo was a detailed account of the atomic bomb test at Alamogordo two days earlier. "For the first time in history there was a nuclear explosion. And what an explosion!" Groves reported enthusiastically. "The test was successful beyond the most optimistic expectations of anyone."[1]

On that same date ten years later, Atomic Energy Commission (AEC) Chairman Lewis L. Strauss presided over a ceremony marking the first commercial transmission of nuclear-generated electricity. On the velvet-trimmed table beside him, a huge electrical switch stood poised upright between two opposite encasements. If he threw this "two-way switch" in one direction, Strauss explained, it would launch a nuclear submarine. "But when I throw it in the other direction, as I am about to do, it will send atomic electric power surging through transmission lines to towns and villages, farms and factories – power not to burst bombs or propel submarines, but to make life easier, healthier, and more abundant." Reminding his audience that this switch represented "the great dilemma of our times," Strauss grasped the handle and threw it "to the side of the peaceful atom."[2]

The problems attending nuclear energy proved to be far more complex than this simple ceremony suggested, yet Strauss was more correct than he realized when he called his two-way switch a symbol of the social choices surrounding the atom. Despite its dramatic appearance, the switch was only a prop; both the transmission lines and the submarine had already been prepared for activation, regardless of the commissioner's ceremony. Like Strauss's switch, the commission he chaired only appeared to offer separate choices. The same agency that controlled production of the weapons had been assigned supervision of nuclear power – with many of the same aims and methods. No matter which way Chairman Strauss threw the atomic switch, the AEC was compelled to light up the towns and launch nuclear submarines – and to perform both tasks with similar urgency.

Although the environmental controversy over nuclear power did not attract sustained national attention until the 1970s, the seeds of that crisis were sown in the decade between Groves's memo and Strauss's ceremony. Like every other aspect of nuclear policy, safety standards for the development of the peaceful atom were profoundly affected by the prevailing military and political pressures surrounding the Manhattan Project and the postwar arms race. In its first commitment to nuclear technology, the federal government gambled that lavish funding, unprecedented scientific staffing, and absolute secrecy could overcome all technical uncertainties. The dramatic success of that undertaking left a powerful legacy for administrators. Postwar nuclear policy retained the Manhattan Project's penchant for secrecy, its equation of nuclear objectives with national identity, its sense of urgency, and its faith in the ability of government scientists to find last-minute solutions to any technical problems. Each of these tendencies militated against the complex and time-consuming process of establishing and enforcing reliable environmental standards for nuclear power.

After Hiroshima, Congress had to devise a new administrative framework for the development and application of nuclear technology. The Atomic Energy Act of 1946 created a civilian Atomic Energy Commission, to be composed of five presidential appointees. To provide for congressional monitoring of the AEC, the act also authorized a Joint Committee on Atomic Energy (JCAE), consisting of nine senators and nine representatives. A Military Liaison Committee would coordinate AEC policy and Defense Department objectives, while a General Advisory Committee of scientists and technical experts would contribute its own assessment and perspectives.[3]

A primary object of the 1946 act was to maintain the US government's monopoly on the atomic bomb; that goal established an administrative link between nuclear weapons and the peaceful atom. Because nuclear power plants would use and generate fissionable material that could be applied to producing nuclear weapons, Congress assigned control of nuclear power to the same agency that directed the production of nuclear weapons. As a result, nuclear power became bureaucratically attached to the geopolitical status of the military bomb, and the AEC's power to classify virtually any information pertaining to the weapons applied equally to nonmilitary projects.[4]

For the first three years, the AEC concentrated on the production of atomic weapons, forbidding commercial applications of nuclear technology as a security risk. The Soviet Union's first successful detonation of an atom bomb in 1949 signaled shifts in policy emphasis. Alarmed by the rapidity with which the Soviets had broken America's atomic monopoly, and denounced at home for failing to prevent the Communists' victory in the Chinese revolution that same year, the Truman administration committed itself to a greatly accelerated defense budget, with the nation's nuclear stockpile as the centerpiece. The JCAE urged the AEC to proceed with the vastly more powerful hydrogen bomb; the General Advisory Committee strongly dissented, claiming that such a weapon would only trigger a far more deadly arms race. In 1950, the president announced the nation's intention to develop a hydrogen bomb. A renewed sense of emergency and expediency permeated nuclear policy.[5]

The Soviet bomb also set the stage for enlisting nuclear-generated electricity as a new element in atomic diplomacy. To most US officials, the Soviet bomb minimized the utility of nuclear weapons as instruments for settling global disputes. Instead, both sides increasingly sought symbolic deployments, employing nuclear technology as an emblem of military and ideological superiority. The Soviets now had the capacity to develop a nuclear power program of their own. And the United States, as principal architect of the North Atlantic Treaty Organization (NATO, also established in 1949), was under new pressure to share nuclear technology with its allies. Atomic bombs as well as nuclear power plants would soon be within the grasp of Britain and France. Could the United States afford to be the only nuclear nation without an atomic power program? Between 1950 and 1953, the JCAE prodded the AEC toward a redefinition of civilian nuclear power as a necessity, rather than a threat, to national security.[6]

During the early 1950s, several disagreements persisted concerning the nature of the arms race and its relation to nuclear power; yet nearly all disputants agreed, for their own reasons, that an aggressive nuclear power program was desirable. For those who considered atomic energy to be primarily a military necessity for containing Soviet power, civilian nuclear power plants represented a possible source of fissionable material for weapons, as well as a domestic justification for an aggressive nuclear policy. One of the most prominent advocates of this point of view, Dr Edward Teller, also sounded one of the first warnings about the environmental safety risks accompanying nuclear power. Best known as the principal developer and champion of the hydrogen bomb, Teller also chaired the AEC's Reactor Safeguards Committee. In a letter submitted to the JCAE in July 1953, Teller warned that "no legislation will be able to stop future [nuclear power plant] accidents and avoid completely occasional loss of life." Nevertheless, particularly in light of the "great and increasing need for fissionable materials in the military field," Teller concluded that "the unavoidable danger which will remain after all reasonable controls have been employed must not stand in the way of rapid development of nuclear power."[7]

A number of other administrators and scientists, however, advocated a nuclear power program as a way of transcending rather than augmenting nuclear technology's military image. David Lilienthal, the AEC's first chair, recalled the widespread conviction among early atomic administrators "that somehow or other the discovery that had produced so terrible a weapon simply *had* to have an important peaceful use." Such an attitude, he noted, "led perhaps to wishful thinking, a wishful elevation of the 'sunny side' of the Atom."[8] Glenn Seaborg, one of the codiscoverers of plutonium, was one of a number of Manhattan Project scientists who, in contrast to Teller, devoted their postwar careers to nonmilitary applications of nuclear technology. As chairman of the AEC from 1961 to 1971, Seaborg became the government's most tireless publicist for the peaceful atom.

Perhaps the greatest number of nuclear power proponents viewed nuclear-generated electricity as a propaganda weapon in the ideological struggle between the United States and the Soviet Union. In June 1953, JCAE Chairman Sterling Cole and Vice Chairman Bourke Hickenlooper released a statement calling for American supremacy in the impending "atomic power race." In the "battle for the minds of men" between the free world and "the Soviet atheistic materialists," Cole and Hickenlooper warned, atomic weapons were no longer enough. "It is urgent – and we use the term in its truest sense – for our national warfare and for our national defense" that we deploy the peaceful atom to "show ourselves and the world that the industrial vigor of America continues to lead the way to a decent standard of living."[9] Two months later, when the Soviet Union exploded its first hydrogen bomb only months after the United States had done so, AEC Commissioner Thomas Murray urged AEC Chairman Strauss to announce a civilian nuclear power program to counter the propaganda value of the Soviet bomb. In a speech before a public utilities conference in October, Murray characterized nuclear power plants as comparable to the H-bomb in strategic importance. If the Soviet Union developed nuclear power first, and offered it to developing nations in exchange for their allegiance, Americans would discover that the "nuclear power race," as surely as the arms race itself, was "no Everest-climbing, kudos-providing contest."[10]

Commissioner Strauss represented a group of administrators and members of Congress, mostly Republicans, who shared Murray's view of the importance of nuclear power, but disagreed with the contention by Murray and his allies, mostly Democrats, that the government should develop nuclear power as a public enterprise in the interest of expediency. A former Wall Street investment banker, Strauss firmly believed that nuclear power should be "opened to the genius and enterprise of American industry." The government might provide generous subsidies and access to government-developed technology, but private utilities should develop nuclear power as a showcase for the free enterprise system. The JCAE tended to share Strauss's view; its hearings on

"Atomic Power Development and Private Enterprise" in the summer of 1953 were designed primarily to demonstrate the feasibility of a government-subsidized, privately developed nuclear power program.[11]

Thus by late 1953, nuclear administrators and advisers with a wide range of differing priorities agreed that nuclear power should be developed as quickly as possible. In December, President Eisenhower announced in a speech to the United Nations that the United States would embark on a new, international "Atoms for Peace" program that would reverse the common perception of atomic energy as a destructive force. In an effort "to serve the needs rather than the fears of mankind," America's nuclear technology would "provide abundant electrical energy in the power-starved areas of the world" as well as at home.[12]

The revised Atomic Energy Act of 1954 authorized the AEC to encourage, rather than forbid, the ownership, construction, and operation of nuclear power plants by private companies; such plants, however, had to be licensed by the AEC, and the government retained its technical ownership of all nuclear fuels. In effect, the 1954 act assigned two contradictory tasks to the AEC – promotion and regulation of nuclear power.

It was a lopsided mandate. For the next twenty years the JCAE, the Congress, and nearly all the AEC commissioners pushed for rapid development and promotion. Regulation might impede that development – particularly if it imposed lengthy test periods or costly safety procedures. In Commissioner Strauss's words, "The AEC's objective in the formulation of the regulations was to minimize government control of competitive enterprise."[13] The only political threat to minimal regulation was adverse public opinion toward nuclear power. The best insurance against public criticism was aggressive promotion of the benefits of the peaceful atom. Given its bureaucratic origins and the political pressures surrounding it, the AEC discovered that the public opinion was easier to regulate than the nuclear industry itself.

The 1954 act also increased the JCAE's powers. The only joint committee with legislative authority, it controlled virtually every bill in either house that related to atomic energy. The usual disagreements and alterations that occurred between committees, and between the House of Representatives and the Senate, were missing from nuclear issues. The JCAE also constituted the only informed overseers of the AEC. Members of Congress, however, were even more vulnerable to the political pressures for swift development than the commissioners. Having designed the 1954 revisions that made a nuclear power industry possible, the JCAE continued to press the AEC for an aggressive program and tangible results.[14]

For the first few years after passage of the 1954 act, hesitation over nuclear power was more likely to come from industry than from the government. Three tiers of companies were involved. Most influential were the vendor corporations, notably Westinghouse and General Electric, which had dominated earlier, defense-related contracts for nuclear reactors. These companies saw the construction and sale of nuclear power plants as a lucrative new market. Next came the private utility companies that would buy the plants and sell the electricity. With other cheap, plentiful sources of energy available, nuclear power seemed less attractive to these companies without strong incentives from the government and the vendor companies. In the early years, the utilities were drawn to nuclear power more out of fear that the government would operate it as a public utility than out of eagerness to develop it. Finally, there were the companies indirectly affected by the emergence of a nuclear power industry. Most significant among these were the insurance companies, which found the risks attending nuclear power too uncertain to warrant coverage. Without insurance, the utilities could not proceed.[15]

The AEC responded to the insurance problem by instructing its scientists at Brookhaven National Laboratory to undertake a detailed study of nuclear power plants. Over their brief period of operation, nuclear reactors had logged a good safety record, but no one had established how likely an accident might be, or how serious the consequences. In 1957, the Brookhaven staff reported its findings to the commissioners in a report titled "Theoretical Possibilities and Consequences of Major Accidents in Large Nuclear Power Plants," but commonly referred to by its document number: WASH-740. Their report hypothesized that an accidental release of radioactive material from a nuclear plant could cause 3,400 deaths, 43,000 injuries, and $7 billion in damage. The Brookhaven scientists were unable to determine the likelihood of such an accident, but deemed it only possible, not probable.[16]

No safety evaluations eventuated from WASH-740. Instead, the JCAE drafted the Price-Anderson Act of 1957, which exempted the nuclear power industry from lawsuits for injuries sustained in a nuclear accident. In place of corporate liability, Congress set aside an arbitrary sum of $560 million. By the AEC's own estimate, this amount could not begin to cover damage claims from a significant nuclear accident. The figure was large enough to remove the issue of liability as an obstacle, yet small enough to prevent public alarm at the anticipated scope of accidental damage.[17]

WASH-740 had based its estimates on a hypothetical nuclear power plant with a power capacity of 185 megawatts – about twice the size of the nation's first nuclear plant in Shippingport, Pennsylvania, which began operation in 1957. Nuclear plants in this first generation, to paraphrase Mark Twain, were to their larger successors as the lightning bug is to lightning. By the mid-1960s, Westinghouse and General Electric were proposing 1,000-megawatt plants. With the Price–Anderson Act due for renewal in 1967, the AEC asked Brookhaven in 1964 to reexamine the WASH-740 findings in light of the newer, larger reactor proposals. Expecting more favorable results than those in the original report, the commissioners found the updated estimates distressing. A major accident at one of the new reactor plants might cause 45,000 deaths, according to the Brookhaven staff; property damage could approach the $400 billion mark. And although probability was impossible to calculate accurately, the new report found "nothing inherent in reactors or in safeguard systems as they now have been developed which guarantees either that major reactor accidents will not occur or that protective safeguard systems will not fail."[18]

After discussing with industry representatives the negative public relations impact of such findings, the AEC elected to classify the WASH-740 update as secret and to approve applications for the new plants. No significant changes in reactor safety accompanied these actions. Instead, the AEC's annual reports to Congress from 1954 to 1969 reflected the political priorities and public concerns of the time. By and large, operational safety and environmental protection received much less attention than the educational and informational programs by which the AEC promoted nuclear power. These promotional efforts illustrate the political and social assumptions underlying the emblematic role of nuclear power in its formative years; ironically, they also help explain the emergence of grassroots environmental opposition to nuclear power in the 1970s.

Atomic Advertising, 1954–1969

With the advent of a federal nuclear power program, the AEC undertook the most extensive government public relations effort since the Office of War Information had closed its doors in 1945. A positive image of nuclear power was important for several reasons. Members of Congress and their constituents had to be assured of the wisdom of continuing appropriations; utility companies needed to be persuaded to participate in the government's nuclear power program. Most important, however, was the emblematic nature of atomic energy policy in general. Like nuclear weapons, nuclear power had been assigned a crucial symbolic role by its proponents. Nuclear power plants were to serve as badges of

American technological and political superiority at home, and as adjuncts of atomic diplomacy abroad. The display value of nuclear technology could be only as effective as the publicity surrounding it. From the outset, then, the question was not whether to promote nuclear power aggressively, but how best to go about it.

Officially, as well as informally, disciples of the nuclear gospel sought each other's advice on how best to proceed. Just after Eisenhower's election in November 1952, former AEC Commissioner T. Keith Glennan proposed "a national association of atomic industries" to encourage "the development and utilization of the peaceful applications of atomic energy in accordance with the best traditions of the American system of free competitive enterprise."[19] The following spring, Glennan's suggestion resulted in the formation of the Atomic Industrial Forum (AIF). In the years to come, the AIF provided one of the key settings for government-corporate cooperation in nuclear power development and promotion.

In 1956, the AIF sponsored the first national conference on public relations for nuclear power. Its proceedings offer an instructive glimpse of nuclear power advocacy in its formative stage. AIF Executive Manager Charles Robbins called the conference to order with the question of the hour: "How do we overcome the doubts and apprehensions of the wartime atom and replace these with confidence and a ready acceptance of peaceful atomic enterprise?"[20] AEC personnel addressed the conference on the progress of reactor development and discussed promotional materials provided by the federal government. Frank Pittman, the AEC's deputy director of the Division of Civilian Application, suggested that "in its civilian uses the energy of the atom should be described as 'nuclear energy' rather than 'atomic energy.' This might help eliminate the fearful feeling that is brought to the minds of many members of the public by the word 'atomic.'" Pittman also warned his audience that "it must be made clear that there is no such thing as an absolutely safe operating nuclear reactor, just as there is no such thing as an absolutely safe operating chemical plant, oil refinery, automobile, airplane, or anything else."[21]

At least one speaker commented on the diversity of motives for developing nuclear power. *Nucleonics* magazine editor Jerome Luntz noted the degree to which "atomic energy" had permeated American culture, with no clear sense of its nature or purpose. The Manhattan telephone directory for 1956, for example, contained "41 entries with the word 'atom' or 'atomic,' going from Atom Fuel Company, which is probably a coal company, to Atomic Undergarment Company." Part of the uncertainty, Luntz speculated, might be due to "the confusion among our own top level atomic energy policy makers as to why we are developing atomic power and how fast we should move in that development." Some spoke of atomic power's "propaganda" value, or of opportunities it provided to "make gains in the cold war," Luntz noted. For his own part, the editor felt that the most important issue was making nuclear power profitable.[22]

Luntz's comments provided a rare moment of candor at the public relations conference. Presumably, all the industry representatives shared his preference for profits first, geopolitics later. As is often the case when differing motives surround similar goals, the various advocates tended to speak in each other's language. Many of the participants from nuclear and public relations industries spoke as if they were in the State Department. LeBaron Foster, editor of *Public Opinion Index for Industry*, attempted to bridge economic and ideological motives, explaining that the nuclear power question was "really a problem of preserving our system of values." One sure sign of alien ideologies polluting the nuclear issue, Foster maintained, was public support for government ownership of nuclear power plants. In a public opinion study entitled "Free Market versus Socialist Thinking," Foster's Opinion Research Corporation had determined that blacks, unskilled workers, those with only an eighth-grade education, low-income individuals, and the foreign-born were in the "strongly socialistic" column (because they approved of public ownership), whereas business executives, upper-income individuals, Republicans, college teachers, and government employees favored the "free market" (that is, government subsidies without government control). The nuclear industry's task would be to explain its special needs to this unevenly informed public.[23]

The public relations community's message to the assembled industry and government representatives was one that would only grow in significance in the decades to follow: it is easier to develop public "tolerance for accidents" than to avoid the accidents themselves – more expedient to offer strategies for "Developing Consumer Acceptance of Radioactivity" than to establish and enforce radiation standards. Nearly all the public opinion surveys cited during the conference revealed a general public willingness to embrace nuclear power. Nonetheless, one of those same surveys warned that "'danger' lies not simply in the presence of a hazard," but also in the loss of public faith in the problem-solving ability of experts. "In all likelihood, it would take but one highly dramatic and well publicized event – a major plant catastrophe – to upset this faith."[24]

The government and the nuclear power industry thus faced potentially conflicting choices: to maintain safety standards at possible risk to public confidence, or to maintain appearances at possible risk to safety. The AEC pursued both safety and public relations, but found the latter much easier and more welcome. By the late 1950s, reactor safety guidelines and nuclear waste disposal policy remained unresolved; but the AEC and the industry were already well embarked on a massive campaign to celebrate the peaceful atom.

To create a positive public image of nuclear power, the AEC relied on two closely related techniques: secrecy and advertising. Supervision of nuclear weapons had already conditioned the AEC to classify information routinely; as the WASH-740 update demonstrates, the commission simply transferred that procedure to the peaceful atom, suppressing documents and accident reports that questioned the safety or economic feasibility of nuclear technology. What not to say seemed clear enough; the new problem was what to present to the public, and how to reach it. Through booklets, films, press releases, lectures, and exhibits, the educational arm of the AEC undertook to reach the entire nation, and much of the rest of the world.

It proved to be a highly successful campaign. The AEC's educational pamphlets enjoyed nationwide distribution. One series alone – the *Understanding the Atom* booklets – began to appear in 1952; by the end of the decade, over eight million copies were in print. Between 1960 and 1970, over forty million people attended AEC screenings of films, and nearly four times that number viewed them on television. Traveling exhibits, high school lecture-demonstrations, science fairs, and even Boy Scout merit badges in atomic energy brought the message to tens of millions of school children. In addition, the AEC participated in joint promotional efforts with the AIF and other trade associations. The major nuclear vendors were quick to mount their own publicity drives; eventually, they were joined by the private utility companies. From the mid-1950s to the late 1960s, public expectations for the peaceful atom grew and flourished in the bright light of nuclear publicity.[25]

Because the peaceful atom represented a new and complex technology, atomic advocates were free to characterize it in almost any way they chose. The images they selected warrant scrutiny, for they had a profound effect on public attitudes toward nuclear power, on AEC policies, and even on cultural attitudes toward technology and expertise in general. Like the AIF, the AEC perceived the need to dissociate the peaceful atom from the bomb. One of the earliest – and most quoted – examples of this tendency was the speech delivered by AEC Chairman Strauss in September 1954. Within fifteen years, Strauss predicted, the peaceful atom would lead us to "transmutation of the elements – unlimited power.... It is not too much to expect," he claimed, "that our children will enjoy electrical energy too cheap to meter... will travel effortlessly over the seas and under them and through the air with a minimum of danger and at great speeds – and will experience a lifespan far longer than ours."[26] This was more than Commissioner Lilienthal's "sunny side of the Atom." Strauss was invoking a vision of technological optimism, grounded in the magical properties of the atom. Words like "magic," "wonder," and "mystery" appeared routinely in the titles of countless AEC booklets, films, and magazine articles. In 1955, President Eisenhower activated the nation's first commercial nuclear power plant by waving a radioactive "magic wand." "Unlimited power" might, however, have frightening implications if the magician ever lost control. The task facing nuclear publicists was to invoke the magical possibilities of the atom while at the same time domesticating it, reducing its mysterious powers to the palpable dimensions of daily life.[27]

One of the most vivid and most widely viewed examples of this domesticated magic appeared in *Our Friend the Atom*, a Walt Disney production that first appeared on nationwide television in 1956 and soon became one of the most popular items in the AEC film library. Disney assures his listeners that "the atom is our future," and introduces us to Dr Heinz Haber, Disneyland's new expert on "scientific development." Haber says that the development of nuclear technology has been "almost a fairy tale," illustrating his point with a cartoon update of the Arabian Nights tale of the genie and the fisherman. In the Disney version, a fisherman finds a magic bottle in his nets. When he uncorks it, a fierce, slant-eyed genie appears in a huge mushroom-shaped cloud. Furious at having been pent up for so long, the genie announces that he will destroy his liberator. The fisherman uses verbal trickery to recapture him. Chastened, the genie reemerges to grant his new master's wishes. In case the viewers missed the point, the film superimposes the genie onto reverse footage of an atomic explosion, so that the bomb appears to implode harmlessly back into the lamp. Atomic power was thus domesticated – in the form of a powerful but docile servant.

Like Strauss's two-way switch, or Ike's wand, Disney's genie converts the fury of the atom into the power to perform tasks. What should those tasks include? Readers of the August 1955 issue of *Ladies' Home Journal* learned of an impending nuclear world

> in which there is no disease . . . where hunger is unknown . . . where "dirt" is an old-fashioned word and routine household tasks are just a matter of pushing a few buttons . . . a world where no one stokes a furnace or curses the smog . . . and the breeze from a factory is everywhere as sweet as from a rose. . . .

The author of that article was President Eisenhower's special assistant on disarmament, Harold Stassen – a man seldom praised for his ability to predict the future. Stassen carefully tailored his image of nuclear magic to include "routine household tasks" as well as global transformations.[28]

Those household tasks became the focus of the atom's domesticated magic in *The Atom and Eve*, a 1965 film produced by a consortium of New England utility companies and distributed through the AEC. *The Atom and Eve* traced the parallel development of the electrical industry and "little Eve," who was fortunate enough to be born into a modern-day "electrical garden of Eden." As she approaches puberty, Eve acquires an expanding array of electrical appliances; she also eats from the tree of electrical knowledge ("Eve learned a new word: hydroelectricity"). As Eve reaches maturity, the electrical industry grows with her, finally developing nuclear technology "to meet Eve's never-ending needs." Fully grown and draped in a flowing, low-cut evening gown, Eve twirls from one nuclear-generated electrical appliance to another, lovingly embracing the refrigerator and the electric range, lying supine against the smooth expanse of the electric washer-dryer. Eve's coming-of-age culminates in her Dance of the Nuclear Light Bulb. Destined to burn for "a million years" with its inexhaustible nuclear storehouse of energy, the bulb becomes consumer culture's eternal flame, which Eve caresses as she spins and pirouettes across the screen.[29]

Electricity for household appliances was not the only way in which nuclear enthusiasts proposed to alter Eve's domestic realm. In a feature article titled "You and the Obedient Atom," the September 1958 issue of *National Geographic* echoed Disney in its observation that "these unimaginably tiny particles work like genii at man's bidding." Visiting the AEC's various national laboratories, the magazine staff found even the smallest details of daily life were being transformed by this new servant. Brookhaven National Laboratory sought to create bold new hybrids of carnations in its radioactive "Gamma Garden." Unfortunately, some less pleasing mutations, such as two-colored "schizophrenic carnations" produced "flowers of evil" alongside the "flowers of good." Meanwhile, researchers at Argonne Laboratory were testing the food of the future. Potatoes, bread, and hotdogs left exposed to air for several months – predictably – rotted. Yet irradiated samples of these same foods remained fresh and "germ-free." Argonne reported that "changes in taste [in irradiated food] are scarcely noticeable." Samples had already been fed to rats, military volunteers, and congressmen "without harmful effect." *National Geographic* concluded that "the atomic revolution" would "shape and change our lives in ways undreamed of today – and there can be no turning back."[30]

In addition to the AEC's projects and promotional efforts, the very language it used emphasized both the power and the subservience of "the obedient atom," often through the familiar analogy of parent and child. In February 1966, the AEC commemorated the twenty-fifth anniversary of the "birth" of plutonium with a highly publicized ceremony. The commission's press release described how the element's five fathers had gone about creating their "new baby." (Clearly, this "nuclear family" remained decidedly patriarchal.) Glenn Seaborg, one of the five and now chairman of the AEC, minimized the danger and difficulty involved with plutonium by characterizing it as "the ornery element" – a "difficult child" among the older, more sanguine elements. "It may be because I am so well acquainted with plutonium's early childhood that I am inclined to view it as one might consider a 'bad' child," he observed in the press release for the commemoration, "difficult and even exasperating in its conduct at times, but replete with fascinating possibilities." For Seaborg, the childlike qualities of the atom permitted its master to recapture his own youthful sense of wonder. "In a homely sense," he wrote, "the atom is like one of those old many-sided jackknives that can do almost anything a kid would want to do – whittling, screwdriving, bottle-opening and so on."[31]

The language of nuclear promotion deleted most of its cold war references whenever it moved from JCAE hearings and AEC meetings to press releases, information booklets, and films. Both versions of the atom were intended to represent "our system of values," as LeBaron Foster put it. Nonetheless, while most government officials continued to see nuclear power as a symbol of national prestige, the public information offices of the AEC and the nuclear industry recast those values into a more accessible setting: household consumer goods powered by cheap, abundant nuclear electricity. In part, these more personalized depictions of nuclear prestige reflected atomic energy's entry into the parlance of the marketplace: utility companies, as well as their customers, had to be convinced of the need for this new source of electricity; and the principal nuclear vendors, General Electric and Westinghouse, marketed electrical appliances as well as nuclear power plants. But the AEC gained more than corporate interest by applying one set of nuclear images on Capitol Hill and another on Main Street. Trading the geopolitical lance and shield for a washer-dryer or an atomic jackknife might sacrifice some of the global stature of nuclear technology, but it had the advantage of distancing its audience as far as possible from the bomb and its attendant lexicon of national security. For most Americans, this translation of "unlimited power" from the international arena to the household removed the atom from a social environment in which they felt helpless, to the familiar trappings of a consumer culture where their choice of products conveyed the illusion of control. For those developing nations to which the AEC brought its exhibits and films, nuclear-powered appliances provided a vision of abundance to associate with American largesse.

The domesticated magic of nuclear power promotion, however, retained a certain Sorcerer's Apprentice quality; it was as if the endless proliferation of appliances and benefits would finally allay any fears that the nuclear genie might burst from its lamp again, or that the fisherman might be incompetent. In the 1950s and 1960s, such fears focused on nuclear explosives, rather than on nuclear power. As public concern over fallout and the arms race mounted, promotional images of a nuclear Garden of Eden offered a comforting respite from the perils of the military atom. The AEC went even beyond nuclear power plants in its efforts to domesticate the atom. During the same years that it launched its promotion of nuclear-generated electricity, the government sought ways of applying the bomb itself for civilian uses through Project Plowshare. An examination of that project will help to clarify the relation between the AEC's early promotional and environmental priorities, since it demonstrates, in David Lilienthal's words, "how far scientists and administrators will go to try to establish a nonmilitary use [for the atom]."[32]

Plowshare and "Planetary Engineering"

The first environmental issue over which the AEC confronted significant public dissent was fallout from nuclear weapons testing. The controversy began in the mid-1950s, when information questioning the environmental safety of the tests first became available, and subsided after the 1963 signing of the US-Soviet Limited Test Ban Treaty, which forbade atmospheric testing. In the course of the debate, it became apparent that the AEC had underestimated, sometimes dramatically, the potential environmental and health effects of radioactive fallout. Part of the government's difficulty derived from lags in scientific procedure. The AEC based its calculations of public exposure, for example, on the assumption that fallout would disperse equally throughout the global atmosphere; more advanced understanding of world climate patterns revealed uneven concentrations in the temperate zones. In addition, the controversy challenged the credibility of the AEC itself on three counts. First, the government had not arranged for adequate monitoring and follow-up testing of radiation exposure in the areas where weapons were detonated (primarily at the Nevada Testing Grounds and on island sites in the Pacific). Second, the AEC had approached radiation danger almost exclusively as a matter of short-term, external exposure, despite growing evidence of the long-term hazards of internal exposure, such as concentrations of strontium 90 and iodine 131 in the food chain. Finally, the AEC attempted to suppress evidence of fallout-induced health problems among exposed persons and animals, and classified or tried to discredit scientific studies suggesting that official exposure standards were unsafe.[33] At the same time, at least one AEC laboratory explored civilian engineering tasks for thermonuclear explosives.

When President Eisenhower announced his Atoms for Peace program in December 1953, he characterized nuclear-generated electricity as a means of converting the "greatest of destructive forces" into "a great boon for the benefit of mankind."[34] Project Plowshare (1956–1971) essentially pushed claims for the peaceful atom one step further by approaching nuclear weapons as a tool for large-scale environmental modification, such as excavation, mining, and drilling. The idea first gained support during the 1956 Suez Canal crisis, when scientists at the AEC's Lawrence Radiation Laboratory (LRL) in Livermore, California, proposed blasting a new canal across Israel with nuclear explosives. The crisis passed before any tests could be initiated; the idea, however, survived to attract various levels of AEC sponsorship for the next fifteen years.

The evolution of Plowshare was to some degree a product of the geography of AEC decision making. Like the other AEC national laboratories, the LRL staff could submit projects to Washington for approval. They saw themselves as competing with their more conventional counterparts at Los Alamos for funding and staffing. For its successful proponents, Plowshare could open a new realm of project supervision.[35]

Beyond this bureaucratic incentive, scientists and administrators brought a variety of related objectives to their support for the peaceful bomb. Edward Teller championed a broad and vigorous thermonuclear applications policy as an issue of national security. To people concerned about fallout from Plowshare experiments, he maintained that the upcoming generation of nuclear explosives would be safer than their predecessors. (Elsewhere, Teller argued that radiation from fallout "might be slightly beneficial" and that any mutations it might induce should be welcomed for accelerating the evolutionary process.)[36]

Other scientists initially embraced nonmilitary uses of nuclear explosives as a way of redeeming nuclear technology as a social force. Speaking of Project Orion, a plan for a spacecraft propelled by nuclear explosions, Freeman Dyson wrote: "We have for the first time imagined a way to use the huge stockpiles of our bombs for better purposes than for murdering people."[37]

Even from the outset, however, an overriding concern regarding nonmilitary use of nuclear explosives was their public relations impact. Harold Brown, who first submitted LRL's proposal for Plowshare, wrote to Herbert York in 1957: "It is plain that many of the difficulties involved in non-military uses [of nuclear explosives] are not technical but have to do with questions of public opinion." Peaceful applications of these weapons might generate local "nuisance problems"; yet "such programs if successful might produce a change in attitude." After all, who would object to nuclear weapons testing (or nuclear power plants) in the vicinity if mines, harbors, canals, and even cities were being carved from the earth with thermonuclear bombs? Plowshare might set the stage for "an altered public relations program" – one that publicized projects rather than conceal them.[38]

Perhaps the most enthusiastic defender of Plowshare was AEC Chairman Glenn Seaborg, who envisaged nuclear technology as the key to a "three-dimensional" future in which people would "cut the umbilical cord that ties us precariously to [the Earth's surface]" and begin to populate the moon, the ocean floor, and the Earth's interior ("The Nether Frontier").[39] Seaborg saw Plowshare as part of a more immediate program of "planetary engineering," whereby nuclear explosives and other nuclear technologies would irrigate the deserts, remove mountains, carve "instant harbors" and canals, desalinate ocean water, and through the benefits of "Hardiman," a nuclear-powered "man-amplifier," make an ordinary man as powerful as a forklift. Like "Paul Bunyon and Babe, his Great Blue Ox," Seaborg observed, we could transform our surroundings with a well-placed (nuclear) gesture. Nuclear excavation would be much quicker and cheaper than conventional methods, and "the dangers of radioactivity from the new, *nearly fission-free* explosives are small."[40]

Project Plowshare's various projects highlighted a number of political and environmental issues. The Suez Canal crisis prompted interest in a second, sea-level canal in Panama: a "Panatomic Canal" to absorb increased shipping traffic and to minimize the national security risk of relying on a single interoceanic canal. The AEC began investigating the Isthmus of Panama for likely canal sites as early as 1956. Participants in the Second Plowshare Symposium in 1959 were assured that "the cost of excavating a canal by nuclear means is only a small fraction – [in this case] only some 16 percent – of conventional costs." Marine biologists argued, however, that a sea-level canal would create disastrous ecological imbalances by inducing contact between the separate Atlantic and Pacific marine species. But other biologists disagreed, and Seaborg observed that "tempers are short and arguments long, and great advantages of a new canal to the human species are often underestimated or forgotten in the heat of conflict."

Seaborg conceded that there was a further difficulty with projects such as the Panatomic: "Nuclear excavation might entail the temporary removal of tens of thousands of people at the very least. Such operations," he lamented, combined with fears of radioactivity and of induced earthquakes, could lead to considerable apprehension, regardless of the great saving to world commerce and substantial benefits a canal could bring to the area.

After $17 million in feasibility studies, the Panatomic Canal was finally shelved in 1970.[41]

Private industries found the AEC's claims for nuclear excavation sufficiently enticing to propose some projects of their own. One of the more ambitious ideas was the North American Water and Power Alliance, a proposal submitted in 1964 by an engineering firm to create a coast-to-coast waterway across the United States by nuclear blasting, particularly through the Rockies. Nuclear-powered water pumps would sustain the transcontinental flow, with the added advantage that thermal pollution from the pumps would keep the waterways ice-free.[42]

More often than not, Plowshare projects became entangled in a web of political considerations. In 1963 the Santa Fe Railroad proposed the use of Plowshare explosives to crease a "Nuclear Right-of-Way" for rail lines across the Bristol Mountains between Barstow and Needles in California. The project (dubbed "Carryall" by the AEC), like all Plowshare undertakings after 1963, was hindered by the new Limited Test Ban Treaty, which forbade above-ground nuclear explosions. Critics claimed that such projects were disguised efforts to continue weapons testing. But Carryall's fate was further complicated by support from Secretary of the Army Stephen Ailes. In a December 1964 letter to Seaborg, Ailes linked Carryall to the success of the Panatomic Canal. "All of us involved in the sea-level canal studies have recognized from the outset that a major nuclear excavation project would have to be carried out within the US before we would ask another country to permit one on its territory," Ailes explained. Presumably because of its relative isolation and private industrial support, "The Carryall Project appears to be ideal for this purpose."[43]

Project Plowshare never got beyond a series of cratering experiments. The lifespan of Plowshare, however, covered crucial years in the development of AEC policies (roughly 1956 to 1971). Its history reveals several assumptions underlying these policies. Like all peaceful applications of the atom, Plowshare was important for its public relations impact on the cold war, on military nuclear policy, and on government use of nuclear technology in general. As image and credibility became increasingly significant in postwar policymaking, all nuclear technology served as a weapon of impression management.

More important for future nuclear policy was the relationship that Plowshare revealed between the AEC's imperatives for aggressive development and its recognition of environmental hazards. In the mid-1950s, of course, information concerning the environmental risks accompanying radiation remained inadequate and poorly circulated, even within the AEC. But in 1970, the commission's chairman still looked favorably on plans to detonate thermonuclear devices in densely populated areas to reduce industrial excavation costs.[44] In such a climate, how could the commission be expected to attach much significance to the far less dramatic environmental consideration of a nuclear power plant?

Ironically, Plowshare's anomalous bureaucratic status led the AEC to conduct some of its first significant environmental impact studies, which helped to establish the project's infeasibility. Project Chariot, an LRL proposal to create a harbor on Alaska's north coast by nuclear excavation, is a case in point. Ordinarily, the proposals of the weapons scientists, couched in national security mandates, were approved with little or no resistance by the AEC. In the case of Chariot, however, the scientists could not invoke military necessity, because the project called for non-military use of nuclear explosives. Against the strenuous opposition of the project's LRL sponsors, the AEC ordered a preliminary assessment of the effect of Chariot on the region's ecosystem. The environmental scientists assigned to the task were so alarmed by their estimates that they were instrumental in organizing opposition to the proposed blast. As Irvin Bupp has noted,

> neither the Commission nor the laboratory knew how to proceed when it was unable to justify an undertaking on grounds of national security. All prior Commission experience with opposition to its nuclear testing activities had been conducted in the tacit understanding that opposition could, in the end, simply be ignored.[45]

In October 1969, Alaska's Senator Mike Gravel joined Senator Edmund Muskie in introducing legislation to establish a commission to examine the environmental effects of Plowshare projects. In that same month, two LRL scientists, John Gofman and Arthur Tamplin, announced that, according to their findings, permissible radiation exposure levels were twenty times more carcinogenic than their AEC employers claimed. Less than three months later, President Nixon signed into law the National Environmental Policy Act. That inchoate cluster of social forces known as the environmental movement had caught up with Plowshare and with the rest of the government's nuclear energy policies.

The Rise of Environmentalism

In the 1970s, nuclear power stood squarely at the intersection of two of the decade's prevailing concerns: energy and the environment. Born in an era of cheap energy and a booming economy, the nuclear power industry encouraged rapidly increasing consumption of electricity, while warning of future scarcity as a result of that consumption. The 1973–74 Arab oil embargo seemed custom-made for strengthening the industry's prospects. President Nixon's Project Independence called for nuclear power to provide 50 percent of the nation's electricity by the end of the century. The industry and the AEC faced, however, a simultaneous environmentalist challenge that threatened to counterbalance the gains promised by the energy crisis. The manner in which government and industry responded to this challenge was in many ways as significant as the substance of the debate.

At an AIF-sponsored conference on "The Nuclear Controversy" in 1972, AEC and industry representatives pointed to 1969 as the year the trouble began. "If we look back at the national controversy over nuclear power in the United States," the first speaker noted, "we don't have to look far. There was none on the national level before 1969."[46] In January of that year, *Sports Illustrated* published an article criticizing the effects of thermal pollution from nuclear power plants on fish and marine life. In that same year, two books attacking reactor safety and nuclear hazards captured national attention: *The Careless Atom* by Sheldon Novick and *Perils of the Peaceful Atom* by Richard Curtis and Elizabeth Hogan. *Esquire* published an article based on Dr Ernest Sternglass's claims that the risks of low-level radiation had been dramatically underestimated. In October, the JCAE began the hearings at which Gofman, Tamplin, and other scientists challenged the AEC's radiation standards. A public forum in Burlington, Vermont, brought AEC and industry representatives face to face with their critics for a highly publicized debate. The environmental implications of nuclear power had become a national issue.[47]

At the JCAE's hearings on "Environmental Effects of Producing Electric Power" in late 1969 and early 1970, several commissioners and members of Congress made it clear that they considered more than technical issues to be at stake. AEC Chairman Seaborg warned the JCAE that a wave of "unsubstantiated fear-mongering" accompanied the public's recent interest in the environment. "In the years ahead," he predicted, "today's outcries about the environment will be nothing compared to cries of angry citizens" in future energy-starved cities, where prolonged blackouts would leave people to "shiver while imprisoned in stalled subways" in a world of "spoiled food," "darkened skyscrapers," and paralyzed police and medical services. "Fortunately," Seaborg observed, "most people are not willing to sit in the dark." AEC Commissioner James T. Ramey noted that public meetings on nuclear power issues always attracted "some professional 'stirrer-uppers'" and "phonies" who criticized AEC policy. When a scientist testified that the long-term effects of low-level radiation were unknown and suggested that the burden of proof should rest with the AEC, JCAE Chairman Chet Holifield asked, "Can we live in a society where every fact has to be proven?"[48]

Some commissioners and nuclear industry leaders viewed the environmentalist challenges to nuclear power as part of a nationwide epidemic of distrust of technology and government in general. At a January 1970 conference on Plowshare, AEC Commissioner Theos J. Thompson warned that "a danger that is perhaps greater than that of the threat to our environment" was the "growing rejection of those American ideals that have made this relatively young country a leader in the world today." To oppose nuclear technology because low-level radiation might be detrimental struck Thompson as woefully enervated: "It is as though we decided not to get out of bed anymore because we might slip on the way to the bathroom." Just as development of nuclear power had been equated with national identity, so the commissioner saw criticism of nuclear technology's environmental safety as an attack on "the American philosophy of life."[49]

General Electric nuclear executive Bertram Wolfe elaborated on Thompson's argument, charging that antinuclear critics had a "hidden agenda," manipulating antinuclear sentiment to attack corporate capitalism, centralized power, a vigorous growth economy, and the culture of abundance. Antinuclear environmentalists, Wolfe maintained, felt "that energy should be used as a means for societal change not directly connected with energy." Not just nuclear power, but "the whole structure of our society" was the target, Wolfe explained; "it's another Jonestown they're talking about."[50]

With fifteen years of experience in inspiring public confidence, why did nuclear advocates interpret specific environmental criticisms as general attacks on technology, government, and "American ideals?" No doubt some antinuclear critics did want to see broader social changes; but the AEC itself was so accustomed to approaching nuclear power as an ideological emblem that it repeatedly did what it accused its opponents of doing: judging technical issues on political grounds. The AEC was also slow to acknowledge that the most compelling environmentalist criticism came from AEC scientists, nuclear industry engineers, and even former AEC commissioners who believed that nuclear power would have to overcome the mistakes of its past in order to provide the energy of the future.

Ultimately, nuclear advocates may have been right to sense a larger social change behind the emerging antinuclear movement, but wrong about its origins. At a time when civil rights, antiwar, and feminist movements articulated a broad agenda for social change, many defenders of nuclear power saw their detractors as just another dissident group. . . . Samuel P. Hays examines twentieth-century environmentalism in light of a broad cultural shift in consumer demands from conveniences to amenities. Perhaps the electrical Garden of Eden projected by nuclear advocates presented a prewar celebration of abundance to a postwar culture that was in the process of replacing that vision with a new concern for the environment as a commodity in its own right.[51]

Congress responded more favorably than the AEC to the public's growing interest in the environment. On January 1, 1970, the National Environmental Policy Act (NEPA) went into effect. For the nuclear power industry, this meant that the new Environmental Protection Agency would determine radiation and safety standards and would require an environmental impact statement prior to the licensing of all nuclear power plants. The AEC's initial response to NEPA was not entirely cooperative. In 1971, the AEC refused to consider citizen challenges to Baltimore Gas and Electric's Calvert Cliffs nuclear plant on Chesapeake Bay on the basis of thermal pollution; the AEC further claimed that NEPA did not apply to this case. The US Court of Appeals in Washington, DC, ruled against the AEC, instructing it to comply with NEPA requirements.[52]

Meanwhile, documentation of problems with reactor safety and radioactive waste disposal mounted. Daniel Ford and Henry Kendall led the Union of Concerned Scientists investigation of failures in the AEC-approved Emergency Core Cooling System, the power plants' major protection against a meltdown. The resulting hearings, which began in 1972 and continued for eighteen months, focused national attention on the issue of reactor safety. In 1973, Ralph Nader called for a national moratorium on nuclear plant construction, and Friends of the Earth won access to internal AEC documents exposing the AEC's cover-up of the WASH-740 update in 1964.[53]

By the early 1970s, nuclear friends and foes alike spoke of the damaging effect of the largely uncritical nuclear advocacy espoused by the AEC and the JCAE. Environmental concerns had warranted institutional innovation; now Congress sought an institutional redefinition of the federal atomic establishment. The Energy Reorganization Act of 1974 split the AEC into two new agencies: a Nuclear Regulatory Commission (NRC) to oversee licensing and regulation of nuclear power plants, and an Energy Research and Development Administration (ERDA) to cover the development and promotion of energy and the production of nuclear weapons. In 1977, President Carter's Department of Energy Organization Act incorporated ERDA into a new cabinet-level agency. Meanwhile, Congress stripped the JCAE of its legislative powers and divided its tasks among five different committees.

These new institutions, however, inherited old problems. In 1975, the new NRC released the results of a two-year Reactor Safety Study, also referred to as WASH-1400 and as the Rasmussen report (after MIT nuclear engineer Norman Rasmussen, the study's director). Although the report contained mixed reviews, it largely reaffirmed the safety of nuclear reactors, comparing the likelihood of a major accident to that of being struck by a meteor. At first, the Rasmussen report provided the favorable publicity required to prop up the utility companies' sagging confidence in the economic viability of nuclear reactors. *The Bulletin of Atomic Scientists*, however, denounced the Rasmussen report as "an in-house study" of questionable value; and in 1977, the Union of Concerned Scientists published a detailed critique, challenging its methods as well as its findings. In 1979, the NRC itself finally rejected the report's optimistic findings.[54]

On March 28, 1979, a series of malfunctions occurred at Unit 2 of the Three Mile Island (TMI) nuclear power plant near Harrisburg, Pennsylvania. In the next few days, several thousand people evacuated the area, and hundreds of millions of others watched and read updates on the worst accident in nuclear power's brief history. TMI was not the first serious accident at a nuclear plant; nor was it the first accident to present a serious risk of meltdown. In October 1966, for example, a partial fuel meltdown occurred at the Enrico Fermi Fast Breeder Reactor in Detroit. In March 1975, a worker at the TVA's Brown's Ferry nuclear power plant was checking for air leaks with a lighted candle when some electrical cables caught fire; in the seven-hour fire that ensued, all of the safety backups for one of the reactor's cooling systems were impaired.

The most important aspects of TMI were the publicity it received, and the timing of that publicity. At the time, many critics considered it the Tet offensive of the nuclear power controversy, swinging the press over to the antinuclear perspective and solidifying the de facto moratorium on new reactor orders. The industry's defenders charged – with justification – that the news media sensationalized and distorted the events and the significance of Three Mile Island. The media's sense of betrayal was, however, predictable. Metropolitan Edison first delayed reporting the accident, then misrepresented its scope. In the absence of substantive information, the press was as unprepared as the general public for fine gradations of technology assessment. Unexamined nuclear fear in 1979 was a direct product of the unexamined nuclear optimism of the 1950s and 1960s.

In the long run, however, TMI had a revitalizing effect on pronuclear publicity. The Atomic Industrial Forum responded to the accident by creating the US Committee on Energy Awareness (USCEA). Sponsored by nuclear vendors, engineering firms, and utility firms, the USCEA conducted a $25- to $30-million-per-year advertising campaign to restore the image of nuclear power's legitimacy among scientists and policymakers. In May and June 1983, a congressional subcommittee conducted the first hearings to investigate the Department of Energy's (DOE) nuclear public relations campaign and its connection with private efforts like that of the USCEA. Promotion of nuclear power, if not nuclear power itself, had made a vigorous comeback.[55]

Conclusion: Pondering the Nuclear Future

On the morning of April 28, 1986, the dust on a Swedish worker's shoes set off the alarm on a radiation detector at the Forsmark nuclear power plant north of Stockholm. Safety inspectors combed the plant for leaks, and tested the seven hundred other employees. The workers' clothing registered radiation exposure at five to ten times normal background levels; yet the plant looked clean. The source of radioactivity appeared to be outside the power plant; ironically, the workers were carrying traces of radioactivity into a nuclear facility from the streets. By that night, all the world knew the source: an explosion had occurred at another nuclear power plant, in the Soviet Union. Forsmark, like much of Europe, found itself in the shadow of Chernobyl.

The environmental dimensions of nuclear power were dramatically underscored by the Chernobyl accident. Radiation from the damaged reactor observed no political boundaries, traveling farther (over a thousand miles) and dispersing less uniformly than expected. The evacuation of 135,000 people within a nineteen-mile radius of the reactor underscored the increasing concern in the United States over emergency evacuation procedures.

Chernobyl also presented a delicate public relations problem for Washington. The Soviets failed to notify the world of the accident until Swedish reports of radiation forced them to explain what had happened. Some government officials seized upon Chernobyl as proof of Soviet duplicity and secrecy; to them, the unsubstantiated (and, as it turned out, groundless) reports of two thousand fatalities were much more credible than the Soviet Union's claim (later verified) that there had been only two immediate deaths.

For the US Department of Energy and the Nuclear Regulatory Commission, Chernobyl threatened to discredit nuclear power. Even the Soviets' initial reticence was uncomfortably reminiscent of Metropolitan Edison's conduct during the TMI accident (a parallel that General

Secretary Gorbachev noted during a May 14, 1986, speech on Soviet television). Thus, while NRC and DOE officials criticized the Soviet Union for withholding or delaying information, they instructed their own employees, scientists, and contractors to avoid the press, and specifically to refrain from making comparisons between American and Soviet reactors. Joined by the Atomic Industrial Forum and the US Committee on Energy Awareness, NRC and DOE spokespersons also released statements that contributed to a number of misconceptions: that the Chernobyl reactor had no containment structures (it had two); that all American reactors have such structures (the DOE operates five reactors with no regular containment domes); and that the Chernobyl plant's design was too dissimilar to any American reactor to warrant comparison (a claim that dissenting NRC member James Asseltine contested before a congressional committee).[56]

Predictions of nuclear power's future in the United States vary greatly, depending primarily on how one interprets the past. Some nuclear analysts argue that the twin plagues of unresolved safety issues and escalating costs, coupled with the declining demand for electricity, will consign nuclear power to an early grave. "Hard, cold economics is now doing to nuclear power what thousands of hot-blooded demonstrators never could," claims Christopher Flavin. "It is slowly, painfully shutting down the world's nuclear industries." Others, as widely divergent in outlook as the Atomic Industrial Forum and nuclear critic Mark Hertsgaard, foresee a resurgent nuclear industry. The amount of capital already invested is great enough to suggest that the major nuclear corporations are willing to wait it out; and the far greater scope of their nonnuclear assets indicates that they can afford that luxury.[57]

The nuclear industry has maintained that the main cause of the atom's enlarging price tag is delays in plant construction and operation that result from excessive government safety and environmental regulations. Some critics and industry analysts disagree, claiming that the main reason for escalating costs was the intense competition for control of the nuclear market during the 1970s by the four largest vendors (General Electric, Westinghouse, Combustion Engineering, and Babcock and Wilcox).[58] Like auto makers in the 1950s, these corporations produced ever-larger new models, thereby forfeiting the benefits of standard production and accumulated operational experience with a given design.

If nuclear power can weather the present economic crisis, we must look to the relationship between policy and expertise, institutions and technology, for our projections. We could argue that the AEC, a politically vulnerable agency overseeing a highly politicized technology, created such a gap between expertise and policy that the environmentalists of the 1970s were able to rush into the resulting power vacuum. Such an analysis would permit some reassurance from the fact that those who challenged the institutional expertise of fifteen years ago have since institutionalized their own environmental critique into the regulatory expertise of the present. Thus the conflict of interest between federal overseers and corporate developers would appear to have been reduced. To be sure, the traditional alliance between government and industry has been strained by the environmental revolution. Even at its best, however, the regulatory process has severe limitations. It can sound the alarm, but it cannot put out the fire. The most dangerous threat to an environmentally sound nuclear policy today may be the inability of any regulatory process to extract both safety and productivity from current nuclear technology.

The AEC and its successors, like all agents of government power, became increasingly preoccupied with credibility in the postwar era. Its bureaucratic proximity to nuclear weapons rendered nuclear power especially susceptible to emblematic, rather than substantive, policies; and as with nuclear weapons, the magnitude of risks accompanying an inadequate nuclear power policy has subjected it to far greater public concern, once the facts became available, than most arenas of government authority. Today's nuclear power plants are artifacts of a generation's misplaced trust in an unexamined technology; tomorrow's plants may encapsulate within their cooling towers the next generation's misplaced trust in the regulatory process. In both cases, a certain expediency has triumphed over the nuclear mandate for socially responsible technology.

Notes

1   Martin Sherwin, *A World Destroyed: The Atomic Bomb and the Grand Alliance* (New York: Vintage, 1977), 308.
2   "Commercial Electric Power from Atomic Energy," *Science*, July 29, 1966, 192.
3   Morgan Thomas, *Atomic Energy and Congress* (Ann Arbor: University of Michigan Press, 1956), 13–16.
4   Stephen Hilgartner, Richard C. Bell, and Rory O'Connor, *Nukespeak: The Selling of Nuclear Technology in America* (New York: Penguin, 1982), 60–62.
5   Mark Hertsgaard, *Nuclear, Inc.: The Men and Money Behind Nuclear Energy* (New York: Pantheon, 1983), 25–26.
6   Harold P. Green and Alan Rosenthal, *Government of the Atom: The Integration of Powers* (New York: Atherton Press, 1961), 9–12.
7   Edward Teller to Sterling Cole, July 23, 1953, *Atomic Power Development and Private Enterprise: Hearings before the Joint Committee on Atomic Energy*, 83d Cong., 1st sess., 1953, 633.

8   David E. Lilienthal, *Change, Hope, and the Bomb* (Princeton: Princeton University Press, 1963), 109, 110; Glenn Seaborg and William Corliss, *Man and Atom* (New York: E. P. Dutton, 1971).

9   JCAE Hearings, *Atomic Power Development and Private Enterprise*, 2.

10 Hertsgaard, *Nuclear, Inc.*, 26; Richard G. Hewlett and Francis Duncan, *Nuclear Navy 1946–1962* (Chicago: University of Chicago Press), 237–38.

11 Lewis L. Strauss, "My Faith in the Atomic Future," *Reader's Digest*, Aug. 1955, 17; JCAE Hearings, *Atomic Power Development and Private Enterprise*.

12 *New York Times*, Dec. 9, 1953, 2, cited in Hilgartner et al., *Nukespeak*, 43.

13 George T. Mazuzan, "Conflict of Interest: Promoting and Regulating the Infant Nuclear Power Industry, 1954–1956," *The Historian*, Nov. 1981, 1–14; Daniel Ford, *The Cult of the Atom* (New York: Simon and Schuster, 1982), 42.

14 Green and Rosenthal, *Government of the Atom*, 26, 12.

15 Hertsgaard, *Nuclear, Inc.*, 20–60; Steven L. Del Sesto, *Science, Politics and Controversy: Civilian Nuclear Power in the United States, 1946–1974* (Boulder, Colo.: Westview Press), 58–59.

16 U.S. Atomic Energy Commission, *Theoretical Possibilities and Consequences of Major Accidents in Large Nuclear Power Plants*, WASH-740 (Washington, DC: Government Printing Office, 1958).

17 Ford, *Cult of the Atom*, 45.

18 Ibid., 71.

19 *Forum Annual Report for the Year Ended June 30, 1954* (New York: Atomic Industrial Forum, 1954), 5.

20 Charles Robbins, "Uses of Atomic Industry," *Public Relations for the Atomic Industry: Proceedings of a Meeting for Members, March 19 and 20, 1956* (New York: Atomic Industrial Forum, 1956), 1.

21 Robert Charpie, "Power Reactors," *Public Relations*, 4–20; Shelby Thompson, "Sources of Atomic Energy Information in Government," *Public Relations*, 66–70; Frank K. Pittman, "Safety Requirements of the Atomic Energy Commission," *Public Relations*, 94–95.

22 Jerome Luntz, "Address," *Public Relations*, 40, 41.

23 LeBaron Foster, "Address," *Public Relations*, 79, 82–83.

24 William A. Stenzel, "Developing Consumer Acceptance of Radioactivity," *Public Relations*, 110–114; Harold A. Beaudoin, "Locating a Reactor in a Populated Area," *Public Relations*, 105.

25 For the AEC's public relations efforts I have relied on the AEC *Annual Reports*.

26 AEC Press Release, Sept. 16, 1954, cited in Ford, *Cult of the Atom*, 50.

27 Hilgartner et al., *Nukespeak*, 44.

28 Harold Stassen, "Atoms for Peace," *Ladies Home Journal*, Aug. 1955, 48.

29 Produced by the Connecticut Yankee Atomic Power Consortium, *The Atom and Eve* featured a scale model of the Haddam Neck plant, where "even the colors chosen for the structure were selected from the natural hues of the surrounding valley" (brown) and color-coordinated to "recall the New England tradition" (white).

30 Allan C. Fisher, Jr., "You and the Obedient Atom," *National Geographic*, Sept. 1958, 303, 311, 329, 352.

31 AEC Press Release, Feb. 20, 1966; Seaborg and Corliss, *Man and Atom*, 22.

32 Lilienthal, *Change*, 110.

33 H. Peter Metzger, *The Atomic Establishment* (New York: Simon and Schuster, 1972), 112, passim; US Atomic Energy Commission, *Radioactive Fallout from Nuclear Weapons Tests*, AEC: CONF-765, Nov. 1965.

34 Hilgartner et al., *Nukespeak*, 41.

35 Irvin C. Bupp, "Priorities in Nuclear Technology: Program Prosperity and Decay in the United States Atomic Energy Commission, 1956–1971" (PhD diss., Harvard, 1971), 181.

36 Edward Teller and Allen Brown, *The Legacy of Hiroshima* (Garden City, NJ: Doubleday, 1962), 180.

37 Freeman Dyson, *Disturbing the Universe* (New York: Harper and Row, 1979), 112.

38 Bupp, "Priorities," 196.

39 Seaborg and Corliss, *Man and Atom*, 234.

40 Ibid., 183. (Emphasis in original.)

41 L. J. Vortman, "Excavation of a Sea-Level Ship Canal," *Proceedings of the Second Plowshare Symposium, May 14, 1959*, Part II: Excavation (AEC: UCRL-5671), 88; Seaborg and Corliss, *Man and Atom*, 184, 195.

42 Ibid., 113.

43 Stephen Ailes to Glenn Seaborg, December 30, 1964, Carryall folder, Plowshare Papers, Department of Energy Archives.

44 Seaborg and Corliss, *Man and Atom*, 234.

45 Bupp, "Priorities," 196.

46 Bill Perkins, "The US Controversy – Issues of Concern," *The Nuclear Controversy in the USA* (Atomic Industrial Forum and Swiss Association for Atomic Energy, Lucerne, Apr. 30–May 3, 1972), 1.

47 Gofman, a graduate student of Seaborg's at Berkeley, and Tamplin were both AEC scientists who became outspoken critics of nuclear policy as a result of their research for the AEC; for an account of Tamplin's assignment to discredit Ernest Sternglass, see Metzger, *Atomic Establishment*, 276–78, n. 17. See also John W. Gofman and Arthur R. Tamplin, *Poisoned Power* (Emmaus, Pa: Rodale Press, 1971).

48 US Congress, Joint Committee on Atomic Energy, *Environmental Effects of Producing Electric Power*, 2 pts, 91st Cong., 1st and 2d sess., 1969–70.

49 Theos J. Thompson, "Improving the Quality of Life – Can Plowshare Help?" *Symposium on Engineering with Nuclear Explosives, January 14–15, 1970*, vol. 1 (AEC: CONF-700101), 104.

50 Bertram Wolfe, "The Hidden Agenda," in *Nuclear Power: Both Sides*, ed. Michio Kaku and Jennifer Trainer (New York: Norton, 1982), 240–43; Hertsgaard, *Nuclear, Inc.*, 181.

51 Samuel P. Hays, *Beauty, Health, and Permanence: Environmental Politics in the United States, 1955–1985* (New York: Cambridge University Press, 1987).

52 Metzger, *Atomic Establishment*, 270.
53 Paul Turner, "Introductory Remarks," in *The Nuclear Controversy in the USA II*: Conference Papers, Atomic Industrial Forum and Swiss Association for Atomic Energy, Lucerne, May 5–8, 1974 (New York: Atomic Industrial Forum, 1975), 1–3; Ford, *Cult of the Atom*, 115–30.
54 Ford, *Cult of the Atom*, 172.
55 Daniel Ford, *Three Mile Island: Thirty Minutes to Meltdown* (New York: Penguin, 1981); Committee on Energy and Commerce, *Nuclear Public Relations Campaign: Hearings before the Subcommittee on Energy Conservation and Power*, 98th Cong., 1st sess., 1983, 53, 87, 98–117, 192–98, 351, passim.
56 *New York Times*, May 22, 1986.
57 Christopher Flavin, "Reassessing the Economics of Nuclear Power," in Lester R. Brown et al., *State of the World, 1984* (New York: Norton, 1984), 132.
58 Hertsgaard, *Nuclear, Inc.*, 63–65.

Documents

Atomic Power Development and Private Enterprise

UNIVERSITY OF CALIFORNIA,
RADIATION LABORATORY,
Livermore, Calif., July 23, 1953.

Hon. STERLING COLE,
  Chairman, Joint Committee on Atomic Energy,
  Congress of the United States, Washington, DC
DEAR SIR: In response to your invitation to make a statement in connection with the development of atomic energy by private enterprise, I should like to discuss two topics concerning which I have some specific experience. These are the safety of nuclear reactors and the connection between power production and military application.

Taken from Hearings before the Joint Committee on Atomic Energy, Congress of the United States, Eighty-third Congress, First Session on Atomic Power Development and Private Enterprise. June 24, 25, and 29; July 1, 6, 9, 13, 15, 16, 20, 22, 23, 27, and 31, 1953. Printed for the use of the Joint Committee on Atomic Energy. United States Government Printing Office, Washington, DC, 1953.

Briefly, my opinion can be stated as follows: First, nuclear power-producing units will be dangerous instruments and careful thought will have to be given to their safe construction and operation and, second, there is a great and increasing need for fissionable materials in the military field.

I should like to recommend, first, that an advisory committee should be set up to review planned reactors and supervise functioning reactors under the control of private enterprise. Instead of setting up a new committee, the present Advisory Committee on Reactor Safeguards of the Atomic Energy Commission might serve this purpose; and second, that the Government stimulate power production by private enterprise by guaranteeing to buy militarily useful byproducts at a pre-determined price and in limited but large quantities for a period of 5 or 10 years.

Safety of Nuclear Reactors

For the past 6 years I have served as the Chairman of the Reactor Safeguard Committee. Recently, this committee and the Industrial Committee on Reactor Location Problems have been merged into the Advisory Committee on Reactor Safeguards, and I am participating in the work of this new committee.

Up to the present time we have been extremely fortunate in that accidents in nuclear reactors have not caused any fatalities. With expanding applications of nuclear reactions and nuclear power, it cannot be expected that this unbroken record will be maintained. It must be realized that this good record was achieved to a considerable extent because of safety measures which have necessarily retarded development.

The main factors which influence reactor safety are, in my opinion, reasonably well understood. There have been in the past years a few minor incidents, all of which have been caused by neglect of clearly formulated safety rules. Such occasional accidents cannot be avoided. It is rather remarkable that they have occurred in such a small number of instances. I want to emphasize in particular that the operation of nuclear reactors is not mysterious and that the irregularities are no more unexpected than accidents which happen on account of disregard of traffic regulations.

In the popular opinion, the main danger of a nuclear pile, is due to the possibility that it may explode. It should be pointed out, however, that such an explosion, although possible, is likely to be harmful only in the immediate surroundings and will probably be limited in its destructive effects to the operators. A much greater public hazard is due to the fact that nuclear plants contain radioactive poisons. In a nuclear accident, these poisons may be liberated into the atmosphere or into the water supply. In fact, the radioactive poisons produced in a powerful nuclear reactor will retain a dangerous concentration even after they have been carried downwind to a distance of 10 miles. Some danger might possibly persist to distances as great as 100 miles. It would seem appropriate that Federal regulations should apply to a hazard which is not confined by State boundaries. The various committees dealing with reactor safety have come to the conclusion that none of the powerful reactors built or suggested up to the present time are absolutely safe. Though the possibility of an accident seems small, a release of the active products in a city or densely populated area would lead to disastrous results. It has been therefore the practice of these committees to recommend the observance of exclusion distances, that is, to exclude the public from areas around reactors, the size of the area varying in appropriate manner with the amount of radioactive poison that the reactor might release. Rigid enforcement of such exclusion distances might hamper future development of reactors to an unreasonable extent. In particular, the danger that a reactor might malfunction and release its radioactive poison differs for different kinds of reactors. It is my opinion that reactors of sufficiently safe types might be developed in the near future. Apart from the basic construction of the reactor, underground location or particularly thoughtfully constructed safety devices might be considered.

It is clear that no legislation will be able to stop future accidents and avoid completely occasional loss of life. It is my opinion that the unavoidable danger which will remain after all reasonable controls have been employed must not stand in the way of rapid development of nuclear power. It also would seem that proper legislation at the present time might make provisions for safe construction and safe operation of nuclear reactors. In case an accident should occur which involved the lives of many people, pressure for such legislation would become overwhelming. Proper steps taken at the present time could reasonably prepare for accidents and minimize the suffering that is caused, when and if they should occur.

It would seem reasonable to extend the Atomic Energy Commission procedures on reviewing planned reactors and supervising functioning reactors to nuclear plants under the control of private enterprise. To what extent these functions should be advisory or regulatory is a difficult question. I feel that ultimate responsibility for safe operation will have to be placed on the shoulders of the men and the organization most closely connected with the construction and the operation of the reactor.

Power Production and Military Application

The first- and best-known military application of atomic energy was connected with strategic bombing. In the popular mind, such strategic bombing has been identified with the destruction of cities. The belief is widely held that a relatively limited number of atomic bombs cannot only cause terrifying destruction but would produce saturation, that is, only a limited number of atomic bombs would be needed. It is my conviction that this opinion is based on a misconception and that indeed a great stockpile of fissionable material could be usefully applied in warfare. Furthermore, it seems to me that a more general use of fission weapons will not result necessarily in a more thorough destruction of cities but might rather be used against military targets of the more conventional type. It seems to me, therefore, that a less expensive source of fissionable materials would be desirable. Such a less expensive source could be obtained if atomic reactors were constructed for the dual purpose of providing power and producing fissionable materials.

Strategic targets include industrial plants and military installations far behind the enemy's lines. Depending on the vulnerability of these targets and on their contribution to the enemy's war effort, one may well be justified in using atomic bombs against these targets. The size of the target need not be decisive and the number of such targets may be quite appreciable.

The possible tactical targets are even more numerous. Any concentration of fighting forces or of materiel near the fighting lines constitutes tactical targets. Strongly defended positions might be attacked by atomic bombs. Atomic weapons could be used against beachheads or against enemy forces attempting to cross a natural obstacle. Conversely, atomic weapons could be employed to prepare a landing on a beachhead or the attack of a parachute force. The vulnerability of naval vessels to atomic bombs has been demonstrated in the Bikini tests. Vehicles less expensive than naval units may present atomic-bomb targets, particularly if the cost of the bomb is lower than the cost of the vehicle which one attempts to destroy. An enemy bomber or even an enemy fighter plane might be considered as a possible target for an atomic bomb.

It might seem extravagant to use atom bombs for all these different types of targets. The question of extravagance or of sound economy must be considered, however, in connection with the ease of delivery, with the expense of delivery, and with the expense of the fissionable materials. I can think of no exception to the rule that the cost of delivery will be less if one produces a certain damage by atomic weapons rather than by more conventional means. It is therefore the cost of fissionable materials which will decide how extensively one can use atomic weapons in warfare. The more the cost of atomic weapons can be reduced, the greater will be the number of applications where relatively cheap delivery systems can replace the much more expensive conventional methods. Increase in our stockpile of fissionable materials may therefore reduce the military expenditure without reducing military potential.

It seems to be doubtful whether, on the basis of present technology, atomic energy can produce power in an economically profitable manner. Power production can, however, be conducted in such a manner as to produce militarily useful materials. It would seem to me reasonable to stimulate the construction of power-producing reactors by guaranteeing a price at which the Government will buy the militarily useful by-products. This price should of course be set lower than the price at which the Atomic Energy Commission is producing fissionable materials at the present time. It probably will be necessary to set a limit to the amount of fissionable material which the Government is prepared to purchase and also to set a limit to the time during which such purchases will be made at the fixed price. Nevertheless, it seems probable that if a fair price is guaranteed for a period like 5 or 10 years, this will be an effective stimulant to the Nation's atomic-power industry. This industry is likely to become a factor in national defense which may not be second even to the steel or aircraft industries.

The above contains the substance of the testimony which I have prepared for the joint congressional committee. I should like to express my very great regret that at the date set for the hearing it was completely impossible for me to leave Livermore. It would be a great pleasure to appear before the joint congressional committee at any time to amplify the above statements or else to help in any other way that you can think of.

Yours very truly

EDWARD TELLER.

Environmental Effects of Producing Electric Power

CONGRESS OF THE UNITED STATES,
JOINT COMMITTEE ON ATOMIC ENERGY,
Washington, D.C., May 5, 1969.

Hon. ROBERT C. TUVESON,
Chairman, Minnesota Pollution Control Agency,
Albert Lea, Minn.

DEAR MR. TUVESON: It has recently come to the attention of the Joint Committee on Atomic Energy that the Minnesota Pollution Control Agency has under consideration a proposal to include in any waste disposal permit it may issue for the Monticello Nuclear Generating Plant of Northern States Power Co. conditions or limitations relating to radioactive waste discharges from the plant, both gaseous and liquid. These limitations, I understand, are considerably different from those which the Atomic Energy Commission would impose pursuant to the Atomic Energy Act and regulations promulgated thereunder, and would be in addition to limitations on conventional wastes, including waste heat, which state water pollution control agencies traditionally control.

My purpose in writing is to express my very deep concern that, with respect to the proposal to regulate radiological effluents from the Monticello plant, the Minnesota Pollution Control Agency would be attempting to exercise control in an area that has been specifically preempted to the Federal Government. As a charter member of the Joint Committee, and as a member of the House Military Affairs Committee which drafted the original Atomic Energy Act, I can assure you that it was the intent of Congress that this important area should be regulated by the national government, and not by each of the individual states. This action was not taken simply out of a desire for uniformity in regulation, although this certainly was a motivating factor; in large measure this action was taken out of recognition of the Atomic Energy Commission's and the Federal Radiation Council's vastly greater expertise respecting the potential hazards of radiological effects, and the control thereof, than any single state reasonably could be expected to have or acquire. I am enclosing for

---

Taken from Hearings before the Joint Committee on Atomic Energy, Congress of the United States, Ninety-first Congress, Second Session on Environmental Effects of Producing Electric Power. January 27, 28, 29, 30; February 24, 25, and 26, 1970. Part 2 (Vol. I). Printed for the use of the Joint Committee on Atomic Energy. United States Government Printing Office, Washington, DC, 1970.

your information a summary legal analysis prepared by my staff which discusses in somewhat greater detail the legal situation in this regard. As you will note from the memorandum, virtually every court, legal scholar and state attorney general who has ever considered this question has concluded that the regulatory control of the radiological effects of the various atomic energy materials is vested exclusively in the Atomic Energy Commission, vis-a-vis the states, except where the Commission has undertaken to relinquish certain of this authority to qualified states pursuant to provisions of the Atomic Energy Act.

I fully recognize your concern for the health and safety of the people of Minnesota, including safety from the potential hazards associated with the use of atomic energy materials. Congress also recognized that concern by specifically requiring in the Atomic Energy Act that the AEC give prompt notice to interested states of any application for a Commission license, and by further requiring that the AEC "afford reasonable opportunity for State representatives to offer evidence, interrogate witnesses, and advise the Commission as to the application. . . ." I know from personal knowledge that in almost every AEC proceeding to date involving an application for a permit to construct a nuclear power plant affected States have availed themselves of this opportunity to express their views on those matters within the cognizance of the Commission.

I would be interested in discussing this matter with you and any other members of your agency if it would be convenient for you to visit Washington in the near future. I would also be interested in learning why, and the basis on which, your agency apparently believes it is necessary to establish radiological discharge standards different from and evidently even more restrictive than those of the Atomic Energy Commission. If there is actual reason to believe the Commission's standards, and the internationally-recognized standards on which they are based, are deficient in certain respects, I would certainly like to have any such information brought to my attention and that of my colleagues on the Joint Committee.

I look forward to hearing from you at your earliest convenience.

With warm personal regards, I am,

  Cordially yours,   CHET HOLIFIELD, *Chairman.*

P.S. – I assume that Governor LeVander is aware of and interested in this important matter, so I am taking the liberty of sending him a copy of this letter.   C. H.

———

STATE OF MINNESOTA,
OFFICE OF THE GOVERNOR,

MR. GLENN T. SEABORG,   *St. Paul, May 12, 1969.*
Chairman, U.S. Atomic Energy Commission,
Washington, D.C.

DEAR MR. SEABORG: This is to inform you that the Minnesota Pollution Control Agency today issued a permit setting the emission standards with which Northern States Power Company would have to comply to operate a nuclear power plant at Monticello, Minnesota.

These regulations are considerably more restrictive than standards set by the Atomic Energy Commission. Our Agency is extremely sensitive to maintaining Minnesota's reputation for clear air and pure water, which constitute our most valuable natural resource. The position of the State of Minnesota with respect to the Monticello generating plant, in effect, limits radioactive discharge to about 1/50th the level allowed by the AEC. This decision was made only after many months of study, review by professional consultants, and in-depth discussion.

Because the AEC was aware before May 12 that regulations stricter than your own were likely to be imposed, and if, as you claim, the AEC has preempted the nuclear field, I would have anticipated that AEC would have acted affirmatively to assert your exclusive jurisdiction before our Agency acted. Not having done so, I hope that you will now support our Agency's action.

The AEC representatives stated at the May 12 hearing that only a construction permit had been issued NSP by the Atomic Energy Commission and that an operating permit will still need issuance.

I now sincerely urge that the AEC not issue any operating permit for nuclear power generation in the State of Minnesota which does not respect the stringent regulations the State Pollution Control Agency requires.

We are most hopeful that the AEC will concede that regulations more stringent than those demanded by the Federal agency can only result in greater safety to the health and welfare of the people of Minnesota and to the continued excellent condition of our natural resources.

Sincerely,   HAROLD LE VANDER, *Governor.*

Nuclear Public Relations Campaign

Appendix "E"
Contract No. 31-109-38-6410
Argonne National Laboratory

Statement of Work
for
The Revision, Updating, Illustration,
Technical Review, Design, Typesetting,
and Mechanics to Provide A Camera-
Ready Copy of *Nuclear Power Plants*

April 1981

I. Background

Nuclear Power Plants was a key title in the "Understanding the Atom" series of booklets developed by the Atomic Energy Commission and distributed by ERDA. Along with the rest of the series, it was discontinued in the late 1980s [*sic*], leaving a vacuum in public information about nuclear energy available from the Government.

The objective of this project is the revision and updating of *Nuclear Power Plants*. Additional pertinent information about developments affecting nuclear power in the eight years since the booklet was last revised is considered necessary for this revised booklet. The Contractor shall also be responsible for the design, layout, and mechanicals necessary for the production of a camera-ready copy. It is anticipated that final publishing or printing and dissemination shall be accomplished by existent US Government facilities.

II. Scope

The update will be similar to the original in format, tone and content. The presentation will be non-adversarial, avoiding advocacy and

---

Taken from Hearings before the Subcommittee on Energy Conservation and Power of the Committee on Energy and Commerce, House of Representatives, Ninety-eighth Congress, First Session. May 23 and June 30, 1983. Serial No. 98–48. Printed for the use of the Committee on Energy and Commerce. US Government Printing Office, Washington, DC, 1983.

minimizing defensive material about such issues as radiation and waste management. The length of the text will be approximately the same as in the 1973 edition (6,000–7,000 words), though the emphasis and basic story line will change considerably (see below).

The amount of art work will also be roughly the same, with a few changes: Drawings illustrating the fission process and the workings of a nuclear power plant will be improved; photographs and illustrations will be scattered logically through the text, with less clustering of them in a single section; there will be no attempt to include a photo of every operating nuclear plant, but a cross-section representing regions, reactor types, etc.; and it will include some livelier art work – such as a clipping or book page showing early (1950s) wild-eyed expectations for nuclear energy.

December 3, 1982

Argonne National Library
Argonne, IL 60439

Appendix "B"
Contract No. 31-109-3B-7032

Statement of Work
Pamphlets for the Nuclear Energy Public Information Program

This pamphlet is one of a series intended to provide the public with candid, factual, no-advocacy information on nuclear energy subjects of interest or concern to the public. The subject is "Nuclear Power: A Woman's Perspective" and is intended to present information of particular concern to women; i.e. health effects on present and future generations, safety, moral and ethical issues.

Each pamphlet is to be an eight to twelve page booklet (including covers) approximately four inches by nine inches, in medium stock paper, printed in two colors of ink. The front panel is the title page and will have colors and/or a styling common to all pamphlets to identify the series. The individual title (which must be somewhat intriguing or provocative) will identify the particular topic in an eye-catching manner. Space will be reserved on the last panel for references to other DOE material, the DOE logo, and the theme statement "Nuclear Electricity: Part of our Everyday World."

The text is to be prepared from an outline provided by IEP/ANL, the purpose of which is to express the ideas and features which are to be included. The author is free to rearrange or otherwise change the material presented in the outlines as long as the essential ideas and topics are retained. The titles submitted are to indicate the subject only and are not necessarily to be used. The author's list of references used for the text should also be included with the first draft. After review of the first draft by ANL/IEP staff, the author is required to submit a final text revised to comply with the review comments.

The style of writing must engage the interest of the average reader who has been characterized as reading at the ninth grade level. The degree of detail and vocabulary should be consistent with this requirement. The total text should contain about 2,000 to 3,000 words with five or six illustrations. The text should be sectioned under several headings which might, for example, be in question form – questions in the public's mind.

The artwork, including cover design, line drawings, diagrams and layout will be done by artists at ANL, who will incorporate the author's suggestions and IEP's guidelines into original work. The author is requested to submit his ideas for illustrations (or word description of the illustrations) with the first draft of the text.

Proposal for a Nuclear Energy Public Affairs Program

I. Introduction

To assure an informed public opinion on nuclear energy, the Federal Government needs to implement a comprehensive public information program. First, we need amplification and explanation of the Presidential statement on nuclear policy. Mechanisms to do that with the help of Cabinet-level officials are prescribed in Section II below. Next, more information needs to be brought to the public. Section III of this paper describes a public information program designed to be complementary to ongoing non-government efforts. . . .

II.   Exposition of Administration Policy

The statement of the President of Administration policy in support of nuclear energy will be an important part of the process of building public acceptance. The public information program set forth herein is designed to help implement the Administration policy. While public elaboration and justification of the policy would primarily be the responsibility of DOE, nuclear energy is not a narrow issue affecting only DOE. The use or non-use of nuclear energy is linked to national and international economic well-being, to foreign affairs, to national security, and to environment and public health. As such, nuclear energy is a national issue which cuts across a number of government departments.

Defense and State could assert the effect on national security of decreased dependence on OPEC. The Departments of Commerce, Labor, and Treasury, as well as OMB, could speak to the economic advantages. The Surgeon General and the President's Science Advisor might commission blue ribbon scientific panels to certify the negligible radiation effect of nuclear power reactors. The Department of the Interior might comment on the several environmental advantages of nuclear power. DOE and NRC would need to address safety and waste management concerns, and to stress the assurance of supply resulting from greater use of nuclear energy.

Coherent support for nuclear energy across the top level of government should help to restore much needed credibility. Utilities, financial institutions, state governments, the media and the public need to be assured that we have a firm policy, that we are in no doubt about it, that we *need* the policy not only for assurance of energy supply, but for reasons of economic well-being, national security, environment, and public health and safety.

The question of adequate public information concerning nuclear power could usefully be addressed by some kind of high-level government/industry working group in support of the Presidential Nuclear Power Policy Statement. . . .

III.   Recommended Public Information Program

Association of nuclear energy with economic well-being, national security, clean environment, and public health and safety would do much to demonstrate that the benefits of nuclear energy outweigh the risks. We must present information which shows the contribution NE programs are making to safety and waste management. We need also to speak to the essential role of nuclear energy in the overall US electric energy mix; solar will not be available in time, if ever, and coal brings with it difficulties and risks which preclude exclusive reliance on coal as the electric energy alternative of the future. Work needs to be done at the outset of our program to pull together studies of these major issues.

Following is a list of public information activities which DOE/NE should undertake. Where it seems appropriate, a description is included of how the proposed NE activity might be linked with the ongoing non-government programs.

1 *Op-ed pieces.* We should monitor the leading newspapers and magazines. Articles and editorials which comment on nuclear power, pro or con, should selectively be responded to. The Atomic Industrial Forum (AIF) sometimes does this, but its response is often ignored or appears as a letter to the editor, rather than as op-ed article. A DOE response would merit greater attention, especially if directed to an article or editorial which dealt with an aspect of government policy. DOE-initiated op-ed pieces should be signed by officials of the rank of Deputy Assistant Secretary or higher. In most cases they should be signed by the ASNE.

2 *Granting of interviews to selected journalists.* There are some important journalists who might agree to interview the ASNE or other high-level DOE managers about nuclear energy policy, and to write a column about the interview. Representative journalists include Hugh Sidey, George Will, William Buckley, and James Reston. We might also seek to arrange interviews for more liberal journalists such as Carl Rowen; nuclear energy has populist appeal which is generally overlooked, e.g., jobs, environment, anti-inflationary.

3 *Editorial boards.* The ASNE should seek to meet with selected editorial boards, or at least the science and/or energy editorialists. Among those newspapers whose editorial policies may have national influence are the *New York Times, The Washington Post, The Wall Street Journal, The Christian Science Monitor,* and *The Los Angeles Times.*

4 *Articles.* Preparation of articles about nuclear energy by ASNE or other qualified officials would be useful. Journals which should be considered include Foreign Affairs, Foreign Policy, New York Times Magazine, Atlantic, Harpers, Time (Essay), Readers Digest, and Parade.

5 *Attend meetings of state and local government officials.* Mayors, governors, state legislators, and state Public Utility Commissions periodically meet as national groups. They have national organizations which represent them on a continuing basis, e.g., the National Conference of Mayors, the National Governor's Conference, the National Association of Regulatory Utility Commissions. We should be sure that our nuclear energy policies are known to these organizations, and we should offer to provide spokesmen to attend their conferences and describe our policies and programs. In addition, many states have designated energy or nuclear affairs representatives; we must assure systematic contact with them to be sure they are fully informed of Federal policies and programs, and that we are fully informed of their activities as they relate to nuclear energy.

6 *Public appearances.* Speeches before civic organizations and social groups, appearances on TV or radio talk shows and speeches to university audiences are easily arranged, and would be useful in communicating our policies and programs both to community leaders and to the general public. Some of this is done. More should be done. There are organizations which (for a fee) specialize in arranging public appearances, and which can coach the speaker beforehand. There are others who could provide speechwriting support.

7 *Enlist civic organizations.* An effort should be made to follow-up appearances before certain civic organizations with a program which will enlist their active cooperation with our public information program. Organizations such as Kiwanis and Lions exist for public service. If they agree that nuclear energy public information activity is worthy of their active support, they might be willing to work in their communities to improve understanding of nuclear energy issues.

8 *Financial community.* Banks and investment institutions are sophisticated analysts of the nuclear energy situation. As such they probably do not require much additional information about either the geopolitical or technical aspects of nuclear energy. They do, however, need information on a sustained basis about Federal nuclear energy policies and programs. The financial community needs to be made aware in detail about regulatory changes, rate structure changes, changes in construction lead time, and about plans and actions for implementation of the Presidential statement on nuclear energy policy. Information contacts should be made at various levels of the financial community, and top-level contacts should be done by top-level administration officials. Working level contacts should be broad and sustained.

9 *Nuclear industry trade organizations.* Information about federal nuclear energy policy and programs (including such things as regulatory and rate structure information) should be made available to organizations which represent various segments of the nuclear electric power industry. Such organizations include the Atomic Industrial Forum, Edison Electric Institute, National Rural Electric Cooperative Association, American Public Power Association. Their membership includes utility chief executive officers, who collectively will determine the future role of nuclear energy in electric power generation, and the nuclear supply industry whose future viability is linked in part to federal policies and programs. . . .

13 *Scientists and Engineers for Secure Energy (SE-2).* This is a pro-nuclear organization organized to offset the anti-nuclear Union of Concerned Scientists. SE-2 membership includes such eminent scientists as Bethe, Teller, Van Allen, Weinberg, and Seaborg; it is chaired by Frederick Seitz, President Emeritus of Rockefeller University. SE-2 mem-

bers have done very effective pro-nuclear pieces used by Pacific Gas and Electric in an advertising campaign for the Diablo Canyon reactor. SE-2 is represented locally by Mark Mills. SE-2 will perform contract studies, the results of which could be released as SE-2 findings. This group should be kept informed of our policies and programs. We should invite them to study selected safety and waste management issues; their results if positive should be announced to support our work; if negative, their results should serve as a basis for redirection of our work.

14 *Professional organizations.* Information about federal nuclear energy policy and programs should be made available to those professional organizations whose interests extend to nuclear power. Such organizations should include the American Nuclear Society, American Association for the Advancement of Science, American Physical Society, American Association of Engineering Societies, American Association of Radiological Physicians, Health Physics Society, American Society of Nuclear Medicine, American Chemical Society, American Society of Mechanical Engineers, Institute of Electrical and Electronics Engineers and Scientists and Engineers for Secure Energy. Our purpose would be not only to inform technical opinion makers but also to seek announced support of these organizations for our policies and programs.

15 *Congressional relations.* Responsibility for Congressional relations within NE is organizationally separate from responsibility for other aspects of nuclear energy public information. Reference is made herein to Congressional relations only because the need to inform Congress of our policies and programs is so vital that failure to identify that central requirement would result in an incomplete overview of our public information program. An important collateral aspect of Congressional relations would be to inform the American Nuclear Energy Council of our work. ANEC lobbies Congress on nuclear energy matters.

16 *Labor organizations.* For economic reasons, labor is generally sympathetic to nuclear power. Through information programs to labor, we should seek to perpetuate and strengthen existing sympathies. It should be made clear to labor through informational visits and appearances before labor groups that this administration is uniquely supportive of nuclear energy. Labor should be kept aware of our policies and programs. Note: CEA has a law firm which advises them on labor organization views re nuclear energy. CEA has provided a film and exhibits to labor organization meetings. Labor is represented on the AIF Board.

Further Reading

Atomic Café. New York: First Run Features, 1982.

Boyer, Paul. *By the Bomb's Early Light: American Thought and Culture at the Turn of the Atomic Age*. Chapel Hill: University of North Carolina Press, 1994.

Broad, William J. *Star Warriors: a Penetrating Look into the Lives of the Young Scientists Behind Our Space Age Weaponry*. New York: Simon and Schuster, 1985.

Franklin, H. Bruce. *War Stars: the Superweapon and the American Imagination*. New York: Oxford University Press, 1988.

Pool, Robert. *Beyond Engineering: How Society Shapes Technology*. New York: Oxford University Press, 1997.

York, Herbert. *The Advisors: Oppenheimer, Teller and the Superbomb*. San Francisco: W. H. Freeman and Co., 1976.

8

Race and Technological Change

1876	Alexander Graham Bell demonstrates his newly invented telephone.
1915	First transcontinental telephone call made between New York and San Francisco.
1950	Telephone operators number 208,139 nationwide.
1963	First TSP equipped office opens in New York City.
1973	AT&T signs Consent Decree.
1973	CWA union opposes Consent Decree.
1976	AT&T installs first electronic switching machine for long-distance calls.
1981	Telephone operators number 88,599 nationwide.

Introduction

The historian Venus Green drew from her own experience as a switching equipment technician for the New York Telephone Company to inform her study of how a history of racist hiring practices and company culture, technological innovations in telephone switching equipment, government policy, union resistance, and worker aspirations combined to both create and destroy job opportunities for African-American women at the phone company. The role of race in technological change has as yet been little studied, but in this case at least, Green concludes that it trumps both class and technology.

Race and Technology: African American Women in the Bell System, 1945–1980

Venus Green

Telephone operators in America's largest cities experienced a dramatic technological transformation of their work process during the mid-1960s when the Bell System (AT&T and its associated companies) replaced cord switchboards with Traffic Service Positions – computerized equipment.[1] Martia Goodson, a former operator who worked on both types of equipment, described how astonishing the change was for her:

> [Cord board operators] get calls [at a] switchboard [which] is full of holes and over every hole there is a light. When the light lights up [it] shows that someone is calling. You stick the plug in that hole; but how fast you get the cord up there is up to you. . . . Every three or four positions the switchboard repeats itself . . . so you might start to go for a light and somebody else picks it up, . . . the light goes out.

> How fast you pick it up . . . how fast you handle the call depends. . . . If no one puts their hand up there to pick up the light, the call would never get answered. . . . That's different from having [a call] come in your ear . . . and the customer is there, you see what I'm saying, that's why TSP blew my mind so bad because all of a sudden the customer was there . . . where we used to go in, see how it sounded, if it didn't sound right . . . we'd come out . . . [with TSP] the customer was in your ear.[2]

Goodson's testimony is rich for interpretation by those who study labor, women, and technology. Scholars who examine questions of skill, deskilling, the degradation of work, and job loss or gain due to new technology would be alarmed at the elimination of the physical and mental tasks associated with TSPS. They would argue over whether TSPS divides skilled labor into smaller tasks that require less skill, less knowledge, and less initiative or whether this new technology augments, broadens, and upgrades older skills in a new work environment. The loss of the operators' limited ability to decide when to insert the plug is a concern for historians who analyze issues of workers' control.[3] Has

Excerpted from Venus Green, "Race and Technology: African American Women in the Bell System, 1945–1980," *Technology and Culture*, 36 (1995), pp. S101–S143. © 1995 The Society for the History of Technology. All rights reserved.

TSPS taken away the operator's ability to use his or her own initiative and judgment in completing tasks, or has it helped to organize the work process to enhance the operator's decision-making possibilities? Goodson's gender and employment in a job that had been feminized for well over a century certainly make her comments of interest to historians who study wage discrimination, work segregation, career possibilities, union representation, male/female solidarity, women's work culture, and women's responses and resistance to the introduction of new technologies.[4] Methods of analysis that utilize these issues are important for an understanding of the technology/labor/gender nexus, but alone they tend to elide race as a significant analytic category. Martia Goodson is an African American woman.

Although black women's limited presence or total exclusion from a specific workplace is duly noted, labor history paradigms in general, including those that analyze the impact of technology on the workplace, have left the working lives of black women largely unexplored. Periodized before World War II, models based on male craft culture, union membership/militance, and large male-dominated industries have simply pointed to African American women workers' prewar concentration in agricultural and domestic work to fulfill any obligation for a more thorough investigation.[5] Women's labor historians, anxious to construct models that include gender, often fail to acknowledge differences among women or they study occupations and issues that marginalize the experiences of African American women workers. Scholars of black labor have also shown that race alone as a category is inadequate for the study of African American women workers. And, finally, historians who examine issues related to technology and work rarely consider the question of race, even when they include an analysis based on gender.[6]

Black and white workers of both genders are affected differently by managerial decisions to introduce new workplace technologies.[7] For this reason, the impact of technology on African American women's work experience demands specific attention within the analytic frameworks of the skill/deskilling, worker control, work segmentation/segregation, and union/management paradigms. This article makes no attempt to retheorize these paradigms or to replace them with one based solely on race. Rather, it posits that an analysis of the unique race/sex ideology expressed toward African American women in the workplace is crucial to the history of all workers, whether black women were present or not. From this point of view, the discussion goes beyond a mere victimization story or the "compensatory" inclusion of black women to demonstrate how a racialized concept of gender can increase our understanding of all workers' history. For instance, the technological fragmentation of white male telephone craft work is better understood when we know why managers selected not just women, but mostly African American women, to perform the deskilled work caused by that fragmentation.[8] An essential component of the managerial ideology that guided the employee selection process is a distinct combination of concepts about race and gender.

The salience of gender in this ideology is indisputable, but gender must be racialized to capture African American women workers' unique history.[9] Racializing gender avoids creating a false dichotomy between race and sex. Black women's history as workers in the United States precludes such a separation. From the moment black women were subjected to special tithes, relegated to fieldwork on plantations, and finally designated as slaves, they experienced racism, sexism, and the lowest-class status simultaneously.[10] This 17th-century slaveholders' construction of the African American woman as an inferior being (at the bottom of a hierarchy based on social and economic domination) has permeated American social ideology and is reflected in the attitudes and actions of many corporate managers, union leaders, and white workers today.

These attitudes are not simply notions about biological inferiority; they include rationalizations for discrimination based on racial identity and they entail antiblack sentiments and practices that define black people as "outsiders"/"others" who should not enjoy the privileges and "rights" of institutions supposedly won and built by whites.[11] Consequently, African American women, who share the sexism of job segregation with white women, are further segregated into the lowest-level "women's" jobs that subordinate them to white women in wages and status even when education and training levels are similar. The same racial ideology guides the employment of African American women in the lowest occupational positions and determines how new technologies will affect their experience in these positions.

For telephone operators, this ideology was most vividly illustrated when computerization caused a severe reduction in their numbers and led to conditions which facilitated the transformation of the operating force from white to black. In less than ten years, black operators in the larger cities replaced white operators as a result of a hiring policy that deliberately segregated most of the African American women into one job – telephone operating. At the same time, the push to automate all local, long-distance, and even international calls received an electronic boost. In effect, as soon as the job opportunity opened for large numbers of African American women, the introduction of high-speed computerized equipment closed it.[12] Traffic Service Positions Systems and Electronic Switching Systems (ESS) are the computer-driven machines most responsible for the changes in women's work that coincided with African American women's entrance into the Bell System as operators.

This article analyzes how technology specifically affected African American women's employment possibilities in the post-World War II telephone industry.[13] As it acknowledges the significance of demographic, political, labor market, and other economic forces, it explores the hypothesis that when technology converges with gender- and race-related dynamics in the workplace, race becomes the overriding variable in determining policy.[14] The discussion centers around the ways in which technology shaped Bell System hiring and promotion practices within the context of the Civil Rights movement, AT&T/EEOC Consent Decrees, and union responses to affirmative action. The impact of technology on skills, health, worker control, working conditions, and job loss in relation to gender and race is examined along with the operators' responses to these issues.

What, then, of the machines that put the customer "in your ear" and "blew" Martia Goodson's mind "so bad"?

Computerization: Traffic Service Position Systems Replace Switchboards

Although the installation of machines designed to connect local calls automatically began in the World War I era, the most significant change in operators' tasks involved a totally new concept in their work and equipment. As part of the continuous Bell System quest to develop equipment that would minimize labor costs and at the same time provide quick and reliable service, telephone technology evolved gradually and culminated with the introduction of new machines to replace switchboards. Referred to as TSP, these new machines completely eliminated the need for operators to make connections. *Bell Telephone Magazine* described the new concept in telephone operators' work as follows:

> The switching or connecting of telephones is done in the dial equipment. Calls do not go through the TSP as they go through a switchboard. With the TSP, the calls go through the dial equipment. The only time the TSP is connected is when it is necessary for the operator to assist the customer or to exercise control over the call. It is for this reason that the TSP is cordless.
>
> Also, the TSP utilizes the call distributing principle which has been in use on information and intercept desks for some years. Calls which come into a TSP-equipped office are automatically directed to any position in the office where there is an operator who is not handling a call at the moment. Should all operators be occupied, the incoming calls are stored briefly and then distributed to the operators in proper sequence as they become available.[15]

The first TSP office opened in New York City in October 1963. The TSP equipment automatically displayed to the operator the telephone numbers of called and calling parties. It also computed time and charges and disconnected completed calls without an operator. Despite Bell System managers' attestations to the contrary, TSP reduced local and long-distance operating to a matter of selecting the correct buttons to push. "Some 39 separate work steps" formerly required to complete an operator-dialed call, according to one Bell System publication, were simply replaced by "a matter of moments, a few words, [and] a few movements of her fingers."[16] Renamed "service specialist," the TSP operator really functioned as an adjunct to a machine rather than as a controller of machinery. Consciously, managers perpetuated the idea that the freshly deskilled "service specialists" required a more office-like atmosphere, and, since the new consoles resembled desks, this appeal to modernity and class was reinforced.[17]

With the operators marginalized, it became necessary, from the managers' point of view, to increase the rate at which the operators could work and at which calls could be processed through the equipment. Engineering efforts materialized in the No. 1 Electronic Switching Systems (No. 1 ESS), a new computerized switching system that operated in time factors of milliseconds, easily replacing the electromechanical systems (crossbar and panel). The Bell System applied electronic switching technology to TSP and to long-distance switching systems. In 1965, TSPs were transformed into TSPSs, which provided the same services as the regular TSP but surpassed it in speed, economy, and flexibility. Eleven years later, AT&T installed in Chicago its first electronic switching system designed for long distance, No. 4 ESS (4E). This machine processed 550,000 long-distance calls per hour, four times as many as the 4A crossbar system.

Computerization completely transferred connecting responsibilities from the telephone operator to the subscriber and the new machines. The advent of 4E and other more sophisticated electronic switching systems made possible the closing of many toll centers and the routing of the calls to much larger regional or national centers which utilized fewer operators to cover wider areas. During the mid-1970s, New York Telephone and other operating companies introduced the practice of charging for Directory Assistance, thereby decreasing the number of requests and further reducing the need for operators. By 1980, the Bell System had successfully established customer direct dialing to most places in the world, and it had also made successful inroads into the reduction of the remaining information, intercept, and overseas operating forces. Between 1960 and 1981, women operators in the Bell System had been reduced by one-half, and the total number of operators by close to 40 percent.[18] It was into this rapidly changing technological environment that the Bell System began to hire significant numbers of African American operators.

African American Women Enter the Bell System

Ironically, the decision to hire African American women as telephone operators reflected neither a long-lasting and genuine corrective to past unfair practices nor the opening of new opportunities offered by rapid technological change. Despite the 1960s' rhetoric and publicity stating otherwise, Bell System hiring policies and practices had long been guided by a racial ideology that viewed African American women as inferior and unintelligent "outsiders" who should only be employed in jobs designated as undesirable for white workers. While the attractiveness of jobs for whites changes depending on economic and social factors, the idea that black women should be at the bottom of the hierarchy, preferably in subservient roles, remains relatively constant over time. Consequently, the same racial ideology that had excluded black women from the Bell System operating forces also led to their inclusion and the continuation of race/sex discrimination in a different form. Evidence of this ideology can be found in company publications, public statements made by managers, and a statistical analysis of the Bell System workforce.

Images of African Americans, particularly women, found in advertisements and other literature depict historically familiar stereotypes. These images were so unquestionably common that the New York *Telephone Review* had two covers in 1911 portraying African American females in subservient roles.[19] The April cover shows a black girl who has delivered the wrong hat to a white woman. It is unclear whether the girl has misunderstood the written instructions or simply could not read them. The October–November issue portrayed the stereotypical "Aunt Jemima" serving dinner to a white family. She, of course, is amazed by both the telephone and a young white boy's ability to use it.

Belittling portrayals of African Americans were not restricted to simple cartoons and drawings in Bell literature. Throughout the 1920s, 1930s, and 1940s, Bell publications contained pictures of whites in "blackface" providing entertainment for company functions. Most common are pictures of blackfaced white women dressed in male and female costumes acting out skits that ridiculed African American intelligence, speech, and other behavior.[20] In 1939, the *Telephone Review* reported that the "old south," complete with plantation, Aunt Jemima, and "Lazybones," was a "principal feature" of the annual Christmas party

held for operators in Buffalo, New York.[21] Ten years later, the April
1949 issue of the same magazine disclosed that thirty-three women from
the Commercial Department performed "a real 'ol' time' minstrel show,
featuring the familiar Dixieland songs and dances to the accompaniment
of a fast banjo and a hot piano" for 1,300 persons at the Walton High
School in the Bronx.[22] As late as September 1955, the "Sodus Minstrels" were staging "minstrel shows for Pioneer parties, the Business
and Professional Women's Club and the Grange."[23]

The *Bell Laboratories Record* also printed pictures of entertainment
offered by its male employees. The July 1949 issue, for example,
revealed that educated and professional Bell Laboratories men celebrated the end of a colloquium season by performing skits at a restaurant
for their colleagues. One of these skits was an imitation of "Amos 'n'
Andy" discussing "in their inimitable manner, the development of
microwave system."[24] The writers at Bell Laboratories thought that
"this skit was one of the many which made the evening a memorable
one."[25] Demeaning images of African Americans can also be found in
the *Western Electric News* and other Bell System journals. Print and
dramatic caricatures of African American people were merely a graphic
representation of an ideology Bell System managers frequently expressed
in other more subtle but effective ways.

Managers used language to obfuscate their own opinions and behavior
and to shift responsibility away from themselves. Before the World War
II era, Bell managers' explanations for the exclusion of African American
women from the operating forces ranged from vague references to tradition and custom to statements that blamed either white women telephone workers or black women applicants. In 1920, when the telephone
industry suffered a tremendous labor shortage and advertised for 1,000
operators, New York Telephone Company refused an offer to supply it
with "neat and intelligent... colored girls," free of charge, made by
Eugene McIntosh, proprietor of the Harlem Employment Agency.[26]
To this offer of "100 per cent American" girls who would "prove
competent and loyal," E. J. Anderson, the employment manager,
blandly replied that while the company had "given consideration to
employing colored girls as telephone operators," it was "not in a position
to do so at the present time."[27] Anderson gave no further explanation,
but a Mr. Schultz, assistant to the vice president, responded to a similar
offer made by the League for Democracy by disclaiming any personal
objection to black workers, asserting that the white operators would quit
if they had to work next to black women and further claiming that white
women would not train black women.[28]

New York Telephone's position seemed to harden over time. In 1927,
when George S. Schuyler of the *Messenger* inquired about the number of

blacks employed by the company, Vice President T. P. Sylvan replied
that there were some blacks on the payroll "assisting . . . in the conduct
of . . . restaurant and lounge facilities."[29] To Schuyler's follow-up letter
asking why there were no black operators, Sylvan answered that he had
already discussed this matter with other "distinguished" blacks and that
he believed he had "satisfied them that the position which we have taken
with reference to their employment has been a proper and necessary
one."[30] According to a New York City Mayor's Commission Study in
1935, "Mr. R. H. Boggs, Vice-president in charge of personnel of the
New York Telephone Company did not regard the exclusion of
Negroes . . . , as discrimination but only as a customary practice."[31]

Even after New York State passed a law in 1933 that forbade public
utilities to "refuse to employ any person in any capacity, in the operation
or maintenance of a public service on account of the race, color or
religion of such person," the exclusion of black women from the operating forces continued.[32] Indeed, during the 1930s, in testimony given
before government investigators, New York managers insisted that the
absence of African American women from operating and clerical work
was an indication of black women's incompetence.[33] Consider the testimony of Walter D. Williams, New York Telephone general traffic manager in New York City before the New York State Temporary
Commission on the Condition of the Urban Colored Population in
1937:

> Q. What explanation have you for the failure of any Negro telephone
> operator to be employed out of those 4500? A. That in the opinion of
> the interviewers, they are not qualified to fill the position of telephone
> operator. . . .
> Q. Have you ever had a Negro Telephone Operator who has been quali-
> fied, in your experience? A. Not in my experience.
> Q. What prevents them from being qualified, in your opinion? A. Our job,
> of course, in the Central Offices, is to give telephone service; that is done
> by a group of girls and we work together. They are white girls, and in our
> judgment it would not be possible to give a proper grade of telephone
> service if we put the Negro girls in with the white girls.
> Q. Upon what is your judgment based, Mr. Williams, what fact, if any,
> have you in your possession upon which you base your judgment? A.
> Business judgment over a number of years.
> Q. I ask you if you are in possession of any facts? A. I am not.[34]

Throughout his testimony, Williams asserted the right of the company
to exclude black people and that the company was not in violation of the
law to do so.[35] Furthermore, he stated that his judgment was in no way
affected by the knowledge that black and white women worked side by

side in civil service and other government jobs.[36] He even acknowledged the justice of hiring African Americans but concluded that "it is a matter of a practical condition that we have before us, and unfortunately all the things in this world are not decided on straight questions of justice."[37] Williams's views are clearly based on the notion that custom and tradition dictate that African American women remain in subordinate social and economic positions.

The evidence presented here applies specifically to New York Telephone Company, but there is ample evidence that these notions were prevalent throughout the Bell System, despite AT&T claims that the associated companies enjoyed total independence in the selection of personnel. What may not have been explicit in company rules was certainly implicit in AT&T's own policy of excluding black women. Indeed, a study of forty-four cities conducted by the Urban League concluded that "available information is sufficient to substantiate the fact that Negro workers have been systematically excluded from employment in this industry in many cities."[38] Consequently, the report continued, "prior to 1940, no Negro switchboard operators were employed in any of the exchanges" investigated. And, "in fact, there is no record of the employment of Negro operators in any city in the country before that date."[39] Since the Bell System trained all of its newly hired employees, neither special training nor work experience weighed more heavily than race as a prerequisite to employment. A statistical analysis of African American employment in the Bell System further evidences this requirement and the ideas that supported it.

African Americans had worked for different Bell operating companies before the large-scale hirings of the 1960s but in 1940, when blacks numbered 10 percent of the American population, they comprised only .7 percent of telephone workers and were segregated into the most menial jobs. Prior to World War II, the Bell System virtually ignored challenges to its policy against hiring any but white women as operators.[40] In the war period, the Fair Employment Practices Committee (FEPC), pressured by African American complaints, filed several suits against the various operating companies in an effort to break down this institutional racism. A sprinkling of African American women gained entry into AT&T Long Lines (the long-distance company) and some of the operating companies, but it is not clear whether this resulted from FEPC actions or the scarcity of labor during and immediately following the war.[41] It is likely that the alternative opportunities offered to white women, extraordinarily high turnover, and the general expansion of telephone usage in the war period all combined to create an economic motivation for the introduction of African American women into Bell System operating.

Bell System economic conditions, rather than a desire to eradicate racist practices, moved the operating companies to increase the number of black women to 1 percent of all women workers in the telephone industry by 1950. The demand for operators in large urban areas led to another small percentage increase in black women operators between 1950 and 1960. In this period 2.5 percent of the telephone workforce consisted of black workers, concentrated in New York City, Philadelphia, Detroit, Chicago, and Los Angeles. Southern operating companies hired no black women and actually reduced the number of black men. The trend toward hiring black women only as operators and mostly in northern industrial centers had clearly emerged by 1960. Up to this time black males had outnumbered black females.

At the height of the Civil Rights era (1960–70), the Bell System hired significant numbers of African Americans without changing its pattern of occupational and geographical segregation. The percentages increased rapidly: 4.0 percent of the workforce in 1963, 4.6 percent in 1966, and 9.8 percent in 1970. As operating companies in other areas of the country reluctantly hired blacks, Southern Bell and Southwestern Bell continued to exclude blacks from all except the most menial jobs. A look at their record during the 1960s is illustrative:

> In the entire state of Mississippi, Southern Bell employed no blacks in any entry-level job above service worker or laborer until June, 1965. In New Orleans, Southern Bell hired its first black above service worker or laborer in November, 1963, and its first black Operator one year later. The Company hired its first black Operator in Florida in March, 1964; and in South Carolina in July, 1964. Southwestern Bell hired its first black Operator anywhere in Kansas in 1963. The first black Installer employed in Kansas was hired in June, 1969. No black above service worker or laborer was hired in Arkansas until 1964. The first black Operator in Oklahoma was hired in March, 1964.[42]

General employment trends and the Civil Rights Act (1964) hardly affected southern employment policies before 1970. Of course, when they did hire blacks, they duplicated the segregated work patterns practiced in the North.

New York operators, interviewed for a larger study, stated that the transformation to a black operating force happened in no more than the last four or five years of the 1960s. According to Bernard E. Anderson, an expert on black telephone industry employment, the Bell System hired 53,903 black employees between 1965 and 1971 while the entire industry had hired only 54,000 between 1950 and 1960.[43] Furthermore, an EEOC investigation demonstrated that in nonsouthern urban areas, women composed between 72 and 92 percent of black telephone workers in 1967 whereas white women made up only 48 to 61 percent of the white workforce. In New York, for example, while 92 percent of black employees of the New York Telephone Company were women, only 50 percent of its white employees were women.[44]

The Bell System deliberately hired African American women into an occupation that not only paid low wages but was becoming technologically obsolete. Managers, infused with a racist ideology, implemented new technologies in an urban setting in order to exploit changing urban demographics.[45] Between 1960 and 1970 the number of young black city dwellers increased by 78 percent while young whites increased by only 22.8 percent.[46] The nation's largest urban areas presented the Bell System with an untapped labor pool. In October 1969, AT&T vice president Walter Straley delivered a report to a conference of Bell operating company presidents in which he stated:

> Population and labor force projections are not at all encouraging. The kind of people we need are going to be in very short supply. . . . Most of our new hires go into entry level jobs which means we must have access to an ample supply of people who will work at comparatively low rates of pay. That means city people more so than suburbanites. That means lots of black people.
>
>   There are not enough white, middle class, success-oriented men and women in the labor force – or at least that portion of the labor force available to the telephone companies – to supply our requirements for craft and occupational people. And from now on, the number of such people who are available will grow smaller even as our need becomes greater. It is therefore perfectly plain that we need nonwhite employees. Not because we are good citizens. Or because it is the law as well as national goal to give them employment. We need them because we have so many jobs to fill and they will take them.[47]

Faced with unusually high turnover and white flight from operating, managers in their sexist thinking had to find another group of women to keep their system replenished. The racial ideology of these managers impelled them to hire the women who were deemed socially inferior and who could be paid the least.

Vice President Straley questioned who would be "available for work paying as little as $4,000 to $5,000 a year." Noting that two-thirds of the people in urban areas available for such low rates would be black, he answered, "It is therefore just a plain fact that in today's world, telephone company wages are more in line with black expectations – and the tighter the labor market the more this is true."[48] These "expectations," limited by what a labor market controlled by white managers actually offered, created a tidal wave of black applications for telephone operating. African American women, many of them recent emigrants from the South searching for an escape from agricultural and domestic labor, were unwitting but willing victims of a Bell System hiring policy that consciously chose them for exploitation.[49]

Instead of raising wages and creating less stressful work environments to attract people of all races, the Bell System segregated black women into departmental ghettos (operators and low-level clerks) where there was little opportunity for advancement. The insidiousness of this racism is that the higher-paying, less stressful, and more varied job opportunities that did become available for telephone women opened mostly for white women. White men and white women who lived in the suburbs gladly commuted to the cities to earn the higher salaries offered in craft and upper-level jobs. It was not the lack of white workers but the lack of white workers who would work for low wages that motivated the Bell System to hire black urban dwellers.

African American women and men, in addition to large groups of Spanish-surnamed and other nonwhite people in various parts of the country, were systematically excluded from craft and upper-management positions. Arbitrary testing procedures and irrelevant academic credentials barred most nonwhites from the higher-paying and more desirable jobs in the telephone industry. Craft jobs – the highest-paying nonmanagement jobs and the almost exclusive domain of white men – opened to a few nonwhite men, but black operators, like white operators, did not have a real chance at these jobs before the 1970s. And the few black men who did achieve craft status remained in the lower crafts. Even in companies like New York Telephone, where a significant number of blacks had worked since the 1940s, they were underrepresented in management jobs. At the end of 1969, only 4.4 percent of New York Telephone's black employees had achieved management titles, while 27.2 percent of the white employees worked as managers. In the South, .6–.9 percent of the blacks held management titles. Regardless of location, the Bell System's racial ideology trapped black women both as women, who would only obtain the lower-paying operating or clerical jobs available to women, and as blacks, who would only obtain the lowest-paying jobs available to blacks. Government policies and union activities, also affected by this ideology, hardly improved African American women's position in the telephone industry.

AT&T and the EEOC

Despite AT&T's highly publicized equal opportunity programs, an EEOC investigation completed in 1971 concluded that AT&T and its associated companies had in fact systematically discriminated against women and "minorities." Without admitting to any unfair practices, AT&T signed a Consent Decree with the government in 1973. The decree awarded workers a $38 million wage compensation and called for complete reorganization of personnel procedures to reduce the racial and sexual job segregation so long practiced in the telephone industry. Subsequently, two more Consent Decrees became necessary when the Bell System failed to fully implement the intent of the original agreement.

The Consent Decree granted AT&T and its operating companies six years to hire, transfer, and promote a "targeted" number of women and minorities into higher-paying management and craft jobs and also to place men in some of the female-dominated jobs. The Bell System constructed an Upgrade and Transfer Program, and it utilized government-approved seniority "overrides" to obtain the targets. General economic conditions, union legal interferences, local managers' pertinacity, and technological displacement make it difficult to assess the decrees' impact on the employment and promotion of women and minorities. Nevertheless, evidence does indicate some improvement in opportunities for both groups.

White women, regardless of their educational levels, moved more rapidly and in larger numbers into the higher-level and expanding occupations than "minority" women. As the more educated white women moved into upper management and sales positions, inexperienced and unskilled white women advanced into craft jobs.[50] After a detailed statistical analysis by region and occupational group, Herbert R. Northrup and John A. Larson concluded that when these women were hired, promoted, or transferred into craft jobs, the percentage of white male applicants entering these jobs decreased from 83 percent in 1973 to 56.3 percent in 1979. They also noted that some less educated white women may have lost clerical and administrative opportunities to men since the percentage of white males in introductory clerical jobs increased from 17 percent in 1973 to 43.7 percent in 1979. Affirmative action had favorable results for both white men and white women, even though some occupational shifting did occur.

Despite severe losses in several occupational groups, African American and other minority women also experienced some occupational advancement during the years of the Consent Decrees. Like white women, the more educated nonwhites made significant gains in both numbers and percentages in the higher job categories. Improvements in craft jobs were remarkable in that nonwhite women who totaled ninety-three outside craft workers in 1973 increased to 1,175 in 1979. The occupational shifting of white women away from low-level clerical work is illustrated in the increase in nonwhite women who numbered 39,818 in 1973 and 53,158 in 1979. Despite these improvements, the occupational groups in which African American and other minority women were concentrated suffered enormous losses. Between 1973 and 1979, the number of operators decreased by 28.7 percent and service workers by 53.8 percent.

Interpretations of the decline in telephone women's work vary according to the variables analysts weigh. Economists Northrup and Larson, for example, applauded the results of the Consent Decree since the results had been obtained in a period of employment stagnation (total Bell System employment increased by less than 2,000 employees) and at a time when the total percentage of telephone women declined by .6 percent (from 51.5 to 50.9 percent). Unlike these analysts, who viewed technology as a basically benign progression (an independent variable), sociologist Sally L. Hacker identified "technology as an intervening variable" in her examination of sex stratification in the telephone industry. Her research "discovered [that] planned technological change would eliminate more jobs for women than affirmative action would provide."[51] While computerized systems eliminated operating and many lower-level clerical jobs, lower-level managers, mostly women, who supervised these women also lost their jobs. Thus, states Hacker, technological change displaced both management and nonmanagement women.

Affirmative action protected only middle-management women, while it opened entry-level, traditionally female, jobs to men. Indeed, according to Hacker, nonmanagement women suffered excessively since "affirmative action placed thousands more men in traditionally women's work than it placed women in traditionally men's work." Many women felt that not only were men moving into traditional female jobs, men were also moving up and out of these very jobs at a faster rate than women had. Dead-end jobs for women became stepping-stones for men. Sex discrimination decreased, but mostly because men replaced women in their work, not the reverse. Race discrimination, even in the context of equal opportunity, continued.

Locally, many lower-level managers found ways to subvert the spirit of affirmative action. Frequently, local managers left African American women's Upgrade and Transfer applications unprocessed. A completed application would be rejected at a later stage in the bureaucracy either because a manager intentionally failed to fill it out properly or because he simply did not care enough to follow it through. In many cases, by the time all of the paper shuffling was finished, someone who had completed the application later had filled the job. African Americans also complained that even after their applications had been successfully recorded, unfair testing procedures often eliminated them. These local practices stunted even the limited advances planned by Bell System executives.

For different reasons, white and black women telephone workers decreased in numbers during this period. African American women replaced white women in the lowest and most populated levels of telephone work. Hacker's findings indicated that jobs in which large numbers and proportions of minority women worked best predicted "slow growth or decline."[52] Minority women were concentrated in operating and clerical jobs – jobs most dramatically affected by technological change. Hence, she concluded that "displacement struck most sharply where minority women worked."[53] Although sexist managers continued to place white women in jobs that were already segregated by sex or in low-level craft work that would later be negatively affected by technology, these jobs were better-paying, with more opportunities for advancement, than those for which African American women were selected. Racial ideology severely eroded any opportunities based on sex for African American women.

Managers' racial attitudes also determined how the Bell System used affirmative action targets to maneuver women into rapidly changing male craft jobs. Under the guise of upgrades and promotions, managers placed both white and black women in jobs that new technologies changed. Personnel departments across the country hired women as pole climbers, installers, and frame technicians at the very time that the Bell System planned to eliminate this work by the introduction of new technologies and by changes in customer services.[54] As the Bell System encouraged women, mostly white, to utilize the Upgrade and Transfer Programs to enter these higher-paying craft jobs, they also encouraged minority women to accept targeted upgrades and transfers into clerical jobs created by the fragmentation and deskilling of male craft work.

Dave Newman, a switching equipment technician at New York Telephone Company, described this process in the case of deskmen or testers who had been responsible for locating trouble on customer lines:

> This has been one of the most highly skilled craft jobs. It is being virtually eliminated by MLTs (Mechanized Loop Testers), which are operated by clerks earning significantly lower wages. But money is not the only loss incurred by the workers involved. Testers utilize their knowledge and experience to interpret meter readings and to work with other craftspeople, while a clerk simply dials a line into the machine, cross-references the response against a chart without knowing what it means, and dispatches the trouble to the appropriate craftsperson without knowing what that person's job involves or understanding how it is related to the trouble.

Also, testers are overwhelmingly white and male; the maintenance administrators who operate the MLTs tend to be black and female.[55]

Similar fragmentation and deskilling of switching technician's work and other crafts have led to the creation of whole departments at New York Telephone Company in which only black women work. More than 75 percent of these jobs require women to remain seated at video terminals where they key in data at company-established productivity rates. White men (who had been skilled craftsmen) and frequently white women supervise these departments. Computerized work measurements and strict supervision combine frequently with racism and sexism to form a virtual hell for most of these women.[56]

Objectively these women work in degraded, deskilled, and dehumanized jobs, but subjective conditions compel some caution in presenting this point of view. African American and other minority women who had worked in the low-paying operator and clerical jobs jumped at the opportunity to work in the deskilled craft jobs, just as they had when the opportunity to work as operators first became available. Higher wages and in some cases more routine hours made these jobs highly attractive to women who in many instances were single mothers. They earned less than skilled craftsmen, but their wages were higher than most other clerical workers. And significantly, they had not been the ones to see their jobs deskilled. The difference between a tester and a maintenance administrator had little meaning to women who had worked in highly segregated environments where there was little knowledge about work in "male" departments. These new jobs represented an upgrade into higher-paying craft work long unobtainable for minority women.

Regardless of the women's own subjective perceptions and conditions, the new jobs amounted to nothing more than another set of positions from which there was little upward mobility. There is no question that Bell managers used racial and sexual divisions to achieve their aims or that they diverted and manipulated equal-opportunity goals to insure that African American and other minority women remained at the bottom of the Bell System hierarchy in jobs adversely affected by new technologies. Managers not only decided which new technologies would be introduced, they also decided who would work in which occupations. Upgrades and targets merely placed a numerical goal on positions planned and designed by Bell engineers. The government did not concern itself with whether or not these jobs were slated for technological displacement or whether they offered few possibilities for promotion. Telephone company strategies succeeded to a large degree because unions chose to fight the government over affirmative action rather than to fight management over technological displacement.

Communications Workers of America Oppose the Consent Decrees

Unions, particularly the Communications Workers of America (CWA), which had already failed to protect operators from technological displacement, openly challenged affirmative action. The CWA refused to attend the EEOC negotiations although it, along with the International Brotherhood of Electrical Workers (IBEW), had been asked to participate in the formulation of the Consent Decrees.[57] Instead, the CWA sought "to block the implementation of the decrees on the grounds that: (1) it infringed upon their bargaining rights and (2) [CWA] was not consulted on areas in which it had a vital interest such as issues affecting wages, hours, and conditions of employment."[58] Unsuccessful in this strategy, the CWA initiated a lawsuit in 1973 against AT&T to reverse the Consent Decrees, especially the "override," which it charged violated contractual seniority clauses and permitted the company to engage in unlawful discrimination based upon race and sex, that is, "reverse discrimination."

After five years and numerous appeals up to the Supreme Court, the CWA lost, and the override remained in place along with the other provisions of the Consent Decree. Why had the CWA spent, at least partially, the dues of African Americans, other minorities, and women to finance an attack on the rights of these very members? Why did the CWA choose not to participate in the construction of an agreement that would protect all of its workers and insure fair treatment to those who had been most disadvantaged?

The answers to these questions lie in the composition of the CWA leadership and the priorities they chose to pursue. Like most high-level company executives, the CWA national leadership has been mostly white and male. Many of these leaders shared management's racial ideology. Not only were they antiblack but they were also prowhite, in the sense that they believed that the union was theirs and therefore meant to serve their interests exclusively. Bell System manipulation of women and nonwhites into jobs adversely affected by technological change caused no union uproar because this policy adhered to union policy of protecting white male jobs. Automation, in its initial stages (when it only affected women), was welcomed by the national leadership. In 1965, CWA president Joseph A. Beirne expressed only slight concern over the loss of 80,000 jobs because he believed "frankly, most of the losses had been handled by attrition since technological innovations affected telephone operators and clerical operations where turnover was high."[59] Beirne admitted that "what most disturbed us [CWA] in 1963 was that we saw where future innovations might affect the more highly skilled occupations where turnover was much slower."[60] In 1963, white men dominated the "highly skilled occupations."

On the local level, white male and female union leaders, protective of their power bases, discouraged nonwhite union participation. Union leadership feared the voting power of nonwhites, especially women, so much that they left many nonwhite employees unorganized well into the 1970s. This was especially true in those places where the membership had rapidly changed from white to black and where the leadership still consisted of long-entrenched white union bosses. In Atlanta, for example, where the traffic department had been better organized than the plant twenty years earlier, most of the black operators remained nonunion in 1970 because local leaders would not ask them into the union.

In northern cities, white female leaders who had historically headed the operators' locals fought against nonwhite leadership and participation while they also failed to represent the nonwhites fairly. Union membership, however, did not always help. New York Telephone operators (approximately 75 percent of whom were black), belonged to the Telephone Traffic Union (TTU) whose white leadership, according to former operator Lessie Sanders, never sent the operators out on strike.[61] The TTU membership resorted to wildcat strikes at the end of their contracts because their leadership did not fight for black operators' demands. The actions of the TTU's white women leaders demonstrate that America's racial ideology crosses gender lines.

Indeed, the desire to exclude African American women from the better-paying jobs crossed gender and union lines. Not only did union leaders and individuals challenge black female promotions with the cry of "reverse discrimination," in many shops whites unified so that white women could be used to block the promotion of nonwhites. Often, with union acquiescence, white male managers promoted white females to the disadvantage of nonwhites. Of course, this tended to destroy any unity based on gender and class solidarity.

Although there may have been exceptions among individuals and local leaders, telephone unions in general throughout the 1960s and most of the 1970s never pursued strong equal opportunity goals. Without concerning themselves with unfair racist and sexist hiring and promotion practices, most union leaders insisted that African Americans and other minorities received the same union protections and benefits won through national contractual provisions for all workers. Indeed, the CWA gained a public reputation for bargaining contracts that included high wages, above-average benefits, and, in the 1980s, significant protections against technological change.

The CWA Bargains Technology Clauses

The CWA, mostly concerned about the impact of technology on its craft workers, bargained several new contract provisions in 1977 and 1980. These clauses included such income protections as the Supplemental Income Protection Plan (SIPP) to workers "declared" surplus (technologically displaced), Reassignment Pay Protection Plan (RPPP) to workers downgraded, and Technological Displacement allowances to workers who chose termination rather than transfers or downgrading. Other provisions upgraded the service representatives in 1977 and the operators in 1980 (both jobs dominated primarily by black women at that time and increasingly besieged by technology), eliminated certain types of remote monitoring, and prohibited outside contractors from telephone work.

The 1980 contract contained letters of agreement that established joint Technology Change Committees in the Bell operating companies, Western Electric Company, and AT&T Long Lines, a national CWA/AT&T Working Conditions and Service Quality Improvement Committee, and a national CWA/AT&T Occupational Job Evaluation Committee.[62] Another provision of the contract obligated the company to give the union six months advance notice of any technological change that might affect its members. These committees and the other contractual provisions have been applauded by many in the labor movement as a real advance in the technological struggle.

Dave Newman, a CWA steward, critic, and activist, also acknowledged that the CWA had "pioneered in winning contract language which [sought] to minimize the harmful impact of technological changes."[63] Still, he voiced several objections:

> While virtually the entire membership supports such protections as RPPP, SIPP, layoff procedures by inverse seniority, etc., there is increasing concern and understanding that the amelioration of negative company actions is not the same thing as fighting the actions. These programs and procedures do not constitute job security, nor do they protect job content or skills. The three committees... are seen as impotent (having advisory power only), and the high union officials on these committees are viewed with skepticism, since they are the same officials who are seen as having done nothing previously to combat technological change and its negative effects.[64]

Ideally, the new but inadequate technology clauses should have protected any group of workers experiencing technological change. But frequently, managers unfairly manipulated these clauses against the interests of women and nonwhites, just as they had done with the EEOC targets. During the 1980s, well after nonwhites and women had not only become union members but together represented the majority of its members, union neglect and apathy created conditions conducive for the continuation of company racism and sexism. The closing of the AT&T New York City International Operating Center (IOC) (a workplace with a majority of black women) in 1983 and the continued technological displacement of low-level clerical workers in the operating companies provide examples that demonstrate how even these objective clauses can be administered in a subjective and racist manner.

Management Administers the Clauses: The Closing of the New York IOC

Long-distance, particularly overseas, operators were the last large group of operators to experience technological displacement. International Direct Distance Dialing (IDDD) and International Service Position Systems eliminated overseas operators in the 1970s and 1980s just as dial, direct distance dialing, and TSPS had eliminated local and long-distance operators in earlier periods. These technologies allowed operators anywhere in the country to place overseas calls and led to the shifting of work from one part of the country to another. Nationally, the company operated at least a half dozen International Operating Centers to process calls from different parts of the country to various overseas points.

Gradually, AT&T began to phase out these centers for reasons that indicated priorities other than an excess of equipment or a surplus of workers.[65] When AT&T decided to close its New York IOC and move the work to other regions, Pat Meckle, who was an operator and also secretary treasurer of CWA Local 1150 during this period, attributed the move to the company's desire to pay lower operating costs and the desire to close before the upcoming divestiture of the Bell operating companies.[66] Equally as important, Meckle stated, "they also felt they didn't have such militant people in some of the other locations."[67] Ron Tyree, vice president of Local 1150, one of the first male operators and a steward at that time, also suspected that the company especially wanted to get rid of the black operators because of their resistance to company policies.[68]

His suspicions were borne out by the way AT&T manipulated the contract to create confusion, fear, and frustration among the operators. Anne H. Walden, CWA Local 1150 Section vice president of traffic in 1983, recalled that when the company first notified the union of the closing on August 30, 1982, management indicated that it would "make an attempt to place the employees in other jobs including a few thousand downgraded . . . clerical jobs in New York Telephone without the benefit of the Reassignment Pay Protection Plan."[69] The company gave no explanation for why the operators would not have received RPPP benefits (a contract violation). By February 1983, the company announced that these jobs would not be available since New York Telephone company also had a surplus.

Other possible opportunities proved equally elusive. Few women received upgrades to service representative or craft jobs. Eventually AT&T pressured some operators into entry-level clerical jobs that were often great distances from their homes or former jobs. In many cases the company induced others to quit with a "Separation Payment." Since many of these women had already achieved an operator's top salary, moving into entry-level clerical positions entailed a reduction in salary. The RPPP protected the pay of those with fewer than fifteen years of service for only one year. Many black women did not have that level of seniority. Others, hired in the late 1960s and early 1970s, did not have enough seniority to take advantage of the retirement benefits under SIPP. The closing of the IOC caused over 1,200 women to be transferred to new locations, downgraded, or forced to resign. The company eventually laid off as many as 300 of these women. Pat Meckle stated that none of the IOCs before or after New York had been closed in the same manner. Somehow all of the people in the other IOCs received other jobs.

Union behavior in this tragedy requires scrutiny. Meckle defended the union, which had been criticized for the layoffs, scattered transfers, and the lack of demonstrations and other forms of protest. Acknowledging that many of the union officers had been craftsmen who were not immediately affected by the closing, she still argued that the criticisms had been misdirected since "so many did get jobs because [the union] persisted and persisted and argued and fought."[70]

Tyree voiced a considerably different assessment of how the union handled the closing. He did not think anyone actually had investigated how to stop the closing or to save as many jobs as possible. Neither the national nor local leadership made any plans or took any aggressive action on behalf of these black operators. He did not believe that they "could have completely changed what happened," but he thought that the union "could have made it easier . . . could have prepared people a lot better."[71]

According to Tyree, union officers Anne Walden and Pat Meckle were the only operators who voted for a strike at a Local 1150 meeting held in May 1983. He attributed this disaster to the actions of Chester (Chet)

L. Macey, the local president at the time, who told the operators that if they voted for a strike the company would simply close the IOC earlier. Angry but afraid, operators defeated the strike vote. A local president, either through a lack of concern, ineptitude, or perhaps ambition for a position in the company, asserted his authority to suppress dissent instead of rallying and directing the workers toward resistance.

Chet Macey, a white male who had never been an operator and who after leaving union office went directly into management, had failed to protect black women workers. As a result, the company, as Walden demonstrated, was allowed to abuse contract provisions by simply ignoring them (RPPP) or using them (Separation Payments) to force the operators to quit. And more important, the provisions themselves had been conceptualized with seniority prerequisites when black women with lower seniority worked in the very jobs slated for technological displacement – supposedly the type of jobs intended for protection.

Contrast this AT&T closing with the introduction of MLTs, which displaced test desk technicians, a largely white male group. According to Newman, some of these men retired under SIPP, and others accepted downgrades under RPPP or transferred to test bureaus in areas yet unaffected. Significantly, Newman observed "that whatever the inadequacies of the union's response, no testers lost their jobs as Bell System employees."[72] Other major work organization changes due to technological changes also did not lead to craftsmen losing their jobs. Crossbar switchmen, for example, have been retrained for the latest digital switching systems. The majority of white men have suffered few pay reductions and no loss of individual jobs. On the other hand, white men's jobs have suffered massive deskilling as centralization and computerization have increasingly diminished their control over their work. Computerization has made it possible for management to encroach on more and more of the craftsperson's work under the guise of "supervision" and "analysis." These same processes have also made it possible to get the jobs done with fewer people. In the long run, craft jobs will experience the same technological displacement operating has. For the moment, however, the protections (although small and inadequate) of the union's technological provisions have been greater for white male craft workers than for women and nonwhites.

Union performance was not uniformly poor. On an individual basis and in some regions, the CWA provided strong representation for nonwhites and women. In the case of the MLTs, the women who replaced the men achieved higher salaries (though significantly less than testers) than they would have as regular clerks. Even operators' salaries increased as their numbers decreased. One study stated that in 1985, the CWA-represented operators earned "wages that equalled those of the average male worker in the labor force as a whole" and "significantly more than the average woman earns in the US."[73]

The CWA has also sought to improve the wages and working conditions of women by its participation in special committees, conferences, and community coalitions.[74] A more diverse membership agitated for policies that would relieve the effects of both management's and the union's race/sex policies. As a result, in the early 1980s the CWA began to adjust its outlook to reflect an awareness of the special problems presented by its female and nonwhite membership. Working with AT&T in the Occupational Job Evaluation Committee and the Quality of Worklife Committees established in 1980, it sought to establish principles of "comparable worth" and to address other problems in the workplace. The national CWA leadership also expanded its previously established Women's Committees and Committees on Equity.

Despite union cooperation and the signing of new EEOC Consent Decrees in 1982, statistics released by New York Telephone Company demonstrate that women and minorities, albeit to a lesser extent, continued to be segregated in the lower-paying, powerless positions. Just as in the early 1970s, women's percentage and numbers in the female-dominated occupations decreased at a faster rate than their growth in male-dominated crafts. Overall, unionism and affirmative action helped to increase the percentages of women and nonwhite people in jobs from which they had been historically excluded. Yet new technologies continuously erode future employment possibilities while they create even more stressful work environments.

New Technology: The Cost to Bell System Women

Although job loss is a major concern in any discussion of the technological transformation of work, health and job satisfaction are equally important considerations. Most Bell System women work in closed environments at some type of video display terminal (VDT) where their mobility is severely limited. As a result, significant health hazards are encountered, including miscarriage, eye strain, backaches and strain, headaches, stress, burning and itching eyes, and environmental problems such as extremes in temperature, exposure to hazardous and toxic chemicals used in photocopiers, printers, duplicators, and other office machines, inadequate illumination, insufficient fresh air ventilation, and poorly designed work spaces. Worse still is the pervasiveness of carpal tunnel syndrome among VDT workers. The *CWA News* described the symptoms as "tingling and numbness in the hands and fingers, sharp pain in the hands and wrists while performing tasks, and throbbing, sleep robbing pain at night from the shoulder on down."[75]

Usually "associated" with work such as "meatcutting, assembly line work, and sorting mail," carpal tunnel syndrome among telephone women is believed to be caused by "a constant motion of fingers and wrists while working at improperly designed VDT stations, combined with the elements of high job stress and lack of rest breaks." The result is a "swelling of muscle tendons running through the wrist bones – the 'carpal tunnel' – which produces pressure on, and eventually damage to, the median nerve."[76] Tendinitis, ganglionitis, bursitis, painful disorders of the neck and back, and other musculoskeletal illnesses also occur as a result of VDT work. Directory Assistance operators, confined to one position up to $2\frac{1}{2}$ hours without a break and who work at a constant repetitive pace under extreme surveillance, have been especially suscept-ible to VDT illnesses.

Mental health has also become an important concern. Whether work-ing as operators, clerks, or skilled craftspeople, few women receive the job satisfaction they thought would come with transfers or promotions. As a result of management's continuous separation of knowledge from execu-tion, most women work all day in front of VDTs performing jobs frag-mented to the extent that the women know relatively little about how their work fits into the total picture. When they do know, they are powerless to correct system design problems created by their "superiors." One National Institute for Occupational Safety and Health (NIOSH) study "found that people who work on VDTs face higher stress than any other occupational group, including air traffic controllers."[77] Other NIOSH research concluded that VDT workers suffered from "anxiety, depres-sion, irritability, monotony, fatigue, and lack of inner security."[78]

The operators' job, always stressful, became nearly intolerable with the new Traffic Service Position Systems. The TSPS operators automat-ically receive calls sent to them by an Automatic Call Distributor. They have no control over when to take the next call because the machine recognizes the microsecond the prior call is finished and sends another one to the position immediately. Unlike the flashing-light signals on the cord boards, TSPS operators know they have another call when they hear a "beep" in their earphones. Keep in mind that these operators are still working according to the pre-World War I standard under which they are expected to answer the "electronic beep" within three seconds and no later than ten seconds.

The TSPS stole even the few seconds of peace that cord board oper-ators had been able to pilfer in between the physical operations of plug-ging and unplugging cords. Even worse, computers made it possible to measure automatically the amount of time spent on each call. Operators' average work times (AWT) could be measured every fifteen minutes, and AWTs above thirty seconds per call could result in disciplinary actions. Computerization, of course, only enhanced Bell System methods for secretly monitoring operators to insure courteous behavior at all times.

Bell System monitoring and production standards have created such highly stressful work environments that drug abuse and alcoholism among workers have become problematic. Robert Howard, in a 1981 article entitled "How AT&T's Workers Are Drugged, Bugged and Coming Unplugged," gave the following example of telephone workers' pervasive use of drugs: "A survey conducted by Connecticut Union of Telephone Workers of more than 200 service representatives at Southern New England Telephone found that 37.2 percent were taking tranquilizers or other nerve medicine, 39.3 percent had increased their consumption of alcohol since starting on the job and 12.3 percent were using both – a potentially lethal combination."[79] In recognition of workers' stress but also to get them back on the job, company medical offices, perhaps illegally, dispensed "greenies" (aspirin and caffeine packaged under the Bell logo), Valium, Darvon, Lomotil, codeine, and other drugs. Nervous breakdowns and disorders have been frequent occurrences among service representatives and operators who have computer-monitored preset time limits in which to answer and service calls.[80] The Bell System, of course, did not publicize these problems.[81]

For several reasons, African American women are especially susceptible to both the physical and mental health problems associated with telephone work. Racist ideology significantly increases mental stress for African American women in a variety of ways. They are concentrated in VDT-intensive jobs where unfair treatment based on race usually results in delayed and postponed relief periods, which can exacerbate physical problems.[82] Second, black women experience the effects of racist ideas held by many of their fellow workers and management. African American women suffer abusive attitudes and remarks when they are in the lower positions, and they experience hostility, rejection, and sabotage when they hold positions formerly believed to be exclusively for whites. Both groups of women feel that they are watched more closely by management, that they are more likely to be "ratted on" by their co-workers, and that they are punished more swiftly, more frequently, and more severely for their mistakes.[83]

Women Cope and Resist

All telephone workers, of course, did not succumb to drugs or to the pressures of technological change. They exhibited a wide range of responses to the introduction of new technologies and the restructuring of their occupations. Despite the working conditions, some welcomed the new opportunities. Many African American women felt that they now had a long overdue chance at better-paying jobs. Other believed that the new machines represented "progress," a force over which they had no control.

Whether they accepted the new technology or not, telephone workers worked under extremely stressful conditions, and they found methods of resisting and coping. Geneva Tucker, for example, who had worked in restaurants, dry cleaners, and factories before becoming an operator and who thought the company had treated her fairly in the twenty years she was employed, expressed the desire to just get out and go back down South to live. Upgraded to a clerical position created by automation in the Repair Service Bureau, she does not expect to advance any further and she does not even have a request in for an upgrade to craft work. Her way of coping is to make plans for her escape. She typifies many of the women in the clerical force.[84]

While others sit out their time toward retirement, many workers "play" the Absence Control Plan.[85] The plan is a progression of five steps leading to termination. Every absence (of any duration) creates a step that has to be cleared by a three-month period of perfect attendance, otherwise the step progresses to the next one. To play the plan, employees take days off as sick days, get paid, and wait until their step clears before they are absent again. Obviously, the company has had to revise the plan as a means of deterring this type of resistance. But for those who use absence as a means of resistance, the plan merely controls the frequency, not the number, of their absences.

Another passive form of resistance is simply to do one's job and nothing more. With the new technology assigning tasks, instructions are frequently inaccurate due to last-minute changes, computer difficulties, and other reasons. Women have taken the attitude that they will just do what they are assigned, even when they know that it is wrong and will cause future problems with the system. Sometimes employees perform their tasks strictly according to the procedures described by the Bell System Practices (manuals that tell how to do everything from climbing stairs to using an oscilloscope), which results in a significant increase in the amount of time to complete a job. In effect, they are refusing to use shortcuts and other techniques they have learned as a result of experience on the job.

Rare, but more overt, resistance includes damaging the equipment, willfully performing the work incorrectly, and simply not performing assigned duties. In order to avoid punishment, workers must apply these methods strategically; and the high ratio of management to worker lessens their frequency. None of these tactics, however, prevents the introduction of new machinery. Individual resistance, no matter how pervasive, has done little to counter the effects of technological change.

Union activities, on the other hand, have been equally ineffective. Strikes and other more militant acts have rarely been initiated. Job pressures and work satisfaction are important enough for the company and the union to form joint discussion committees, but these issues are not strike issues in the opinion of the union leadership. Even when stewards on the shop floor initiate grievances against work pressures, local and national leaders cannot give them the support needed to win the individual grievance. Crippled by their own sanction of the company's "right" to reorganize work according to "the needs of the business," union leaders often do not have any grounds on which to launch a fight against the continuous process of deskilling, fragmentation, and degradation of their work.

Trade unions, government investigators, and other reformers have not been able to pierce the Bell System's wall of power. Through its control over its research and development, the company has been able to keep the union ignorant of both its intentions and the true impact of new technologies. Clauses bargained to notify the union when new technology is about to be introduced are almost meaningless in light of the union's inability to stop the introduction of the new technology or to determine how it will be applied. Left out of the developmental stage, the best the union can do is to haggle over retraining or job transfers.

Conclusion

To conclude, let us return to the hypothesis that race is an overriding variable in determining policy when it converges with gender in the workplace. This article has argued that, despite the Civil Rights movement, EEOC Consent Decrees, and dilatory union cooperation, AT&T and its operating companies pursued policies that in the long term disproportionately subjected African American women to technological displacement and/or dead-end jobs even when these jobs represented opportunities formerly closed to nonwhite women. And this article has argued that these personnel policies reflected a distinct race and sex ideology specifically applied to African American women.

How does race become the overriding variable? How were black women affected differently than any other women? The technology was not designed to eliminate only African American women. Bell System research and development goals were no different than any other company desirous of lower operating expenses. And white women, after all, had suffered enormous technological displacement as operators before the computer era. What, then, distinguishes black women's experiences in the telephone industry?

First, the Bell System limited the employment of African American women. Telephone companies offered black women employment only as operators or low-level clerks at the very time that white women's opportunities expanded. Because of their sex and race, black women had been deliberately hired into low-paying occupations in which they would be rapidly displaced by technology. When technologically fragmented craft work became available, these jobs, at least in New York City, became black women's domain. Rarely, however, did African American women become supervisors in the newly created departments, whereas white men and frequently white women did supervise an all-black workforce.

Second, shop-floor implementation of policies adopted by company executives and government agencies often subverted the very intention of these policies. Throughout the tenure of the Consent Decrees, lower-level supervisors and foremen continued to delay the processing of African American women's Upgrade and Transfer requests, and test administrators continued to unfairly administer the tests required for upgrades. In effect, lower-level managerial practices narrowed even further the limited opportunities designed by corporate executives.

Third, many union leaders and individuals who viewed black women as others and outsiders not only failed to protect black women because they were women, but actually attacked them because they were black. Believing that the union should serve only white interests, union officials failed to adequately represent African American women who had grievances against the company. These officials, alleging reverse discrimination, also initiated grievances and court cases against black female promotions. In one of the most perverse convolutions of affirmative action goals, union officials and lower-level white male managers colluded to block the promotion of nonwhite women by promoting white women.

Finally, I would argue, at the risk of stating the obvious, that the real difference in women's experiences in the telephone industry is no more than a reflection of the attitudes and behavior of American society. Historically, African American women are the least defended population in this country. It should come as no surprise that their disempowerment would be mirrored in the microcosm of the Bell System. National racism motivated both the company's and the union's responses to equal opportunity. AT&T achieved its service goals and increased its control over *all* of its workers by using black people, especially women, to intimidate the white workers.[86]

Race became the overriding variable when white people believed that any rights won by black people meant a loss of privilege for them. In this context, management versus nonmanagement has no meaning. When white workers believe that African American women belong on the bottom, they do not endorse equal rights. This lack of working-class unity creates an environment in which managers can apply technology in ways that adversely affect African American women's employment possibilities.

Notes

1   After further computerization, Traffic Service Positions (TSP) became known as Traffic Service Position Systems (TSPS). This equipment automatically measured the length of time an operator spent on a call and the number of calls handled per hour. The machines also calculated changes and determined call routing without any operator input. This equipment will be described more fully in the next section.

2   Martia Goodson made this statement in an interview conducted with Lessie Sanders in September 1975. I am indebted to her for the tape.

3   A fundamental component of the deskilling and work degradation debate is the issue of workers' control. Few labor historians after Harry Braverman have failed to consider these questions. Consequently, there are dozens of books that refine various points of interpretation regarding the interconnections of skill, work degradation, and workers' control. . . .

4   Women's labor historians not only have had to make a point of including women in the study of labor, they have also had to create different analytical frameworks to analyze women's experiences and simultaneously evaluate the models created for males. . . .

5   See Ava Baron, "Gender and Labor History: Learning from the Past, Looking to the Future," in *Work Engendered: Toward a New History of American Labor,* ed. Ava Baron (Ithaca, NY, 1991), for a strong analysis of how male-defined models marginalize women's work experience and distort periodization.

6   When race is included it is simply added as an issue that must be noted but not analyzed or explained. . . .

7   For a history of the decision-making process in the evolution of telephone switchboards and other equipment combined with an analysis of the effects on black and white workers, see Venus Green, "The Impact of Technology upon Women's Work in the Telephone Industry, 1880–1989" (PhD diss., Columbia University, 1990). . . .

8   The Bell System occupational groups fall within the following hierarchical categories: white-collar: (1) officials and managers, (2) administrative staff, (3) sales workers, (4) clerical staff, and (5) operators; blue-collar: (1) inside crafts, (2) outside crafts, and (3) service workers. Traditionally

female-dominated, operators and clerical staff were the majority of tele-phone workers up to the early 1980s when the Bell System was split into regional operating companies. Inside crafts (frame attendants, switching-equipment technicians, deskmen, and others who installed, maintained, and repaired equipment inside telephone buildings) and outside crafts (repair service technicians, installers, cable splicers, and others who installed, repaired, and maintained outside equipment and subscriber lines) were historically male jobs. Switching-equipment technicians, deskmen, special-equipment installers, and cable splicers were among the upper-craft and higher-paying jobs. Frame attendants and regular installers were the lower-craft workers.

9   Gender is racialized, of course, when studies of women omit or marginalize African American women. For the purpose of this article, however, I am using the racialization of gender to refer to the specific history of African American women.

10 See A. Leon Higginbotham, Jr, *In the Matter of Color: Race and the American Legal Process* (New York, 1978); Winthrop D. Jordan, *White over Black: American Attitudes toward the Negro, 1550–1812* (1968; reprint, New York, 1977); and Deborah Gray White, *Ar'n't I a Woman: Female Slaves in the Plantation South* (New York, 1985), for the legal, economic, social, and political development of the American racial ideology about African American women.

11 For the purposes of this article, I have chosen to keep the definition focused on workplace discrimination. Spatial limitations make it impossible to examine fully how racism and racial ideologies are expressed differently along class, ethnic, regional, and gender lines.

12 Black women hired into the Bell System as operators between 1964 and 1969 temporarily reversed a post-Korean War decline in operators due to the introduction of dial or automatic call connecting. Although white women experienced this particular displacement, they had long been the operating force, and they had not been deliberately chosen after the com-pany decided to automate. I argue elsewhere that the Bell System's depend-ence on women's personalized service actually helped to delay the introduction of dial. Below are the total number of Bell System operators for selected years.

Year	Operators	Year	Operators	Year	Operators
1940	108,375	1965	148,046	1974	141,923
1946	223,824	1966	154,585	1975	128,500
1950	208,139	1967	153,133	1976	109,368
1956	203,285	1969	163,506	1977	102,001
1960	159,954	1970	165,628	1978	100,333
1961	146,069	1971	157,498	1979	97,723
1962	140,194	1972	149,179	1980	92,740
1963	139,347	1973	148,043	1981	88,599
1964	142,205				

These numbers are taken from American Telephone and Telegraph Company, *Bell System Statistical Manual, 1920–1964* (New York, 1965), p. 708, and *Bell System Statistical Manual, 1950–1981* (New York, 1982), p. 705.

13 The Bell System is an excellent setting for this type of case study because of its high concentration of women in gender-specific jobs and because of its pioneering history in technology.

14 This thesis has been implied but not analyzed in studies of the computerization of clerical work. Without investigating the employment policies that confirm their postulations, these studies simply assert that African American women will be more adversely affected by new office technologies because black women work in the low-level jobs that are most subject to computerization.

15 Leonard C. Briggs, "TSP – as New as Tomorrow's Telephone Service!" *Bell Telephone Magazine*, 1 (1962): 48.

16 "Operators: Their Wide New World," *Telephone Review*, 6 (1963): 4.

17 Evelyn Holton, former New York Telephone Company operator interviewed for this study, liked the TSP because it was something new, prettier, desklike, and spacious compared to the "elbow room only" at the old cord switchboards. Although many operators liked these aspects, they did not like the speed-up facilitated by this new equipment.

18 There were a total of 159,954 Bell System operators (eight males and 159,946 females) in 1960 and in 1981 a total of 88,599 (9,776 males and 78,823 females). See American Telephone and Telegraph Company, *Bell System Statistical Manual 1950–1981*, p. 705....

19 The *Telephone Review*, 4 (April 1911): cover; and *Telephone Review*, 10–11 (1911): cover.

20 See "The Minstrelettes at the Richmond Hill, Virginia and Cleveland Central Office Party," *Telephone Review*, 3 (1928): 97; and "Sorry, Wrong Number," *Telephone Review*, 11 (1949): 20–21.

21 " 'Would Be Minstrels' Amuse Buffalo Toll Party-Goers," *Telephone Review*, 1 (1939): 21.

22 " 'Gentlemen . . . Be Seated!' " *Telephone Review*, 4 (1949): 4–5.

23 "Sodus Minstrels," *Telephone Review*, 9 (1955): 17.

24 "Deal-Holmdel Party," *Bell Laboratories Record*, 7 (1949): 280.

25 Ibid.

26 "Phone Co. Won't Hire Negroes to Meet Shortage," *New York Call*, March 1920, p. 2.

27 Quoted in ibid.

28 Ibid.

29 George S. Schuyler, "Negro Labor and Public Utilities," *Messenger*, January 1927, p. 4.

30 Ibid....

31 The Mayor's Commission on Conditions in Harlem, *The Negro in Harlem: A Report on Social and Economic Conditions Responsible for the Outbreak of March 19, 1935* (New York, 1936), p. 24.

32 New York State Temporary Commission on the Condition of the Urban Colored Population, *Report to the Legislature of the State of New York* (New York, 1937), p. 64.

33 New York State Temporary Commission on the Condition of the Urban Colored Population, *Public Hearings*, 1937. See, e.g., the testimonies of Walter D. Williams, general traffic manager, New York Telephone Company, New York City, and Peter D. Lowrie, auditor of the Bronx-Westchester area, New York Telephone Company, Bronx, New York.

34 Ibid., pp. 1512–13.

35 Ibid., p. 1514.

36 Ibid., p. 1513.

37 Ibid., p. 1522.

38 National Urban League, Department of Industrial Relations, *Number Please? Employment of Negro Workers in the Telephone Industry in 44 Cities* (New York, 1946), pp. 1–2. The cities covered the entire United States. . . .

39 Ibid., p. 5.

40 African Americans had challenged Bell System discrimination since World War I. Between 1937 and 1939, activists intensified their campaign for the employment of black women as operators in several large cities. Boycotts and other protests raised the issue but had no results.

41 African American women also pressured the Bell System to hire them. In New York, Baltimore, Chicago, and other cities they held twenty-four-hour picket lines around buildings and mass bill pay-ins and phone-ins to tie up Bell equipment. . . .

42 David Copus, Lawrence Gartner, Randall Speck, William Wallace, Marjanette Feagan, and Katherine Mazzaferri, " 'A Unique Competence': A Study of Equal Employment Opportunity in the Bell System," submitted before the Federal Communications Commission, 1971, pp. 179–81.

43 Bernard E. Anderson, "Equal Opportunity and Black Employment in the Telephone Industry," in *Equal Employment Opportunity and the AT&T Case*, ed. Phyllis A. Wallace (Cambridge, Mass., 1976), p. 183.

44 Copus et al., p. 200.

45 The Bell System consciously installed its switching systems in cities to tap the black labor pool. In 1977, 81.1 percent of its workforce was concentrated in large cities or close to them. . . .

46 Anderson, p. 196.

47 Walter Straley, vice president AT&T, "Report on Force Loss and the Urban Labor Market," paper delivered at the Bell Systems Presidents' Conference, October 9, 1969, p. 50, in the Records of the Equal Employment Opportunity Commission, Numeric Subject Files Relating to the Litigation against American Telephone and Telegraph Company, 1965–73, Classified Files, 1971–73, Record Group 403, box 99, National Archives, Washington, DC (hereafter cited as EEOC, NA).

48 Ibid., pp. 20–22, 32.

49 In interviews conducted by the author, ten black women (New York Telephone and AT&T employees included) hired between 1946 and 1971 stated that when they were hired they thought their starting salaries were good. They all said that the company had only offered them the operating job. They did not know of other jobs. A few women did begin as clerks, but this was extremely rare. It should also be mentioned that operators were not the lowest-paid workers in the Bell System. There were low-grade clerks who received a few dollars less than operators. Not surprisingly, however, black women who were not operators held these jobs.

50 Herbert R. Northrup and John A. Larson, *The Impact of the AT&T-EEO Consent Decree* (Philadelphia, 1979), pp. 45–47, 49–50, 55, 59, 60–61, 64–66, and tables III-4, 6, 7, 8, 9, 10, 12, and 13. . . .

51 Sally Hacker, "Sex Stratification, Technology, and Organizational Change: A Longitudinal Case Study of AT&T," *Social Problems*, 5 (1979): 539.

52 Ibid., pp. 549–50.

53 Ibid.

54 Ibid., p. 550.

55 David M. Newman, "New Technology and the Changing Labor Process in the Telephone Industry: The Union's Response" (1982, typescript), pp. 4–5.

56 These statements are based on my own experience as a switching equipment technician at New York Telephone Company for over fifteen years. As a steward I have been involved in countless discussions, grievances, and other battles with and on behalf of many of these women.

57 Phyllis A. Wallace, "The Consent Decrees," in Wallace, ed. (n. 43 above), p. 276. The IBEW did not participate.

58 Ibid., p. 275.

59 Joseph A. Beirne, "Foreword," in *Automation: Impact and Implications, Focus on Developments in the Communications Industry*, by The Diebold Group, Inc. (Washington, DC: Communications Workers of America, AFL-CIO, 1965), p. 7.

60 Ibid.

61 Lessie Sanders, interviewed by Venus Green (telephone) on October 14, 1989, in New York City. Sanders, an engineering studies clerk, is a former telephone operator who has worked for New York Telephone Company since 1969.

62 Technology Change Committees discussed retraining and employment opportunities for Bell employees whose jobs were affected by technology. They also discussed the appropriate administration of SIPP, RPPP, and transfers in the event of technological displacement.

63 Newman (n. 55 above), p. 21.

64 Ibid., pp. 23–24.

65 Pat Meckle, interviewed by Venus Green on July 27, 1989, in New York City, second interview. Meckle is the only white operator interviewed for this study. Local 1150 included AT&T operators and craftsmen working in New York City. According to Meckle, the Oakland IOC "did not stay open

too long" because the company took "a beating" from the militant operators out there.

66 Ibid. On January 1, 1984, as a results of an antitrust settlement with the federal government, AT&T divested itself of its twenty-two operating companies. These companies reorganized into seven regional companies while AT&T kept its long-distance business, and Western Electric and Bell labs, their manufacturing and research units.

67 Ibid.

68 Ron Tyree, interviewed by Venus Green on July 27, 1989, in New York City.

69 Anne H. Walden, "Anne Walden on the IOC Closing," *Local Spirit*, Newsletter of Local 1150, Communications Workers of America (April 1983), p. 1.

70 Pat Meckle, interviewed by Venus Green.

71 Ron Tyree, interviewed by Venus Green.

72 Newman (n. 55 above), p. 25.

73 National Organization for Women, "Women's Wages: A Key to Preserving Middle Income Jobs" (Washington, DC, August 1986), updated November 1986 by Judith Gregory, George Kohl, Leslie Loble, Louise Novotny, and Karen Sacks, pp. 18, 23. This study does not mention the weekend and out-of-hours premiums that may be included in the figures given. An interesting point, but another story, is that by this time the operating job has begun to attract white women again. Divestiture and the rise of competition created new opportunities.

74 Alone and in conjunction with the Coalition of Labor Union Women, the CWA has sponsored several National Women's Conferences to discuss such issues as pay equity and new technology.

75 "Carpal Tunnel Syndrome," *CWA News*, 4 (1989): 6.

76 Ibid.; and US Department of Labor, Occupational Safety and Health Administrator, *Working Safely with Video Display Terminals*, rev. ed. (Washington, DC, 1991), pp. 2–3.

77 Cited in Jane Fleishman, "The Health Hazards of Office Work," in *Double Exposure: Women's Hazards on the Job and at Home*, ed. Wendy Chavkin (New York, 1984), pp. 65, 69.

78 Cited in Mary Sue Henifin, "The Particular Problems of Video Display Terminals," in Chavkin (n. 77 above), p. 73.

79 Robert Howard, "Strung Out at the Phone Company: How AT&T's Workers Are Drugged, Bugged and Coming Unplugged," *Mother Jones*, 7 (1981): 39.

80 Ibid., p. 44.

81 Nevertheless, I can assure the reader that there are numerous psychiatric, alcohol, and drug treatment centers with which the company has agreements. In the past, I have witnessed dozens of coworkers go in and out of these treatment programs. The problem is immense.

82 Operators, e.g., could not rise from their positions to relieve themselves without the supervisors' permission. All of the women I interviewed

complained about this practice. African American women felt that supervisors took longer to grant them breaks and that their breaks were closely monitored. These women offer countless stories about miscarriages and the aggravation of serious illnesses caused by the refusal of supervisors to grant relief breaks. AT&T operators believed that one such incident resulted in the death of a sister operator. . . .

83 Green (n. 7 above), chap. 11. During the EEOC investigation, Cathy Dennis, a black sales representative in New York, testified that management harassment included forcing sick women to work under the threat of punishment through the Absence Control Plan (box 4, vol. 35, p. 3640, EEOC, NA). . . .

84 Geneva Tucker, interviewed by Venus Green on June 21, 1989, in New York City.

85 Winifred King, interviewed by Venus Green. King stated "as long as they pay me my salary, I will stay here and do what I can, but I have no incentive to be outstanding . . . or gung ho . . . or motivated to do anything more than I have to do." She also looks forward to when she has "enough time [seniority] . . . where [she] can retire and relax."

86 Many white employees believed that black women satisfied two quotas and therefore were more likely to be promoted. These misconceptions created fears that made shop-floor unity almost impossible in many places.

Documents

It's the Wrong *Hat!*

Front cover of *The Telephone Review*, 2, 4 (April 1911).

Telephone Industry Employment by Race and Sex, 1930–1970

	1970	1960	1950	1940	1930
All Employees	899,997	692,480	594,120	316,600	578,602
Black	71,469	17,127	7,920	2,320	3,995
Percent	7.9	2.5	1.3	0.7	0.7
Male	427,463	303,884	220,380	126,920	267,354
Black	18,096	6,121	4,290	1,940	3,478
Percent	4.2	2.0	1.9	1.5	1.3
Female	472,534	388,596	373,740	189,680	311,248
Black	53,373	11,006	3,630	380	517
Percent	11.3	2.8	1.0	0.2	0.2

Source: US Census of Population:
- 1930: Vol. V, General Report on Occupations, Chapter VII, Table 2. (Gainful workers, 10 years old and over.)
- 1940: Sample Statistics, The Labor Force, Industrial Characteristics, Table 1.
- 1950: Special Report P-E No. 1D, Characteristics of the Population, US Summary, Table 2.
- 1960: PC(2) 7F, Industrial Characteristics, Table 3.
- 1970: PC(1)-D1, US Summary, Detailed Characteristics, Table 236.

Includes telegraph employment in 1930.

Further Reading

Fischer, Claude S. *America Calling: a Social History of the Telephone to 1940.* Berkeley: University of California Press, 1992.

Hacker, Sally L. *"Doing It the Hard Way": Investigations of Gender and Technology.* Boston: Unwin Hyman, 1990.

Rakow, Lana F. *Gender on the Line: Women, the Telephone, and Community Life.* Urbana: University of Illinois Press, 1992.

Wajcman, Judy. *Feminism Confronts Technology.* University Park: Pennsylvania State University Press, 1991.

Wright, Barbara Drygulski, ed. *Women, Work, and Technology: Transformations.* Ann Arbor: University of Michigan Press, 1987.

Excerpted from Phyllis A. Wallace, ed., *Equal Employment Opportunity and the AT&T Case* (Cambridge, MA: MIT Press, 1976), Table 8.1, p. 182. Reprinted with permission.

9

Appropriate Technologies

1854	Daniel Halladay patents first American commercially successful windmill.
1935–41	Over 25,000 solar units installed in the Miami, Florida, area.
1949	President Harry S. Truman announces his Point-Four program.
c.1950	Over 800,000 Aermotor Co. windmills in the country.
1952	Dr Maria Telkes given Achievement Award by Society of Women Engineers.
1973	*Small Is Beautiful* by E. F. Schumacher published.
1976	California forms the Office of Appropriate Technology.
1979	President Carter has solar panels placed on the White House.
1982	President Reagan removes solar panels from the White House.

Introduction

It is commonly observed that technologies not only appear to be becoming more complex, but are gathered into ever more intricate networks. We are no longer surprised when we learn that a failed O-ring causes the catastrophic failure of a space launch, a failed relay blacks out virtually the entire northeastern section of the country, or a computer software bug can, a half-century later, threaten chaos in all manner of devices from gasoline pumps to pacemakers. It is the signal characteristic of modernity that it leads to, indeed seeks, the annihilation of time and space. Not only can one access a bank account in America from an ATM in Europe, one can trade on a stock market somewhere in the world 24 hours a day. One can eat asparagus in the middle of winter and ice cream on the hottest day of summer. The complexity and integration of networks that allow all these to happen are, by their very nature, at the same time simple and vulnerable. In the 1970s a movement formed around the idea that technologies which took time and place seriously could improve both the quality and sustainability of life on the planet. The idea of "appropriate technologies," like so much else, proved to be both contingent and contested.

The Rise and Fall of the Appropriate Technology Movement in the United States, 1965–1985

Carroll Pursell

Anchored in a period of social ferment and reform at one end, and in the Reagan years at the other, the two decades which saw the flourishing and the foundering of the Appropriate Technology movement in America encompassed also the end of the Vietnam War, a major energy crisis, and the first years of the environmental movement. The Appropriate Technology movement had its origins in perceived failings of the post-World War II technical aid efforts (by the United States and other northern hemispheric powers) in Third World countries but also quickly developed into a critique of American domestic technology. A welter of institutions were created: public and private; state, federal, and local; high-tech and low; aimed at underdevelopment overseas and overdevelopment at home. By the mid-1980s, however, most of these institutions had either disappeared or lost their momentum. The technologies themselves – solar energy, the generation of electricity by windmills, the utilization of abandoned dams for low-head hydroelectric generation, the development of methane gas and gasahol for fuel, a reemphasis on bicycles and mass transit, recycling and the use of natural materials, composting and sustainable (often organic) agriculture – survive, but without an ideological context which could give them political meaning.

To explain the rise of Appropriate Technology, one must take into account the convergence of a broad countercultural movement, a reassertion of doubts about the role of technology in American life, and the burgeoning environmental movement. This rich nexus was easily labeled "antitechnology" but, in fact, embodied a critique of certain technologies and certain definitions of the word, rather than a rejection of technology as such. The decline of the movement can be attributed to a combination of political and cultural factors. On the one hand, despite initiatives at the state level and by President Jimmy Carter, there was a lack of political commitment to changing the economic subsidies (including federally funded research and development budgets) that underwrote nuclear power, for example, but not the direct conversion

Taken from Carroll Pursell, "The Rise and Fall of the Appropriate Technology Movement in the United States, 1965–1985," *Technology and Culture*, 34 (July 1993), pp. 629–37. ©

of sunlight into electricity. Culturally, the campaign of the 1980s to "remasculinize" America after its defeat in Vietnam was profoundly antithetical to a movement that believed "Small Is Beautiful" and advocated "Soft Energy Paths," to cite the titles of two of the most influential books in the literature of Appropriate Technology.[1] It is difficult to imagine Rambo deliberately choosing to ride a bicycle, or recycle his cartridges, simply because such practices would be gentle on the earth.

The debate over Appropriate Technology was rich in cultural meaning and ideological intent, as well as being a material and economic challenge to existing social interests. These interests were committed to a certain kind and understanding of technology which operated as a hegemonic culture, and to that privileged position the oppositional culture of Appropriate Technology mounted a profound challenge. Since technological change can be understood in terms of not only social forces but also of cultural meanings, it pays to look especially at the contested definitions of words. In so doing one finds often enough that Appropriate Technology was represented as more feminine than the hegemonic technology and therefore seen by some as a threat to accepted notions of masculinity. The eclipse of Appropriate Technology in the 1980s became an important part of the so-called remasculinization of America.

Post-World War II American aid programs can conveniently be dated from President Harry S Truman's Point Four program, laid out in a speech on June 24, 1949. After warning that the "grinding poverty" of the underdeveloped world might cause its populations to "turn to false doctrines which hold that the way of progress lies through tyranny," he called for the United States to provide the "technical assistance [that] is necessary to lay the groundwork for productive investment." There would be two parts to this assistance: first, what he called "the technical, scientific, and managerial knowledge necessary to economic development," and second, "production goods – machinery and equipment – and financial assistance in the creation of productive enterprises."[2]

To a significant degree, the American aid programs, and those of other developed nations, were captive to the notion that ideally all countries should follow the same pattern of industrialization, in both urban and rural settings, which had presumably been traced by the donor nations. Thus, large factories, a mechanized agriculture, the rapid exploitation of natural resources, and the making of an engineering infrastructure (especially large electrical power projects) were seen as critical. Often, as it turned out, such efforts ignored or misunderstood local environments, both natural and cultural. Dams that destroyed fisheries, dual economies that privileged local elites, and machinery that lay idle because of a lack of fuel or maintenance eventually led to the realization that many technologies that might be useful in donor countries might be worse than useless in different places and circumstances.

In 1973 the British economist E. F. Schumacher published his widely influential book *Small Is Beautiful*, subtitled *Economics as if People Mattered*. In this book he developed his vision of what he called an "intermediate" technology, one which fit between the primitive and poverty-reinforcing tools of much of the southern hemisphere and those large, powerful technological systems of the northern. Addressing a Unesco Conference on the Application of Science and Technology to the Development of Latin America, he defined the goal as creating workplaces that were located where people live, that would be cheap enough for common use, and that used relatively simple techniques and local materials to make things for local use.[3] The intermediate technologies that met these criteria could be considered "appropriate" for that time and place.

Even before the appearance of Schumacher's book, some private groups in the United States had been formed to address the problem. In 1959 Volunteers in Technical Assistance (VITA), a body of scientists and engineers, organized to provide the technical assistance needed to help "enable low-income communities to use locally available and appropriate resources to meet their own needs for economic and social development."[4] A similar group, Volunteers in Asia, concentrated on appropriate development on that continent.

Almost immediately, however, the terms intermediate, alternative, and appropriate, often used interchangeably, proved to be almost infinitely malleable in meaning: intermediate between what, an alternative to what, appropriate to what? Referring to what it called "an illusion of consensus" around the term "alternative," the Volunteers in Asia quoted one fellow worker as believing that "the meaning becomes established by convention within the community that uses it...the term 'alternative technology' has acquired an illicit content narrower than a strict interpretation would call for...which seems to be conditioned by the connotations of the word 'alternative' in the counter-culture of the West."[5]

In the 1960s and 1970s new groups were springing up which advocated the application of a broader, and culturally challenging, understanding of appropriate technology to American society as well. Believing that the overdevelopment of the United States was as destructive of social and natural health as was underdevelopment in much of the rest of the world, such groups as the New Alchemy Institute in Massachusetts and the Farallons Institute in California advocated what the latter called "self-reliance, local autonomy, and respect for Nature. We demonstrate land use and living patterns that improve the quality of life by reducing energy consumption and dependence on fossil fuels. We design self-sustaining living patterns that increase our awareness of the balance between the realities of Nature and the needs of Man."[6] Appropriate technologies they defined as those "that are: 1) cheap enough to be accessible to nearly everyone, 2) simple enough to be easily maintained and repaired, 3) suitable for small-scale application, 4) compatible with man's needs for creativity, and 5) self-educative in environmental awareness."[7]

Private initiatives were soon followed by efforts of government, at all levels, to help develop appropriate technologies. Sim Van der Ryn, the architect who was president of the Farallons Institute in 1974, was appointed state architect by Governor Jerry Brown of California, and in 1976 his agency became the home of the new Office of Appropriate Technology (OAT), also established by Brown. The OAT was housed in the Gregory Bateson Building, a state office structure designed by Van der Ryn and called "the most energy-efficient office building in the nation."[8] At the federal level, President Carter, in response to the 1973–74 oil embargo, initiated several energy-conservation programs which became associated with the Community Action Agencies, which, in turn, in 1976, became the core around which a National Center for Appropriate Technology (NCAT) was established.

Neither of these governmental initiatives survived the arrival of Republican administrations in Sacramento and Washington. In California the Office of Appropriate Technology was abolished by Governor George Deukmejian when he replaced Brown in 1982, and in 1981 the newly elected President Ronald Reagan terminated the federal Community Services Administration, leaving NCAT without institutional or financial support.[9] In 1982, during repairs to the roof of the west wing of the White House, solar panels installed there by President Carter in 1979 were taken off, stored for a decade, then disposed of to a college in Maine.[10] It was a symptomatic, but not a unique, rolling back of the progress Appropriate Technology had made over the past decades.

In part this eclipse of the Appropriate Technology movement was attributable to its political failure to bring sufficient power to bear against entrenched advocates of the dominant American technologies of agribusiness, large private utilities, multinational construction and manufacturing firms, and the military-industrial complex, all of which had a vested interest in perpetuating and elaborating the large technological systems already in place. In part, however, it was also an example of the triumph of hegemonic culture over deliberate subversion by a truly oppositional culture. Indeed, those institutions showed a remarkable ability to expropriate emerging technologies for their own benefit. *Science* magazine charged, for example, that "despite the diffuse nature of the resource," the federal "research program has emphasized large central stations to produce solar electricity in some distant future." It quoted one critic as claiming that this was "creating solar technologies in the image of nuclear power."[11] In 1976 the Boeing Aerospace Company beat out both Rockwell and Grumman to receive a $970,000 research grant from the National Aeronautics and Space Administration and the Energy Research and Development Administration to study the feasibility of orbiting solar "power stations."[12]

The meanings of words are frequently contested, and the discourse over the "true" definition of "technology" is as old as the word itself. Some have attempted to narrow its meaning, others have taken a more expansive view of the matter. Those who were eager to broaden the usage of the word tried to expand it in two directions: first, to disconnect it from the narrow and privileged discourse of engineering, and, second, to reach beyond recognizable tools and devices to include larger social systems.

For example, the 1976 publication *Radical Technology* included an essay entitled "Inner Technologies" which, after asserting that "the present technological paradigm is clearly in need of replacement," warned that "it is unlikely that a truly holistic-ecological ethic can be built into technology if it is not already built into us as well."[13] To give a more recent example, the *New York Times* reported in 1992 that the Sacramento [California] Municipal Utility District (SMUD) was giving away shade trees to its customers. For every four cents of the cost of these trees, air conditioners would need one kilowatt hour less of electricity. Since generation costs were much higher than four cents per kilowatt hour, the program was billed as a "hard-headed, cost-effective" part of SMUD's efficiency program, not the dreams of "a bunch of do-gooders, greenies." Whether trees and "inner technologies" deserve to be considered as a part of technology is clearly a contested issue. Significantly, the general manager of SMUD in 1992 had not come up through industry ranks but had been, in the 1970s, head of an energy project for the Ford Foundation.[14]

The engineer and social commentator Samuel C. Florman, on the other hand, asserts that "to the engineer in the United States, the debate about whether technologies should in principle be large or small, hard or soft, high or low, is almost incomprehensible" since "engineering solutions have been inherent in the very scheme of things" rather than "arbitrarily decided." Indeed, he believes "the technological issue is found to be a diversion, not at the heart of the matter."[15] By his definition, technology stands outside the social, political, and cultural struggle over what sort of country America should be, and what sort of lives its citizens should live. Appropriate Technology was, therefore, at the "heart," not a technology at all. Our continuing failure to find one single, satisfactory definition for technology is directly tied to the fact that the stakes are high. In attempting to redefine technology, advocates of Appropriate Technology were directly challenging the power of those who shaped the hegemonic notion of that subject.

Another critical aspect of Appropriate Technology was that it was perceived as less manly, more feminine, than the nation's dominant technological culture. I cannot make the case as completely as I would like on this occasion, but perhaps a few examples will suffice to suggest the nature of my argument. The persistent and central claim of Appropriate Technology, that it worked in gentle partnership with nature and fostered intimate personal relationships, linked it to the powerful cultural identification of nature and the personal with the feminine. A study of farmers in Wisconsin who were dedicated to the practice of what they called "sustainable agriculture" revealed that an overwhelming number of them did so in the name of family farms, of domestic rather than market values. As the investigator explained it, "They believe the principles of sustainable agriculture that could help preserve family farming (the reliance on small-scale, labor-intensive production using nonsynthetic chemicals, for example) are inseparably related to values that sustain farm families. These values include the integration of work life and family life, and environmental conservation."[16]

Schumacher himself had labeled supporters of the conventional viewpoint "the people of the forward stampede," and those who advocated appropriate technology, the "home-comers." The operator of a low-head hydroelectric plant, quoted by John McPhee in 1981, insisted that "every machine is an individual.... A turbine is a symphony of noise. You listen. You know if something is missing. Being able to listen to a waterwheel is something that is not in the books."[17] Comments like this reveal attitudes far from the rhetoric of conquest and domination, rationality and control, that are often associated with masculine constructions of technology. In 1952 when the newly established Society of Women Engineers bestowed its first Achievement Award on Dr. Maria Telkes, it reported that "since 1945 she has devoted herself chiefly to further research in the field of solar energy," a field, according to her citation, "which has not been developed nearly as fast as, for instance, nuclear energy. She has been known to remark wistfully, 'You see, sunshine isn't lethal.' "[18]

Critics of Appropriate Technology often linked it to notions powerfully associated, in our culture, with the feminine. The Canadian architect Witold Rybczynski charged advocates with appealing to the "emotions" rather than to "reason," and Florman accused them of "passive" resistance and wanting to "withdraw" from the prevailing culture. Their ideas, he warned, conjured up "Oriental attitudes," a powerful image of otherness.[19]

Concepts of masculinity and femininity, of course, like those of technology itself, are socially constructed and are being constantly reproduced and modified. None are unchanging or universally agreed on. Indeed, the culture of Appropriate Technology, as it was expressed from the mid-1960s to the mid-1980s, was more than a little reminiscent of two constructions of masculinity which were widely adhered to in the United States at the beginning of the 19th century: that attached to the republican gentleman, with its ideal of proportion and self-restraint, discipline of self and generosity toward others, and that associated with the independent producer, drawing pride of manliness from work, skill, the ownership of tools, self-reliance, and technical competence. Both were eclipsed as the 19th century wore on by the manly figure of the self-made, acquisitive entrepreneur, but neither disappeared completely. During the 1980s, however, it was easy for the dominant culture of American masculinity, which still drew heavily on the 19th-century entrepreneurial style, to see Appropriate Technology as a part of the experience of feminization that was read out of a recently resurgent civil rights movement, a growing women's movement, a new environmentalism, and, most of all, a humiliating military defeat in Vietnam.

Reagan and Rambo were the perfect representatives of a masculine backlash against all of these, including what could be characterized by them as a cowardly and self-indulgent refusal to embrace technological vanguardism as the finest expression of national virility. It is significant that Rybczynski, in his book on Appropriate Technology, dismissively titled *Paper Heroes*, links the German-born Schumacher with the *Jugendkultur* which flourished in the defeated Germany between the wars.[20]

The questions raised by the Appropriate Technology movement, and by its critics, are still very much with us. Our responsibility for aid to development extends now to the states of eastern Europe and the republics of the former Soviet Union as well as to the southern hemisphere. The environment is in even more danger from destructive technologies, and the geopolitics of oil still claim lives and treasure. The question of which technologies will be developed in the United States in the future, and which exported to newly developing and redeveloping nations, is a matter partly of technical feasibility, is very much an issue of social and political advantage, but is also, in ways that we do not well understand, the result of deeply held cultural perceptions.

Notes

1 I take the phrase from Susan Jeffords, *The Remasculinization of America: Gender and the Vietnam War* (Bloomington, Ind., 1989). In doing so I do not mean to suggest that masculinity is a single and immutable concept.

2 "Truman's Four Point Program, June 24, 1949," in *Documents of American History*, ed. Henry Steele Commager, 7th ed. (New York, 1963), pp. 558–59.

3 E. F. Schumacher, *Small Is Beautiful: Economics as If People Mattered* (New York, 1973), p. 165.

4 Angela Sinclair, *A Guide to Appropriate Technology Institutions* (London, 1984), p. 101.

5 Ken Darrow and Rick Pam, *Appropriate Technology Sourcebook* (Stanford, Calif., 1976), p. 14.

6 *The Farallons Institute* (Point Reyes, Calif., 1974), p. 3.

7 Ibid., p. 5.

8 *Office of Appropriate Technology*, brochure issued by OAT (n.d.).

9 "An Introduction and a History," leaflet produced by the National Center for Appropriate Technology (n.p., n.d.).

10 Letter from Rex W. Scouten, White House curator, to author, July 20, 1992; "College Uses Panels Discarded by White House," *Chronicle of Higher Education*, 38 (July 1, 1992): A5.

11 "Solar Energy Research: Making Solar after the Nuclear Model?" *Science*, 197 (July 15, 1977): 241.

12 "US Seeks Way to Plug in to Sun," *Los Angeles Times*, December 10, 1976.

13 Peter Russell, "Inner Technologies," in *Radical Technology*, ed. Geoffrey Boyle and Peter Harper (New York, 1976), p. 234.

14 "An Energy Prophet Who Guessed Right," *New York Times*, September 27, 1992.

15 Samuel C. Florman, *Blaming Technology: The Irrational Search for Scapegoats* (New York, 1981), pp. 82–83, 88.

16 Michael A. Gordon, "Oral Documentation and the Sustainable Agriculture Movement in Wisconsin," *Public Historian*, 11 (Fall 1989): 94.

17 John McPhee, "Minihydro," *New Yorker*, 57 (February 23, 1981): 49.

18 Society of Women Engineers, *Achievement Award, 1952–1974* (n.p., n.d.).

19 Witold Rybczynski, *Paper Heroes, Appropriate Technology: Panacea or Pipe Dream?* (New York, 1991), p. 13; Florman, pp. 81, 93.

20 Rybczynski, p. 16.

Documents

Technical Assistance for the Underdeveloped Areas of the World

Message
from
The President of the United States
transmitting

A recommendation for the enactment of legislation to authorize
an expanded program of technical assistance for the underdeveloped
areas of the world

JUNE 24, 1949. – Referred to the Committee on Foreign Affairs,
and ordered to be printed

To the Congress of the United States:

In order to enable the United States, in cooperation with other countries, to assist the peoples of economically underdeveloped areas to raise their standards of living, I recommend the enactment of legislation to authorize an expanded program of technical assistance for such areas, and an experimental program for encouraging the outflow of private investment beneficial to their economic development. These measures are the essential first steps in an undertaking which will call upon private enterprise and voluntary organizations in the United States, as well as the Government, to take part in a constantly growing effort to improve economic conditions in the less-developed regions of the world.

The grinding poverty and the lack of economic opportunity for many millions of people in the economically underdeveloped parts of Africa, the Near and Far East, and certain regions of Central and South America, constitute one of the greatest challenges of the world today. In spite of their age-old economic and social handicaps, the peoples in these areas have in recent decades been stirred and awakened. The spread of industrial civilization, the growing understanding of modern concepts of government, and the impact of two World Wars have changed their lives and their outlook. They are eager to play a greater part in the community of nations.

All these areas have a common problem. They must create a firm economic base for the democratic aspirations of their citizens. Without such an economic base, they will be unable to meet the expectations which the modern world has aroused in their peoples. If they are frustrated and disappointed, they may turn to false doctrines which hold that the way of progress lies through tyranny.

For the United States the great awakening of these peoples holds tremendous promise. It is not only a promise that new and stronger nations will be associated with us in the cause of human freedom, it is also a promise of new economic strength and growth for ourselves.

With many of the economically underdeveloped areas of the world, we have long had ties of trade and commerce. In many instances today we greatly need the products of their labor and their resources. If the productivity and the purchasing power of these countries are expanded, our own industry and agriculture will benefit. Our experience shows that the volume of our foreign trade is far greater with highly developed countries than it is with countries having a low standard of living and inadequate industry. To increase the output and the national income of the less developed regions is to increase our own economic stability.

In addition, the development of these areas is of utmost importance to our efforts to restore the economies of the free European nations. As the economies of the underdeveloped areas expand, they will provide needed products for Europe and will offer a better market for European goods. Such expansion is an essential part of the growing system of world trade, which is necessary for European recovery.

Furthermore, the development of these areas will strengthen the United Nations and the fabric of world peace. The preamble to the Charter of the United Nations states that the economic and social advancement of all people is an essential bulwark of peace. Under article 56 of the Charter, we have promised to take separate action and to act jointly with other nations "to promote higher standards of living, full employment, and conditions of economic and social progress and development."

For these various reasons, assistance in the development of the economically underdeveloped areas has become one of the major elements of our foreign policy. In my inaugural address I outlined a program to help the peoples of these areas to attain greater production as a way to prosperity and peace.

The major effort in such a program must be local in character; it must be made by the people of the underdeveloped areas themselves. It is essential, however, to the success of their effort that there be help from abroad. In some cases the peoples of these areas will be unable to begin their part of this great enterprise without initial aid from other countries.

The aid that is needed falls roughly into two categories: The first is the technical, scientific, and managerial knowledge necessary to economic development. This category includes not only medical and educational knowledge, and assistance and advice in such basic fields as sanitation, communications, road building and governmental services, but also, and perhaps most important, assistance in the survey of resources and in planning for long- range economic development.

The second category is production goods – machinery and equipment – and financial assistance in the creation of productive enterprises. The underdeveloped areas need capital for port and harbor development, roads and communications, irrigation and drainage projects, as well as for public utilities and the whole range of extractive, processing, and manufacturing industries. Much of the capital required can be provided by these areas themselves, in spite of their low standards of living. But much must come from abroad.

The two categories of aid are closely related. Technical assistance is necessary to lay the groundwork for productive investment. Investment, in turn, brings with it technical assistance. In general, however, technical surveys of resources and of the possibilities of economic development must precede substantial capital investment. Furthermore, in many of the areas concerned, technical assistance in improving sanitation, communications, or education is required to create conditions in which capital investment can be fruitful.

This country, in recent years, has conducted relatively modest programs of technical cooperation with other countries. In the field of education, channels of exchange and communication have been opened between our citizens and those of other countries. To some extent, the expert assistance of a number of Federal agencies, such as the Public Health Service and the Department of Agriculture, has been made available to other countries. We have also participated in the activities of the United Nations, its specialized agencies, and other international organizations to disseminate useful techniques among nations.

Through these various activities we have gained considerable experience in rendering technical assistance to other countries. What is needed now is to expand and integrate these activities and to concentrate them particularly on the economic development of underdeveloped areas.

Much of the aid that is needed can be provided most effectively through the United Nations. Shortly after my inaugural address this Government asked the Economic and Social Council of the United Nations to consider what the United Nations and the specialized international agencies could do in this program.

The Secretary General of the United Nations thereupon asked the United Nations Secretariat and the secretariats of the specialized international agencies to draw up cooperative plans for technical assistance to underdeveloped areas. As a result, a survey was made of technical projects suitable for these agencies in such fields as industry, labor, agriculture, scientific research with respect to natural resources, and fiscal management. The total cost of the program submitted as a result of this survey was estimated to be about $35,000,000 for the first year. It is expected that the United Nations and the specialized international agencies will shortly adopt programs for carrying out projects of the type included in this survey.

In addition to our participation in this work of the United Nations, much of the technical assistance required can be provided directly by the United States to countries needing it. A careful examination of the existing information concerning the underdeveloped countries shows particular need for technicians and experts with United States training in plant and animal diseases, malaria and typhus control, water supply and sewer systems, metallurgy and mining, and nearly all phases of industry.

It has already been shown that experts in these fields can bring about tremendous improvements. For example, the health of the people of many foreign communities has been greatly improved by the work of United States sanitary engineers in setting up modern water-supply systems. The food supply of many areas has been increased as the result of the advice of United States agricultural experts in the control of animal diseases and the improvement of crops. These are only examples of the wide range of benefits resulting from the careful application of modern techniques to local problems. The benefits which a comprehensive program of expert assistance will make possible can only be revealed by studies and surveys undertaken as a part of the program itself.

To inaugurate the program, I recommend a first-year appropriation of not to exceed $45,000,000. This includes $10,000,000 already requested in the 1950 budget for activities of this character. The sum recommended will cover both our participation in the programs of the international agencies and the assistance to be provided directly by the United States.

In every case, whether the operation is conducted through the United Nations, the other international agencies, or directly by the United States, the country receiving the benefit of the aid will be required to bear a substantial portion of the expense.

The activities necessary to carry out our program of technical aid will be diverse in character and will have to be performed by a number of different Government agencies and private instrumentalities. It will be necessary to utilize not only the resources of international agencies and the United States Government, but also the facilities and the experience of the private business and nonprofit organizations that have long been active in this work.

Since a number of Federal agencies will be involved in the program, I recommend that the administration of the program be vested in the President, with authority to delegate to the Secretary of State and to other Government officers, as may be appropriate. With such administrative flexibility, it will be possible to modify the management of the program as it expands and to meet the practical problems that will arise in its administration in the future.

The second category of outside aid needed by the underdeveloped areas is the provision of capital for the creation of productive enterprises. The International Bank for Reconstruction and Development and the Export-Import Bank have provided some capital for underdeveloped areas, and, as the economic growth of these areas progresses, should be expected to provide a great deal more. In addition, private sources of funds must be encouraged to provide a major part of the capital required.

In view of the present troubled condition of the world – the distortion of world trade, the shortage of dollars, and other aftereffects of the war – the problem of substantially increasing the flow of American capital abroad presents serious difficulties. In all probability novel devices will have to be employed if the investment from this country is to reach proportions sufficient to carry out the objectives of our program.

All countries concerned with the program should work together to bring about conditions favorable to the flow of private capital. To this end we are negotiating agreements with other countries to protect the American investor from unwarranted or discriminatory treatment under the laws of the country in which he makes his investment.

In negotiating such treaties we do not, of course, ask privileges for American capital greater than those granted to other investors in underdeveloped countries or greater than we ourselves grant in this country. We believe that American enterprise should not waste local resources, should provide adequate wages and working conditions for local labor, and should bear an equitable share of the burden of local taxes. At the same time we believe that investors will send their capital abroad on an increasing scale only if they are given assurance against risk of loss through expropriation without compensation, unfair or discriminatory treatment, destruction through war or rebellion, or the inability to convert their earnings into dollars.

Although our investment treaties will be directed at mitigating such risks, they cannot eliminate them entirely. With the best will in the world a foreign country, particularly an underdeveloped country, may not be able to obtain the dollar exchange necessary for the prompt remittance of earnings on dollar capital. Damage or loss resulting from internal and international violence may be beyond the power of our treaty signatories to control.

Many of these conditions of instability in underdeveloped areas which deter foreign investment are themselves a consequence of the lack of economic development which only foreign investment can cure. Therefore, to wait until stable conditions are assured before encouraging the outflow of capital to underdeveloped areas would defer the attainment of our objectives indefinitely. It is necessary to take vigorous action now to break out of this vicious circle.

Since the development of underdeveloped economic areas is of major importance in our foreign policy, it is appropriate to use the resources of the Government to accelerate private efforts toward that end. I recommend, therefore, that the Export-Import Bank be authorized to guarantee United States private capital, invested in productive enterprises abroad which contribute to economic development in underdeveloped areas, against the risks peculiar to those investments.

This guaranty activity will at the outset be largely experimental. Some investments may require only a guaranty against the danger of inconvertibility, others may need protection against the danger of expropriation and other dangers as well. It is impossible at this time to write a standard guaranty. The bank will, of course, be able to require the payment of premiums for such protection, but there is no way now to determine what premium rates will be most appropriate in the long run. Only experience can provide answers to these questions.

The bank has sufficient resources at the present time to begin the guaranty program and to carry on its lending activities as well without any increase in its authorized funds. If the demand for guaranties should prove large, and lending activities continue on the scale expected, it will be necessary to request the Congress at a later date to increase the authorized funds of the bank.

The enactment of these two legislative proposals, the first pertaining to technical assistance and the second to the encouragement of foreign investment, will constitute a national endorsement of a program of major importance in our efforts for world peace and economic stability. Nevertheless, these measures are only the first steps. We are here embarking on a venture that extends far into the future. We are at the beginning of a rising curve of activity, private, governmental, and international, that will continue for many years to come. It is all the more important, therefore, that we start promptly.

In the economically underdeveloped areas of the world today there are new creative energies. We look forward to the time when these countries will be stronger and more independent than they are now, and yet more closely bound to us and to other nations by ties of friendship and commerce, and by kindred ideals. On the other hand, unless we aid the newly awakened spirit in these peoples to find the course of fruitful development, they may fall under the control of those whose philosophy is hostile to human freedom, thereby prolonging the unsettled state of the world and postponing the achievement of permanent peace.

Before the peoples of these areas we hold out the promise of a better future through the democratic way of life. It is vital that we move quickly to bring the meaning of that promise home to them in their daily lives.

HARRY S. TRUMAN.

THE WHITE HOUSE, *June 24, 1949.*

Purpose, Organization, and Activities
State of California Office of Appropriate Technology

Purpose

The recognition that we live in a world of limited resources requires development of a conserving technology. As government tries to adapt to the new realities of diminishing resources and changing values, we must find ways to carry out our responsibilities in ways that are less wasteful, less costly and bureaucratic, less harmful to people and our environment. We need to encourage tools, techniques and processes in our economy – as well as in our communities and institutions – that are simple, direct, small-scale, and inexpensive: a balanced technology that is appropriate to maintaining the health of California's people, economy, and environment.

On May 12, 1976, Governor Brown created the Office of Appropriate Technology by Executive Order. The Office was created to assist the government and people of California in this period of social transition, dealing with changing personal values, environmental stress, and diminishing resources. The Office of Appropriate Technology will act as a catalyst for change in government in the areas of:

- job development
- resource conservation

Taken from "Purpose, Organization, and Activities," Press release, State of California Office of Appropriate Technology, Sacramento, June 1976.

- environmental protection
- community development

through the introduction of cost-saving alternatives to present practices.

The Office is intended to be active especially in assisting low-income groups and cultural minorities to achieve more self-reliance and improve their real quality of life without government handouts. The actions of the Office will be directed toward developing human-scale technologies and ways of thinking which promote wise use of resources, more harmonious connections with the natural world, and smaller, more workable governmental and social institutions.

These actions will include working to change administrative and legal barriers to decentralization, change, and small-scale, self-reliant enterprise. In most areas of life, for example: housing, education, professional training, health, water, waste management, transportation, banking, and real estate – State laws and standards tend to institutionalize high-technological values in such a way that make it difficult for more appropriate forms to compete fairly or even exist. Additionally, in many areas, public policy favors and often subsidizes large scale standardized activity at the expense of diversified local enterprise. The Office will seek out and document overt and covert subsidies of both wasteful practices and deterrents to local and individual self-reliance. It would call to the attention of the executive and legislative branches of government those regulations which make intelligent alternatives difficult or impossible to realize.

OAT intends to catalyze change in State government by introducing new perspectives of social and ecological well being, resource conservation and economic redevelopment into State policies, programs and projects. Government now intervenes in just about every area of people's lives and yet our problems remain unsolved. Through appropriate technology there can be less need for government intervention to control the myriad and often unanticipated effects of "advanced" technology. Appropriate technology is here now that can be applied to many areas of our everyday life in ways that create new and satisfying jobs, save energy, and improve the quality of life:

- inexpensive, simply constructed solar hot water heaters can replace our present dependence on natural gas and electricity.
- renewable energy sources can be put to work to heat and cool our homes and work places.
- small-scale intensive agriculture and farmers' markets on unused land in and around our cities can provide families with fresh vegetables and healthy exercise.
- non-polluting mini-transit systems and bicycle ways can make getting around the city easy and inexpensive.
- finding new uses for old buildings saves energy and maintains neighborhood stability.
- plumbing and sewage systems can be simplified using modern biological techniques to reduce pollution, conserve water and materials, and rebuild the soil.
- use of locally available materials and careful climate-based design can reduce housing costs and improve quality through greater individual choice and diversity.

Objectives

The Office has five major objectives:

- Bring the message and perspectives of appropriate technology to State government;
- Introduce significant cost-savings in government programs;
- Document and evaluate economic, social, and technical feasibility of alternative technologies;
- Demonstrate and implement working alternative technologies in State government operations; and
- Encourage implementation of appropriate technology throughout California.

Organization

Sim Van der Ryn, State Architect, is Director of OAT. The Office is located administratively in the Governor's Office of Planning and Research, headed by Bill Press. Professional/technical back-up will be provided by consultants. Judy Michalowski is the Coordinator of OAT and is responsible for special programs, office operations, and program continuity.

OAT is also assisted in its work by a number of people in other State agencies who contribute their time, perspectives, and energies in various ways to help the office in its work.

OAT intends to remain small, relying on a small core staff, supplemented by cooperative working agreements with other State agencies and occasional use of outside consultants on specific projects (funded mainly by federal grants) to perform most of the work.

Program

The Office intends primarily to serve as a coordinator for a network of people using appropriate technology in State government. In this context, "Appropriate Technology" characterizes small-scale/human-scale, simple and understandable, non-violent, science and skill-intensive but low-capital tools, systems and techniques, designed to help people to move towards lighter living more in keeping with finite resources, ecological harmony, personal growth and cooperative effort: a way of life attuned to a human and environmental philosophy whose operating principles also have been called gentle, soft, and intermediate technology, or biotechnics. The concepts inherent in this work may be called "Whole Life Systems".

A Whole Life System implies: 1) a more integrated and steady relationship between the man-made and the natural environment so we do not overpower the self-healing capacities of natural systems to maintain themselves and support life, 2) developing social, economic, and environmental diversity so that communities and regions can provide for many of their own needs without putting all their eggs in the single shrinking basket of imported and depleting resources, and 3) creating and managing systems that require less capital, less outside energy and transportation, but more personal involvement and direct production.

We will use appropriate technology that has already been developed in many areas important to the future of our society, including energy conservation, solar energy use, wind power generation, use of biofuels such as methane, new waste management and wastewater reuse practices, small-scale rural and urban agriculture and aquaculture, ecological habitat restoration and environmental protection techniques, integrated pest control, and bicycle paths. In all of these cases, implementation of appropriate technologies has led to more employment, less resource waste, and more livable human communities. It is our expectation that this kind of "appropriate technology" has an increasingly important role to play in the lives of all the people of California and we intend to give it space, resources, and direction.

An Introduction and a History
National Center for Appropriate Technology

Appropriate Technology: Economics as if People Mattered

When looking for the origins of appropriate technology, most point to the book *Small Is Beautiful: Economics as if People Mattered* by E. F. Schumacher. In this book, Schumacher, a British economist, critiques traditional economics which have put the world and its very limited

---

Excerpted from National Center for Appropriate Technology, "An Introduction and a History," Butte, MT, undated.

resources on a "collision course." He suggests instead an economics of permanence, one which will result in a "profound reorientation of science and technology."

Schumacher provides examples that include agricultural methods which are biologically sound and build up soil fertility. In industry, he calls for the evolution of small-scale technology which is non-violent (that is, it does not destroy the environment) and has "a human face," allowing individuals to work with dignity and satisfaction.

In this approach to technological development, process is as important as the technology itself. Schumacher is concerned with a world of diminishing resources, but he is just as concerned that modern techno-logy has dehumanized work, "making it a merely mechanical activity."

This approach led to what Schumacher calls "intermediate technol-ogy," his way of distinguishing between high technology (or "the super technology of the rich") and the primitive technology of the past. He also refers to it as self-help technology, democratic technology, and technology with a human face. As he explains it, "any third-rate engineer or researcher can increase complexity; but it takes a certain flair of real insight to make things simple again."

Schumacher applied his principles in developing countries, by found-ing the Intermediate Technology Development Group in London. This group promotes development using technologies which are "cheap enough so that they are accessible to virtually everyone; suitable for small-scale application; and compatible for man's need for creativity." So, instead of introducing diesel generators in the Pacific Islands, for example, where residents, who cannot afford to use or maintain them are forced to become dependent on outside resources, sustainable alternat-ives are encouraged, such as solar water heating, photovoltaics, and wind generators.

The need is clear in developing countries to wisely use limited resources and small-scale technologies, but how do these criteria fit into a resource-abundant society such as ours?

Appropriate Technologies: an American Perspective

During the oil embargo of 1973–74, Americans were rudely awakened. Oil, which had been cheap and abundant, and had fueled economic development and an affluent life-style, was unexpectedly turned off.

Suddenly, Americans were faced with shortages and long lines at the gas pump.

Then President Carter responded by initiating several energy conser-vation measures including a weatherization program for low-income housing which was carried out through the Community Services Administration (CSA).

However, despite a handsome budget and genuine interest on the part of Community Action Agencies who were assigned the work, little was known about how to apply weatherization technologies in low-income neighborhoods. And, to compound the problem, what was "appropriate" for one application might be inappropriate in another.

It also became clear that although billions of dollars were being spent to develop high-technology solutions to the energy crisis, little was being dedicated to research, develop, and implement small-scale technologies which could directly address the energy needs of the poor.

In 1974, a one-and-a-half day meeting on solar and other alternative energy sources was held in Washington, DC. Energy leaders from around the country attended, including Dr Jerry Plunkett, who was to become the Director of the Magnetohydrodynamics (MHD) facility in Butte (MHD is a high-technology coal conversion technology which was enthusiastically supported by former Montana US Senator, Mike Mansfield).

At this and subsequent meetings, it was decided that inexpensive, non-energy intensive technologies should be developed to help low-income communities through the energy crisis. What was needed was a mechanism or organization that would work with Community Action Agencies around the country to develop appropriate technologies for low-income communities.

Having already established a relationship with Senator Mansfield while developing the MHD Institute in Butte, Dr. Plunkett convinced the Senator to support a bill to fund a national center for appropriate technology. The center would, for the first time, develop technologies as a way to combat poverty.

In 1975 and 1976, language was included in the Appropriations Reports which supported such a center under the Community Services Administration. In June 1975, an initial planning grant was issued by CSA to explore:

1   the potential benefits to be derived from encouraging the development of technologies appropriate to the needs of the poor;
2   the different methods which might be effective in disseminating such information;
3   the advantages or disadvantages of a single national center compared to regional centers;
4   the relationship of such a center or centers to the community action network and the CSA administrative structure.

In September 1976, a proposal for the National Center for Appropriate Technology was submitted to the Community Services Administration and a grant of $3,086,546 was approved for Fiscal Year 1977.

The CSA Years: 1977–1981

Appropriate technology can mean many things to many people, partly because by definition it involves the idea that a technology "appropriate" to one set of circumstances is not necessarily appropriate for another.

When NCAT was organized, the concept of appropriate technology was narrowed to technologies – and processes – that are appropriate to the resources and needs of low-income communities. It was in this context that NCAT outlined the following profile of appropriate technologies:

- simple to apply.
- not capital intensive.
- not energy intensive (requiring little non-renewable energy to do, build, or maintain).
- use local resources and labor.
- nurture the environment and human health.

Using these criteria, the goal was for NCAT to "help low-income communities find better ways to do things that will improve the quality of life, and that will be doable with the skills and resources at hand. This will involve problem identification and information sharing, problem solving and research and development, and the support of local testing and demonstrations in the communities themselves."

Because one of the biggest concerns to low-income people at the time was the energy crisis, NCAT agreed to dedicate the first year of its program to the research and development of energy-related technologies to help the poor, and to provide technical assistance to the CSA Weatherization Project. The initial program included three areas:

1   Information exchange, outreach, education and technical assistance, where NCAT staff met with community action leaders, identifying local needs.
2   Research, development, and technical support of technologies identified as a result of this information exchange.
3   A grants program for technology demonstrations that included technical support and evaluation.

From 1977 to 1981, NCAT funded 370 appropriate technology demonstration projects, held more than 50 hands-on workshops and training
sessions for community action leaders and low-income people, and
published over 100 technical and consumer publications.

Although the main focus of the program was on renewable energy and
conservation, NCAT also worked on housing issues, food production,
transportation, economic development, and jobs.

Solar Energy Research: Making Solar after the Nuclear Model?

Allen L. Hammond and William D. Metz

A point about solar energy that government planners seem to have
trouble grasping is that it is fundamentally different from other energy
sources. Solar energy is democratic. It falls on everyone and can be put
to use by individuals and small groups of people. The public enthusiasm
for solar is perhaps as much a reflection of this unusual accessibility as it
is a vote for the environmental kindliness and inherent renewability of
energy from the sun.

But the federal program to develop new energy technology is giving
only belated recognition to solar energy's special characteristics. Despite
the diffuse nature of the resource, the research program has emphasized
large central stations to produce solar electricity in some distant future
and has largely ignored small solar devices for producing on-site power –
an approach one critic describes as "creating solar technologies in the
image of nuclear power." The program contains virtually no significant
projects to develop solar energy as a source of fuels and only modest
efforts to exploit it as a source of heat. The massive engineering projects
designed by aerospace companies which dominate much of the program
seem to have in mind the existing utility industry – rather than individuals
or communities – as the ultimate consumer of solar energy equipment.

One consequence of this R & D emphasis on large-scale, long-range
systems is to distort economic and policy assessments of solar energy
based on the current program, both within the Energy Research and
Development Administration (ERDA) and in higher levels of the

Taken from "Solar Energy Research: Making Solar after the Nuclear Model?" *Science*,
vol. 197, July 15, 1977, pp. 241–4. © 1977 *Science*.

government. Indeed, the potential of solar energy is still regarded with skepticism by many government energy officials and publicly discounted by spokesmen for oil and electric utility companies. Funds for solar research are leveling off, because of cuts made by the outgoing Ford Administration and confirmed, with minor overall changes but some shift in emphasis, by the Carter Administration. Agency officials concede that even the present federal program – representing an investment less than one-half of that for new coal technologies and a small fraction of that committed to the nuclear field – has survived only because of the immense popular appeal of solar energy and consequent pressure from Congress.

In contrast to this official skepticism is the virtual explosion of optimism and activity elsewhere. Dozens of pieces of proposed solar legislation and hundreds of companies now manufacturing solar components reflect this interest. The number of solar-heated houses built in the United States has doubled approximately every 8 months since 1973, and the rate shows no signs of slackening. The rapid buildup of a fledgling industry has been matched or even exceeded by a staggering rate of technical innovation in designs for solar equipment and in research on advanced methods for capturing and using solar energy. Measured by the number of new ideas or the rate of progress, solar energy has become the hottest property and the most sought-after action in the energy field. The burden of criticism from the solar energy community and from independent analysts is that the federal program has lagged rather than led many of these developments and that it has directed its research toward goals that betray a lack of understanding of the solar resource.

Coming to Grips with Solar

The government's difficulty in coming to grips with solar energy is understandable because the solar program was born, in an institutional sense, only about 5 years ago. The early work on solar energy was scattered among various government agencies, but much of it was an outgrowth of the National Aeronautics and Space Administration (NASA) effort to find practical spin-offs from space technology. After the 1969 Apollo moon landings, four different NASA labs began to do modest amounts of solar energy research. In 1972 the National Science Foundation (NSF) became the lead agency for solar energy research, which was funded at only $2 million per year. Many of the early program managers came from NASA and much of the contracted research went to aerospace companies.

In early 1975, all the solar research programs were shifted from the NSF, which has not been organized for commercial technology development, to the newly formed Energy Research and Development Administration, where solar was cast into competition with the nuclear breeder, the government's newly invigorated coal program, and the growing program for fusion. In its first 2 years the ERDA solar program was greatly understaffed and overworked – at one time 60 percent of the mail for the entire agency concerned solar energy. But in spite of institutional handicaps, the program grew rapidly because Congress authorized large increases in the solar research budget – as much as 80 percent above what the agency officially requested.

The program under ERDA moved into a mode of design, construction, and testing of various types of solar power pilot plants on an aggressive timetable. Feeling pressure to build up the solar program rapidly, ERDA delegated a large – some critics would say dominant – role to its national laboratories and to various NASA laboratories. The different subprograms were evaluated in a series of "mission analysis" studies, largely performed by aerospace contractors, and new priorities were set. Much of the evaluation was based on the capability of various solar technologies to approach base-load electric power supply – under the assumption that anything else would fall short of a major contribution. During this crucial period of solidification, the program had no regular review by an outside advisory board and there were no congressional oversight hearings. One of the strongest outside influences on the shape of the program, according to well-informed observers, was the utility industry.

Today, government solar research is a $290 million effort spread among four subprograms for electric applications, one for fuels, and two for heating, cooling, and related direct applications, with a professional staff of about 70 persons. In fiscal 1978, the program recommended by the Carter Administration will grow only modestly to $320 million. Because the various solar technologies are generally unrelated to each other, there is not a great deal of overlap between the research bases needed for the subprograms. The result is that the different solar options are at an even greater disadvantage vis-à-vis other energy programs than the total solar research budget would indicate.

The largest allotment of ERDA funds and staff resources has been for solar electric technologies. The concept which the utility's research arm – the Electric Power Research Institute – sees as the most likely candidate for central electricity generation is the power tower, a system with a boiler on a high tower heated by the sunlight reflected from a field of hundreds or thousands of sun-following mirrors. The power tower with its related solar thermal systems is still the leading subprogram in dollar priority – $79 million in fiscal 1977. Next is research on photovoltaic power systems – an effort to develop low-cost versions of the silicon cells used on space satellites for converting sunlight directly to electricity. Wind-power research, although it is the solar electric technology closest to being economically competitive, receives only about 8 percent of the solar budget. Approximately 5 percent goes to develop methods of extracting energy from the small temperature differences between surface and deep seawater – a concept usually referred to as OTEC (ocean thermal energy conversion) and conceived to produce electricity or perhaps an energy-intensive chemical in a huge floating plant that would provide about 200 megawatts of power. Still less money presently goes to the solar resource that could be most versatile of all – plant matter or biomass, which can be converted into either heat, fuels, or electricity. ERDA officials are generally agreed that biomass is one area in which they have yet to get a strong and coherent program under way.

The solar heating and cooling subprogram is funded at $86 million at present and $96 million in the fiscal 1978 budget. Solar home and hot water heating is nearly competitive in some areas of the country already. However, the ERDA program has paid little attention before now to the benefits of passive solar heating – the capture of solar heat that can be achieved from a well-sealed south-facing window as opposed to a roof-top solar collector used with a water or airflow system to carry the heat downstairs. Such systems are now widely thought to be capable of filling a large fraction of the winter heating needs in many areas at costs generally less than those of active systems.

As the Carter Administration prepares to shift energy research to yet another agency – the proposed Department of Energy – solar energy is still in search of a proper institutional home. Noting that skepticism of the solar program is one of the proper functions of ERDA's management, Henry Marvin, solar program director, nevertheless says that the program has been subject to tight controls by the agency's upper echelons and by the Office of Management and Budget. In his words, "Congress has been the corrective factor" in the growth of the program. According to Marvin, the solar program now has all the money it needs, "but we are still somewhat staff limited and travel-money limited – that has been the mechanism of OMB control." He foresees a program that may have already reached its broadest extent and will focus more narrowly as early decisions are made about solar hardware development projects in 1978 to 1981 and successful technologies are transferred to private industry.

Marvin is credited by several observers with having sought to limit the role in the program of the national laboratories – which, he says, "are not natural stopping places" enroute to developing commercial technologies

– and with having managed the program competently within the guidelines set by the agency.

Centralized versus On-site Solar

But critics believe those guidelines still reflect the narrow set of preconceptions with which the program began. One of these preconceptions is the preferred role of centralized energy systems. Several pieces of evidence suggest that the ERDA program has given inadequate attention to the issue of the appropriate scale for solar technologies and, in so doing, has failed to exploit the most promising characteristic of solar systems. A report recently issued by the Congressional Office of Technology Assessment (OTA), for example, points out that federal research on electric generating equipment of all kinds has been focused almost exclusively on a centralized approach and has neglected what OTA sees as a significant potential for on-site power production. The report – one of the most comprehensive studies of emerging solar technologies yet made – concludes that "devices having an output as small as a few kilowatts can be made as efficient as larger devices" and that on-site solar systems capable of generating electricity at prices competitive with those charged by utilities may be available "within 10 to 15 years." "Onsite solar energy," the report declares, "must be regarded as an important option."

The solar thermal subprogram provides an instance of how ERDA's choices of scale were established. Initially, the subprogram was conceived of exclusively in terms of central power stations, as large as possible. Charles Grosskreutz, an analyst with the engineering firm of Black and Veatch during the period when it was involved in the initial program analysis of power towers for ERDA, says that "everyone started by considering a 1000 megawatt size and quickly scaled it down to about 100 megawatts" when it became clear that the tower height and the land acquisition problem were impractical for the larger sizes. "To my knowledge," he says, "there are no good studies of the optimum size of these facilities." Little serious consideration appears to have been given to solar thermal generating facilities in conjunction with community-scale energy systems or biomass fuel refineries – applications for which the optimum size, according to Princeton University physicists Robert Williams and Frank von Hippel, will probably be much less than 10 megawatts. According to Marvin at ERDA, "it may well be that 10 megawatts is the unit size for the power tower – we used 100 megawatts for our calculations."

Likewise, the wind-power program, according to early program documents, did not look carefully at the prospects for improved versions of small wind turbines for distributed applications, or at the potential economies of mass production that might apply to small devices but not to large ones. Instead, the program plunged ahead to build a large, 100-kilowatt prototype as a first step toward a commercial size conceived to be as large as possible with the materials available – 1.5 to 2 megawatts.

Williams and his colleagues point out that the ERDA solar program throughout concentrates its main efforts on the largest and smallest scales of energy production, but they contend that an intermediate size may turn out to be the natural scale for many solar technologies. Their analysis points to community-size systems, equivalent to a few hundred or a few thousand houses, as the most cost-efficient, in that they would allow storage of solar energy on an annual basis – something impractical for an individual house – and would also allow the coproduction of solar heat and electricity in a manner that would be impractical for large central power plants.

Other independent analyses have come to similar conclusions. The noted British radio astronomer Martin Ryle, in a study of the applicability of solar energy to that country, concludes that a distributed network of small wind turbines provides the best match of potential supply to demand and would be competitive with coal-fired or nuclear generating stations. Ryle concluded that windpower, used with storage systems, could provide a substantial part of the power needs of the British Isles.

Another criticism of the solar program is that its management has been unnecessarily restrictive. During the last $2\frac{1}{2}$ years, while ERDA has directed the program, it has been guided by a management philosophy of "aggressive sequential" development. In practice, this has meant a policy of giving priority to one solar technology in each subprogram, such as the power tower in the solar thermal program, and pushing it to quickly develop hardware and test its feasibility. What the policy has ruled out – reportedly because of skepticism from the agency leadership and budget-cutting by the Office of Management and Budget – is the parallel development of competing concepts. It is, of course, possible that the best candidates were not chosen initially, but nevertheless a whole solar subprogram could be phased out because of poor performance by an ill-advised solar concept. In particular, features such as scale and type of application have been heavily influenced by the original choices for development, and there is considerable danger that values derived from those choices will be the ones on which engineering and economic evaluations of future support will be made. It is just such considerations that lead environmentalists to make the charge that solar energy is being "set up" to fail.

Commenting on the desirability of pursuing parallel concepts, Marvin says that "it is not clear that we would not be more productive if we could pursue multiple paths." But he believes that it would be disruptive, if not politically impossible, to stop existing programs. He says he has attempted to correct what may be imbalances by bringing in a new group of managers (two of whom just arrived this month), and by supporting some of the neglected options as secondary, follow-on efforts when the budget allows. For instance, the fiscal 1978 budget includes $8 million for small-scale windmills. Marvin notes, however, that "it doesn't gain us time lost."

Another problem with the solar program has been lack of flexibility, leading to too little integration of different solar technologies with each other and with the energy needs they might ultimately satisfy. Storage is a problem with many solar systems, but the program has given little attention to applications in which biomass fuels would provide the storage element, or in which the need for storage is obviated by using solar energy in conjunction with another energy source. Solar-coal and solar-hydroelectric systems offer tantalizing possibilities for combinations that could approach around-the-clock power, and there is some evidence that direct solar energy and wind energy might complement each other well. Little attention has been given to on-site application of photovoltaic and solar-thermal devices, in which the utility grid could be used as a buffer and thus storage would not be required. In addition, a generally acknowledged problem with the ERDA program is that its sharply divided subprogram structure has limited the development of systems that serve two purposes at once, such as total energy systems that produce both heat and electricity with a considerable improvement over the efficiency of single-purpose systems. The program has only belatedly begun to look at projects that do not fall into any of the predefined categories, such as solar irrigation, which ERDA developed no sooner than did the state of Guanajuato, Mexico.

The organizational structure of the energy agency, moreover, appears to be at cross-purposes with many novel or noncentralized applications. The solar energy division, for example, is effectively prohibited from working on community-scale solar systems because the agency management has decreed community-oriented projects to be in the domain of the conservation directorate.

Cost is the stumbling block most often cited by solar skeptics, and there is no doubt that few of the solar options are competitive today. But current cost estimates are almost certainly deceptive, in the absence of a real market. Furthermore, no one really knows what the costs of small-scale systems will be because so little research has been done on them. The conventional wisdom at the solar program planning office is that, compared to electricity at current prices, wind generators are competitive today or within a factor of 2 of being competitive, biomass fuels are a factor of 2 to 4 away from a competitive price, ocean thermal power systems a factor of 4 to 5, power towers a factor of 5 to 10, and photovoltaics a factor of 20 to 40 away. The opportunities for price reduction among these different technologies are controlled by quite different factors, however. Even the technologies for which a market does exist – hot water heating, for example – do not yet benefit from the kinds of implicit subsidies enjoyed by most other energy sources or the advantages of mass production by a well-established industry.

Probably no question about solar energy is more controversial than whether it can become a major energy source in the near term or should be regarded (and funded) as a limited, long-range option. Assessments of this question tend to get swept up into what has become a highly polarized debate between environmental advocates and the defenders of coal and nuclear power – a debate whose terms are more nearly philosophical or ethical than economic. The one view holds that a transition to a predominantly solar economy is not only feasible but *necessary* – to avert climatic disaster from the buildup of carbon dioxide that would accompany massive use of coal, and to prevent the danger of nuclear warfare attendant on the proliferation of the plutonium economy. The other dismisses solar energy and holds that coal and nuclear are essential on the grounds that even if costs were to drop dramatically, it would still be many decades before enough solar-heated houses and solar power stations could be built to make any dent in this country's huge and growing appetite for energy.

But these tactical positions obscure a number of things that tend to argue the importance of solar energy on purely economic grounds, as well as some substantial problems. One of the key problems is that solar equipment tends to be capital-intensive, with high initial costs that are a deterrent to consumers unaccustomed to making decisions on a life-cycle basis. Another is that many existing institutional arrangements, from building codes to utility rate structures to federal tax policies, discriminate against unconventional energy sources. But some institutional barriers are being removed by legislation, and the prices of many solar components are already dropping sharply in response to steadily growing demand. It seems evident that the growth of distributed solar systems, for which equipment can be mass-produced, can be far more rapid than the growth of centralized power plants, which must be laboriously assembled in the field. Frost and Sullivan, a respected market research firm, predicts that 2.5 million US homes will be solar heated by 1985. The government itself may become a major market for solar energy – a Department of Defense report done for the Federal Energy

Administration estimates that a DOD market for up to 100 megawatts of photovoltaic devices a year may exist at the prices expected to prevail in the early 1980s.

Political fortunes may also play a role in determining the short- or long-term impact. Solar energy fared badly under a Republican administration. President Ford had many opportunities to attend solar project ribbon cuttings but did not do so. Under his administration, the OMB strenuously opposed and nearly gutted the major short-term elements of the government's solar energy program – the demonstration projects for solar heating. ERDA appealed to President Ford but, according to one observer, had the misfortune to argue its case during a week in which Ford was preoccupied with the Angolan crisis. In any case, the OMB position largely prevailed – a circumstance that apparently contributed substantially to the resignation of ERDA assistant administrator John Teem – and the proposed demonstration program, modest though it was, was drastically cut back.

The government program is having some effect – ERDA's work on photovoltaics and wind has stimulated some private investment. And quite apart from the government's program there appears to be a remarkable amount of momentum in solar thermal devices, wood burning stoves and boilers, and other components of a solar energy industry.

After 5 years of rapid but uneven development, solar energy is in need of reassessment. The present federal program has been as much the product of institutional happenstance and various technical predilections as it has been the product of coherent planning. In a broader perspective, the government policy under Republican administrations characterized solar energy as a long-term option comparable to fusion and the breeder, but in fact it has little in common with these potential leviathans. Solar technology is more diverse, and even the most difficult technologies, such as photovoltaics, may be closer to commercial realization. Many solar technologies already work, even though the best designs have not been found, and they are already facing the economic challenges that other long-range options have yet to confront. It is arguably time to reconsider solar priorities and ask whether the distribution of research resources among nuclear, fossil, and solar options reflects a rational policy.

Further Reading

Butti, Ken, and John Perlin. *A Golden Thread: 2500 Years of Solar Architecture and Technology.* Palo Alto, CA: Cheshire Books, 1980.

Jackson, Wes, Wendell Berry and Bruce Coleman, eds. *Meeting the Expectations of the Land: Essays in Sustainable Agriculture and Stewardship*. San Francisco: North Point Books, 1984.

Lerner, Steve. *Eco-pioneers: Practical Visionaries Solving Today's Environmental Problems*. Cambridge, MA: MIT Press, 1997.

Mills, Stephanie, ed. *Turning Away from Technology: a New Vision for the 21st Century*. San Francisco: Sierra Club Books, 1997.

10

Toward Technoliteracy

1884	Herman Hollerith applies for patent for an "electrical enumerating mechanism" using punch cards.
1945	ENIAC computer completed at University of Pennsylvania.
1945–53	MIT builds Whirlwind, a digital computer.
1949	Whirlwind becomes prototype for SAGE, an air-defense computer weighing 250 tons.
1968	HAL stars in the film *2001: a Space Odyssey*
1969	Research and development begins on Pentagon's ARPAnet.
1971	Article in *Esquire* alerts public to the "phone phreaks."
1972	ARPAnet publicly demonstrated.
1976	Steve Jobs and Stephen Wozniac start Apple Computer.

Introduction

This concluding article is an attempt by Andrew Ross to sketch a path toward what he calls "technoliteracy," a kind of understanding that will allow us "to make a historical opportunity out of a historical necessity." Comparing hackers and the technology of the "Information Age" with the hippies and "appropriate technologies" of the 1960s and 1970s, he insists that what has emerged is "the uneven result of cultural struggles over values and meanings." Importantly, he rejects any easy recourse to notions of technological determinism, and asserts that the "ideological or interpretive dimension of technology as culture" is one that "can and must be used and consumed in a variety of ways." In a society that is saturated with powerful technologies, it is imperative that we each take responsibility for being "technoliterate." Ross's manifesto shows us one way of doing that.

Hacking Away at the Counterculture
Andrew Ross

Ever since the viral attack engineered in November of 1988 by Cornell University hacker Robert Morris on the national network system Internet, which includes the Pentagon's ARPAnet data exchange network, the nation's high-tech ideologues and spin doctors have been locked in debate, trying to make ethical and economic sense of the event. The virus rapidly infected an estimated six thousand computers around the country, creating a scare that crowned an open season of viral hysteria in the media, in the course of which, according to the Computer Virus Industry Association in Santa Clara, California, the number of known viruses jumped from seven to thirty during 1988, and from three thousand infections in the first two months of that year to thirty thousand in the last two months. While it caused little in the way of data damage (some richly inflated initial estimates reckoned up to $100 million in downtime), the ramifications of the Internet virus have helped to generate a moral panic that has all but transformed everyday "computer culture."

Following the lead of the Defense Advance Research Projects Agency (DARPA) Computer Emergency Response Team at Carnegie-Mellon University, antivirus response centers were hastily put in place by government and defense agencies at the National Science Foundation, the Energy Department, NASA, and other sites. Plans were made to introduce a bill in Congress (the Computer Virus Eradication Act, to replace the 1986 Computer Fraud and Abuse Act, which pertained solely to government information) that would call for prison sentences of up to ten years for the "crime" of sophisticated hacking, and numerous government agencies have been involved in a proprietary fight over the creation of a proposed Center for Virus Control, modeled, of course, on Atlanta's Centers for Disease Control, notorious for its failure to respond adequately to the AIDS crisis.

Media commentary on the virus scare has run not so much tongue-in-cheek as hand-in-glove with the rhetoric of AIDS hysteria – the common use of terms like *killer virus* and *epidemic;* the focus on high-risk personal contact (virus infection, for the most part, is spread on

Taken from Andrew Ross, "Hacking Away at the Counterculture," in Constance Penley and Andrew Ross, eds, *Technoculture* (Minneapolis: University of Minnesota Press, 1991), pp. 107–34. © 1991 University of Minnesota Press.

personal computers, not mainframes); the obsession with defense, security, and immunity; and the climate of suspicion generated around communitarian acts of sharing. The underlying moral imperative being this: You can't trust your best friend's software any more than you can trust his or her bodily fluids – safe software or no software at all! Or, as Dennis Miller put it on *Saturday Night Live*, "Remember, when you connect with another computer, you're connecting to every computer that computer has ever connected to." This playful conceit struck a chord in the popular consciousness, even as it was perpetuated in such sober quarters as the Association for Computing Machinery, the president of which, in a controversial editorial titled "A Hygiene Lesson," drew comparisons not only with sexually transmitted diseases, but also with a cholera epidemic, and urged attention to "personal systems hygiene."[1] Some computer scientists who studied the symptomatic path of Morris's virus across Internet have pointed to its uneven effects upon different computer types and operating systems, and concluded that "there is a direct analogy with biological genetic diversity to be made."[2] The epidemiology of biological virus, and especially AIDS, research is being studied closely to help implement computer security plans, and, in these circles, the new witty discourse is laced with references to antigens, white blood cells, vaccinations, metabolic free radicals, and the like.

The form and content of more lurid articles like *Time*'s infamous (September 1988) story, "Invasion of the Data Snatchers," fully displayed the continuity of the media scare with those historical fears about bodily invasion, individual and national, that are often considered endemic to the paranoid style of American political culture.[3] Indeed, the rhetoric of computer culture, in common with the medical discourse of AIDS research, has fallen in line with the paranoid, strategic mode of Defense Department rhetoric. Each language-repertoire is obsessed with hostile threats to bodily and technological immune systems; every event is a ballistic maneuver in the game of microbiological war, where the governing metaphors are indiscriminately drawn from cellular genetics and cybernetics alike. As a counterpoint to the tongue-in-cheek artificial intelligence (AI) tradition of seeing humans as "information-exchanging environments," the imagined life of computers has taken on an organicist shape, now that they too are subject to cybernetic "sickness" or disease. So too the development of interrelated systems, such as Internet itself, has further added to the structural picture of an interdependent organism, whose component members, however autonomous, are all nonetheless affected by the "health" of each individual constituent. The growing interest among scientists in developing computer programs that will simulate the genetic behavior of living organisms (in which binary numbers act like genes) points to a future where the border between organic and artificial life is less and less distinct.

In keeping with the increasing use of biologically derived language to describe mutations in systems theory, conscious attempts to link the AIDS crisis with the information security crisis have pointed out that both kinds of virus, biological and electronic, take over the host cell/ program and clone their carrier genetic codes by instructing the hosts to make replicas of the viruses. Neither kind of virus, however, can replicate itself independently; they are pieces of code that attach themselves to other cells/programs – just as biological viruses need a host cell, computer viruses require a host program to activate them. The Internet virus was not, in fact, a virus, but a worm, a program that can run independently and therefore *appears* to have a life of its own. The worm replicates a full version of itself in programs and systems as it moves from one to another, masquerading as a legitimate user by guessing the user passwords of locked accounts. Because of this autonomous existence, the worm can be seen to behave as if it were an organism with some kind of purpose or teleology, and yet it has none. Its only "purpose" is to reproduce and infect. If the worm has no inbuilt antireplication code, or if the code is faulty, as was the case with the Internet worm, it will make already-infected computers repeatedly accept further replicas of itself, until their memories are clogged. A much quieter worm than that engineered by Morris would have moved more slowly, as one supposes a "worm" should, protecting itself from detection by ever more subtle camouflage, and propagating its cumulative effect of operative systems inertia over a much longer period of time.

In offering such descriptions, however, we must be wary of attributing a teleology/intentionality to worms and viruses that can be ascribed only, and, in most instances, speculatively, to their authors. There is no reason a cybernetic "worm" might be expected to behave in any fundamental way like a biological worm. So, too, the assumed intentionality of its author distinguishes the human-made cybernetic virus from the case of the biological virus, the effects of which are fated to be received and discussed in a language saturated with human-made structures and narratives of meaning and teleological purpose. Writing about the folkloric theologies of significance and explanatory justice (usually involving retribution) that have sprung up around the AIDS crisis, Judith Williamson has pointed to the radical implications of this collision between an intentionless virus and a meaning-filled culture:

> Nothing could be more meaningless than a virus. It has no point, no purpose, no plan; it is part of no scheme, carries no inherent significance. And yet nothing is harder for us to confront than the complete absence of

> meaning. By its very definition, meaninglessness cannot be articulated within our social language, which is a system *of* meaning: impossible to include, as an absence, it is also impossible to exclude – for meaninglessness isn't just the opposite of meaning, it is the end of meaning, and threatens the fragile structures by which we make sense of the world.[4]

No such judgment about meaninglessness applies to the computer security crisis. In contrast to HIV's lack of meaning or intentionality, the meaning of cybernetic viruses is always already replete with social significance. This meaning is related, first of all, to the author's local intention or motivation, whether psychic or fully social, whether wrought out of a mood of vengeance, a show of bravado or technical expertise, a commitment to a political act, or in anticipation of the profits that often accure from the victims' need to buy an antidote from the author. Beyond these local intentions, however, which are usually obscure or, as in the Morris case, quite inscrutable, there is an entire set of social and historical narratives that surround and are part of the "meaning" of the virus: the coded anarchist history of the youth hacker subculture; the militaristic environments of search-and-destroy warfare (a virus has two components – a carrier and a "warhead"), which, because of the historical development of computer technology, constitute the family values of information technoculture; the experimental research environments in which creative designers are encouraged to work; and the conflictual history of pure and applied ethics in the science and technology communities – to name just a few. A similar list could be drawn up to explain the widespread and varied *response* to computer viruses, from the amused concern of the cognoscenti to the hysteria of the casual user, and from the research community and the manufacturing industry to the morally aroused legislature and the mediated culture at large. Every one of these explanations and narratives is the result of social and cultural processes and values; consequently, there is very little about the virus itself that is "meaningless." Viruses can no more be seen as an objective, or necessary, result of the "objective" development of technological systems than technology in general can be seen as an objective, determining agent of social change.

For the sake of polemical economy, I would note that the cumulative effect of all the viral hysteria has been twofold. First, it has resulted in a windfall for software producers, now that users' blithe disregard for makers' copyright privileges has eroded in the face of the security panic. Used to fighting halfhearted rearguard actions against widespread piracy practices, or reluctantly acceding to buyers' desire for software unencumbered by top-heavy security features, software vendors are now profiting from the new public distrust of program copies. So too the explosion in security consciousness has hyper-stimulated the already fast growing sectors of the security system industry and the data encryption industry. In line with the new imperative for everything from "vaccinated" workstations to "sterilized" networks, it has created a brand-new market of viral vaccine vendors who will sell you the virus (a one-time only immunization shot) along with its antidote – with names like Flu Shot +, ViruSafe, Vaccinate, Disk Defender, Certus, Viral Alarm, Antidote, Virus Buster, Gatekeeper, Ongard, and Interferon. Few of the antidotes are very reliable, however, especially since they pose an irresistible intellectual challenge to hackers who can easily rewrite them in the form of ever more powerful viruses. Moreover, most corporate managers of computer systems and networks know that by far the great majority of their intentional security losses are a result of insider sabotage and monkeywrenching.

In short, the effects of the viruses have been a profitable clamping down on copyright delinquency and the generation of the need for entirely new industrial production of viral suppressors to contain the fallout. In this respect, it is easy to see that the appearance of viruses could hardly, in the long run, have benefited industry producers more. In the same vein, the networks that have been hardest hit by the security squeeze are not restricted-access military or corporate systems, but networks like Internet, set up on trust to facilitate the open academic exchange of data, information, and research, and watched over by its sponsor, DARPA. It has not escaped the notice of conspiracy theorists that the military intelligence community, obsessed with "electronic warfare," actually stood to learn a lot from the Internet virus; the virus effectively "pulsed the system," exposing the sociological behavior of the system in a crisis situation.[5]

The second effect of the virus crisis has been more overtly ideological. Virus-conscious fear and loathing have clearly fed into the paranoid climate of privatization that increasingly defines social identities in the new post-Fordist order. The result – a psychosocial closing of the ranks around fortified private spheres – runs directly counter to the ethic that we might think of as residing at the architectural heart of information technology. In its basic assembly structure, information technology is a technology of processing, copying, replication, and simulation, and therefore does not recognize the concept of private information property. What is now under threat is the rationality of a shareware culture, ushered in as the achievement of the hacker counterculture that pioneered the personal computer revolution in the early seventies against the grain of corporate planning.

There is another story to tell, however, about the emergence of the virus scare as a profitable ideological moment, and it is the story of how teenage hacking has come to be defined increasingly as a potential threat to normative educational ethics and national security alike. The story of the creation of this "social menace" is central to the ongoing attempts to rewrite property law in order to contain the effects of the new information technologies that, because of their blindness to the copyrighting of intellectual property, have transformed the way in which modern power is exercised and maintained. Consequently, a deviant social class or group has been defined and categorized as "enemies of the state" to help rationalize a general law-and-order clampdown on free and open information exchange. Teenage hackers' homes are now habitually raided by sheriffs and FBI agents using strong-arm tactics, and jail sentences are becoming a common punishment. Operation Sundevil, a nationwide Secret Service operation conducted in the spring of 1990, involving hundreds of agents in fourteen cities, is the most recently publicized of the hacker raids that have produced several arrests and seizures of thousands of disks and address lists in the last two years.

In one of the many harshly punitive prosecutions against hackers in recent years, a judge went so far as to describe "bulletin boards" as "hi-tech street gangs." The editors of *2600*, the magazine that publishes information about system entry and exploration indispensable to the hacking community, have pointed out that any single invasive act, such as trespass, that involves the use of computers is considered today to be infinitely more criminal than a similar act undertaken without computers.[6] To use computers to execute pranks, raids, fraud, or theft is to incur automatically the full repressive wrath of judges urged on by the moral panic created around hacking feats over the last two decades. Indeed, there is a strong body of pressure groups pushing for new criminal legislation that will define "crimes with computers" as a special category of crime, deserving "extraordinary" sentences and punitive measures. Over that same space of time, the term *hacker* has lost its semantic link with the journalistic *hack*, suggesting a professional toiler who uses unorthodox methods. So too its increasingly criminal connotation today has displaced the more innocuous, amateur mischief-maker-cum-media-star role reserved for hackers until a few years ago.

In response to the gathering vigor of this "war on hackers," the most common defenses of hacking can be presented on a spectrum that runs from the appeasement or accommodation of corporate interests to drawing up blueprints for cultural revolution. (a) Hacking performs a benign industrial service of uncovering security deficiencies and design flaws. (b) Hacking, as an experimental, free-form research activity, has been responsible for many of the most progressive developments in software development. (c) Hacking, when not purely recreational, is an elite educational practice that reflects the ways in which the development of high technology has outpaced orthodox forms of institutional education. (d) Hacking is an important form of watchdog counterresponse to the use of surveillance technology and data gathering by the state, and to the increasingly monolithic communications power of giant corporations. (e) Hacking, as guerrilla know-how, is essential to the task of maintaining fronts of cultural resistance and stocks of oppositional knowledge as a hedge against a technofascist future. With all of these and other arguments in mind, it is easy to see how the social and cultural *management* of hacker activities has become a complex process that involves state policy and legislation at the highest levels. In this respect, the virus scare has become an especially convenient vehicle for obtaining public and popular consent for new legislative measures and new powers of investigation for the FBI.

Consequently, certain celebrity hackers have been quick to play down the zeal with which they pursued their earlier hacking feats, while reinforcing the *deviant* category of "technological hooliganism" reserved by moralizing pundits for "dark-side" hacking. Hugo Cornwall, British author of the best-selling *Hacker's Handbook*, presents a Little England view of the hacker as a harmless fresh-air enthusiast who "visits advanced computers as a polite country rambler might walk across picturesque fields." The owners of these properties are like "farmers who don't mind careful ramblers." Cornwall notes that "lovers of fresh-air walks obey the Country Code, involving such items as closing gates behind one and avoiding damage to crops and livestock" and suggests that a similar code ought to "guide your rambles into other people's computers; the safest thing to do is simply browse, enjoy and learn." By contrast, any rambler who "ventured across a field guarded by barbed wire and dotted with notices warning about the Official Secrets Act would deserve most that happened thereafter."[7] Cornwall's quaint perspective on hacking has a certain "native charm," but some might think that this beguiling picture of patchwork-quilt fields and benign gentlemen farmers glosses over the long bloody history of power exercised through feudal and postfeudal land economy in England, while it is barely suggestive of the new fiefdoms, transnational estates, dependencies, and principalities carved out of today's global information order by vast corporations capable of bypassing the laws and territorial borders of sovereign nation-states. In general, this analogy with "trespass" laws, which compares hacking to breaking and entering other people's homes, restricts the debate to questions about privacy, property, possessive individualism, and, at best, the excesses of state surveillance, while it closes off any examination of the activities of the corporate owners and institutional sponsors of information technology (the almost exclusive "target" of most hackers).

Cornwall himself has joined the lucrative ranks of ex-hackers who either work for computer security firms or write books about security for the eyes of worried corporate managers. A different, though related, genre is that of the penitent hacker's "confession," produced for an audience thrilled by tales of high-stakes adventure at the keyboard, but written in the form of a computer security handbook. The best example of the "I Was a Teenage Hacker" genre is Bill (aka "The Cracker") Landreth's *Out of the Inner Circle: The True Story of a Computer Intruder Capable of Cracking the Nation's Most Secure Computer Systems*, a book about "people who can't 'just say no' to computers." In full complicity with the deviant picture of the hacker as "public enemy," Landreth recirculates every official and media cliché about subversive conspiratorial elites by recounting the putative exploits of a high-level hackers' guild called the Inner Circle. The author himself is presented in the book as a former keyboard junkie who now praises the law for having made a good moral example of him:

> If you are wondering what I am like, I can tell you the same things I told the judge in federal court: Although it may not seem like it, I am pretty much a normal American teenager. I don't drink, smoke or take drugs. I don't steal, assault people, or vandalize property. The only way in which I am really different from most people is in my fascination with the ways and means of learning about computers that don't belong to me.[8]

Sentenced in 1984 to three years' probation, during which time he was obliged to finish his high school education and go to college, Landreth concludes: "I think the sentence is very fair, and I already know what my major will be." As an aberrant sequel to the book's contrite conclusion, however, Landreth vanished in 1986, violating his probation, only to face later a stiff five-year jail sentence – a sorry victim, no doubt, of the recent crackdown.

Cyber-Counterculture?

At the core of Steven Levy's best-seller *Hackers* (1984) is the argument that the hacker ethic, first articulated in the 1950s among the famous MIT students who developed multiple-access user systems, is libertarian and crypto-anarchist in its right-to-know principles and its advocacy of decentralized technology. This hacker ethic, which has remained the preserve of a youth culture for the most part, asserts the basic right of users to free access to all information. It is a principled attempt, in other words, to challenge the tendency to use technology to form information elites. Consequently, hacker activities were presented in the eighties as a romantic countercultural tendency, celebrated by critical journalists like John Markoff of the *New York Times*, by Stewart Brand of *Whole Earth Catalog* fame, and by New Age gurus like Timothy Leary in the flamboyant *Reality Hackers*. Fueled by sensational stories about phone phreaks like Joe Egressia (the blind eight-year-old who discovered the tone signal of the phone company by whistling) and Captain Crunch, groups like the Milwaukee 414s, the Los Angeles ARPAnet hackers, the SPAN Data Travellers, the Chaos Computer Club of Hamburg, the British Prestel hackers, *2600*'s BBS, "The Private Sector," and others, the dominant media representation of the hacker came to be that of the "rebel with a modem," to use Markoff's term, at least until the more recent "war on hackers" began to shape media coverage.

On the one hand, this popular folk hero persona offered the romantic high profile of a maverick though nerdy cowboy whose fearless raids upon an impersonal "system" were perceived as a welcome tonic in the gray age of technocratic routine. On the other hand, he was something of a juvenile technodelinquent who hadn't yet learned the difference between right and wrong – a wayward figure whose technical brilliance and proficiency differentiated him nonetheless from, say, the maladjusted working-class JD streetcorner boy of the 1950s (hacker mythology, for the most part, has been almost exclusively white, masculine, and middle-class). One result of this media profile was a persistent infantilization of the hacker ethic – a way of trivializing its embryonic politics, however finally complicit with dominant technocratic imperatives or with entrepreneurial-libertarian ideology one perceives these politics to be. The second result was to reinforce, in the initial absence of coercive jail sentences, the high educational stakes of training the new technocratic elites to be responsible in their use of technology. Never, the given wisdom goes, has a creative elite of the future been so in need of the virtues of a liberal education steeped in Western ethics!

The full force of this lesson in computer ethics can be found laid out in the official Cornell University report on the Robert Morris affair. Members of the university commission set up to investigate the affair make it quite clear in their report that they recognize the student's academic brilliance. His hacking, moreover, is described as a "juvenile act" that had no "malicious intent" but that amounted, like plagiarism – the traditional academic heresy – to a dishonest transgression of other users' rights. (In recent years, the privacy movement within the information community – a movement mounted by liberals to protect civil rights against state gathering of information – has actually been taken up and used as a means of criminalizing hacker activities.) As for the consequences of this juvenile act, the report proposes an analogy that, in comparison with Cornwall's *mature* English country rambler, is thoroughly American, suburban, middle-class, and *juvenile*. Unleashing the Internet worm was like "the driving of a golf-cart on a rainy day through most houses in the neighborhood. The driver may have navigated carefully and broken no china, but it should have been obvious to the driver that the mud on the tires would soil the carpets and that the owners would later have to clean up the mess."[9]

In what stands out as a stiff reprimand for his alma mater, the report regrets that Morris was educated in an "ambivalent atmosphere" where he "received no clear guidance" about ethics from "his peers or mentors" (he went to Harvard!). But it reserves its loftiest academic contempt for the press, whose heroization of hackers has been so irresponsible, in the commission's opinion, as to cause even further damage to the standards of the computing profession; media exaggerations of the courage and technical sophistication of hackers "obscures the far more accomplished work of students who complete their graduate studies without public fanfare," and "who subject their work to the close scrutiny and evaluation of their peers, and not to the interpretations of the popular press."[10] In other words, this was an inside affair, to be assessed and judged by fellow professionals within an institution that reinforces its authority by means of internally self-regulating codes of professionalist ethics, but rarely addresses its ethical relationship to society as a whole (acceptance of defense grants and the like). Generally speaking, the report affirms the genteel liberal ideal that professionals should not need laws, rules, procedural guidelines, or fixed guarantees of safe and responsible conduct. Apprentice professionals ought to have acquired a good conscience by osmosis from a liberal education rather than from some specially prescribed course in ethics and technology.

The widespread attention commanded by the Cornell report (attention from the Association of Computing Machinery, among others) demonstrates the industry's interest in how the academy invokes liberal ethics in order to assist in the managing of the organization of the new specialized knowledge about information technology. Despite or, perhaps, because of the report's steadfast pledge to the virtues and ideals of a liberal education, it bears all the marks of a legitimation crisis inside (and outside) the academy surrounding the new and all-important category of computer professionalism. The increasingly specialized design knowledge demanded of computer professionals means that codes that go beyond the old professionalist separation of mental and practical skills are needed to manage the division that a hacker's functional talents call into question, between a purely mental pursuit and the pragmatic sphere of implementing knowledge in the real world. "Hacking" must then be designated as a strictly *amateur* practice; the tension, in hacking, between *interestedness* and *disinterestedness* is different from, and deficient in relation to, the proper balance demanded by professionalism. Alternately, hacking can be seen as the amateur flip side of the professional ideal – a disinterested love in the service of interested parties and institutions. In either case, it serves as an example of professionalism gone wrong, but not very wrong.

In common with the two responses to the virus scare described earlier – the profitable reaction of the computer industry and the self-empowering response of the legislature – the Cornell report shows how the academy uses a case like the Morris affair to strengthen its own sense of moral and cultural authority in the sphere of professionalism, particularly through its scornful indifference to and aloofness from the codes and judgments exercised by the media – its diabolic competitor in the field of knowledge. Indeed, for all the trumpeting about excesses of power and disrespect for the law of the land, the revival of ethics, in the business and science disciplines in the Ivy League and on Capitol Hill (both awash with ethical fervor in the post-Boesky and post-Reagan years), is little more than a weak liberal response to working flaws or adaptational lapses in the social logic of technocracy.

To complete the scenario of morality play example-making, however, we must also consider that Morris's father was chief scientist of the National Computer Security Center, the National Security Agency's public effort at safeguarding computer security. A brilliant programmer and code breaker in his own right, he had testified in Washington in 1983 about the need to deglamorize teenage hacking, comparing it to "stealing a car for the purpose of joyriding." In a further Oedipal irony, Morris Sr may have been one of the inventors, while at Bell Labs in the 1950s, of a computer game involving self-perpetuating programs that were a prototype of today's worms and viruses. Called Darwin, its principles were incorporated, in the 1980s, into a popular hacker game called Core War, in which autonomous "killer" programs fought each other to the death.

With the appearance, in the Morris affair, of a patricidal object who is also the Pentagon's guardian angel, we now have many of the classic components of countercultural cross-generational conflict. What I want to consider, however, is how and where this scenario differs from the definitive contours of such conflicts that we recognize as having been established in the sixties; how the Cornell hacker Morris's relation to, say, campus "occupations" today is different from that evoked by the famous image of armed black students emerging from a sit-in on the Cornell campus; how the relation to technological ethics differs from Andrew Kopkind's famous statement, "Morality begins at the end of a gun barrel," which accompanied the publication of the "do-it-yourself Molotov cocktail" design on the cover of a 1968 issue of the *New York*

Review of Books; or how hackers' prized potential access to the networks of military systems warfare differs from the prodigious Yippie feat of levitating the Pentagon building. It may be that, like the JD rebel without a cause of the fifties, the disaffiliated student dropout of the sixties, and the negationist punk of the seventies, the hacker of the eighties has come to serve as a visible public example of moral maladjustment, a hegemonic test case for redefining the dominant ethics in an advanced technocratic society. (Hence the need for each of these deviant figures to come in different versions – lumpen, radical chic, and Hollywood-style.)

What concerns me here, however, are the different conditions that exist today for recognizing countercultural expression and activism. Twenty years later, the technology of hacking and viral guerrilla warfare occupies a similar place in countercultural fantasy as the Molotov cocktail design once did. While such comparisons are not particularly sound, I do think they conveniently mark a shift in the relation of countercultural activity to technology, a shift in which a software-based technoculture, organized around outlawed libertarian principles about free access to information and communication, has come to replace a dissenting culture organized around the demonizing of abject hardware structures. Much, though not all, of the sixties counterculture was formed around what I have elsewhere called the *technology of folklore* – an expressive congeries of preindustrialist, agrarianist, Orientalist, anti-technological ideas, values, and social structures. By contrast, the cybernetic countercultures of the nineties are already being formed around the *folklore of technology* – mythical feats of survivalism and resistance in a data-rich world of virtual environments and posthuman bodies – which is where many of the SF- and technology-conscious youth cultures have been assembling in recent years.[11]

There is no doubt that this scenario makes countercultural activity more difficult to recognize and therefore to define as politically significant. It was much easier, in the sixties, to *identify* the salient features and symbolic power of a romantic preindustrialist cultural politics in an advanced technological society, especially when the destructive evidence of America's supertechnological invasion of Vietnam was being daily paraded in front of the public eye. However, in a society whose techno-political infrastructure depends increasingly upon greater surveillance and where foreign wars are seen through the lens of laser-guided smart bombs, cybernetic activism necessarily relies on a much more covert politics of identity, since access to closed systems requires discretion and dissimulation. Access to digital systems still requires only the authentication of a signature or pseudonym, not the identification of a real surveillable person, so there exists a crucial operative gap between authentication and identification. (As security systems move toward authenticating access through biological signatures – the biometric recording and measurement of physical characteristics such as palm or retinal prints, or vein patterns on the backs of hands – the hackers' staple method of systems entry through purloined passwords will be further challenged.) By the same token, cybernetic identity is never used up – it can be re-created, reassigned, and reconstructed with any number of different names and under different user accounts. Most hacks, or technocrimes, go unnoticed or unreported for fear of publicizing the vulnerability of corporate security systems, especially when the hacks are performed by disgruntled employees taking their vengeance on management. So too authoritative identification of any individual hacker, whenever it occurs, is often the result of accidental leads rather than systematic detection. For example, Captain Midnight, the video pirate who commandeered a satellite a few years ago to interrupt broadcast TV viewing, was traced only because a member of the public reported a suspicious conversation heard over a crossed telephone line.

Eschewing its core constituency among white males of the pre-professional-managerial class, the hacker community may be expanding its parameters outward. Hacking, for example, has become a feature of young adult novel genres for girls. The elitist class profile of the hacker prodigy as that of an undersocialized college nerd has become democratized and customized in recent years; it is no longer exclusively associated with institutionally acquired college expertise, and increasingly it dresses streetwise. In a recent article that documents the spread of the computer underground from college whiz kids to a broader youth subculture termed "cyberpunks," after the movement among SF novelists, the original hacker phone phreak Captain Crunch is described as lamenting the fact that the cyberculture is no longer an "elite" one, and that hacker-valid information is much easier to obtain these days.[12]

For the most part, however, the self-defined hacker underground, like many other protocountercultural tendencies, has been restricted to a privileged social milieu, further magnetized by the self-understanding of its members that they are the apprentice architects of a future dominated by knowledge, expertise, and "smartness," whether human or digital. Consequently, it is clear that the hacker cyberculture is not a dropout culture; its disaffiliation from a domestic parent culture is often manifest in activities that answer, directly or indirectly, to the legitimate needs of industrial R&D. For example, this hacker culture celebrates high productivity, maverick forms of creative work energy, and an obsessive identification with on-line endurance (and endorphin highs) – all qualities that are valorized by the entrepreneurial codes of silicon futurism. In a critique of the myth of the hacker-as-rebel, Dennis

Hayes debunks the political romance woven around the teenage hacker:

> They are typically white, upper-middle-class adolescents who have taken over the home computer (bought, subsidized, or tolerated by parents in the hope of cultivating computer literacy). Few are politically motivated although many express contempt for the "bureaucracies" that hamper their electronic journeys. Nearly all demand unfettered access to intricate and intriguing computer networks. In this, teenage hackers resemble an alienated shopping culture deprived of purchasing opportunities more than a terrorist network.[13]

While welcoming the sobriety of Hayes's critique, I am less willing to accept its assumptions about the political implications of hacker activities. Studies of youth subcultures (including those of a privileged middle-class formation) have taught us that the political meaning of certain forms of cultural "resistance" is notoriously difficult to read. These meanings are either highly coded or expressed indirectly through media – private peer languages, customized consumer styles, unorthodox leisure patterns, categories of insider knowledge and behavior – that have no fixed or inherent political significance. If cultural studies of this sort have proved anything, it is that the often symbolic, not wholly articulate, expressivity of a youth culture can seldom be translated directly into an articulate political philosophy. The significance of these cultures lies in their embryonic or *protopolitical* languages and technologies of opposition to dominant or parent systems of rules. If hackers lack a "cause," then they are certainly not the first youth culture to be characterized in this dismissive way. In particular, the left has suffered from the lack of a cultural politics capable of recognizing the power of cultural expressions that do not wear a mature political commitment on their sleeves.

So too the escalation of activism-in-the-professions in the last two decades has shown that it is a mistake to condemn the hacker impulse on account of its class constituency alone. To cede the "ability to know" on the grounds that elite groups will enjoy unjustly privileged access to technocratic knowledge is to cede too much of the future. Is it of no political significance at all that hackers' primary fantasies often involve the official computer systems of the police, armed forces, and defense and intelligence agencies? And that the rationale for their fantasies is unfailingly presented in the form of a defense of civil liberties against the threat of centralized intelligence and military activities? Or is all of this merely a symptom of an apprentice elite's fledgling will to masculine power? The activities of the Chinese student elite in the prodemocracy movement have shown that unforeseen shifts in the political climate can produce startling new configurations of power and resistance. After Tiananmen Square, Party leaders found it imprudent to purge those high-tech engineer and computer cadres who alone could guarantee the future of any planned modernization program. On the other hand, the authorities rested uneasy knowing that each cadre (among the most activist groups in the student movement) is a potential hacker who can have the run of the communications house if and when he or she wants.

On the other hand, I do agree with Hayes's perception that the media have pursued their romance with the hacker at the cost of under-reporting the much greater challenge posed to corporate employers by their employees. It is in the arena of conflicts between workers and management that most high-tech "sabotage" takes place. In the main-stream everyday life of office workers, mostly female, there is a wide-spread culture of unorganized sabotage that accounts for infinitely more computer downtime and information loss every year than is caused by destructive, "dark-side" hacking by celebrity cybernetic intruders. The sabotage, time theft, and strategic monkeywrenching deployed by office workers in their engineered electromagnetic attacks on data storage and operating systems might range from the planting of time or logic bombs to the discrete use of electromagnetic Tesla coils or simple bodily friction: "Good old static electricity discharged from the fingertips probably accounts for close to half the disks and computers wiped out or down every year."[14] More skilled operators, intent on evening a score with management, often utilize sophisticated hacking techniques. In many cases, a coherent networking culture exists among female console opera-tors, where, among other things, tips about strategies for slowing down the temporality of the work regime are circulated. While these threats from below are fully recognized in their boardrooms, corporations depen-dent upon digital business machines are obviously unwilling to advertise how acutely vulnerable they actually are to this kind of sabotage. It is easy to imagine how organized computer activism could hold such companies for ransom. As Hayes points out, however, it is more difficult to mobilize any kind of labor movement organized upon such premises:

> Many are prepared to publicly oppose the countless dark legacies of the computer age: "electronic sweatshops," military technology, employee surveillance, genotoxic water, and ozone depletion. Among those currently leading the opposition, however, it is apparently deemed "irresponsible" to recommend an active computerized resistance as a source of worker's power because it is perceived as a medium of employee crime and "terrorism."[15]

Processed World, the "magazine with a bad attitude," with which Hayes has been associated, is at the forefront of debating and circulating these questions among office workers, regularly tapping into the resentments borne out in on-the-job resistance.

While only a small number of computer users would recognize and include themselves under the label of "hacker," there are good reasons for extending the restricted definition of *hacking* down and across the caste hierarchy of systems analysts, designers, programmers, and operators to include all high-tech workers, no matter how inexpert, who can interrupt, upset, and redirect the smooth flow of structured communications that dictates their positions in the social networks of exchange and determines the pace of their work schedules. To put it in these terms, however, is not to offer any universal definition of hacker agency. There are many social agents, for example, in job locations who are dependent upon the hope of technological *reskilling*, and for whom sabotage or disruption of communicative rationality is of little use; for such people, definitions of hacking that are reconstructive, rather than deconstructive, are more appropriate. A good example is the crucial role of worker technoliteracy in the struggle of labor against automation and deskilling. When worker education classes in computer programming were discontinued by management at the Ford Rouge plant in Dearborn, Michigan, United Auto Workers members began to publish a newsletter called the *Amateur Computerist* to fill the gap. Among the columnists and correspondents in the magazine have been veterans of the Flint sit-down strikes who see a clear historical continuity between the problem of labor organization in the thirties and the problem of automation and deskilling today. Workers' computer literacy is seen as essential not only to the demystification of the computer and the reskilling of workers, but also to labor's capacity to intervene in decisions about new technologies that might result in shorter hours and thus in "work efficiency" rather than worker efficiency.

The three social locations I have mentioned above all express different class relations to technology: the location of an apprentice technical elite, conventionally associated with the term *hacking*; the location of the female high-tech office worker, involved in "sabotage"; and the location of the shop-floor worker, whose future depends on technological reskilling. All therefore exhibit different ways of *claiming back* time dictated and appropriated by technological processes, and of establishing some form of independent control over the work relation so determined by the new technologies. All, then, fall under a broad understanding of the politics involved in any extended description of hacker activities.

The Culture and Technology Question

Faced with these proliferating practices in the workplace, on the teenage cult fringe, and increasingly in mainstream entertainment, where, over the last five years, the cyberpunk sensibility in popular fiction, film, and television has caught the romance of the popular taste for the outlaw technology of human/machine interfaces, we are obliged, I think, to ask old kinds of questions about the new silicon order that the evangelists of information technology have been deliriously proclaiming for more than twenty years. The postindustrialists' picture of a world of freedom and abundance projects a bright millenarian future devoid of work drudgery and ecological degradation. This sunny social order, cybernetically wired up, is presented as an advanced evolutionary phase of society in accord with Enlightenment ideals of progress and rationality. By contrast, critics of this idealism see only a frightening advance in the technologies of social control, whose owners and sponsors are efficiently shaping a society, as Kevin Robins and Frank Webster put it, of "slaves without Athens" that is actually the inverse of the "Athens without slaves" promised by the silicon positivists.[16]

It is clear that one of the political features of the new post-Fordist order – economically marked by short-run production, diverse taste markets, flexible specialization, and product differentiation – is that the postindustrialists have managed to appropriate not only the utopian language and values of the alternative technology movements but also the Marxist discourse of the "withering away of the state" and the more compassionate vision of local, decentralized communications first espoused by the anarchist. It must be recognized that these are very popular themes and visions (advanced most publicly by Alvin Toffler and the neoliberal Atari Democrats, though also by leftist thinkers such as André Gortz, Rudolf Bahro, and Alain Touraine) – much more popular, for example, than the tradition of centralized technocratic planning espoused by the left under the Fordist model of mass production and consumption. Against the postindustrialists' millenarian picture of a postscarcity harmony, in which citizens enjoy decentralized access to free-flowing information, it is necessary, however, to emphasize how and where actually existing cybernetic capitalism presents a gross caricature of such a postscarcity society.

One of the stories told by the critical left about new cultural technologies is that of monolithic, panoptical social control, effortlessly achieved through a smooth, endlessly interlocking system of networks of surveillance. In this narrative, information technology is seen as the most despotic mode of domination yet, generating not just a revolution in capitalist production but also a revolution in living – "social Taylor-ism" – that touches all cultural and social spheres in the home and in the workplace. Through routine gathering of information about transac-tions, consumer preferences, and creditworthiness, a harvest of informa-tion about any individual's whereabouts and movements, tastes, desires, contacts, friends, associates, and patterns of work and recreation becomes available in the form of dossiers sold on the tradable informa-tion market, or is endlessly convertible into other forms of intelligence through computer matching. Advanced pattern recognition technologies facilitate the process of surveillance, while data encryption protects it from public accountability.

While the debate about privacy has triggered public consciousness about these excesses, the liberal discourse about ethics and damage control in which that debate has been conducted falls short of the more comprehensive analysis of social control and social management offered by left political economists. According to one Marxist analysis, information is seen as a new kind of commodity resource that marks a break with past modes of production and that is becoming the essential site of capital accumulation in the world economy. What happens, then, in the process by which information, gathered up by data scavenging in the transactional sphere, is systematically converted into intelligence? A surplus value is created for use elsewhere. This surplus information value is more than is needed for public surveillance; it is often informa-tion, or intelligence, culled from consumer polling or statistical analysis of transactional behavior, that has no immediate use in the process of routine public surveillance. Indeed, it is this surplus bureaucratic capital that is used for the purpose of forecasting social futures, and con-sequently applied to the task of managing the behavior of mass or aggregate units within those social futures. This surplus intelligence becomes the basis of a whole new industry of futures research that relies upon computer technology to simulate and forecast the shape, activity, and behavior of complex social systems. The result is a possible system of social management that far transcends the questions about surveil-lance that have been at the discursive center of the privacy debate.

To challenge further the idealists' vision of postindustrial light and magic, we need only look inside the semiconductor workplace itself, which is home to the most toxic chemicals known to man (and woman, especially since women of color often make up the majority of the microelectronics labor force), and where worker illness is measured not in quantities of blood spilled on the shop floor but in the less visible forms of chromosome damage, shrunken testicles, miscarriages, prema-ture deliveries, and severe birth defects. Semiconductor workers exhibit an occupational illness rate that by the late seventies was already three times higher than that of manufacturing workers, at least until the federal rules for recognizing and defining levels of injury were changed under the Reagan administration. Protection gear is designed to protect the product and the clean room from the workers, and not vice versa. Recently, immunological health problems have begun to appear that can be described only as a kind of chemically induced AIDS, rendering the T-cells dysfunctional rather than depleting them like virally induced AIDS. In addition to the extraordinarily high stress patterns of VDT operators in corporate offices, the use of keystroke software to monitor and pace office workers has become a routine part of job performance evaluation programs. Some 70 percent of corporations use electronic surveillance or other forms of quantitative monitoring of their workers. Every bodily movement can be checked and measured, especially trips to the toilet. Federal deregulation has meant that the limits of employee work space have shrunk, in some government offices, below that required by law for a two-hundred-pound laboratory pig. Critics of the labor process seem to have sound reasons to believe that rationalization and quantification are at last entering their most primitive phase.

These, then, are some of the features of that critical left position – or what is sometimes referred to as the "paranoid" position – on information technology, which imagines or constructs a totalizing, monolithic picture of systematic domination. While this story is often characterized as conspiracy theory, its targets – technorationality, bureaucratic capitalism – are usually too abstract to fit the picture of a social order planned and shaped by a small, conspiring group of centralized power elites.

Although I believe that this story, when told inside and outside the classroom, for example, is an indispensable form of "consciousness-raising," it is not always the best story to tell. While I am not comfortable with the "paranoid" labeling, I would argue that such narratives do little to discourage paranoia. The critical habit of finding unrelieved domination everywhere has certain consequences, one of which is to create a siege mentality, reinforcing the inertia, helplessness, and despair that such critiques set out to oppose in the first place. What follows is a politics that can speak only from a victim's position. And when knowledge about surveillance is presented as systematic and infallible, self-censoring is sure to follow. In the psychosocial climate of fear and phobia aroused by the virus scare, there is a responsibility not to be alarmist or to be scared, especially when, as I have argued, such moments are profitably seized upon by the sponsors of control technology. In short, the picture of a seamlessly panoptical network of surveillance may be the result of a rather undemocratic, not to mention unsocialist, way of thinking, predicated upon the recognition of people solely as victims. It is redolent of the old sociological models of mass society and mass culture, which cast the majority of society as passive and lobotomized in the face of the cultural patterns of modernization. To emphasize, as Robins and Webster and others have done, the power of the new technologies to transform despotically the "rhythm, texture, and experience" of everyday life, and meet with no resistance in doing so, is not only to cleave, finally, to an epistemology of technological determinism, but also to dismiss the capacity of people to make their own use of new technologies.

The seamless "interlocking" of public and private networks of information and intelligence is not as smooth and even as the critical school of hard domination would suggest. In any case, compulsive gathering of information is no *guarantee* that any interpretive sense will be made of the files or dossiers, while some would argue that the increasingly covert nature of surveillance is a sign that the "campaign" for social control is not going well. One of the most pervasive popular arguments against the panoptical intentions of the masters of technology is that their systems do not work. Every successful hack or computer crime in some way reinforces the popular perception that information systems are not infallible. And the announcements of military–industrial spokespersons that the fully automated battlefield is on its way run up against an accumulated stock of popular skepticism about the operative capacity of weapons systems. These misgivings are born of decades of distrust for the plans and intentions of the military–industrial complex, and were quite evident in the widespread cynicism about the Strategic Defense Initiative. The military communications system, for example, worked so poorly and so farcically during the US invasion of Grenada that commanders had to call each other on pay phones: ever since then, the command-and-control code of ARPAnet technocrats has been C^5 – Command, Control, Communication, Computers, and Confusion. Even in the Gulf War, which has seen the most concerted effort on the part of the military–industrial–media complex to suppress evidence of such technical dysfunctions, the Pentagon's vaunted information system has proved no more, and often less, resourceful than the mental agility of its analysts.

I am not suggesting that alternatives can be forged simply by encouraging disbelief in the infallibility of existing technologies (pointing to examples of the appropriation of technologies for radical uses, of course, always provides more visibly satisfying evidence of empowerment), but technoskepticism, while not a *sufficient* condition for social change, is a *necessary* condition. Stocks of popular technoskepticism are crucial to the task of eroding the legitimacy of those cultural values that prepare the way for new technological developments: values and principles such as the inevitability of material progress, the "emancipatory" domination of nature, the innovative autonomy of machines, the efficiency codes of pragmatism, and the linear juggernaut of liberal Enlightenment rationality – all increasingly under close critical scrutiny as a wave of environmental consciousness sweeps through the electorates of the West. Technologies do not shape or determine such values. These values already preexist the technologies, and the fact that they have become deeply embodied in the structure of popular needs and desires then provides the green light for the acceptance of certain kinds of technology. The principal rationale for introducing new technologies is that they answer to already-existing intentions and demands that may be perceived as "subjective" but that are never actually within the control of any single set of conspiring individuals. As Marike Finlay has argued, just as technology is possible only in given discursive situations, one of which is the desire of people to have it for reasons of empowerment, so capitalism is merely the site, and not the source, of the power that is often autonomously attributed to the owners and sponsors of technology.

There is no frame of technological inevitability that has not already interacted with popular needs and desires, no introduction of new machineries of control that has not already been negotiated to some degree in the arena of popular consent. Thus the power to design architecture that incorporates different values must arise from the popular perception that existing technologies are not the only ones, nor are they the best when it comes to individual and collective empowerment. It was this kind of perception – formed around the distrust of big, impersonal, "closed" hardware systems, and the desire for small, decentralized, interactive machines to facilitate interpersonal communication – that "built" the PC out of hacking expertise in the early seventies. These were as much the partial "intentions" behind the development of microcomputing technology as deskilling, monitoring, and information gathering are the intentions behind the corporate use of that technology today. The growth of public data networks, bulletin board systems, alternative information and media links, and the increasing cheapness of desktop publishing, satellite equipment, and international data bases are as much the result of local political "intentions" as the fortified net of globally linked, restricted-access information systems is the intentional fantasy of those who seek to profit from centralized control. The picture that emerges from this mapping of intentions is not an inevitably technofascist one, but rather the uneven result of cultural struggles over values and meanings.

It is in this respect – in the struggle over values and meanings – that the work of cultural criticism takes on its special significance as a full participant in the debate about technology. Cultural criticism is already fully implicated in that debate, if only because the culture and education industries are rapidly becoming integrated within the vast information service conglomerates. The media we study, the media we publish in, and the media we teach within are increasingly part of the same tradable information sector. So too, our common intellectual discourse has been significantly affected by the recent debates about postmodernism (or culture in a postindustrial world) in which the euphoric, addictive thrill of the technological sublime has figured quite prominently. The high-speed technological fascination that is characteristic of the postmodern condition can be read, on the one hand, as a celebratory capitulation on the part of intellectuals to the new information technocultures. On the other hand, this celebratory strain attests to the persuasive affect associated with the new cultural technologies, to their capacity (more powerful than that of their sponsors and promoters) to generate pleasure and gratification and to win the struggle for intellectual as well as popular consent.

Another reason for the involvement of cultural critics in the technology debates has to do with our special critical knowledge of the way in which cultural meanings are produced – our knowledge about the politics of consumption and what is often called the politics of representation. This is the knowledge that demonstrates that there are limits to the capacity of productive forces to shape and determine consciousness. It is a knowledge that insists on the ideological or interpretive dimension of technology as a culture that can and must be used and consumed in a variety of ways that are not reducible to the intentions of any single source or producer, and whose meanings cannot simply be read off as evidence of faultless social reproduction. It is a knowledge, in short, that refuses to add to the "hard domination" picture of disenfranchised individuals watched over by some scheming panoptical intelligence. Far from being understood solely as the concrete hardware of electronically sophisticated objects, technology must be seen as a lived, interpretive practice for people in their everyday lives. To redefine the shape and form of that practice is to help create the need for new kinds of hardware and software.

One of the aims of this essay has been to describe and suggest a wider set of activities and social locations than is normally associated with the practice of hacking. If there is a challenge here for cultural critics, then it might be presented as the obligation to make our knowledge about technoculture into something like a hacker's knowledge, capable of penetrating existing systems of rationality that might otherwise be seen as infallible; a hacker's knowledge, capable of reskilling, and therefore of rewriting the cultural programs and reprogramming the social values that make room for new technologies; a hacker's knowledge, capable also of generating new popular romances around the alternative uses of human ingenuity. If we are to take up that challenge, we cannot afford to give up what technoliteracy we have acquired in deference to the vulgar faith that tells us it is always acquired in complicity, and is thus contaminated by the poison of instrumental rationality, or because we hear, often from the same quarters, that acquired technological competence simply glorifies the inhuman work ethic. Technoliteracy, for us, is the challenge to make a historical opportunity out of a historical necessity.

Notes

1   Bryan Kocher, "A Hygiene Lesson," *Communications of the ACM*, 32 (January 1989), 3.
2   Jon A. Rochlis and Mark W. Eichen, "With Microscope and Tweezers: The Worm from MIT's Perspective," *Communications of the ACM*, 32 (June 1989), 697.
3   Philip Elmer-DeWitt, "Invasion of the Body Snatchers," *Time* (September 26, 1988), 62–67.
4   Judith Williamson, "Every Virus Tells a Story: The Meaning of HIV and AIDS," *Taking Liberties: AIDS and Cultural Politics*, ed. Erica Carter and Simon Watney (London: Serpent's Tail/ICA, 1989), 69.
5   "Pulsing the system" is a well-known intelligence process in which, for example, planes deliberately fly over enemy radar installations in order to determine what frequencies they use and how they are arranged. . . .
6   "Hackers in Jail," *2600: The Hacker's Quarterly*, 6 (Spring 1989), 22–23.
7   Hugo Cornwall, *The Hacker's Handbook*, 3rd ed. (London: Century, 1988), 181, 2–6. In Britain, for the most part, hacking is still looked upon as a matter for the civil, rather than the criminal, courts.
8   Bill Landreth, *Out of the Inner Circle: The True Story of a Computer Intruder Capable of Cracking the Nation's Most Secure Computer Systems* (Redmond, Wash.: Tempus, Microsoft, 1989), 10.
9   *The Computer Worm: A Report to the Provost of Cornell University on an Investigation Conducted by the Commission of Preliminary Enquiry* (Ithaca, NY: Cornell University, 1989).
10 Ibid., 8.
11 Andrew Ross, *No Respect: Intellectuals and Popular Culture* (New York: Routledge, 1989), 212. . . .
12 John Markoff, "Cyberpunks Seek Thrills in Computerized Mischief," *New York Times* (November 26, 1988), 1, 28.
13 Dennis Hayes, *Behind the Silicon Curtain: The Seductions of Work in a Lonely Era* (Boston: South End, 1989), 93. . . .
14 "Sabotage," *Processed World*, 11 (Summer 1984), 37–38.
15 Hayes, *Behind the Silicon Curtain*, 99.

16 Kevin Robins and Frank Webster, "Athens without Slaves... or Slaves without Athens? The Neurosis of Technology," *Science as Culture*, 3 (1988), 7–53.

Further Reading

Edwards, Paul N. *The Closed World: Computers and the Politics of Discourse in Cold War America.* Cambridge, MA: MIT Press, 1996.

Hanson, Dirk. *The New Alchemists: Silicon Valley and the Microelectronics Revolution.* Boston: Little, Brown and Co., 1982.

Hayes, Dennis. *Behind the Silicon Curtain: the Seductions of Work in a Lonely Era.* Boston: South End Press, 1989.

Lubar, Steven. *InfoCulture: the Smithsonian Book of Information Age Inventions.* Boston: Houghton Mifflin Co., 1993.

Riordan, Michael and Lillian Hoddeson. *Crystal Fire: the Birth of the Information Age.* New York: W. W. Norton and Co., 1997.

Ullman, Ellen. *Close to the Machine: Technophilia and Its Discontents.* San Francisco: City Lights Books, 1997.

Index